An Anonymous Karaite Commentary on Hosea from the Cairo Genizah

Études sur le Judaïsme Médiéval

Fondées par

Georges Vajda

Rédacteur en chef

Paul B. Fenton

Dirigées par

Phillip I. Lieberman
Benjamin Hary
Katja Vehlow

TOME LXXXVII

The titles published in this series are listed at *brill.com/ejm*

Cambridge Genizah Studies

Edited by

Ben Outhwaite
Geoffrey Khan
Michael Rand
Eve Krakowski

VOLUME 13

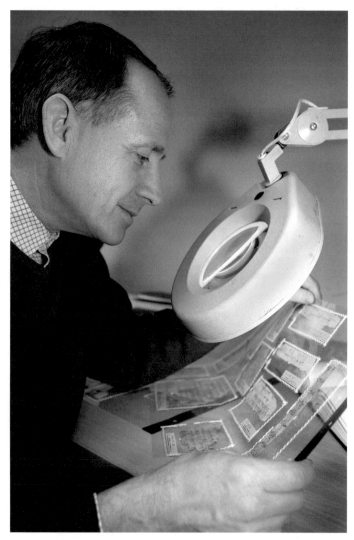

The late Dr Friedrich Niessen at work in the Genizah Research Unit, Cambridge University Library, 2005
REPRODUCED BY PERMISSION OF THE SYNDICS OF CAMBRIDGE UNIVERSITY LIBRARY

An Anonymous Karaite Commentary on Hosea from the Cairo Genizah

By

Friedrich Niessen

BRILL

LEIDEN | BOSTON

Library of Congress Cataloging-in-Publication Data

Names: Niessen, Friedrich, translator, editor, writer of added commentary. |
   Outhwaite, Ben, series editor. | Khan, Geoffrey, series editor, writer of added
   preface. | Rand, Michael (Michael Chaim), series editor. | Krakowski, Eve, 1978-
   series editor. | Cambridge University Library. Taylor-Schechter Genizah
   Collection.
Title: An Anonymous Karaite commentary on Hosea from the Cairo Genizah / by
   Friedrich Niessen.
Other titles: Etudes sur le judaïsme médiéval.
Description: Boston : Brill, 2021. | Series: Cambridge genizah studies, 0169-815x ; 13 |
   Includes bibliographical references and index.
Identifiers: LCCN 2021012884 (print) | LCCN 2021012885 (ebook) |
   ISBN 9789004460034 (hardback) | ISBN 9789004460027 (ebook)
Subjects: LCSH: Bible. Hoseah–Commentaries. | Cairo Genizah. | Karaites.
Classification: LCC BS1565.53 .A56 2021 (print) | LCC BS1565.53 (ebook) |
   DDC 296.8/1–dc23
LC record available at https://lccn.loc.gov/2021012884
LC ebook record available at https://lccn.loc.gov/2021012885

Typeface for the Latin, Greek, and Cyrillic scripts: "Brill". See and download: brill.com/brill-typeface.

ISSN 0169-815X
ISBN 978-90-04-46003-4 (hardback)
ISBN 978-90-04-46002-7 (e-book)

Copyright 2021 by Ranee Niessen and Geoffrey Khan. Published by Koninklijke Brill NV, Leiden, The Netherlands.
Koninklijke Brill NV incorporates the imprints Brill, Brill Nijhoff, Brill Hotei, Brill Schöningh, Brill Fink, Brill mentis, Vandenhoeck & Ruprecht, Böhlau Verlag and V&R Unipress.
Koninklijke Brill NV reserves the right to protect this publication against unauthorized use. Requests for re-use and/or translations must be addressed to Koninklijke Brill NV via brill.com or copyright.com.

This book is printed on acid-free paper and produced in a sustainable manner.

For Ranee, Benjamin and Daniel

Contents

Preface   XI

Introduction   1

Text and Translation   14

Textual Notes   118

References   261
Index of Cambridge University Library, Taylor-Schechter
    manuscripts   264
Index of Biblical Verses   266

Preface

This volume contains an edition, translation and analysis of an important medieval Karaite exegetical text which was discovered and prepared for publication by Friedrich Niessen before his untimely death on 16 January, 2009.

Friedrich Niessen began his university studies with a BA degree in Theology at Bonn University, which he completed in 1967. From an early age he had been fascinated with the Bible and this remained one of his central interests throughout his career. He continued his studies in Theology at Bonn University for an MA degree, which he was awarded in 1969. These degrees in theology offered a solid philological training, including courses in Biblical Hebrew and Biblical Aramaic and textual studies of the Hebrew Bible. Friedrich's later academic studies and research show us that he had a remarkable linguistic ability and was a philologist at heart rather than a theologian. It is not surprising, therefore, that for his MA in Theology he wrote a thesis on 'The nominal sentence in David's succession narrative'.

Subsequently between 1970 and 1972 Friedrich studied at the Cologne Seminary for Catholic Priests. He did not, however, pursue a career in theology or the Church, but rather went into a school-teaching career. He worked until 1995 in a series of schools in northern Germany. From 1972 to 1974 he was in a school in Cologne, in which he taught pupils ranging in age between 10 and 14. Between 1974 and 1977 he taught in a school in Recklinghausen (near Essen and Dortmund), where his pupils ranged from 15 to 17 years old. In 1977 he moved to a school in the neighbouring town of Castrop-Rauxel, where he remained until 1995.

In 1992 he returned to university studies and began a BA degree in Cologne university. The majority of the period of the study for this degree coincided with that of his position as school-teacher at Castrop-Rauxel, so it appears that he did most of his university studies part-time. He graduated in Cologne only two years later in 1994 with what was called a BA in Philosophy. He went on to study for an MA in Philosophy at Cologne and obtained this degree in 1996.

The title of the BA and MA degrees in Cologne mask the remarkable linguistic scope of his studies there. These embraced all the major Semitic languages, including Hebrew (classical, mishnaic, medieval, modern), numerous types of Aramaic (Biblical Aramaic, Targumic Aramaic, Talmudic Aramaic, Syriac, Mandaic), Arabic, Akkadian, Ugaritic and Ethiopic; as well as the languages of Egyptology such as Middle-Egyptian and Coptic (Sahidic, Sub-Akhmimic, Bohairic). During this period he studied, in addition, other ancient languages such as Hittite. Such a range is far beyond what can now be studied in most universities.

Only two years later, in 1998, he had completed a PhD thesis. This was in the field of Samaritan studies, which was also the subject of his MA thesis. His PhD thesis was a critical edition and analysis of sections of one of the so-called 'Samaritan Chronicles', specifically sections from what is known as Samaritan Chronicle number 2 relating to the Joshua narrative, together with the Shobak legend, which is a separate tradition embedded within it. This work was subsequently published in Germany in 2000 (*Eine samaritanishce Version des Buches Yehošuaʿ und die Šoḇaḵ-Erzählung*, Hildesheim: Georg Olms).

In 1998 Friedrich was appointed as a researcher at the Taylor-Schechter Genizah Research Unit in Cambridge University Library, where he worked until his death in 2009. His appointment in Cambridge introduced him into the world of manuscripts from the Cairo Genizah. He was well qualified to undertake work on the Genizah on account of his excellent knowledge of all the major languages of the manuscripts, which included Hebrew, Arabic (mainly Judaeo-Arabic, i.e. Arabic written in Hebrew script) and Aramaic. The Genizah opened new vistas in his research. His main duty was to catalogue the Judaeo-Arabic manuscripts of the Taylor-Schechter New Series, in collaboration with Avihai Shivtiel. Their catalogue was published in 2006: *Arabic and Judaeo-Arabic Manuscripts in the Cambridge Genizah Collections, New Series* (Cambridge University Library Genizah Series 14), Cambridge, 2006.

In the course of his cataloguing duties Friedrich made numerous important discoveries. During the years he worked in Cambridge he began to publish a number of them, but many more remained unpublished at the time of his death. Some of this unpublished work was already in press when he died and has subsequently appeared.

Friedrich's major discovery and the main focus of his personal research in the Genizah was the Karaite commentary on the book of Hosea that appears in this volume. He reconstructed the Judaeo-Arabic text of the commentary from scores of tiny fragments, some of them no bigger than a postage stamp, in a brilliant *tour de force* of philological scholarship. The work is anonymous, but Friedrich was able to identify the Karaite affiliation of the author due to parallels in style and content to the works of other known Karaite scholars. The work is of immense importance to the field of Karaite studies, since it was previously unknown to scholarship and has not survived elsewhere. He described this work together with sample extracts in the first paper that he published in Cambridge: 'An Anonymous Karaite Commentary on the Book of Hosea', in Geoffrey Khan (ed.), *Exegesis and Grammar in Medieval Karaite Texts* (Journal of Semitic Studies Supplement 13), Oxford, 2001, pp. 77–126. By the time of his death he had prepared the Judaeo-Arabic text and its English translation for publication but was not able to see it through the press.

It has been my privilege to prepare the volume for the press. This has involved copy-editing the volume and checking readings, translations and references. Friedrich's work was remarkably accurate and precise, so my intervention was minimal. The introduction was left by Friedrich without any description of the content and background of the commentary, so I added several paragraphs about these based on his aforementioned 2001 article about the work. Also full bibliographical references were missing, so these had to be assembled.

In his textual notes Friedrich referred to Birnbaum's edition of Yefet's commentary on Hosea (1942). Since Friedrich's death a new greatly improved edition of Yefet's commentary was published by Polliack and Schlossberg (2009). References to this edition have been added with the assistance of Joseph Habib. We now also have available an edition of Ibn Nūḥ's grammatical commentary on Hosea (Khan 2011), which was unknown to Friedrich.

Geoffrey Khan
Cambridge, November 2020

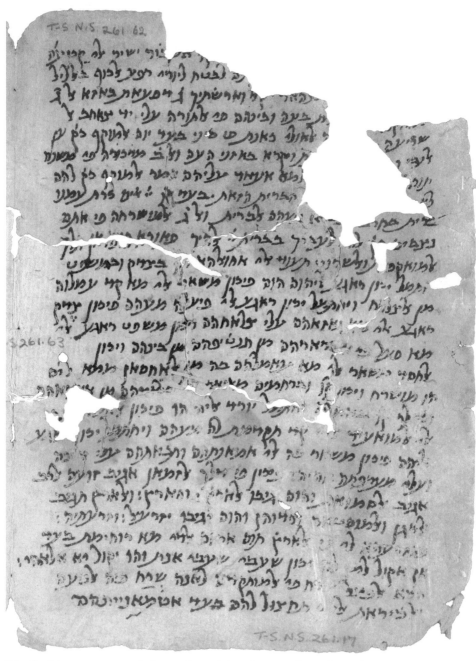

Folio 6b of the commentary, which is made up of three fragments (top to bottom): T-S NS 261.62, T-S NS 261.63, and T-S NS 261.17

REPRODUCED BY PERMISSION OF THE SYNDICS OF CAMBRIDGE UNIVERSITY LIBRARY

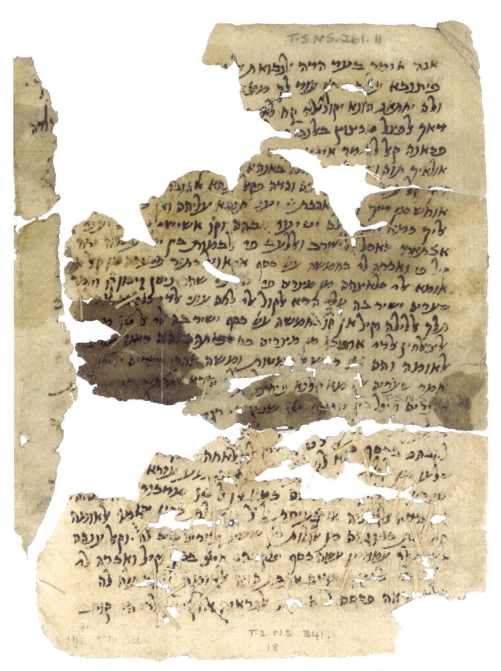

Folio 7b of the commentary, which is made up of four fragments (top to bottom): T-S NS 261.11, T-S NS 261.38, T-S NS 241.18, and the thin strip on the left, T-S NS 261.59

REPRODUCED BY PERMISSION OF THE SYNDICS OF CAMBRIDGE UNIVERSITY LIBRARY

Introduction

The medieval Karaite commentary on Hosea that is published here has been reconstructed from manuscript fragments that were identified in the Taylor-Schechter Genizah collection in Cambridge University Library.

It can be assumed that the pages referring to Hosea represent only a part of a more comprehensive commentary on the Minor Prophets and other biblical books by the same author, since the commentary on the last verses of Hosea 14 is immediately followed by the translation of Joel 1:2–6. Furthermore, another eleven leaves and fragments have been identified that are of the same paper size, in the same handwriting and in the same style of translation and interpretation, including translations, commentaries and grammatical notes on Malachi,[1] Jeremiah[2] and Psalms.[3]

Most of the fragments were found in folder T-S NS 261, some in T-S NS 341 and in various folders of T-S AS. They are written on paper in a semi-cursive script with sporadic Tiberian vocalization. In total 131 fragments have been identified and these form an almost complete commentary on Hosea. The 30 pages of the original work formed a booklet consisting of three quires with five bifolia each, i.e. ten leaves, 'the regular composition of quires in the Orient.'[4] The first

---

1 T-S NS 261.13: commentary on Malachi 3:18–21, followed by grammatical notes on Malachi 1:1–2:13.
2 T-S Ar.21.137 fol. 1: translation of Jer. 38:2–13, followed by commentary on Jer. 38:3–7; fol. 2: commentary on Jer. 40:1–6, translation of Jer. 40:7–12, followed by commentary on Jer. 40:7–8 (see Baker and Polliack 2001:98); T-S Ar.31.221: commentary on Jer. 51:51, translation of Jer. 51:52–53, followed by commentary and grammatical notes; translation of Jer. 51:54–55 (see Baker and Polliack 2001:228).
3 T-S NS 261.9: translation of Psa. 73:19*–28, followed by commentary on Psa. 73:1–3; T-S Ar.1c.24: translation of Psa. 77:14–21, followed by commentary on Psa. 77:1–5 (see Baker and Polliack 2001:22); T-S Ar.23.18: commentary on Psa. 80:2–3 (see Baker and Polliack 2001:112); T-S Ar.31.228 fol. 1: commentary on Psa. 80:15–20 and grammatical notes on Psa. 80:11–17; fol. 2: commentary on Psa. 82:4–8 and grammatical notes on Psa. 82:1–8; translation of Psa. 83:1–5* (see Baker and Polliack 2001:228); T-S NS 261.61: commentary on Psa. 83:4–11; T-S Ar.21.179 fol. 1: grammatical notes on Psa. 83:4–12; translation of Psa. 84:1–13, followed by commentary on Psa. 84:1–2; fol. 2: translation of Psa. 86:7*–17, followed by commentary on Psa. 86:1–2 (see Baker and Polliack 2001:101); T-S Ar.22.119: commentary on Psa. 86:2–11 (see Baker and Polliack 2001:109); T-S NS 261.46: commentary on Psa. 89:1, comparing parallels from other biblical books. Two further fragments written by the same hand as the Hosea commentary (T-S Ar.9.5: *Seder ha-Simanim*, a masoretico-grammatical work datable to the tenth century, and T-S Ar.54.1: Hay Gaon, *On the Laws of Commerce*, table of contents, including chapters 1–28) attest to the wide scope of the scribe's activity.
4 Beit-Arié (1976:44). See also Beit-Arié (1993a:28); Beit-Arié (1993b:222 figure 24).

quire comprises pages 1–10, the second quire pages 11–20, and the third quire pages 21–30. This is clear from the fact that T-S NS 261.48 recto, being part of page 11a, has on the top margin the Hebrew number ב, and T-S NS 261.31 fol. 1 recto, being part of page 21a, the Hebrew number ג, marking the beginning of the second and third quires and thus ensuring the correct order of the codex.[5] Unfortunately the first and last bifolia of the first quire are missing: pages 1–2, dealing with the translation of chapter 1 and the exegesis of Hosea 1:1–4, and pages 9–10 which contained the translation of Hosea 4:13–19 and the exegesis of Hosea 4:1–15.

The pages of the commentary have been reconstructed from the following fragments:

pages 1–2 are missing

page 3

(1)	T-S NS 261.43:	7 lines
(2)	T-S NS 261.67:	23–24 lines
(3)	T-S AS 167.217:	3–4 lines
(4)	T-S NS 29.173	9 lines

page 4

| (1) | T-S NS 261.8: | 8–9 lines |
| (2) | T-S NS 261.59 fol. 1: | 24 lines |

page 5

(1)	T-S NS 261.17 fol. 1	10 lines
(2)	T-S NS 261.62 fol. 1	10 lines
(3)	T-S NS 261.63 fol. 1	12 lines
(4)	T-S NS 261 minute fragment (12/1)	2 lines
(5)	T-S NS 341 minute fragment (2/1)	4 lines
(6)	T-S AS 167.209:	6–7 lines
(7)	T-S AS 167.325 6/2	3 lines

---

5 See Beit-Arié (1976:50, 60).

INTRODUCTION 3

page 6

(1) T-S NS 261.17 fol. 2   22 lines
(2) T-S NS 261.62 fol. 2   10 lines
(3) T-S NS 261.63 fol. 2   10 lines

page 7

(1) T-S NS 261.11:   7 lines
(2) T-S NS 261.38:   13–14 lines
(3) T-S NS 261.59 fol. 2   7 lines
(4) T-S NS 341.18:   4–5 lines

page 8

(1) T-S NS 261.44:   9–10 lines
(2) T-S NS 261.50:   22 lines
(3) T-S NS 261 minute fragment (14/1)   5 lines
(4) T-S NS 261 minute fragment (16/3)   6 lines

pages 9–10 are missing

page 11

(1)   T-S NS 261.16:   6 lines
(2)   T-S NS 261.21:   7–6 lines
(3)   T-S NS 261.45:   13 lines
(4)   T-S NS 261.48:   12–14 lines
(5)   T-S NS 261.60:   7 lines
(6)   T-S NS 261 minute fragment (1/2)   8 lines
(7)   T-S NS 261 minute fragment (1/3)   2 lines
(8)   T-S NS 261 minute fragment (8/1)   6 lines
(9)   T-S NS 261 minute fragment (18/4)   5 lines
(10) T-S AS 164.307 2/10:   3–4 lines
(11) T-S AS 167.325 2/5:   3 lines
(12) T-S AS 173.444 2/1   5 lines

page 12

(1) T-S NS 261.39:   10–11 lines
(2) T-S NS 261.55:   18 lines
(3) T-S NS 341.13:   7–8 lines
(4) T-S AS 159.51:   7 lines
(5) T-S AS 218.301 6/2   2 lines
(6) T-S AS 221.313 7/5   2 lines
(7) T-S AS 224.208 5/9   3 lines

page 13

(1) T-S NS 261.53:   16–17 lines
(2) T-S NS 261.66:   13 lines
(3) T-S NS 261 minute fragment (11/2)   3 lines
(4) T-S NS 261 minute fragment (17/3)   4 lines
(5) T-S AS 140.113 3/2   5 lines
(6) T-S AS 159.303 2/6   2 lines
(7) T-S AS 202.95   7 lines
(8) T-S AS 202.490 7/9   4 lines

page 14

(1) T-S NS 261.15:   11 lines
(2) T-S NS 261.57:   23–24 lines
(3) T-S NS 261 minute fragment (13/2)   3 lines
(4) T-S NS 261 minute fragment (16/1)   5 lines

page 15

(1) T-S NS 261.23:   12 lines
(2) T-S NS 261.36 fol. 1   14 lines
(3) T-S NS 261.47 fol. 1   13 lines

page 16

(1) T-S NS 261.36 fol. 2   15 lines
(2) T-S NS 261.47 fol. 2   15 lines
(3) T-S NS 261 minute fragment (11/3)

page 17

(1) T-S NS 261.5:   10 lines
(2) T-S NS 261.7:   13–14 lines
(3) T-S NS 261.12:   8 lines
(4) T-S NS 261.29:   8–9 lines
(5) T-S NS 261.65:   11–12 lines
(6) T-S NS 341 minute fragment (1/3)   3 lines
(7) T-S NS 341 minute fragment (1/4)   2 lines

page 18

(1) T-S NS 261.14:   10 lines
(2) T-S NS 261.34:   10 lines
(3) T-S NS 261.56:   23–24 lines
(4) T-S NS 261 minute fragment (13/1)   5 lines

page 19

(1) T-S NS 261.26:   27–28 lines
(2) T-S NS 261 minute fragment (18/1)   7 lines
(3) T-S AS 201.310   5 lines

page 20

(1) T-S NS 261.24:   10–12 lines
(2) T-S NS 261.32:   11 lines
(3) T-S NS 261 minute fragment (10/1)   6 lines
(4) T-S NS 261 minute fragment (15/2)   5 lines
(5) T-S NS 261 minute fragment (15/3)   2 lines
(6) T-S AS 169.93

page 21

(1) T-S NS 261.25:   11–12 lines
(2) T-S NS 261.30:   4 lines
(3) T-S NS 261.31 fol. 1   24 lines
(4) T-S NS 261.33:   9 lines
(5) T-S NS 261.49
(6) T-S NS 261 minute fragment (1/1)   4 lines

(7)	T-S NS 261 minute fragment (8/3)	2 lines
(8)	T-S NS 261 minute fragment (16/2)	6 lines
(9)	T-S NS 29.199	4 lines
(10)	T-S NS 29 minute fragment (5/10)	4 lines

page 22

(1)	T-S NS 261.42 fol. 1	23 lines
(2)	T-S NS 261 minute fragment (7/1)	2 lines
(3)	T-S NS 261 minute fragment (9/1)	6 lines
(4)	T-S NS 261 minute fragment (14/3)	5 lines
(5)	T-S AS 156.162	4 lines
(6)	T-S AS 156.443 4/2	4 lines
(7)	T-S AS 164.138	8 lines
(8)	T-S AS 164.308 7/4	5 lines
(9)	T-S AS 172.378 6/2	4 lines
(10)	T-S AS 175.152 5/6	3 lines
(11)	T-S AS 217.172 7/1	4 lines

page 23

(1)	T-S NS 261.10:	15–16 lines
(2)	T-S NS 261.52:	25 lines
(3)	T-S NS 341 minute fragment (1/1)	5 lines
(4)	T-S AS 155.450 4/1	5 lines
(5)	T-S AS 167.34	5 lines
(6)	T-S AS 225.265 9/3	3 lines
(7)	T-S AS 225.272 7/2	3 lines

page 24

(1)	T-S NS 261.6:	15–16 lines
(2)	T-S NS 261.35:	9 lines
(3)	T-S NS 261.41 fol. 1	15 lines
(4)	T-S NS 261.51:	8 lines
(5)	T-S NS 261 minute fragment (2/1)	5 lines
(6)	T-S NS 341 minute fragment (1/2)	3 lines

page 25

(1) T-S NS 261.4 fol. 1   19 lines
(2) T-S NS 261.40 fol. 1   11 lines
(3) T-S AS 140.113 1/3   3 lines
(4) T-S AS 154.79 fol. 1   5 lines
(5) T-S AS 222.241 6/5   5 lines

page 26

(1) T-S NS 261.4 fol. 2   18 lines
(2) T-S NS 261.28:   9 lines
(3) T-S NS 261.40 fol. 2   11 lines
(4) T-S NS 261 minute fragment (13/3) 4 lines
(5) T-S AS 154.79 fol. 2   6 lines

page 27

(1) T-S NS 261.41 fol. 2   16 lines
(2) T-S NS 261.58:   6–7 lines
(3) T-S NS 261.64:   16–17 lines
(4) T-S NS 261 minute fragment (18/2) 5 lines
(7) T-S AS 90.189   13 lines
(8) T-S AS 221.315 8/12   3 lines

page 28

(1) T-S NS 261.18:   10 lines
(2) T-S NS 261.27:   13 lines
(3) T-S NS 261 minute fragment (17/2) 3 lines
(4) T-S NS 261 minute fragment (18/3) 1 line
(5) T-S AS 140.87   9 lines
(6) T-S AS 140.114 3/5   2 lines
(7) T-S AS 156.443 6/9   4 lines

page 29

(1) T-S NS 261.19:   17–18 lines
(2) T-S NS 261.20:   7–8 lines
(3) T-S NS 261.37:   7 lines

(4)	T-S NS 261.42 fol. 2	19 lines
(5)	T-S NS 261 minute fragment (14/2)	
(5)	T-S NS 261 minute fragment (15/1)	6 lines
(6)	T-S NS 339 minute fragment (4/1)	3 lines

page 30

(1)	T-S NS 261.22:	13–14 lines
(2)	T-S NS 261.31 fol. 2	4 lines

The size of the original pages was 20.7–21 cm (length) × 15.5–16 cm (width). From the number of lines of the almost completely reconstructed pages, it can be assumed that each page originally comprised twenty-five to thirty lines.

The fragments are written in black ink on thick, dark, pre-watermarked oriental Arabic paper with a rough surface and without visible wirelines.[6] On some fragments the script is well preserved, on others it is rubbed and faded in places and hardly legible.

The script is an oriental semi-cursive script[7] probably of the late eleventh or the twelfth centuries.[8] Among the main features of this script are the serif added to the left end of the top of the letters ב, ד, כ, and ר, the stroke ('mast') attached to ל, the 'horn' in מ and the prolonged downstrokes of ע and ח; א sometimes resembles the Latin letter 'K.'[9]

A diacritic is generally marked over the letters צ and ט to represent Arabic *ḍād* and *ẓāʾ* respectively. Supra- or sublinear diacritics, however, are omitted on the letters ג, ד and ת to mark the consonants *jīm*, *ghayn*, *dhāl* and *thāʾ*; very rarely a supralinear dot appears on כ to represent *khāʾ*.[10] Sometimes the consonantal ה is marked by a supralinear short line, especially when representing the suffix pronoun of the 3rd person masculine singular. There are only a few ligatures, for example אל and ני.

---

6 See Beit-Arié (1976:26–29).

7 According to Engel (1999:374–377), this type of script should be named 'semi-square script' (כתב מרובע-למחצה), which 'seems to have dominated the style of writing' in Syria and Palestine during the eleventh century (p. xxxi).

8 See Birnbaum (1971, vol. 1: 312–316), Birnbaum (1954–1957, vol. 2, plates 383–396) on Karaite scripts; Engel (1999: 374–377).

9 See Yardeni (1997:149). Some similarities can be noted between the script of the fragments and the handwriting of writers of the first half of the eleventh century, e.g. the Gaon Shelomo ben Yehudah (e.g. T-S 13J11.5; see Engel 1999:400 plate 2a) or Shelomo ben Ṣemaḥ (e.g. T-S 18J3.9, dated December 1033; see Gil 1983 vol. 2: 382–384).

10 See Blau (1978:124–125 = Blau 1988:88–89).

The orthography of the Genizah fragments is characterized by the sporadic spelling with *waw* as a *mater lectionis* (*scriptio plena*) of *u* vowels that are short according to the syllable structure of Classical Arabic,[11] and by the marking of consonantal *y* in medial position with double *yodh*,[12] thus suggesting that it belongs to the later type of Judaeo-Arabic orthography.[13]

Some words are completely or sporadically vocalized with Tiberian vowel signs,[14] especially in the section containing the grammatical notes. As far as words of the biblical text are concerned, their vocalization is identical with the Tiberian Masoretic Text, with a few occasional exceptions.

The vocalization of the Judaeo-Arabic words reflects Classical Arabic pronunciation in the majority of cases. Sometimes the *shewa* sign occurs where Classical Arabic has a short *a* vowel in an unstressed[15] or stressed syllable.[16] It is preferable to assume that *shewa* in initial position represents a full short vowel and reflects a largely Classical Arabic syllable structure[17] rather than to interpret it as a sign for the reduction or complete elision of the vowel.[18] In four cases the *ḥireq* sign occurs where Classical Arabic has short *a*, once in an open unstressed syllable[19] and twice in closed syllables, as often found in Arabic dialects.[20] The pronominal suffix of the 1st person singular with the form *-yi* is used after final *-ī* instead of the expected *-ya* according to Classical Arabic.[21]

The Tetragrammaton is replaced by a symbol composed of three *yodh*s arranged in a triangle.

Custos/custodes, i.e. the first catchword or first few catchwords, appear regularly at the foot of the verso of some folios to ensure the right order of the

---

11 E.g. אומכם 'your mother' (page 3a line [25] = T-S NS 261.43 r5); תום 'then' (page 3b line [2] = T-S NS 261.67 v2) or the suffix pronoun *-hum*: תגדהום 'she finds them' (page 3b line [8] = T-S NS 261.67 v8). See Khan (1992b:228).

12 E.g. פכזיית (page 3b line [4] = T-S NS 261.67 v4), גייד (page 3b line [9] = T-S NS 261.67 v9), לתוגטייה (page 3b line [13] = T-S NS 261.67 v13), פְּתַזִיֵּנַת (page 3b line [19] = T-S NS 261.67 v19). See Khan (1992b:229).

13 On the characteristics of the later orthography see Hary (1990, 1992).

14 On some aspects of vocalization of Genizah fragments see Sharvit (1992).

15 פְּאַגְדַר (page 3b line [7]) = CA *fa-'ajdaru*; פְּתַזִיֵּנַת (page 3b line [19]) = CA *fa-tazayyanat*; פירכ[בה] (page 5b line [9]) = CA *fa-yurakkibahu*.

16 קָדַר (page 4a line [17]) = CA *qadara*; רְהַג (page 4a line [28]) = CA *rahaj*.

17 Khan (1992a:106).

18 Blau and Hopkins (1985:472 = Blau 1988:250).

19 כָּרְמָל (page 3a line [20]) = CA *ka-raml*.

20 רְהַג (page 4a line [28]) = CA *rahaj*; אלחג (page 5b line [11]) = CA *'al-ḥajj*. See Blau and Hopkins (1985: 453 = Blau 1988:231).

21 מוחבִּיי (page 3b line [5]) = CA *muḥibbī-ya*. See Blau (1980:58, § 50א); Blau and Hopkins (1985: 463–464 = Blau 1988; 241–242).

quires,[22] or at the foot of the recto of each folio to ensure the right order of the leaves within the quire, respectively.[23]

In the edition, lacunae in the manuscript are indicated by square brackets, e.g. []. They have been restored where possible, e.g. בנ[ישׂ]ראל. A series of dots within square brackets indicates that some script has been preserved, but is not legible, e.g. [.....]. Redundancies in the manuscript, e.g. dittographies, are enclosed in curly brackets, e.g. {}.

The content, style and grammatical terminology in the commentary indicate that work is of Karaite origin. Though it has not been possible to identify the original author, it is a significant contribution to the understanding of early Karaite techniques of translation and exegesis. It represents the tradition of the tenth century Karaite Jerusalem school and reflects the primary principle of all Karaite Bible translation and exegesis, namely to elucidate the precise literal meaning (*peshaṭ*) of the biblical text. It exhibits the familiar threefold structure of Karaite commentaries: Hebrew source text or Hebrew incipit(s), translation and exegesis, and provides also some additional grammatical notes.

(1) The literal, simple translation of the biblical source-text, contrasting e.g. with Saadiah Gaon's non-literal rendition,[24] is as faithful as possible, highlighting its syntactic and grammatical structures and interpreting it from its immediate context.[25] Literalism does not mean, however, that the author provides a totally imitative rendering of the biblical text by offering a word-for-word translation into Arabic, but his intention is 'to express the grammatical and lexical

---

22 See page 20b (= T-S NS 261.24v), page 30b (= T-S NS 261.22v).

23 See page 5a (= T-S NS 261.17 fol. 1r), page 6a (= T-S NS 261.17 fol. 2r), page 8a (= T-S NS 261.50r), page 11a (= T-S NS 261.45r), page 13a (= T-S NS 261.53r), page 17a (= T-S NS 261.29r), page 18a (= T-S NS 261.56r), page 19a (= T-S NS 261.26r), page 20a (= T-S NS 261.24r), page 23a (= T-S NS 261.52r), page 24a (= T-S NS 261.51r; T-S NS 261.4r), page 25a (= T-S NS 261.40 fol. 1r), page 26a (= T-S NS 261.28r). The left corners at the bottom of page 3a (= T-S NS 261.43r), page 4a (= T-S NS 59 fol. 1r), page 7a (= T-S NS 341.18r), page 12a (= T-S NS 261.55r), page 14a (= T-S NS 261.57r), page 15a (= T-S NS 261.47 fol. 1r), page 16a (= T-S NS 261.47 fol. 2r), page 21a (= T-S NS 261.49r), page 22a (= T-S NS 261.42 fol. 1r), page 27a (= T-S NS 261.58r), page 28a (= T-S NS 261.27r) and page 29a (= T-S NS 261.37r) are torn off or illegible; page 30a consists actually only of two small fragments. See Beit-Arié (1993b:79–82).

24 Saadiah (882–942) never aimed to produce a literalist translation in the manner of the Karaites and was more concerned with a rendering of the biblical text in conformity with Arabic style. His translation style admitted addition, alteration and even countenanced omissions, and incorporated Rabbinic tradition. For Saadiah's concept of translation see Polliack (1996a:78–79).

25 See Polliack (1997:28–29).

structure of the Hebrew source language as accurately as possible in the Arabic target language, and to communicate this structure to the reader or the hearer of the Arabic translated text.'[26] This includes, for example, the use of the Arabic particles *thumma* and *fa-* to convey the semantic range of biblical *waw* conversive (*we-/wa-*), the addition of a suffix pronoun (Hosea 2:9) or a relative clause (Hosea 2:11) for clarification purposes and the insertion of an explanatory gloss, introduced by the technical term *yaʿnī*, to solve a grammatical difficulty (Hosea 2:3).

Though the translator is influenced by the distinctive methodology that was developed in the Karaite Jerusalem school and shared by all Karaite translators, and similarities between his rendering and that of Yefet ben ʿEli can be established, his translation is not an adaptation of Yefet, but an independent approach to the biblical text.

(2) The commitment to a literal translation is paralleled by a philologically oriented exegesis (*maʿnā/maʿānī*), which 'bears strong affinities to the contextual or *peshaṭ* reading'[27] and makes an effort to seek the 'plain sense' (*ẓāhir*) of the biblical text.[28] More precisely, the exegesis can be characterized as 'literary-contextual exegesis,'[29] i.e. a type of exegesis that is closely bound to the text and concerned with its structure and language, considering the grammatical, syntactic, stylistic and thematic dimensions of the biblical verses as well as their connection with neighbouring verses and sections of the text, i.e. the close and wider context in which they occur. Though closely bound to the precise meaning of the biblical text and never going beyond its literary and linguistic boundaries, the exegesis presents at the same time 'more than is offered directly by the text itself,'[30] i.e. it uncovers the intention 'behind' the plain wording. The author, however, is exclusively concerned with the internal logic of the biblical text and avoids deviating from the intention of the biblical author by appealing to external, i.e. extra-textual, considerations of a theological or ideological character.

The literary-contextual exegesis, which is characteristic of all Karaite approaches to biblical texts, stands in contrast to midrashic or halakhic forms of interpretation or allegorization which are motivated by extra-textual, theological and ideological concerns. The anonymous commentator works with the

---

26   Polliack (1996b:191).
27   Frank (2000:111).
28   See Frank (2000:117).
29   Polliack (1999:xv).
30   Khan (2000:134).

exegetical tools developed in the Karaite Jerusalem School and shares a certain common ground of exegetical traditions. Therefore it is not surprising that some parallels or affinities with the exegetical ideas of Daniel al-Qumisī (second half of the ninth century) and Yefet ben ʿEli (second half of the tenth century) can be perceived in his work. Nevertheless, on the whole, he has developed his individual style and his distinctive ideas of interpretation, and his exegesis can be regarded as his own intellectual performance.

(3) A distinctive feature of this commentary is the fact that after his translation and exegesis the author provides an additional aid for understanding the biblical text by adding some grammatical notes, which are more comprehensive and detailed than the grammatical notes supplied by Yefet ben ʿEli. Those notes concentrate on some biblical words the understanding of which are potentially difficult or problematic.

A crucial influence on the author must have been ʾAbū Yaʿqūb Yūsuf ibn Nūḥ (second half of the tenth and beginning of the eleventh centuries), known in Hebrew as Joseph ben Noah. Ibn Nūḥ was the founder of the 'House of Learning' (*dār li-l-ʿilm*) in Jerusalem[31] and was one of the most important exponents of the so-called 'early Karaite grammatical tradition,' whose grammatical teachings have been preserved in his grammatical commentary on the Bible known as the *Diqduq*. The selected grammatical comments in the Genizah text are based on and reflect the grammatical concepts of the early Karaite tradition.

Some of the grammatical terms are identical with those used by Ibn Nūḥ in his *Diqduq*. This is evident from the technical terms *rakkaba* 'to prefix inflectional elements' (e.g. verbal prefixes) and *al-ʾiḍāfa* 'conjoined status,' which belong undoubtedly to his terminology.[32] On the other hand, some of the grammatical terms that appear in the text are generally not used by Ibn Nūḥ, e.g. *murakhkham* instead of *mukhtaṣar* 'apocopated,' 'elided,' *ʾasqaṭa* 'to cause elision' instead of *ʾikhtaṣar*[33] and *māḍī* instead of *ʿābar* for 'perfect,' 'past form of verbs.' The last case reflects the replacement of the Hebrew terminology of

---

31 For details of the Jerusalem School see Frank (2000:119–123).
32 See Khan (2000:147–149). Other technical terms of the Genizah text that parallel the terminology of Ibn Nūḥ are *ʾamr bi-raʾsihi* 'imperative in its primary, basic form' (literally: 'in its head'), i.e. the imperative that constitutes the fundamental base, which is not derived from any other base (T-S NS 261.40 fol. 1, r8); *al-ʾaṣl* 'morphological base of a word' (= *ʾaṣl al-kalima*) (e.g. T-S NS 261.45 r10; T-S NS 261.56 v12); also *ḥaqīqa* 'true meaning' (as opposed to *majāz* 'metaphor'), see Versteegh (1993:108, 122), e.g. חקיקתהא (T-S NS 261.32 r5; T-S NS 261.27 r2), חקיקתה (T-S NS 261.40 fol. 1, r10).
33 אסקט is, nevertheless, found in some early Karaite grammatical texts.

the early Karaite grammatical tradition by an Arabic term from the Baṣran tradition, which is a feature of the Karaite grammatical texts from the eleventh century.[34]

The influence of Ibn Nūḥ was not restricted, however, to the technical terminology of the anonymous author. Beyond grammatical terminology, he shared also Ibn Nūḥ's grammatical theories, e.g. the method of defining the meaning of a noun, the concept of *lughah* 'lexical class' and, above all, one of the central ideas of the early Karaite tradition, the derivation of all forms of a verb from an imperative base, which is not necessarily an actually attested form[35] and the distinction between primary and secondary imperatives.[36]

As the grammatical theories of the anonymous author belong mainly to the early Karaite tradition of Hebrew grammatical thought and exhibits close parallels with those of Ibn Nūḥ, who was active in the late tenth century, it is likely that the Genizah commentary originates from a similar period.[37]

---

34 See Khan (2000:23).
35 E.g. the hypothetical passive imperative רֻחַם (*puʿal*) (page 5b line [5]).
36 This distinction is evident from the aforementioned (n. 32) term *ʾamr bi-raʾsihi*; see Khan (2000:53–55).
37 It is notable, however, that both the grammatical analysis and exegesis of the anonymous commentary differ in a number of details from those found in the section of Ibn Nūḥ's grammatical commentary (*Diqduq*) on Hosea; cf. Khan (2011) (GK).

Text and Translation

3a	1	וׅ[קוׅ ופקדת]י את דמי יזרעא]ל [.................]
	2	אלדי [.......] בית אחאב פי [בית יהוא [.................]
	3	פעלו בית [.........] אלטולם [פי בי]ת אח]אב וקוׅ ושברתי א[ת קשת
	4	יש׳ בעמק יזר[עאל] יענ]יׅ] אכ]סר] קוותה]ם [...........] אעז [......]להם ואפכר
	5	מוצ]עהם וקוׅ] בעד הדא [ו]תל]ד ב]ת ידל [אנהם] אטהר פיעל אלא אנה
	6	אצעף מן דאך אלפיעל אלמותקדם כמא אן אלבנת אצעף מן אלאבן
	7	פאורא א]נ]הם יסתחקו לאגלה אן לא יורחמו וקוׅ ללנבי לא אוסיף
	8	עוד ארחם את בית יש׳ יעני לא אמהלתהם כמא אמהלתהם קבל
	9	הדא וקוׅ כי נשא אשא להם ישיר בה אלי חמלהם פי אלגאליה עלי
	10	[...]ה [וקוׅ] ואת בית יהודה ארחם ישיר בה אלי מא עאמל בה
	11	בחקה [ל]אצחאבה מן אלמוהלה וקוׅ והושעתים ביי׳ אלי׳יהם ישיר
	12	ו]...[אלי מא אגׅאתהם מן מלך אשור לאן כדי דעא חזקיה וקאל
	13	ועתה יי׳ אלי׳ינו הושיענו נא מידו וקוׅ ולא [אוש]יעם בקשת ובחר]ב[
	14	[יש]יׅר בה אלי מא קאל ויצא מלאך יי׳ [ויד ב]מחנה אשור לאן כאנת
	15	א]גׅ]אתתהם סמאויה וקוׅ ותלד בן בעד הדא ידל אנהם אטה]ר פיׅ]על
	16	[אלא אנה ... מ]ן דלך פאסתחקו לא]גׅ]לה אן יובעדו מן אלבצוׅץ אל]די כאנו
	17	[.................] וקד קיל אן מעני קוׅ ותהר ותלד [בן וקוׅ] ותהר ותלד בת
	18	[ישיר בה אלי] אלאגיאל אלדי נש]את בעד דלך] אלדי כאן גיל בעד כל גיל
	19	יׅ]גׅיׅ ...[שר מן אלאכבר חתי אס[ראיל .....] ל]גאׅ]ליה: והיה: סא יכון אחצ]א[
	20	בנ]י יש]ראל כרֶמֶל אלבחר אל]די לא יכא]ל ולא יחצא פיכון פי
	21	אלמוצׅע אלדי כאן יוקאל להם ליס שעבי א]נת]ם יוקאל להם בני
	22	טאיק חי: ונקבצו: פיגת]מעו א]ל יהודה ואל [יש]ראל גמיע]א[
	23	פיגעלו להם רייס ואחד [פי]טלעו מן אלארץ לאן כביר
	24	[יום יזר]עאל: אמרו: פקולו [לאכ]ותכם אנתם שעבי ולאכואתכם

Exegesis 3a
Hosea 1:4: [1] [The phrase] *I* [*will avenge*] *the blood-guilt of Jezree*[*l* ...] [2] who [...] the house of Ahab on [the house of Jehu ...] [3] the house of [...] did the iniquity on [the hou]se of Ah[ab].

Hosea 1:5: [The phrase *And I will break*] *the bow of* [4] *Israel in the valley of Jezr*[*eel*] i.e. I [will break] the[ir] strength [...] mightier [than] their [...] and I will despise [5] [their] place.

Hosea 1:6: [And] the following [verse] *And she bore a daughter* indicates [that they are] a very distinct action; however, that it is [6] weaker than this preceding action, as a daughter is weaker than a son. [7] He demonstrates that, therefore, they did not deserve to be pitied. The word to the prophet *I will no* [8] *longer have mercy on the house of Israel* means: I will not show forbearance, as I have shown forbearance before [9] that. The phrase *For I will lift them* alludes to carrying them in exile on [10] his [...].

Hosea 1:7: The phrase *But I will have mercy on the house of Judah* alludes to [11] the forbearance with which He treated his friends. The phrase *And I will save them by YHWH their God* alludes [12] to that He has come to the aid of them against the king of Assur, for thus Hezekiah prayed [13] *And now, YHWH our God, save us please from his hand* (2 Kings 19:19). The phrase *And I will not save them by bow and by sword* [14] alludes to what is said *And the angel of YHWH went out and struck down in the camp of Assur* (2 Kings 19:35), for [15] their help was from heaven.

Hosea 1:8–9: The following phrase *She bore a son* indicates that they are a very distinct action; [16] [however, ...] than that. And therefore they deserved to be excluded from the special relationship they were [17] [in ...]. Some say that the meaning of *And she became pregnant and bore* [*a son*] and *And she became pregnant and bore a daughter* (Hosea 1:6) [18] [allude] to the generations who ro[se after that ...] which was a generation after each generation [19] [...] from the last until Israel [...] to the exile.

Translation
Hosea 2:1: The number [20] of the Israelites will be like the sand of the sea which [cannot be measu]red and not be counted; and it will be [21] in the place where it was said to them, 'You are not my people', it will be said to them, 'Sons [22] of the living Powerful One'.

Hosea 2:2: And the people of Judah and the people Israel will be gathered together, [23] and they will appoint a single leader for themselves, and they will come up from the land; for great is [24] the day of Jezreel.

25 יעני ואחדה מנהם קד רוחי[מ]ת: ריבו: כאצמו אומכם
26 [כ]אצמו לאנהא ליס הי לי במרה ואנא פליס להא ברגול
27 [ותז]יל [טג]יאנאתהא מן וגההא ופגוראתהא מן בין תדי[יהא:]

3b

1 פ[]: כילא אסלכהא ערי[אנה פאוקפהא כיום ול[אד]הא
2 ת[ום אצירהא כאלבר ואג[עלהא כארץ מפא[זה ואקת[ול]הא
3 באלעט[ש: ואת: ובני[הא פ[לא ארח[ם לאן בני [טגיאנא]ת הום:
4 כי: לאן טגת אומהם פבזיית [אל}{חא[בלהם לאן ק[אלת אסלוך ו[רא]
5 מוחביי מועטיין כו[ב]זי ומיאה[י] צופי וכתאנ[י] דוהני
6 ומשרובאתי: לכן: לדלך הודאני מסייג טריקך ב[אלא[שו]אך]
7 פאַגָדֵר גְדַארהא וסובלהא פלא תגד: ורדפה: פתכלב מחביהא
8 ולא תלחקהם תום תטלובהם ולא תגדהום פתקול אלצואב אן אסלוך
9 וארגע אלי רגולי אלאול לאן קד כאן חאלי גייד חין אדן אכתר מן
10 אלסאעה: והיא: והי פמא ערפת באן אנא אעטית[הא אלדגן]
11 ואלמסטאר ואלדוהן ופצֶה כֵתָרת להא ודהב פעמלוה [לל[ותן: לכן:
12 פלדלך ארגע פאכוד דגני פי וקתה ומסטארי פי זמאנה תום
13 אוכלץ צופי וכתאני אלדי געלתה לתגטייה סווחהא: ועתה:
14 [ו]אלסאעה אכשף סקאטתהא חדא מוחביהא ואימר פלא יכלצהא
15 מן [י]די: והשבתי: פאעטל כל סרורהא חיגהא רוס שה[רהא]
16 וסבתהא וכל [א[עיאדהא: והשמותי: תום אוחש גפא[נהא ות[יאנהא]
17 אלדי קאלת געל הם לי אלד[י] א[עטוני מוחביי פאג[עלהם]
18 שערא לתאכלהם וחוש אל[צחר]א: ופקדתי: תום אפתקד [עלי]הא
19 איאם אלאותאן אלדי כא[נת תקתר] להם פְּתַזיֵנת בשונ[פהא]
20 וחלייהא תום מרת ו[ר]א מחביה[א] וא[י]י פנסית זועם אלרב

TEXT AND TRANSLATION   17

Hosea 2:3: And say [to] your brothers, 'You are my people', and to your sisters, [25] i.e. one of them, 'She has been pitied'.

Hosea 2:4: Bring legal action against your mother, [26] bring legal action! For she is not My wife and I am not her husband. [27] And let her remove her harlotries from her face and her adulteries from between her breasts!

Hosea 2:5: [1] [Lest I will strip her na]ked and make her stand as (on) the day   3b of her birth. [2] The[n I will make her like the wilderness and ma]ke her like the land of the des[ert and cause] her [to d]ie [3] of thirst.

Hosea 2:6: [And on] her [children] I will not have mercy. For they are children of [harlot]ry.

Hosea 2:7: [4] For their mother has whored and (she) who con[ceived them] has behaved disgracefully. For she said, I will go af[ter] [5] my lovers who give my bread and my water, my wool and [my] flax, [my oil] [6] and my drinks.

Hosea 2:8: Therefore, behold, I will hedge up your way with [th]orn[s] [7] and I will build up a wall against her, so that she will not find her paths.

Hosea 2:9: And she will pounce on her lovers, [8] and she will not reach them. Then she will seek them, and she will not find them. And she will say, It is right that I go [9] and return to my first man, because my situation was much better then than [10] now.

Hosea 2:10: And she—she did not know that I gave [her the grain] [11] and the new wine and the oil, and I multiplied for her silver and gold. And they have made it to the idol.

Hosea 2:11: [12] Therefore I will return, and I take My grain at its time and My new wine at its season. Then [13] I will withdraw My wool and My flax which I made to cover her nakedness.

Hosea 2:12: [14] And now I will uncover her shame in front of her lovers and no one will deliver her [15] from My hand.

Hosea 2:13: And I will bring an end to all her rejoicing, her pilgrim festival, [her] new moon, [16] and her sabbath and all her festive seasons.

Hosea 2:14: Then I will lay waste [her] vines [and] her [f]igs [17] (of) which she said, They are payment for me, which my lovers have given me. And I will ma[ke them] [18] a scrub country so that the animals of the desert will devour them.

Hosea 2:15: Then I will visit upon her [19] the days of the idols to whom she [has been burning incense], and she adorned herself with [her] earrings [20] and her jewellery. Then she went af[ter] h[er] lovers, and M[e]—she forgot—declaration of the Lord.

21 הדא אלפצל מנתסק אלי מא קב[לה] לאנה למא חט עלי קו׳ כי אתם
22 לא עמי ואנכי לא אהיה לכם ו[...] סאמע הדא יו[ן]ק[ד]ר אן הדא
23 אלכל[א]ם מוובד פאתבעה בקו׳ [והיה] מספר בני יש׳ לי[ו]ר[י] אן
24 הדה אלקטיעה להא נהאיה [ואן] לא בוד להדה אל[...] באן
25 [חי]ת אן תעוד אלי אלכתרה פיכון קו׳ והיה מספר בני ישראל נק[ץ] [קו׳]
26 [והי]ה ביום ההוא ושברתי את קשת ישראל אלדי אורא פי[ה] כס[ר ...]

4a
1 [.. קו׳] בעמק יז[ר]עאל יעני
2 [.. וכ]אן י[...] אלאומר ויקולו קד
3 [..] פי דאך אל[מ]וקע יו[ש]ר[פ]ו ותורפע
4 [..] אנהם סא יוחצ׳ו פי וקת כרוגהם
5 מן אל[...................] פי [........]הם כמא [אוח]צ׳י יוצאי מצרים וכמא
6 אוחצי[ו יוצאי] בבל וכדי קאל אלולי ייי יספר בכתוב עמים וקאל כחול הים
7 לא[ן ...] אברהם פי וקת אלעקידה קיל לה והרבה ארבה את זרעך ככוכבי
8 השמים כאן אלקצד בדלך אלי מא חצל להם פי מא מצא וכדי קאל לה[ם]
9 צאחב [א]לשריעה [ייי] אל׳ יכם הרבה אתכם והנכם היום ככוכבי השמים לרוב וכדלך
10 קאל [אל]מדון דוד כי אמר ייי להרבות את ישראל ככבי השמים תום קאל ה
11 ו[כחול אשר ע]ל שפת הים וכאן אלאישארה בה אלי מא יכון פי אלעתיד
12 פ[קאל] הונא כחול הים ולמא כאן קד גרת עודה אלגלות כאן תוכאל
13 ו[תוחצא כ]אעדאד כילהא יוקאל כדי קפיז וכדי כור חסון
14 אן יקול ען חול הים לא ימד ולא יספר יעני לא תוכאל פתוחצא אכיאלה
15 וקי׳ והיה במקום יחתמל מא קלנאה אנה ישיר אלי אלמכאן נפסה ויחתמל
16 אן קי׳ במקום יעני בדל מא כאן יוקאל לכם כי לא עמי יוקאל לכם בני
17 אל [ח]י וקי׳ אל חי פי הדא אלמו[נ]צ׳[ע] ליורי אן הו אלדי קדר עלי כלאצתהם
18 ו[............] והו אל חי אלדי [........]ם במואעידה: למא כאן קד דכר
19 פי אל[פ]צל א[ל]מתקדם אלאומה מוסמה ישראל נאחיה ויהודה נאחיה
20 בש[ר] פי הדא אלפצל בתוולפהם ואיגתמאעהם גמיעא עלי כדי
21 [...] בקו׳ ונקבצו בני יהודה ובני יש׳ יחדו ו[הדא] איצא [חט] מן
22 נסק הדא אלפצל אלי אלפצל אלמתקדם [.........] עלי ישראל
23 לוגהין לל[ד]לאלה ולאנה חט פי דכרהם [.......] חט ואורא [מ]ן קי׳

Exegesis

Hosea 2:1: [21] This section is closely related to what precedes it; for, since reflecting upon the phrase *For you are* [22] *not My people, and I am not for you* (Hosea 1:9), [somebody] hearing this could assume that this [23] statement was meant to be for ever. So he made the phrase *And the number of Israelites* [*will be*] follow it to demonstrate that [24] there will be an end to this depopulation and [that] this [...] is evident [25] [...] since it will again increase to a great number. *And the number of the Israelites will be* annuls [26] *And it will be at that day that I will break the bow of Israel* (Hosea 1:5) by which he shows the brea[king of ...] | [1] [...] *In the valley of Jezreel* (Hosea 1:5) means [2] [...] and it was [...] the matters. They say, [3] [...] in this situation they will be honoured and [4] [...] will be exalted [...] that they will be counted at the time of their exodus [5] from the [exile ...] in their [...], as those who left Egypt were counted and as [6] [those who left] Babel were counted. Likewise the friend (of God) said *YHWH will count when He records nations* (Psalms 87:6). *As the sand of the sea* is said [7] because [likewise it was said to] Abraham at the time of the Binding (of Isaac), *I will multiply your seed as the stars* [8] *of the heaven* (Genesis 22:17); this is to refer to what has happened to them in the past. Likewise [9] the author of the Torah said to the[m *YHWH,*] *your God, has multiplied you, and behold, you are today as the stars of the heaven for multitude* (Deuteronomy 1:10). Likewise [10] the author David said *Because YHWH had said He would multiply Israel as the stars of the heaven* (1 Chronicles 27:23). The following phrase [11] *And as the sand on the seashore* (Genesis 22:17) alludes to what will happen in the future. [12] And [likewise it is said] here *As the sand of the sea*. After returning from the exile, it will be measured [13] and [counted. According] to the amounts of its measure, it will be said, 'So and so many *qafiz* and so and so many *kurr*'. It is appropriate [14] that it is said about *The sand of the sea: It cannot be measured and not be numbered*, i.e. its measures cannot be numbered nor counted. [15] *It will be in the place* may refer, as we have said, to the place proper, or [16] 'it will be in the place' may mean: instead of what was said to you, (namely) *Not my people*, it will be said to you *Sons of* [17] *the living God*. The term *The living God* in this context is to show that He is able to deliver them [18] and [...] and He is *the living God* who [...] them at His appointed times.

 Hosea 2:2: After mentioning [19] in the previous section the nation called 'Israel' and 'Judah' separately, [20] in this section he heralded their unity and their assembling together in [21] one [notion] by *The sons of Judah and the sons of Israel will be gathered together*. And also [he made the point] with regard [22] to the connection of this section with the previous one [...] on Israel [23] for two reasons: for furnishing evidence and because he made the point by remembering them [...]. He did this in order to demonstrate with the phrase

24	ושמו להם ראש אחד אנהם ינצבו להם [............] בה והו אלמערוף
25	ענד אלאומה במשיח בן יוסף וקו׳ ועלו מן הא[רץ ישי]ר בה אלי טלועהם
26	[מ]ן בלדאן אלגלות נטיר קול אלמצריין ען אלא[ומה ונ]לחם בנו ועלה מן
27	הארץ וקו׳ כי גדול יום יזרעאל יעני אן יום [רגוע]הם אלי בלדהדם
28	יכון כביר אלשאן רָהג מתל יום כרוגה[ם] מן בלדהדם פי אלג[לות]

4b

1	תום קאל אמרו לאחיכם [עמי י]ש[י]ר בה [..................]
2	אלאומה [פי] דאך אלזמאן [אלמ]ונתטֹר [..................]
3	דכר פי אלפצל אלמותקדם ג׳ אסמ[א ....]ל
4	פאורא הונא אינעכאס דלך אלי [...........]
5	לא עמי פקאל הונא בעכסה עמי ואל[י] לא רוחמה [קאל הונא] רוחמה
6	ובההדא אלוגה איצֹ אנתסק הדא אלפצל אלי אלפצל אל[מתק]דם לאנה
7	קד נקץֹ פיה גמיע אלוגוה אלמדכורה פי דאך קו׳ [ר]יבו [בא]מכם
8	בעד הדא אלקול ליורי [הדה אל]בשארה אנמא יסתחקוהא פי וקת גיר
9	הדא אדא מא חצלו טאיעין ואמא אלסאעה פיסתחקו אלתוביך
10	ומתל אלאומה פי הדא אלפצל באלמרה אלדי קד כאן [......] ע]ליהא
11	נעמה טֹאהרה מן גהה רגולהא פאכתארת עליה גי[ר ....]רת
12	עליה פנסבת דלך אלכיר אלי אצדקאהא פאראד אן [..........]
13	מנהא מא אעטאהא לתנבסר ותעלם אן כאן חאלהא מע רגולהא
14	אכיר ממא הי עליה ולמא כאן קד ורד אלפרץֹ פי אלשריעה
15	באן יַלזַם אלרגול ללמרה ג׳ מעאני אלטעאם ואלכסוה ואלתפקוד
16	באלאיגתמאע מעהא דכר פי הדא אלפצל אלג׳ אלדי כאן קד
17	אנעם עליהם בהא פ[א]ורא [..]להא לאגל קולהא אלכה א[חרי] מאהבי
18	נתני לחמי ומימי וחצל אגתמאעהא מעהם בקו׳ ותעד [נז]מה
19	וחל[י]תה ותלך אחרי מאהביה פאומא אלי מנע אלטעאם ואלכסוה
20	בקו׳ ול[ק]חתי [י] ד[גני בע]תו וקאל והצלתי צמרי ופשתי: ואמא
21	אלאגתמאע מעהא [................]ל אלחגוג אלדי כאן יגתמעו פי
22	אלק[וד]ס מע אל[ו]ק[ת] פ[קא]ל ען דלך והשבתי כל משושה חגה [חדשה]
23	ושבתה וכל מו[עדה] פחצל רָפע אלג׳ מעאני קו׳ ללאנביא ר[י]בו
24	באמכם ריבו יעני ובכוהא וכאצמוהא דאים יעני יום בע[ד]
25	[י]ום לאני קד [רפע]ת אלענאיה ענהא וקד בעודת מנהא פלעלהא

5a

1	תנצלח וקו׳ ותסר זנוניה מפניה ישיר בה אלי אלטאהר מן אפעאלהא
2	אלקביחה וקו׳ ונא[פ]ופיה מבין ש׳ ישיר בה אלי אלבואטן ואלאעתקאדאת
3	אלמדֹמומה וקו׳ פ[ן] אפשיטנה ישיר בה אלי ל[.]אכר מן אלדולה ורדהא

[24] *They will appoint themselves a single head* that they appoint for themselves a leader [...] and he is known [25] among the people as 'Messiah son of Joseph'. The phrase *They will ascend from the land* refers to their ascending [26] from the lands of the exile, like the word of the Egyptians concerning the nation *It will fight against us and it will ascend from* [27] *the land* (Exodus 1:10). The phrase *For great is the day of Jezreel* means that the day of thei[r return] to their land [28] will be a great event, enormous as the day of their leaving their land in the e[xile].

Hosea 2:3: [1] The following *Say to your brothers*, [*My People* refers to the ...] [2] the nation [at] this expected time [...] [3] In the previous section he mentioned three nam[es ...] [4] Here he shows the reversal of that into [...]. [There it is said] [5] *Not my people* (Hosea 1:9), and here it is said contrary to that *My people*. [And to] *She has not been pitied* (Hosea 1:8) [it is said here] *She has been pitied*. [6] Also in this respect this section is related to what precedes it, since [7] he has reversed in it all points mentioned there.

Hosea 2:4: The verse *Plead with your mother* [8] after this phrase is to show this good news. But they will deserve it at a different time [9] when they become obedient. As far as now is concerned, they deserve reproval. [10] In this section he compared the nation with the woman whom [He had bestowed] [11] a visible blessing through her husband, however, she preferred [others] to him, [...] [12] on him and attributed that benefit to her friends. He planned to [withdraw] [13] from her what he had given to her so that she should be shattered and realize that being with her husband was [14] better than her present situation. Since in the Law the commandment is quoted [15] that a man is obliged to provide for his wife three things: food, clothing and sexual intercourse (see Exodus 21:10) [16], in this section he mentioned the three things he [17] had bestowed on them. Her [vileness] is shown by her statement *I will go after my lovers* [18] *who give my bread and my water* (Hosea 2:7) and her intercourse with them by *She put on her earrings* [19] *and her jewellery and went after her lovers* (Hosea 2:15). The withdrawal of bread and clothing is indicated [20] by *I will take away My grain in its time* (Hosea 2:11) and *And I will remove My wool and My linen* (Hosea 2:11). Concerning [21] being together with her, [... this refers to] the festivals when they gathered together in [22] the Temple in due time, [as it is said] concerning that: *I will put an end to all her rejoicing, her festival, her [New Moon]* [23] *and her Sabbaths and all her hol[idays]* (Hosea 2:13). Thus the three benefits were withdrawn. His saying to the prophets *Plead* [24] *with your mother, plead* means 'Reprimand her and plead with her permanently', i.e. day after [25] day. For I have [withdrawn] the care from her and I am distant towards her, perhaps | [1] she will be improved. *And she should remove her harlotries from her face* refers to her visible [2] shameful deeds. *And her adulteries from between her breasts* refers to the secrets and the [3] blameworthy thoughts.

4	אלי אלעבודיה וקו׳ כיום הולדה ישיר בה אלי [בקא]הא פי מצרים
5	וקו׳ ושמתיה כמדבר ישיר בה אלי מנע אל[כיראת] ענהא וקו׳ ושתיה
6	כארץ ציה ישיר בה אלי קטע אלנבוה ענהא [וקו׳ והמ]ת[ה] ב[צמא] ידל
7	עלי טול אלגאליה ומותהם גיל בעד גיל בא[............]הם
8	וקו׳ ואת בניה לא ארחם ישיר אלי אלאגיא[ל] אלאי[..... וקו׳] כי בני זנונים ה[מה]
9	יעני א[נה]ם קד ולידו ורוביו עלי רסם עבודה זרה לאן אלכלאם
10	מכצוץ באלחאצ׳רין מע אלאנביא תום אורא כזייהם וכגלהם מן
11	אפעאלהם ואנהם נסבו אלכיר אלדי כאן לה עליהם אלי גירה פאטבק
12	עלי דלך בקו׳ לכן לאגל דלך יעני לאגל מא נסבתום כיראתי אלי
13	גירי הודא אגעל ביני ובינכם סיאג שוך ישיר בדלך אלי אלגאליה
14	אלאולה וקו׳ וגדרתי א׳ גדרה ישיר בה אלי אלגאליה אלתאניה תום
15	א[ור]א באן אדא פסוד בינהא ובין גיראנהא א[ל]די כאן בינהא
16	[ובינה]ם אל[מ]חבה או אלמעבודאת אלדי [...] פי עבודאתהם
17	[אור]א נדמהא בקו׳ ענהא אלכה ואשובה [אלי א]ישי הראשון תום
18	[אור]א אנא אנמא אעטאהא הדא אלכיר ל[ת...ע]/ה פנ]ח] [מנ]הא
19	[בעד] דלך כך׳ עשו לבעל פאורא אנה ימנע מנהא מא כאן קד
20	אנעם בה עליהא פיסקיטהא ענד גיראנהא אלדי כאנת תגתמע
21	מעהם עלי עבאדה אלאותאן וקו׳ ואיש לא יצילנה מידי יעני
22	בה לא אקבל פיהם שפאעה שפיע מן אלאנביא כמא קד גרת
23	אלעאדה אן ישפעו פיהא ויוֹשַׁפַּעוּ ככ׳ לירמיה אם יעמד משה
24	ושמואל לפני אין נפשי אל העם הזה קו׳ והשבתי כל משושה צדר
25	וקדם אלחגוג לכתרה אלאפראח פיהא וכדלך אצאף אליה[א]

5b

1	רוס אלשהר לכתרה אלאפראח פיהא ואקרן אליהא אלסבות תום
2	אעד באקי אלאעיאד אלדי פיהא אפראח תום דכר כראב אלבלד
3	חתי ציר ש[ע]רא מ[רע]א ללוחוש וכתם בקו׳ [ו]פקדתי עליה את ימי

Hosea 2:5: *Lest I undress her* refers to [being removed] from the country and her returning [4] to slavery. *As the day of her birth* refers to her [stay] in Egypt. [5] *I make her as the wilderness* refers to the [blessings] being withdrawn from her. *I set her* [6] *like a dry land* refers to the prophecy being cut off from her. *I will kill her with thirst* indicates [7] the length of the exile and their death, generation after generation, in the [...] their [...].

Hosea 2:6: [8] *And on your sons I will not have mercy* refers to the [...] nations. *For th[ey] are sons of harlotry* [9] means: they were born and raised according to idolatry, for the word [10] is especially associated with those who are together with the prophets.

Hosea 2:7: Then he shows their disgrace and their shame because of [11] their deeds and that they attributed the blessing they owed to Him to somebody else.

Hosea 2:8: He concludes [12] that by the phrase *Therefore* 'because of that', i.e. because you have attributed My blessings to [13] somebody else, behold, I will make a thorn hedge between Me and you, thus referring to the [14] first exile. With the phrase *I will build up her wall*, he refers to the second exile.

Hosea 2:9: Next [15] he shows that then there was a conflict between her and her neighbours between whom was [16] love, or the idols which [...] in their worship. [17] [He shows] her repentance by quoting her announcement *I will go and return [to] my first man*.

Hosea 2:10: Then [18] [he shows] that when He gave her these good, to [...] it [...] [19] [after] that, as it is said *They made into Baal*.

Hosea 2:11: He shows that He will withdraw from her what He had [20] bestowed upon her and make her stumble with her neighbours whom she used to join [21] in worshipping the idols.

Hosea 2:12: The phrase *Nobody will deliver her out of My hand* means: [22] I will not accept for them any intercessions of an interceding prophet, as it was [23] customary that they put in a good word for her and their intercession would be granted, as it is said to Jeremiah *Even if Moses* [24] *and Samuel were to stand before Me, I would have no desire for this people* (Jeremiah 15:1).

Hosea 2:13: The verse *I will cause to cease all her rejoicing* starts [25] by mentioning first the festivals because of the abundance of rejoicing at them. Likewise | [1] he adds the New Moons to them because of the abundance of rejoicing at them, and he connects the Sabbaths with them. Then [2] he enumerates the remaining festivals at which there is rejoicing.

Hosea 2:14: Then he mentions the destruction of the land [3] until it becomes a [scrub] country [as grazing] land for the wild animals.

4	הבעלים ליורי [אן א]סתחקו הדא כולה לאיגל איתבאעהם אלאותאן
5	ותרכהם טא[עתה ר]וחָמָה מן רֶוחֵם ואלמאצִּ[י] רוּחָם ואלמונת רוּחָמה:
6	וירכבה אימנ[ת תקול] אֲרוחָם ירוחם מרוחם: זְנָן אסם אלטוֹגִיאן
7	גמעה [זנונים. נאפוף] אסם פגור גמעה נַאֲפוּפִים: שיקוּי אסם גמעה
8	שיקוּיִם [שיקו]י אסם אכר גמעה שְקוּיִם כק' ושקוּיַ בבכי מסכתי
9	שַד מן שוֹד [פירכ]בה אינת תקול אָשוּדֹ יָשוּד והי לגה אלתֵּסיִג
10	ונטירהא בסמך לגה אלדהֹן: וְרִדְפָה מן רדף פירכב[ה] אימנת:
11	נבלוּת אסם מתל גְבָהוּת: חַגֵה אסם אלחֶג גמעה חַגִים פענד אלאצָאפה
12	צאר חַגַה: שַבַּתָה: אלדיגש אלדי פי אלתיו אסקט אלתיו אלאכר לאן אלאסם
13	שבת פכאן חקהא שבתתה: אֶתְנָה אסם: וַתַּעַד מרכמה הי לאנהא
14	מן הָעֵדָה פאדא רכבהא אימנת תקול אֲעַדֵה יַעַדֵה מעדה בגד:
15	חֵלְיָה אסם אלחֵלִי מונת חֵלִי לאן וַחֲלִי כְתָם אלמפרד מנה חֵלִי:
16	לָכֵן: לדלך הודא אנא מוכדעתהא פאוסלכהא אלי אלבר תום אתכלם
17	עלי קלבהא: ונ[תתי:] פָאַעְטיהא כרומהא מן תַם ומרג ע[כו]ר
18	לפתח רגא פתג[ני] תמה כאיאם צבאהא וכיום צעודהא [מן]
19	ארץ מצר: הדא [אל]פצל מנתסק אלי אלפצל אלמותקדם לאנה
20	קד דכר פיה נדמהא עלי מא גרי מנהא בקו' ענהא אלכה [וא]שובה
21	אל אישי הראשון פ[קו'] לכן יעני לאגל אנכסארהא ות[פת]תהא
22	וקו' מפתיה ישיר בה אלי אלעלאמאת אלדי יטָהֵר להם פי אכר
23	אלגלות חתי ינבדעו בהא ויכרגו אלי אלבר נטיר קו' להם

Hosea 2:15: He concludes with *And I will visit upon her the days* [4] *of the Baalim* to demonstrate [that] they deserved all this because of their heeding the idols [5] and giving up obeying [Him].

Grammatical Notes

רֻחָמָה (Hosea 2:3) (is derived) from (the imperative) רֻחֵם; the past tense is רֻחַם and the feminine רֻחָמָה. [6] If you attach (the affixes) אימנ״ת [you say] אֲרוּחָם, יְרוּחָם, מְרוּחָם, זְנוּן (Hosea 2:4) is a noun (meaning) 'harlotry', [7] its plural is זְנוּנִים. נָאֲפוּף (Hosea 2:4)] is a noun (meaning) 'fornication', its plural being נַאֲפוּפִים. שִׁיקוּי (Hosea 2:7) is a noun, its plural being [8] שִׁיקוּיִם; and [שִׁקּוּי] is a different noun, its plural being שִׁקּוּוִים, like וְשִׁקּוּוַי בִּבְכִי מָסָכְתִּי (Psalms 102:10). [9] שָׂךְ (Hosea 2:8) (is derived) from (the imperative) שׂוּךְ. [If you attach] (the affixes) אימ״ת, you say אָשׂוּךְ, יָשׂוּךְ, and it is the lexical class 'fencing in'; [10] a similar form with *samekh* (i.e. סוּךְ, belongs to) the lexical class 'annointing'. וְרִדְפָה (Hosea 2:9) (is derived) from (the imperative) רְדֹף, and you may attach to it (the affixes) אימנ״ת. [11] נָבְלוּת (Hosea 2:12) is a noun like גַּבְהוּת (Isaiah 2:11, 17). חַגָּה (Hosea 2:13) is a noun (meaning) 'festival'. Its plural is חַגִּים; in the construct state [12] it becomes חַגַּה. שַׁבַּתָּהּ (Hosea 2:13): the *dagesh* in the *taw* causes the elision of the second *taw*, for the noun is [13] שַׁבָּת, and the form according to the rule should be שַׁבַתְּתָהּ. אֶתְנָה (Hosea 2:14) is a noun. וַתַּעַד (Hosea 2:15) is an apocopated form, for it (is derived) [14] from (the imperative) הַעֲדֵה. If you attach (the affixes) אימנ״ת, you say אַעֲדֶה, יַעֲדֶה, מַעֲדֶה בֶּגֶד (Proverbs 25:20). [15] חֶלְיָה (Hosea 2:15) is a noun (meaning) 'piece of jewellery', the feminine form of חֲלִי; for the absolute state of וַחֲלִי־כָתֶם (Proverbs 25:12) is חֲלִי.

Translation

Hosea 2:16: [16] Therefore behold I will deceive her, and I will lead her into the desert. Then I shall speak [17] to her heart.

Hosea 2:17: And I will give her her vineyards from there and (make) the valley of A[kh]or [18] into a door of hope. And she will s[ing] there as (in) the days of her youth and as (on) the day when she came up [from] [19] the land of Egypt.

Exegesis

This section is closely related to what precedes it since [20] he mentions in it her repentance for what she had done, by the phrase spoken by her *I will go and will return* [21] *to my first man* (Hosea 2:9).

Hosea 2:16: The word *Therefore* means: because of her being broken and her [being brayed]. [22] The term *Deceiving* alludes to the signs, which He will reveal to them at the end [23] of the exile so that they are deceived by them

24 והוצאתי אתכם אל מדבר העמים וקו' ודברתי על לבה ישיר
25 בה אלי אלנבואת ואלמובשרין אלדי יַטָהִיר להום פיקויהם בדלך
26 ויעזיהם' ולמא כאן קד חט פי אלפצל אלמֻתְקַדֻם בקו' והשמותי

6a
1 גפנה רפע פי [הד]א [אלפצל] ....
2 אליהא כרומהא עאמרה וקו]' ....[
3 יֻשְׂרְפוּ עלי אלבלד יתסלמוה וקו' וא[ת עמ]ק [עכור]...............
4 אנהם יתסלמו אלבלד כמא תסלמוה אלאבא [..............
5 תסלמוהא אלאבא יתסלמו אלבלד וקו' לפתח ת[קוה] באן אדא
6 תסלמו מן אלבלד פקד צחת להם אלמואעיד [..............] אמלהם
7 וקו' וענתה שמה כימי נע' ישיר בה אלי שיר[ת מרים וקו'] עלותה
8 מארץ מצ' ישיר בה אלי שירת משה ובני [ישראל: והיה: פיכו]ן פי
9 דלך אליום זועם אלרב תנאדי יא רגולי ול[א תנאדי ל]י זאדה בעלי:
10 והסרותי: פאזיל אסמא אלאותאן מן פמהא פ[לא] יודכרו זאדה
11 באסמאהם: וכרתי: [ו]אקטע להם עהד פי דלך אליום מע וחוש
12 אלצחרא ומע טאיר אלסמא ומע דביב אלאדמה וקוס וסיף
13 ומלחמה אכסר מן אלארץֿ פַאֲצְּגִעהם באטמאניה: וארשתיך:
14 פאמליכך לי אלי אלאבד תום אמליכך לי בעדל ובחוכם
15 ובאחסאן וברַחְמאת: וארשתיך: פאמליכך לי באמאנה פתערפי
16 אלרב: הדא אלפצל מנתסק אלי אלפצל אלמתקדם לאנה שרח מא
17 י[......]ו [א]ל[ה]ן יום בעד [דכו]ל[הם] פי אלבלד פלמא כאן קד נוכבר
18 מ[ן] גהה אלבעלים אורא אנהם ליס ידכ]ורוהו[ם חתי לה הו
19 לא יסמוה להם בעל לאן בעל צאחב בל ינאדוה באיש:
20 כך ענהא אלכה ואשובה אל אישי. ואורא אנהם ליס ידכרו
21 אלאותאן דיכר פכיף אן ירגעו אלי שי ממא כאנו עליה מן
22 עבאדתהא תום אורא באנה יוסאלם בינהם ובין אלוחוש

and go forth to the wilderness, as it is said to them [24] *And I will bring you forth* [sic] *into the wilderness of the nations* (Ezekiel 20:35). The phrase *And I will speak to her heart* alludes [25] to the prophecies and the good tidings He will reveal to them, and so He will strengthen [26] and console them by that.

Hosea 2:17: After pointing out in the preceding section by *I will lay waste* | [1]   6a
her vine (Hosea 2:14), he emphasizes in this [section that ... and He will restore] [2] to her her prosperous vineyards [...] [3] they overlook the land, which they have taken in possession. The phrase *And the [valle]y of [Akhor]* [...] [4] that they will take possession of the land as the fathers have taken possession of it [... as] [5] the fathers have taken possession, they will take possession of the land. The phrase *For a door of hope* is evident: When [6] they took possession of the land, the promises had been fulfilled for them [...] their hope [7]. The phrase *She will sing there as in the days of her youth* alludes to the song [of Miriam], and the phrase *Her ascent* [8] *from the land of Egypt* alludes to the song of Moses and the [children of Israel].

Translation

Hosea 2:18: And it will be on [9] that day, declaration of the Lord, you will call out 'My man' and [you will no] more [call M]e 'My Baal'.

Hosea 2:19: [10] And I will remove the names of the idols from her mouth, and they will no more be mentioned [11] by their names.

Hosea 2:20: I will make a covenant for them on that day with the animals [12] of the desert and with the birds of the sky and with the reptiles of the earth. And bow and sword [13] and warfare I will break off from the earth, and I will make them lie down in peace.

Hosea 2:21: [14] I will betroth you to Me forever. Then I will betroth you to Me with righteousness and with justice [15] and with kindness and with mercy.

Hosea 2:22: And I will betroth you to Me with faithfulness, and you will know [16] the Lord.

Exegesis

Hosea 2:18: This section is closely related to what precedes it, since he explains what [17] [will happen to] them after [entering] the land. And after we have been informed [18] about the Baalim, he demonstrates that they [will] not rem[ember] them so that [19] they do not call Him 'Baal' since 'Baal' is 'owner', rather they call him 'man', [20] corresponding to her statement *I will go and return to my man* (Hosea 2:9).

Hosea 2:19: And he demonstrates that [21] they will not even mention the idols, let alone return to any of [22] their former worship.

23	ואלטיור ואלדביב פלא יתאדّו בשי מנהא בעכס מא כאן קד
24	אטלק אדّאהם פיהם פי זמאן אלסכّט כך׳ פי אלתואעוד ושן
25	בהמות אשלח בם עם חמת זחלי עפר. תום אקרן אלי מנע
26	אַדَّא אלמודّיאת מן אלוחוש ואלטיור קטע אדא אלמודّיין

6b

1	[מן אלנאס .... וקו׳ אש]בّור ישיר אלי קטעה
2	[......... וקו׳ והשכב]תّי[]ם לבטח ליורי רפע אלכוף באלליל
3	[......... ....בא]ל[נהאר. קאל וארשתיך ג׳ דפעאת באזא אלג׳
4	[אלדפעאת ....]ת בינה ובינהם פי אלתורה עלי יד צאחב אל
5	שריעה [אלדפע]ה אלאולי כאנת פי סיני בעד יום אלמוקף כך׳ ען
6	אלנבי ו]יקח ספר הברי[ת ויקרא באזני העם ואלב׳ מדכורה פי משנה
7	תור[ה ....] למא אעאד עליהם [א]מר אלמוקף כך׳ להם
8	לא [את אבותינו כרת יי את] הברית הזאת. בעד קו׳ אלינו כרת עמנו
9	ברית בחרב [...]א[......... מע]הם אלברית ואלג׳ אלמושרחה פי אתם
10	נצבים כך׳ ל[]הם] לעברך בברית יי [א]להיך פאורא הונא אן תלך
11	אלמואקפ[א]ת ואלשרוט תעוד אלי אחואלהא וקו׳ בצדק ובמשפט
12	[י׳]חתמל יכון ראגע אליהום הום פיכון משאר אלי מא קד עמלוה
13	מן אלצّל[א]ח ויחתמל יכון ראגע אלי פיעלה מעהם פיכון צֶדק
14	ראגע אלי מא גאזאהם עלי צלאחהם ויכון משפט ראגע אלי
15	מא פעל פי א[ק]רארהם מן תנטיפהם מן בינהם ויכון
16	אלחסד משאר אלי מא עאמלהם בה מן אלאחסאן ממא ליס
17	הו מושרח ויכון קו׳ וברחמים משאר אלי כלאצתה מן א[ע]דאהם
18	וכדלך קו׳ באמונה [י׳]חתמל יורד אליה הו פיכון אל[אשארה] ב[ה]
19	אלי אלמואעיד אלדי כד תקדמת לה מעהם ויחתמל יכון [ר]אגע
20	אליהם פיכון משאר בה אלי אמאנתהם ותבאתהם עלי דינה
21	ועלי מערפתה: והיה: פיכון פי דלך אלזמאן אגיב זוע אלרב
22	אגיב אלסמואת והום יגיבו אלארץֶ: והארץ: ואלארץ תגיב
23	אלדגן ואלמוסטאר ואלדוהן והום יגיבו יזרעאל: וזרעתיה:

Hosea 2:20: Then he shows that He makes peace between them and the wild animals, [23] the birds and the reptiles; they will not be harmed by them in contrast to the way [24] He caused them to be harmed in the time of the anger, as it is said in 'The threat' *And the tooth* [25] *of beasts I will dispatch against them with the venom of those who creep in the dust* (Deuteronomy 32:24). Then he links the prevention [26] of the harmful wild animals and birds with the prevention of the harmful | [1] pe[ople. The phrase] *I will break* alludes to him breaking [2] [... . The phrase *And I make them lie down] in safety* is to demonstrate the elimination of the fear during the night [3] [and ... during] the day.

6b

Hosea 2:21: He says *And I will betroth you* three times, corresponding to the three [4] [times when the covena]nt between Him and them [is mentioned] in the Torah by the author of the [5] Law. The first [time] was at Sinai after the day of the stopping, as it is said about [6] the prophet [*And he took the book of the covena]nt and read (it) before the people* (Exodus 24:7). The second (time) is mentioned in Deuteronomy [7] [...] when he repeated the stopping for them, as it is said to them [8] *Not [with our fathers* YHWH *sealed] this covenant* (Deuteronomy 5:3) after YHWH *our God sealed* [9] *a covenant with us at Horeb* (Deuteronomy 5:2) [... with] them the covenant. And the third (time) is the one described in (the parashah) 'You are [10] standing', as it is said to them *For you to pass into the covenant of* YHWH *your God* (Deuteronomy 29:11). Here he shows that those [11] resting places and agreements are being restored. The phrase *With righteousness and with justice* [12] may refer to them and allude to [13] the righteousness they have done; or it may refer to what He has done to them, (namely:) *Righteousness* [14] refers to what He has rewarded them for their righteousness, and *Justice* refers to [15] what He did to impose (justice) on them by purifying them from their enmity. [16] The *kindness* alludes to the good deeds He has done to them, which are not [17] described. *With mercy* alludes to them being delivered from their en[emi]es.

Hosea 2:22: [18] And likewise the phrase *With faithfulness* may refer to Him and be an allusion [19] to the promises, which He had given to them earlier; or it may refer [20] to them and be an allusion to their faithfulness and their adherence to His law [21] and the knowledge of Him.

Translation

Hosea 2:23: And it shall be in that time, I will respond declaration of the Lord, [22] I will respond to the skies, and they will respond to the earth.

Hosea 2:24: And the earth will respond [23] to the grain and the new wine and the oil, and they will respond to Jezreel.

24	פאזרעהא לי פי אלארץֿ תום ארחם אלדי מא רוחימת בעד
25	אן אקול למן לם יכון שעבי אנת והו יקול יא אלאהי:
26	הדא אלפצל שרח פי אלמותקדם לאנה שְׂרח פיה אלניעם
27	ואלביראת אלדי תחצול להם בעד אטמאנייתהם

7a

1	[............] אענה נאם ייי צדר לי[...ורי] הדה
2	[............] ואלמעני פי קו׳ אענה הו אלחוכם
3	[............] ללמוב[אלגה פרתב מנזלה בעד מנזלה
4	[............] וא[לאמר באלניעם וקו׳ והם יענו
5	[............] אלסמא באלאמטאר
6	[............] א[...........] אגאב[ו ....] ארווהא וקו׳
7	[והארץ תענה] יעני תטהר ניעמהא וקו׳ ו[הם מ]שאר אלי אלדגן
8	[ואלתי]רוש [ואליצ]הר ומעני קו׳ יענו את יזרעאל יע[ני יעו]דו וינפעו הדה
9	אלאומה אל[מל]קבה בהדא אללקב פאן אולא ק[ד] אָמַר אלאנביא
10	אן יבשרוהם בתגַייר הדה אלאסמא מן דֹם אלי חמד פאראד הו
11	הונא יובשר בדלך פדכר [יזרעא]ל אלאסם אלאול אלדי כאן קד אקדמת
12	עליהם עלי טריק אלדֹם פא[ורא] אנעכאסה אלי חמד בק׳ וזרעתיה לי
13	בארץ. וכדלך אַעכֹס אלאסם אלדי כאן סמאהם לא רוחמה בק׳ ורחמתי
14	ואלאסם אלג׳ אלדי כאן לא עמי קאל עמי אתה וקו׳ והוא יאמר אלהי.
15	כת[ם] בה באזא מא כתם פי אלפצל אלאול בק׳ ואנכי לא אהיה לכם.
16	ויא[מר:] וקאל לי אלרב זאד[ה א]מץֿ חב אמראה מחבובה רפיק
17	ופא[גרה כמחבה א]לרב אל אסראיל והום מותגהין אלי אליהה
18	א[...]כר ומוחבי קנאני׳ אלענב: ואכרה: [וא]ת[בתת]הא לי
19	ב[...כמסה עשר] פי אלפצֿה [ובגריב] שעיר ובכורי שעיר.
20	[ואמר: ו]קולת להא א[יאם כ]ת[י]ר תג[לסי] ל[י] לא ת[ז]ני ולא תכוני
21	לאימר גירי ואיצֿא אנא אציר אליך: [כי]: לאן [איאם] כתיר
22	יגלסו אל אסר[אי]ל [...] ליס מלך וליס רייס וליס דביח וליס
23	מצטבה וליס צודרה ולא ציוור: אחר: פבעד דלך ירגעו

Hosea 2:25: [24] And I will sow her for Me in the land. Then I will have mercy on the one who has not been pitied. After [25] I will have said to the one who was not my people: 'You are my people', they will say 'My God'.

Exegesis
[26] He has explained this section in the preceding one, since there he described the good deeds [27] and the benefits that occurred to them after enjoying safety | [1] [...]

7a

Hosea 2:23: He commences with *I will respond word of YHWH* to dem[onstrate ...] this [2] [...] and the meaning of *I will respond* is the judgement [3] [... by exagg]eration and he arranged rank after rank [4] [...] and the instruction to the goods. *And they will respond* [5] [...] the heavens by the rain [6] [...] they answered [...] they watered it.

Hosea 2:24: [7] [The phrase *And the earth will respond* ...] means: it (= the earth) will make its benefactions visible. [The phrase *And they*] refers to the grain, [8] the wine and the oil. And the meaning of the phrase *They will respond to Jezreel* is: [they will ret]urn and help this [9] nation which has been given this name.

Hosea 2:25: Whereas firstly he had given the command to the prophets [10] to announce good news for them by changing these names from derogation into praise, he intended [11] here to announce the good news in that way: He mentions Jezreel as the first name, which was previously said [12] against them derogatively, and he shows its reversal into praise by *I will sow her for Me* [13] *in the land*. And in the same way he reverses the name *'She has not been pitied'*, they were named with, by *'I will have mercy'*. [14] The third name which is *'Not my people'*, he calls *'You are my people'*. He concludes with *And he will say, My God*, [15] corresponding to the conclusion of the first section *And I am not for you* (Hosea 1:9).

Translation
Hosea 3:1: [16] And the Lord said to me, G[o] ag[ain]! Love a woman who is beloved by a companion [17] and an adul[teress, as] the Lord [loves] the people of Israel, though they will turn to [18] other gods [and love jugs] of grapes.

Hosea 3:2: [And I established] her for Me [19] for [fifteen] (pieces) of silver [and for a *jarīb*] of barley and for two *kurr* of barley.

Hosea 3:3: [20] And I said to her, [For ma]n[y] day[s] you will s[it] for [me.] You will not whore and you will not belong [21] to another man than me. And I, also, will come to you.

Hosea 3:4: Because for man[y days] [22] the people of Israel will sit, [...] no king and no leader and no sacrifice and no [23] pillar and no ephod and no statues.

24 אל אסראיל פי[ט] לובו אלרב אלאההם ודויד מליכהם פי[פז]עו
25 פי גהה אלרב [ו]פי גהה כירה פי אכר אלאיאם: הדא אלפצל
26 מנתסק אלי אל[פצ]ל אלמותקדם פי או[ל א]לספר ופיה כול [...]ל

7b
1 אנה אומר בעד הדה אלנבואת אל[................................]ד.
2 פיתנבא על[יהם] בק' עוד לך מצֹא [...........................]ז[
3 ולם יחתאג הונא יקול לה קח לא[ן.........................]ודה
4 דאך אלפצל מכצוץ באלנבו[את...............................]
5 פכאנה קאל לה מר איצֹא [..................................]ז[
6 אוליאך תום ו[....................]ה באנהא [.] [...........] מן [.]
7 [דיד] קאל ענ[הא אשת זנוני]ם והדה פקאל [ע]נהא אהובת [רע..]ו
8 אוחש מן דיך [...וקו' כ]אהבת ייי יעני תנבא עליהם ואן [........]
9 אליך כמא [...] לם יטיעו רבהם וקו' אשישי [ענבי]ם יעני [.....]
10 אכתארו אלאכל ואלשורב ואללעב פי אלבמות בין י[די] עבודה זרה [...]
11 קאל פי ואכרה לי בחמשה עש' כסף אקאויל כתיר פמעהם מן קאל אנה
12 אומא אלי כלאצהם מן מצרים פי ט"ו פי שהר ניסן ויכון קו' וחמר
13 שערים ישיר בה עלי הדא אלקול אלי לחם עוני אלדי כלפה אכל פי
14 תלך אלליל וקיל אן קו' בחמשה עש' כסף ישיר בה אלי אלט"ו מן
15 אלצאלחין אלדי אופיכו מן מצרים בחסנאתהם והום כאנו [...ב].[...]
16 אלאומה והם [י"ב] ראשי [ה]מטות ומשה ואהרן ומרים. ויכון [קו']
17 וחמר שערים עלי מא קלנא פיחצל עלי הדא אל[...] אן פי [......]ת
18 מצרים חצל בין ידיהם ט"ו שכץ [..] רג[..................]
19 [.................................].ט[....]
20 לקבהם [...]ס[..........] ל[...]לאחה[..............................]
21 טלעו מן אלגלות [..................] ט מע עזרא [........................]
22 פי [..................]ם כמא אן אלט"ו מדכור [................]
23 [...] הדה אלגאליה או צֹעיפת אלל' [...]לת [...] ן [...] מֻו אלאומה
24 פי וקת כרוגהם מן אלגלות כך' ששים גבורים סביב לה. וקאל ענהם
25 [בעד] דלך עמודיו עשה כסף פלקבהם איצֹ ב[א]לפצֹא וקיל ואכרה לי
26 [ישיר א[ל]י] אלאכר איאם אתבת הדה אלאומה [.........] ומ[...]תלה לה
27 [בא[ל]אמ]ראה פרסם להא [...] אלגראיב אל[...] אלדי הי קות

8a
1 [.........................] שע[יר מעאיש אלגלותיין ואלתצֹייק עליהם
2 [.........................]ב קו' לה לך אהב אשה
3 [.........................] הדא אלפצֹל מכצוץ ביהודה

Hosea 3:5: And thereafter, [24] the people of Israel will return, and they will seek the Lord, their God, and David, their king, and they will be frightened [25] before the Lord and before His goodness at the end of the days.

Exegesis
This section [26] is closely related to what precedes it in the first part of the book, in it being all [...] | [1] that he gives the command after these prophecies [...] [2] and he will prophesy against [them]. 7b

Hosea 3:1: With *Go again!* 'Go [...]', [3] and it was not necessary here to say to him *Take!* (Hosea 1:2) because [...] [4] this section is special in the prophecies [...]. [5] And as if He said to him, Go again [...] [6] those. Then [...] that she [...] from [...] [7] [...] he says about her [*Woman of harlo*]*try* (Hosea 1:2), and he says about this one *The beloved of a companion* [...] [8] more disgusting than that [...]. [The phrase] *As YHWH loves* means: he prophesied against them and if [...] [9] to you as [...] they did not obey their Lord. *Cakes of grapes* means: [10] they have chosen the food and the drinks and the amusement on the high places in front of idolatry.

Hosea 3:2: [11] There are many interpretations of *I acquired her for Me for fifteen (shekel of) silver.*

One of them holds that it [12] is a reference to their deliverance from Egypt on the fifteenth of the month Nisan. The phrase *And a ḥomer of* [13] *barley* alludes, following this interpretation, to *The bread of affliction* (Deuteronomy 16:3), which He left behind as food in [14] that night.

Another commentator holds that *For fifteen (shekel of) silver* alludes to the fifteen [15] righteous ones who were redeemed from Egypt because of their good deeds, being the [...] [16] of the people, namely the twelve chiefs of the tribes and Moses, Aaron and Miriam. [The phrase] [17] *And a ḥomer of barley* (is to be interpreted) according to what we have said, and it occurs according to this [...] that in [...] [18] Egypt, there were among them fifteen persons who [...] [19] [...] [20] he called them [...] [21] they ascended from the exile [... fif]teen with Ezra [...] [22] in [...] as the fifteen, mentioned [...] [23] [in] this exile or the thirty is doubled [...] the people [24] in the time when they came out of the exile, as it is said *Sixty mighty men round about it* (Song of Songs 3:7), and it is said about them [25] after that *Its pillars he made of silver* (Song of Songs 3:10). And he called them also ['silver'].

Another interpretation is that *I acquired her for Me* [26] [refers to] the end of days; he established this nation [... and he compa]res it [27] [with the wom]an, and he describes her [...] the *jarībs* [...] who are the strength of | [1] [... *bar*]*ley* 8a to the modes of life of the two exiles and the oppression against them [2] [...] the word to him *Go, love a woman!* (Hosea 3:1) [3] [...] this section is special on

4 [.... י]הודה מן אול ספרה ואלי
5 [.... לאן בנימן צ]גיר בנימן
6 עשרה הו שעורים [חומר] בנימן אל[..] פ[...........................]
7 פיכון אלחומר נצף פהו ואללתך חומר הבתים עשרת [כ]י כך אכיאל
8 אלי משאר אלכסף פיכון דרהם אלט״ו באזא כיל ט״ו ד[ת]ואלל אלחומר
9 דכר מוצ׳ל כ] פי [לאן אלתרהיב אלי משאר [ש]ואל[ג]אל[תר]
10 אלקול הדא פעל[י] ותרהיב בתרג׳יב דלך אתבע קד כתאבה פי יהודה
11 משאר ויכון ללאומה אלנבי קול לי תשבי רבים ימים א]מר [א ו]קו ׳ יכון
12 כליפה יטהר נבי ינתטרו אנהם אמרה מן יושאהד הודא מא אלי
13 אליה ואומר יכון אלקול הדא ג׳יר ועלי נסלהם מן אלמרסלין ללאנביא
14 אלגלות הדה פי יצברו באן אומתה ם[ז]אל אלדי אלכ׳אלק אלי ר[אג]ע יכון
15 לא יעני תזני לא קו׳ רבים ימים כי בקו׳ דלך בעד שרח כמא
16 והו אלגאיז טריק עלי תהיי ולא מחטור פי אלדכול תכתארי
17 [נ]בי ולא ג׳ירה מעבוד יתכד׳ו לא אן הו אלגמיע פי ואלמעני אלתזויג׳
18 אשאר יש׳ בני רבים ימים פקאל באלקול פצח תום ביאה[אן ג׳יר]
19 אזואג׳ ליכר׳ג׳ לישראל רבים וימים כק׳ו אלגלות [ה]ם .... אלי בה[
20 פי מוסתעמלה כאנת אלדי והם אלגלות סנין אול פי [בינהם מא] מע
21 ומנהא עליה מחמודין כאנו מא פמנהא דולתהם איאם פי בינהם מא
22 אלגמיע מנהם [מ]ד[מ]ונה [מ]ן אלגלות פי אן פאורא מדמומין כאנו [מ]א
23 להם יכון לא ה[..]מן וכדלך מסכוט ולא מרצ׳י לא מלך להם יכון לא
24 יכון לא וכדלך משכור ולא מדמום לא בגומלתהם אליה ינקאדו רייס
25 להם יכון ולא מדמומה ולא מרצ׳יה מחמודה לא [קרא]בין דביחה להם
26 כמא מדמומה ולא אבינו יעקב עמל כמא מחמודה לא מצ׳בה
27 כמא ולא בה יסאלו ללכהנים כאן כמא אפוד ולא יעמלו הום כאנו

1 [עז ׳כקו מחמובין לא פים[ר]אל[ת ולא אלמחטור אלאפוד מיכה עמל
2 להם כאנת כמא מדמומה ולא ה[מטה] אל התרפים והנה דויד
3 [ירגע .... בע]ד אן אורא תום איצ׳א
4 [...] עליה הום מא מן אלקום
5 [...]ה[.ל].[מ]אל ואל באלדועא
6 [... יעני בו] וא[ל טו] ייי אל ופחדו וקו׳ דויד
7 יבעוד לא אן אלרב [ב]סבב ק[ל]קין פ׳זיעין אבדא פיכונו [י]על[ם גרי
8 תום ענהם [.......] לא אן כירה ובסבב דלך קבל פעל כמא מנהם

Judah [4] [... J]udah from his first journey and to [5] [... s]mall Benjamin, for Benjamin [6] [...] Benjamin. The *Ḥ[omer] of barley* equals ten [7] *kaylas*, as it is said *For ten bats are a ḥomer* (Ezekiel 45:14); the *letek* equals half a *ḥomer*; [8] consequently, the *ḥomer* and the *letek* are fifteen *kayla*s, corresponding to fifteen dirhams. The *silver* is an allusion to [9] the attraction and the *barley* is an allusion to the intimidation, for in each place where [10] he mentions Judah in his book, he lets that to be followed by attraction and intimidation.

Hosea 3:3: On the basis of this verse, [11] the phrase *And I said to her, many days you will sit for me* is the word of the prophet to the people, and it is an allusion [12] to their situation he witnesses here: that they wait for a prophet who appears as a successor [13] of the prophets who were sent from among their descendants. According to another opinion, the phrase *And I said to her* [14] refers to the Creator who compelled His people to endure this exile, [15] as it is explained afterwards by *For many days* (Hosea 3:4). *You will not whore* means: [16] you will not choose to enter in something forbidden. *And you will not be for a man* is a metaphorical expression, i.e. [17] marriage, and the meaning of the whole (context) is, that they must not choose a god other than Him and not another prophet [18] [than] His [pro]phets.

Hosea 3:4: Then he speaks openly and says *For many days the Israelites will sit*; he alludes [19] [by this to ... of] the exile, as it is said *And many days (passed by) for the Israelites* (2 Chronicles 15:3), to bring out pairs [20] together with [what is among them] in the first year of the exile and those which have been established [21] among them in the days of their kingdom, some of them were praiseworthy and some of them [22] were blameworthy. And he shows that in the exile all of them [are blameworthy]. [23] They have no *king*, neither accepted nor hated. And likewise [...] they have no [24] chief to whom they obey altogether, neither blameworthy nor praiseworthy. And likewise [25] they have no offering, neither praiseworthy and accepted nor blameworthy. And they have no [26] *sacred pillar*, neither praiseworthy, as (the one) Jacob our father had made, nor blameworthy, as (the one) [27] they made. And no Ephod, as the one of the priests which they used to consult, and not as | [1] the prohibited Ephod Micah had made. And no *Teraphim* [neither praiseworthy, as it is said about] [2] David *And behold the teraphim (were) on the bed* (1 Samuel 19:16) [and not blameworthy as they had] [3] either.

8b

Hosea 3:5: Then he shows that af[ter ...] [4] the people [will return] from the situation they (were) in, [...] [5] in the prayer and the [request ...] [6] David. The phrase *And they will tremble to YHWH [and to] His [g]oo[dness]* means [...] [7] happened to them and they will always be in fear (and) anxious [because of the Lord] that He is not far [8] from them, as He did before that, and because

9 אורא אן הדא מן בעד זמאן טויל כך' באחרית [הימ]ים: שמעו:
10 אסמעו כטאב אלרב יא אל אסראיל לאן נט֖ר [ל]לרב מע [גל]אס
11 אלארץ לאן ליס חק וליס איחסאן וליס מערפה אללה פי אלארץ֖:
12 אלה: בל תחריג וגחוד וקתל וסרק ופגור פקד תג֖רו ודמא בדמא
13 קד אדְנַו: על: עלי דלך תחזן אלארץ֖ לאן קד קוטע כל גאלס בהא
14 חתי מן וחוש אלצחרא ומן טאיר אלסמא ואיצֿא סמאך אלבחר
15 ינחשרו אלי אליְבַס פיהלכו: אך: כאן אימר ליס יכאצֿם ול[י]ס יווב֖ך
16 אימר ושעבך פקד חצלו כמוכַאצַמי אימאמא: ו[כ]שלתָ: פתנעתר
17 אליום תום יועתַר איצֿא אלנבי מעך אלליה פאֲבְכם אומך: נדמו:
18 אנבכמו שעבי מן עדם אלמערפה לאנך אנת אלמערפה זהדת
19 פאנא אזהדך מן אלתאמום לי וכמא נסית שריע[ה] אלאהך {אנסא}
20 כדלך אנסא בניך איצֿא אנא: כרבם: ככתרת[הם כדלך] אכטו
21 לי פלדלך כרמהם בכזיה[ם] א[ב]ד[ל: חטאת: ק]רבאן חט[אה אלדי
22 לשעבי יאכלו ואלי דנבהם יר[פ]עו אנפוסהם: והיה: פיכון [כאל]שעב
23 כאלאמאם ואנא א[פ]תקד עליה טורקה ושמאילה ארוד
24 לה: ואכלו: פיאכלו ולא ישבעו כמא קד זנו וליס יַתְסְעו
25 יענ[י יכ]תורו לאן אלרב תרכו אלדי וגב עליהם אן יחפטו: זנות:
26 לאן אלזנא ואלכמר ואלמסטאר יקבל אלקלב: עמי: שעבי מן
27 כְשַבה יסאל עצאתה יכברה לאן ריח [טגיאנאת] קד אַטָל

11a
1 [......................ק]אל להם [א]דא כאן מגייכם אלי הדה
2 [אלמואצֿע ....ע]לי הדה אל[צורה ......]תגו ואדא כאנת אימאנכם בי
3 [.......................ל]א תחלפו באסמי: אורא אנהם קד [א]טר[ח]ו אלט[עאם]

of His kindness that it [is not absent] from them. Then [9] he shows that this (will happen) after a long time, as it is said *In the end of the days*.

Translation
Hosea 4:1: [10] Hear the speech of the Lord, people of Israel! For the Lord has a lawsuit with the [inhabi]tants [11] of the land because there is no truth and no beneficence and no knowledge of God [in] the land.

Hosea 4:2: [12] Rather swearing, lying, murder, robbery and adultery have in[creas]ed, and bloodshed [13] has drawn near to bloodshed.

Hosea 4:3: Therefore the land will mourn, because everyone who lives in it will be cut off, [14] including even the wild beasts of the field and the birds of the sky; and also the fish of the sea [15] will be gathered on the dry land and will perish.

Hosea 4:4: In particular, no one will bring legal action and no [16] one will reprimand; and your people were like those who bring legal action against a priest.

Hosea 4:5: And you will stumble [17] by day. Then also the prophet will stumble with you by night, and I will silence your mother.

Hosea 4:6: [18] My people have been silenced for lack of knowledge. For you have rejected the knowledge, [19] and I will reject you from acting as a priest for Me. And as you have forgotten the Law of your God, {I will forget} [20] likewise I, too, will forget your sons.

Hosea 4:7: According to their multitude [likewise] they sinned [21] against Me. Therefore I will re[pla]ce their honour with their shame.

Hosea 4:8: The sin[-offering] of [22] My people they will eat, and they li[ft] their souls to their transgression.

Hosea 4:9: And it will be [like the] people, [23] like the priests. And I will [pu]nish him for his ways, and I will bring back his deeds [24] for him.

Hosea 4:10: And they will eat and will not be satisfied. Just as they have whored, they will not increase, [25] i.[e. mu]ltiply, because they have forsaken the Lord whom they were obliged to keep.

Hosea 4:11: [26] For the harlotry and the wine and the new wine take the heart.

Hosea 4:12: My people [27] ask their wood; their staff informs them. For the spirit of [impiety] has led (them) astray

⟨9a–10b are missing⟩

Exegesis
11a

[1] Hosea 4:15: [… He sa]id to them, When you used to come to these [2] [places …] on this [statue …] and when you used to swear by Me [3] […,] do not swear in My name

4	כ]................. כט]רח אלבקרה אלניר [אלדי הי] תחתה ככ׳ כי כפ[ר]ה סור[ר]ה
5	פ[בעד דלך] מ[ת]ל עקובתהם איצ[א ....אלבהאים [בק׳] כְּבֶשׁ פמעני
6	קו׳ עתה ירעם יוי יעני עלי [.....................] פי אלמוצ׳ע
7	אלואסע והדא נט׳יר ק[ו׳ ....]
8	אלאעדא [......]ל [...]
9	פסרה ב[עד דלך ....] עלי [.......] קד צאר מול]ף ללעצבים
10	אפר[ים] קד [.....] הנח לו יעני א[קר לה ....] אלטריק: וקיל
11	מ[א] דכרנאה פי אלשרח [.................] א]פרים קד אקר לה
12	יעני קד רתב לה [הד]א אל[....................]הם יבכרו אלי
13	ענד אלעצב[ים] אל[.................] יתסע אל]בכו]ר אלי וקת אלטעאם
14	פאדא כאן [..............................]ה סר מן ע[נ]ד אלעצבים אלי סבאם
15	אלי מא קד [אעטוהם] מן אלטעאם ואלשראב פלא יזלו פי אלשרוב
16	[א]לי אן [......ול]מ]א סכרו טלבו אלפגור בכ׳ הזנה הזנו ה[דא] שוגל
17	[......................] ללנהאר וקו׳ אהבו הבו יעני לאגל אנהם
18	[.................] ואעטו אנפסהם [.........א].....] וקראראהא חצל
19	[.................אגלא]הא יעני מלוכהא ורווסאהא אלדי הום להא
20	[.................] וקו׳ צרר רוח א[ות]ה ישיר בה אלי מא אגלאהם אלעדו
21	כאלשי [אלמצרור ב]טרף תוב ויו[.........] יובדד אלי אלאבאעד וקו׳ ויבשו
22	מזבחותהם יעני למא אוגליו דאך אלוקת יכון מן תלך אלדבאיח אלדי
23	כאנו ידבחוהא ללאותאן ויקאל פי צרר רוח אנה מתלהא פי אפעאלהא
24	במן קד צר ריח פי אטראף פי תיאבה יעני מא חצל מעה שי ולא
25	אפאד פאידה פלדלך יכזו יוכגלו הֵבוּ. משתקה מן הַבהַב פאלאצל הַבְ
26	ואלמונ[ג]ת] הֵבָה ואלגמע הָבוּ: שמעו: אסמעו הדה אלנציחה איה אלאיימה
27	ואצגו יא אל אסראיל ויא אהל בית אלמלך אנצתו לאן לכם אלחוכם לאן
28	מקאם פַ קד צרתם עלי אט[ואר] מצפָה ומתל שבכה מבסוטה עלי גבל

11b

1	תבור: ושחטה: ואלדַבח האולי [אלחאידין] גַמקָ[ו ואנא אדב] מן
2	[ג]ומלתהם: אני: אנא קד ערפת [א]פ]רים [ויא ישראל]לם תנכתם]
3	מני ב[א]ן אלסאעתה קד טג׳ית אפרים ואיצ׳א קד [תנגס אל א]סראיל:

Hosea 4:16: He shows [that they have discarded obeying [4] [... like] the cow [thr]ows off the yoke under [which she was], as it is said *Like a stubborn cow*. [5] [After that he co]mpa[res] their punishment also [with ...] the cattle [by saying] *Like a lamb*. The meaning [6] of *Now YHWH will graze them* is: on [...] the [7] open space; and this is like the verse [...] [8] the enemies [...].

Hosea 4:17: [9] He explains it af[ter that ...] [10] Ephraim is [attached] to the idols [...]. *Let him*, i.e. l[et him ...] the way. Another interpretation is [11] what we have mentioned in the commentary [...] Ephraim has let him, [12] i.e. he has arranged for him this [...]. They give incense to me [13] with the idols [...] the incense expands to the time of the food [14] and when it was [...].

Hosea 4:18: *He turned away* from the idols to *their drink* [15], to the food and the drink which [they gave to them.] They will not stop drinking [16] until [they are drunk, and after they] were drunk, they demanded harlotry, as it is said *They took to harlotry*. Th[is] activity [17] [...] for the day. The phrase *They deeply love* means: since they [18] [...] and gave themselves [...] and her confirmation was [19] [...] her [honourables], i.e. her kings and her chiefs who for her [20] [...].

Hosea 4:19: The verse *Wind has bound her up* alludes to (the fact) that the enemy has exiled them [21] like the thing [that is bound in] the fringe of a garment and [it is ...] and spread to the most distant (regions). The phrase *They will be ashamed of* [22] *their sacrifices* means: after they will have been exiled at that time, they will be ashamed of those offerings [23] they used to offer to the idols. Another interpretation of the phrase *Wind has bound up* is that he compares them, as far as their deeds are concerned, [24] with someone who has bound wind in the fringes of his garments, i.e. he had nothing, and [25] he did not have any benefit; therefore they will be ashamed and embarrassed.

Grammatical Note
הֵבוּ (Hosea 4:18) is derived from (the imperative) הַב הַב (Proverbs 30:15); the morphological base is הַב, [26] the feminine form being הֵבָה and the plural הֵבוּ.

Translation
Hosea 5:1: Hear this advice, priests! [27] Listen, people of Israel! And people of the house of the king, hearken! For the judgement is yours. For [28] you have become the place of a snare on the m[ountains] of Mizpah and like a net spread over the mount of | [1] Tabor.   11b

Hosea 5:2: And the slaughter these [deviants] have made deep, [and I am a chastisement] toward [2] all of them.

Hosea 5:3: I know Ephraim. And, Israel, [you was not hidden] [3] from Me. For now you have been impious, Ephraim. And also the people of Israel [have been defiled].

4	[ל]א: ליס יתרוכו שמא[י]להם ללרג[ו]ע אלי אלא[ה]הם לאן [ריח] טגיאנאת
5	פי אחשאהם ואלרב פמא [ערפו: וענה:] פסא ישהד איק[תדאר] אל
6	אסראיל [פי וגהה וא]ל א[ס]ראיל ואל אפרים יתעתרו בדנבהם תום קד
7	א[תעתר איצ'א אל יהודה מעהם: בצאנם: פבגנמהם ובבקרהם
8	יסלוכו לטלב אלרב ולא יגדו לאנה] כלע מנהם: ביי: באלרב
9	קד גד[רו לאן בנין גרבא ולד]ו פלד[ו] לך אלסאעת]ך יפניהם
10	שׁהְר מע [אנצבתהם: הדא א]לפצל מתצל אלי [אלפ]צל אל[די] קבלה
11	לאנה מקאבלה לל[.........]בהם [...]ם אולא[י] אלאיימה אלמקדמין
12	פי אלפצל אלמתקד[ם .... א]לנצי[ח]ה אלדי הודא ינצחהם
13	בהא תום אצ'אף אליה[ם] אלעואם ח[........ מ]ל[ך .... פ]קאל להם אנצתו
14	לאנכם אהל אלחו[ן]כם ו]קו' כי פח [הייתם למצפה ידל אלי אלט'][ולם ואלתע]די
15	עלי אלנאס מתל אלציאדין אלדי [יצטאדו .... ק]ו' פח וקו' רשת
16	ליורי אנהם יצטאדו אחאד ויצטאדו ג[מלה ....כ]...מ[צפה
17	ותבור ליורי אן טולמהם ללנאס טאהר מכ[שוף ....]
18	אקרן אלי הדא אלקול קו' ושחטה שטים. פקיל [אן ראגע אלי ....]
19	לאנה למא ד'כר פח ורשת אלדי המ[א] משהורה בציד [............]
20	אנהם ידבחו מא יצטאדוה אש[א]ר בדלך אלי [............]
21	וקו' העמיקו יעני כתרו ובאלגו פי דלך פיכון עלי [......]ר קו' ואני
22	מוסר לכלם תהדוד להם יעני בעד אן ק[ד פעלו] הדה אלאפעאל אנא
23	איצ'א אכון אדב לגמלתהם אווידבהם עליה וא[צ']רבהם באלצרבאת
24	אלדי יסתחקוהא. וקיל אן ושחטה שטים ראגע אלי אלכהנים יעני
25	האולי אלחאידין ען טאעתי קד כתרו אלדבאיח לגירי ואנא
26	מזאל מנהא כלהא יעני ליס לי פיהא נציב לאן הדא אלקול
27	מכצוץ באיימה עשרת שבטים אלדי כאן ידבחו ללעגלים

12a	
1	[..] וקו' בעדה לא יתנו מעלליהם
2	[..נ]ה אורא אן ליס הום מן יגי מנה
3	[..ו נגא[ר ......] יתנטפו מנהא בעץ'
4	[..ה]..[....]ה אסתעמל כתיר פי [...]
5	[..] קו' כי ר[וח זנונים בקרבם י]דל [...]

Hosea 5:4: [4] [Their] dee[ds] do not permit (them) [to retu]rn to their God. For [the spirit] of impiety [5] (is) inside them, and the Lord [they do] not [know.]

Hosea 5:5: And the strength of the people of [6] Israel will testify [in His face. And the peop]le of I[srael and the people of Ephraim] will stumble through their sin. Then [7] [also the people of Judah stumbled with them].

Hosea 5:6: And with their sheep and with their cattle [8] [they will go to seek the Lord, and they will not find Him; for] He has withdrawn Himself from them.

Hosea 5:7: [9] They have acted treacherously to the Lord [because] they [have beg]otten [foreign sons]. And therefore now [10] a month will consume them with [their allotments].

Exegesis

Hosea 5:1: [This] section is closely related to what precedes it, [11] for it is, as an equivalent for it, [...] these are the priests who are mentioned [12] in the preceding section [...] the [ad]vice, behold, he gives to them [13]. Then he added to them the common people [.... As for the house of the k]in[g,] He said to them, Listen!, [14] since you are the people of the jud[gement]. The phrase *For [you have been] a snare [to Mizpah* refers to the injust]ice and the aggre[ssion] [15] against the people like hunters who [are hunting ...]. The term *Snare* and the term *net* are [16] to show that they hunt single persons and they hunt a g[roup ...]. *Mizpah* [17] and *Tabor* are to show that their iniquity against the people is visible (and) ex[posed ...].

Hosea 5:2: [...] [18] He connects with this word the verse *And slaughter deviants*. Some interpret [that it refers to ...]. [19] For after mentioning *snare* and *net* which are both widely known in hunting [...] [20] that they slaughter what they hunt. By that he makes an allusion to [...]. [21] The phrase *They deepened* means: they increased and exaggerated that, and it is on [...]. The phrase *And I* [22] *am a chastisement for them all* is a threat to them, i.e. after they have done these deeds, I [23] am also chastisement for all of them. I will discipline them for them, and I will strike them with the plagues [24] they deserve. Another interpretation points out that the phrase *And slaughter deviants* refers to the priests, i.e. [25] those who turn aside from obeying Me. They have increased the offerings for somebody other than Me, and I [26] remove all of them from them, i.e. I have no share in them. For this word [27] is especially for the priests of the ten tribes which used to sacrifice to the calves. | [1]   12a [...].

Hosea 5:3–4: [...] and the verse thereafter *Their deeds will not give* [2] [...] he shows that they are not from one who comes from him [3] [...] they cleaned each other from it [4] [...] she used a lot in [...] [5] [...]. [The phrase *For the*

6	דאתהם פאטבק עלי דלך [.....] ....[ ]
7	ויש[ראל ואפר]ים כ[שלו ...]ל [...]ל [...]ל[ ]
8	א[הל בי]ת ....[ ]
9	לאן [................................]
10	אנצב תלך אל[................................]ת[...]
11	עלי אסם אנ[ביאי ....] קו׳ כשל גם [יהודה עמם......]י אלאוכר
12	אנפסדו איצׄא [.....]א[...] אי פיהלכו א[יצא ....] הלכו. למא
13	קאל פי צדר אלפצל ושחטה שטים העמ[י]ק[ו] ישיר אלי דבאיחהם
14	לגירהֿ כתם אלפצל פקאל בצאנם ובבקרם [י]לכו: אורא אן פי וקת
15	אן קד פָּאתֿ אלאמר וחוכם עליהם במא חוכם קד אתו באלקראבין
16	מן אלבקר ואלגנם ליתרצֹו רבהם בהא פליס ינפעהם דלך לאנה
17	קד סבק בקו׳ ולא אריח ריח ניחוחכם. פקו׳ חלק מהם ישיר בה
18	אלי [כלע] אלסכינה מן ב[י]נהם תום אורא אלסבב פי בוע[דה] ענהם
19	[יעני] גֿדר[הם בה ....] לאן ולדו גיל אגנביין מן אלטאעה קד נָשׁו נַשׁו
20	עלי עבאדה אלאותֿאן וקו׳ יאכלם חודש יקאל אנה מכצוץ פי
21	שהר אלדי כאנת נכבתכם פיה ויוקאל אנה מעמום עלי כל
22	שהר [...] עליהם פיה בנכבה: חלקיהם יוקאל אנה ראגע אלי
23	אלבלד ויקאל אנה ראגע אלי אלמעבודאת אלדי אסתכצוהא להם
24	באנצבה: תקעו: אצֹרבו בוק פי אלגבעה ואיצֿא צפארה פי
25	אלראמה תום גֿלבו פי בית און לאן וראך יא אפרים ינגלי
26	בנימ: אפרים: יא אפרים וחשה סא תציר פי יום תוביכה
27	פי אסבאט אל אסראיל קד עַרפת תאבתה: היו: קד צארו

1	רוֹסא אל יהודה כמולחקי [א]ל[ ]תכֿם עליהם אספך כאלמא חלטתי:
2	עשוק[:] מגשום חֶ[֗]ל אפרים בין [............] מרצוץ חוכם לאן
3	א[[מע]ן סָלך ורא וצֿ]יה] אלאנביא [אל.............:. ואני: ואנא
4	[כא]לעותֿ לאפרים וכ[אלנכר] לאל י[הודה: וירא: וראי אפרים

12b

sp]irit of harlotry is in their midst indi[cates that ...] [6] [...] the owner of them, and He agreed on that [...] [7] [...].

Hosea 5:5: [... The phrase *And Isr]ael and Ephra[im will st]um[ble* allud]es to [...] [8] [... peop]le of the hou[se of ...] [9] for [...] [10] I will raise this [...] [11] against the name of My pr[ophets ...]. [The phrase *Judah,] too, will stumble [with them ...]* the others [12] became weakened also by po[verty [...] and they a[lso] will perish [as] they perished.

Hosea 5:6: [13] After stating at the beginning of the section *And slaughter deviants have deepened* (Hosea 5:2), alluding to their offerings [14] for someone else than Him, he concludes the section with the phrase *With their sheep and their cattle they will go*. He shows that (even) [15] after the command had vanished and judgement had been pronounced against them by which they were judged, they (still) brought the offerings [16] of cattle and sheep to satisfy their Lord with them. However, that was of no use for them because [17] He had said already earlier *I will not smell your lovely aromas* (Leviticus 26:31). The phrase *He has withdrawn Himself from them* alludes [18] to the [withdraw]al of the Divine Presence from them.

Hosea 5:7: Then he shows the reason for Him being distant from them, [19] i.e. they acted treacherously toward Him: they procreated a generation of those who were estranged from obeying Him and raised a youth [20] for worshipping the idols. The phrase *A month will devour them* is according to one interpretation to refer especially to [21] [one] month in which their misfortune occurred. Another interpretation holds that it generally refers to every [22] month in which [...] against them with misfortune. Some hold that *Their portions* refers to [23] the land, others that it refers to the idols to whom they assigned [24] their portions exclusively.

Translation
Hosea 5:8: Blow a trumpet in Gibeah and also a siren [25] in Ramah! Then scream in Beth-Awen because after you, Ephraim, [26] Benjamin will be brought into exile.

Hosea 5:9: Ephraim, you will be desolation on the day of rebuke; [27] among the tribes of the people of Israel I have made known what is certain.

Hosea 5:10: [1] The chiefs of the people of Judah have become like those who encroach upon the bou[ndary; upon them I will pour out my wrath like the water.]

Hosea 5:11: [2] Oppressed is [...] of Ephraim between [..., crushed is judgement; for] [3] he willingly went after the command[ment] of the prophets [...].

Hosea 5:12: [And I am] [4] like the moth to Ephraim and like [the decay to the house of Judah].

12b

5 [מר]צّה ויהודה מְדַרהֿ [תום סלך אפרים אלי אלארץ אשור]
6 [ואר]סל יהודה אלי מֶלֶךֿ יָרֵב ו]הו פליס יטיק ישפיכם ולא[
7 [יוברי מנכם מדّר] יעני [גו]רח: כי:]לאן אנא כאלשבל לאל אפרים[
8 [וכאלצרגאם לאל יהודה] אנא [אנא אפתרס ואסלוך אחמל]
9 [וליס מוכליّ: אלךֿ: אסלוך ארגוע] אל]י מוצّעי אלי אן] ינדמו פיטלובו
10 רחמ[תי פי אלצّיק להום] יד]אלגוני: לכ]וֿ: וכדי יקול
11 בעצّהם לב]עْצّ ت]עْא]לו בנא נרגע]אלי אלרב לא]ן הו אלדי אפתרסנא
12 והו ישפינא הו [א]לדי כאן יצّרבנא והו יגّברנא: יחיינו: יחיינא
13 מן יומין פי אליום [אל]תאלת יקימנא ונחיא קודאמה: ונדעה: ונעלם
14 כ]י[ף נכלוב מערפה אלרב כפגר א]לדי[מסתוי מכרגהֿ פיואפי
15 אלינא כאלגית כאללקיש מע אלבכיר עלי אלארץֿ: מה: מא
16 דא אעמל בך יא אפרים מא דא אעמל בך יא יהודה ואחסאנכם
17 אנמא הי כגّמאם צובח וכאלנדא אל]די[הו מודّלג סאלך: על:
18 עלי דלך נחّתֿ באלאנביא קתלתהם באקאויל פי ו]אח[כאמך
19 כאלנור יכרג: כי: לאן איחסאן הֶוَית אגّל]מן ד[ביחה ומערפה
20 אלאה אגّל מן צّואעד: והמה: והום כאדמי עב]רו[עהד תם
21 גדרו בי: גלעד: גלעד קד צّארת קריה פאעלי גّל]גרבז[הֿ
22 מן גהה ספך אלדם: וכחכי: וכצّנאעיר אימר אלדי יצّ]ט[אד בהא
23 אגואק סמך כדלך גמע אימה עלי אלטריק יّקתלّו אלנאס מֶנْכֶב
24 ואחד ומّע דאך פאן פאחשה קד עמלוّ: בבית: פי אל אסّראיל
25 קד ראית פאקרה תם חצّל טוגّיאן לאפרים פתנגّס אל אסّראיל: גם:
26 איצّא אל יהודה קד געל לך חצّאד ענד מא ארדת אן יכון רגועי
27 מע סבי שעבי: הדא אלפצّל מנתסק אלי אלפצّל אלדי קבלה לאנה

Hosea 5:13: [And Ephraim saw] [5] his disease and Judah his rottenness. [Then the people of Ephraim went to land of Assur], [6] [and] Judah sent to the king of Yareb. [And he cannot heal you and] [7] [free you from rottenness,] i.e. a wound.

Hosea 5:14: [For I am like the lion to the people of Ephraim] [8] and like a young lion to the people of Judah.] I, [I will tear apart and I will go away. I will carry away.] [9] [And there is no deliverer].

Hosea 5:15: [And I will go, I will return to [My place until] they will repent and seek [10] [my] merc[y; in their distress, th]ey will set [out to Me at dawn.]

Hosea 6:1: Thus they will say [11] to each [other, Co]me then, let us return [to the Lord] because He is the One who has torn us apart, [12] and He will heal us; He is the One who used to beat us, and He will cure us.

Hosea 6:2: He will bring us to life [13] after two days; on the third day He will cause us to rise, and we will live before Him.

Hosea 6:3: And let us know [14] how we can strive to know the Lord like dawn w[ho]se appearance is regular; and He comes [15] to us like the rain, like the late rain with the early rain upon the earth.

Hosea 6:4: What [16] am I to do with you, Ephraim? What am I to do with you, Judah? And your beneficence, [17] truly it is like morning clouds and like the dew, wh[ich] disappears early in the day.

Hosea 6:5: [18] Therefore I have hewn (them) in pieces through the prophets; I have killed them through the words of My mouth; and your [judge]ments [19] come forth as the light.

Hosea 6:6: For I like beneficence more than sacrifice and knowledge of [20] God more than burnt offerings.

Hosea 6:7: And they like a human being, they have transgressed a covenant; there [21] they have acted treacherously against Me.

Hosea 6:8: Gilead was a city of evil-doers, [treacher]ous [22] because of the bloodshed.

Hosea 6:9: And as fish-hooks of a man [23] with which schools of fish are caught, so the company of priests murder the people on the road [24] unanimously; nevertheless they have committed an atrocity.

Hosea 6:10: Among the people of Israel [25] I have seen destitution; there Ephraim's harlotries took place, and the people of Israel have become unclean.

Hosea 6:11: [26] Also the people of Judah made a harvest for you, when I wished that there would be My return [27] together with the captivity of My people.

13a

1 [קא]ל [......] פי אכר דאך [פצל ו]ישראל ואפרים יכשלו תום קאל כשל גם
2 יהודה ע]מם פי [דאך אלפצל יצף] תעתורהם ובלאהם. קו' תקעו שופר
3 [בגבעה י]שי[ר בה אל]י .... ד]כַר רָמָה ודכר גִבְעָה לעלוּוהם וכדלך
4 [דכר] בית און ו]דכר בנימן י]שיר בה אלי תחצונהם מן אלעדו אלמוקבל
5 [עליהם] ליסביהם ס].................... איש סבב האולי חתי תאמרהם באל
6 תחצון פכאן אלנבי יגיבה [וקא]ל לה אחריך בנימן יע]ני[בעד אן תוגְלָא
7 אנת [.]מ[..]ה י]וג[.]לא ב[עדך .....]ל בן עמך בנימן [קו' בי]ום תוכיחה ישיר
8 בה אלי [אלזמאן] אלדי תחל [בה אלת]וכחות ו]הי א[לו]ת ..... [תום ביין בקו'
9 בשבטי [ישר]אל אנהא [....]לשבטים
10 וקו' הודעתי נאמנה [............. הדא אל]תפסיר נטיר
11 קו' פי אלשריעה ענ] .... [אפרים
12 מא תחלפיך אל]תוכיח]ה[....................... [לאסבאט ישראל
13 קד ערפת אל]תוכיחה] אלדי הי נאמנה ע]לי יד משה ואע]מל במא פיהא
14 פלם תפעל כל ד]לך .....]לת בך אלתוכיחה. מת]ל רווס]א יהודה במולחקי
15 אלתכום ואלאשארה בדלך אלי טולמהם ותעדיהם טאהר מכשוף
16 פלדלך [יס]תחקו אלסכט אלקוי קו' עשוק אפרים רצוץ מש' [בא]זא
17 קו' [פי] אלתוכחות והיית רק עשוק ורצוץ כל הימים תום אורא אלסבב
18 [פי דלך ....]ל בה והו תרכה לוצאיא אלאנביא ומר ורא וצאיא אל
19 אנביא אל[........] אלדי גדבוה אלי עבאדה אלאו]ת[אן. קו' ואני כעש
20 יעני אנא אוותר פיהם כמא יוותר אלע]ו[ת וד]כר ען אפרים אלעות
21 לאן אלבלא אליהם אס]וא[ודכר ליהודה אלרקב אלדי הו אבי[ס] מ]ן[
22 דאך תום אורא קצדה[ם] אלי אלמלוך ליסתעינו בהם ענד [אפא]תהם.
23 דכר ען אפרים אנה קצד מלכי אשור ודכר ען יהודה אנה
24 ארסל אלי מלך ירֵב [ו]הו מלך מצ]ר .... [אסר [.]לד
25 ויקאל אלי מלך יכאצם ע]נ[הם ויקאתל ענהם קו' [יש]יר אלי
26 מלך אשור כאנה קאל לאפרים למא מצא אלי אשור לא יוכל לרפא לכם
27 וקאל ליהודה ולא יגהה מכם מזור [..]תום איצא מלך ירֵב [.]אן יהודה

Exegesis

This section is closely related to what precedes it since he | [1] [sai] d [...] at 13a the end of this [section] *And Israel and Ephraim will stumble* (Hosea 5:5), then he said *Also* [2] [*Judah*] *has stumbled* [*with them* (Hosea 5:5), whereas] in this [section he describes] their stumbling and their misfortune.

Hosea 5:8: With the phrase *Sound a Shofar* [3] [*in Gibeah*] he re[fer]s t[o ...]. He mentioned *Ramah* and he mentioned *Gibeah* because of their altitude. And likewise [4] he mentioned *Beth-Awen* [and he mentioned *Benjamin*, and he] alludes to their fortifying themselves against the enemy who advances [5] [against the]m in order to lead them into captivity [...]. What is the reason for these so that you instruct them [6] to fortify themselves? The prophet gives an answer by saying to him *After you Benjamin*, i.e. after you have been exiled [7] [...], Benjamin will be exiled [...] with you, Benjamin.

Hosea 5:9: The phrase *On the day of rebuke* alludes [8] to [the time] when [the r]e[bu]kes will happen, i.e. curses [...]. Then he explains by the phrase [9] *Among the tribes of Israel* that she [... t]he tribes. [10]. The phrase *And I made known a confirmed thing* [... this] interpretation, like [11] the verse in the Law concerning [...] Ephraim [12]. The [rebuk]e will not happen among you [...] to the tribes of Israel. [13] I made known the [rebuke] which is *confirmed*, th[rough Moses and I will act according to] what is in it. [14] It did not do all this [...] the rebukes [...] among you.

Hosea 5:10: He compares the chiefs of Judah with those who encroach upon [15] the boundaries, thus alluding to their obvious (and) open injustice and aggression. [16] Therefore they deserve the severe wrath.

Hosea 5:11: The phrase *Ephraim is oppressed, judgement is shattered* corresponds to [17] [the verse in] 'The rebukes' *And you will be only oppressed and shattered all the days* (Deuteronomy 28:33). Then he demonstrates the reason [18] [for that ...] in him, namely that he abandoned the commandments of the prophets and followed the commandments of the [...] [19] prophets who lured them to the worship of the idols.

Hosea 5:12: The phrase *And I am like the moth* [20] means: I will affect them like the moth affects [the cloth]. He mentions for Ephraim the moth [21] because the misfortune is very bad for them; and he mentions for Judah the *rottenness* which is [more serious] than [22] that.

Hosea 5:13: Then he shows that they went to the kings to ask them for help in their hardship. [23] He mentions that Ephraim walked up to the kings of Assur, and he mentions that Judah [24] sent to the king of Yareb, i.e. the king of Egypt [...]. [25] Another interpretation is: 'to a king who argues against them and fights with them'. The phrase *And he* alludes to [26] the king of Assur, as if he said to Ephraim who went to Assur *He will not be able to heal you*, [27] and

13b

1 אַצְחַאב אלמַזוֹר יוקאל פי יגהה [......... מ]קאם יִכהה ויקאל א[ן ישתק]
2 מן יטיב גהה יעני יוחסַן ישיר ב[דלך אלי ....ל א]...... ויקאל אן]
3 תשתק מן יגה יעני יניר יְצִי [...]כ]....................] וטהורה [..........]
4 אלאצל גִהֶה פאדא רכבהא יגעלהא א[גהה: מזור אס]ם אלגורח: [תום אורא]
5 אלסבב פי דלך בקו' כי אנכי כשחל וק]ו' וככפיר מתל]ין אלואחד מ[שאר]
6 אלי אפרים [ואלאכר] משאר אלי יהודה [ובאזא א]ני אטרוף לאפרים ואני אטרוף
7 ליהודה וקו' [אלך ואשו]בה אלי טריק אלמ[באלגה] אלמעני פיה רגוע אלנור ואלוקאר
8 אלדי כאן [.....................] אל[..]ם [........].ל ענד [מ]א אלק]ודרה] כך וכל
9 בני ישר[אל ראיס ברדת האיש וכב]וד ייי על [הבית ....]
10 {פִי} יחז[..............................] מ[שאר ב]ק' אל]ך אשובה וקו'
11 אל מקו]מי ....]הם בל [קא]ל עד אשר
12 יאשמ]ו] תום אור]א ....]חות בעצהם בעץ
13 עלי אלרגוע אלי ת]עאלי קו' כי] הוא טרף משאר [אלי אפרים] אלדי קאל להם
14 לא יוכל לרפוא ל]כם קו'] יד ויחבשנו משאר אלי יהו]דה א]לדי דכר פיהם
15 אלמזור והו אלגורח [וקיל] פי יחינו מי]ומ]ים אן מע]נאה] מן בעד יומין ואלאשאר
16 בדלך אלי גלות בית ראשון וגלות בית שיני פיכון חקיקה אללפטה מן בעד
17 זמאנַין ויכון מעני קו' ביום השלישי פי אלזמאן אלתאלת וקו' יקימנו יעני
18 יותבתנא פי דולתנא ונבקא קודאמה אבדא לא יתגייר לנא חאל וקיל יחינו
19 מיומים אנה עלי טריק אלמבאלגה למא קאל קבלה וירפאנו פקאל יברינ]א] מן
20 מעאלגה יומין יעני אלטביב אלאסתאד אלדי פי אקל מא יכון [מ]ן [א]לזמאן
21 יצמד אלגורח ויגב]רנא ובעד] דלך פי אליום אלג' יותבתנא [.]צ]... ו]ק]י']ל יחינו מיומ'
22 אנמא יריד בה [..........] באנה קאל יברינא כאנא אנמא אעתלנא מן
23 יומין] לאן מותעארף בין אלנאס אן מן [יכון אל]עליל מודה יסירה פיכון

(as if) he said to Judah *And he will not heal your wound* [to include] also the king of Yareb because Judah | [1] was affected by *the wound*.

13b

Grammatical Note
Some say that in יִגְהֶה [... in the pl]ace of יִכְהֶה (*He is dim*) (Isaiah 42:4); others say th[a [it is derived] [2] from גֵּהָה יֵיטִיב (*Cure is good*) (Proverbs 17:22), i.e. he cures, th[us] alluding to [...; others say that] [3] it is derived from יִגַּהּ (*He shines*) (Job 18:5), i.e. he illuminates, he shines [...] and his appearance [...] [4] the morphological base (of the imperative) is גְּהֵה. If he attaches it, he forms אֶגְהֶה. [—*Wound* is a nou]n meaning 'injury'.

Hosea 5:14: [Then he demonstrates] [5] the reason for that by *For I am like a lion* and [*Like a young lion*, two similes:] the first [is an allusion] [6] to Ephraim [and the other] is an allusion to Judah, [since] the phrase *I will tear* [refers] to Ephraim, and the phrase *I will tear* [7] to Judah.

Hosea 5:15: [The phrase *I will go, I will retu*]*rn* is a hyperbolic expression whose implicit meaning is the returning of the light and the glory [8] which was in [...] at [...] the Omnipotence, as it is said *And all* [9] *the Israeli[tes watching them when the fire and the glo]ry of YHWH descended upon the te[mple* (2 Chronicles 7:3) ...] [10] {in} [...] by [*I will*] *go, I will return*. And the phrase [11] *To My pl[ace*] [...] their [...]; rather [he say]s *Until* [12] *they will acknowledge their guilt*.

Hosea 6:1: Then he demonstrates [...] each other [13] about the returning to the Ex[alted One ... The phrase *For He*] *has torn* is an allusion [to] Ephraim to whom he said [14] *He will not be able to cure y[ou]* (Hosea 5:13). The verse *He smites and He will bandage us* is an allusion to Ju[dah] about whom [15] he mentioned the wound, i.e. the injury.

Hosea 6:2: [Some say] that the mea[ning] of *He will make us alive from two days* (מִיָּמָיִם) is 'after two days' and [16] that alludes to the exile of the First Temple and the exile of the Second Temple. The basic meaning of the expression is 'after [17] two times'; and the meaning of *On the third day* is 'at the third time'. The phrase *He will raise us* means: [18] he will establish us in our country and we will stay before him always while our situation will not change.

Others say that *He will make us alive* [19] *from two days* is a hyperbolic expression, since he said before that: *And He will heal us* (Hosea 6:1), and it means: He will heal us by means of [20] the treatment of two days, i.e. an experienced physician who [21] will bandage the injury in no time and brings us back to normal. [After] that he establishes us on the third day [...].

Others say that by *He will make us alive from two days* [22] he intends [...] since he says, He will heal us as if we had been ill for only [23] [two days.] For it is well known among human beings, that the patient will walk after a short

24 ב[ר]וה סריע חסב [יחת]אג ואדא כאנת עילה קד טאלת מכתהא וגורח
25 קד טאל עליה אל[....................].ג אלי מודה טוילה חתי יתנטם וינגבר
26 פאו[רא] סור[עה אלבר בקו'] ונחיה לפניו יענ[י] כמא כונא נחצול בין
27 ידיה פי קו[.....] תום אורא אן מע כונתם פי קודסה יכונו עלמא
28 פוהמא כמא יגב עליהם ומע דאך יכונו חריצין נשיטין עלי

14a

1 [מערפה אלרב ....] ובק' כ]שחר אורא איקבאלהם תום אורא
2 [בקו' ויבוא כגשם לנו כמלקוש יורה ארץ] אנה ינמיהם ויכתרהם כמא יפעל
3 [אלמטר ....] אלכתאב אן יוקדם [יור]ה עלי מלקוש
4 [....................] א[ל]מ[לקוש ואן כאן אלמותאבר לאן
5 [....................] קו' כי הנה הסתיו עב[ר] קו' בעד הדא
6 [....................] תוב[תהם פי אל]..... כאן מן גהתהם
7 [....................] קיל] א[ז] קו' ח[צבתי ב]נביאים משאר
8 אלי ....] הדא אלקול [ה]ר[ג]ת]ים בא[מרי פי ... אל]די כאנו
9 [....................] יא[מורו בקתלהם או יתנ]בא[ו .... אן] יקתל וקו'
10 [ומשפטיך אור יצא יעני אן] כאנת גלייה מתל נור וקיל אן קו'
11 [ומשפטיך ראגע אלי נב]וה אלי תום] אורא אנה כאן יקתולהם באמרה
12 קו' כי חסד חפצתי מנתסק אלי קו' [ע]נן בקר וקו' ודעת אלים
13 באזא קו' לדעת את יי קיל אן מעני קו' כאדם [מתל] אלאדמי אלעא[ם]
14 וקיל אנה [רא]ג]ע אלי אדם הראשון אלדי יכאלף וקו' שם משאר אלי
15 אלמוצ'ע אלדי כאן יגב תועמל פיה אלטאעאת פפעלו הום צ'דהא
16 כמא קלנא פי קול ואל תבואו הגלגל ואל תעלו בית און. גלעד הו אסם
17 קריה כק' פי אל[ש]ריעה ויתן משה את הגלעד למכיר בן מנשה וישב
18 בה: פאורא אנהם בעד אן כאנו עלי נהאיה מא יכון מן אלצלאח
19 האולי אהל אלגלעד אנפסדו [.....].נ[.]ו בגד[....] פועלי און וצארו
20 יחתאלו עלי אלנאס פיספוכו דמאהם ויאבדו אמואלהם קיל וכחכי איש
21 אנה יריד בה אלצנאניר אלדי יוצטאד [בה]א אגואק אלסמך וקיל
22 אנהא [.......] לגה אלאנתטאר פיק[אל פי אנ]תטאראת רגול גדודים:
23 [י]עני כמא יכונו אלגד]ודי]ם אגואק אלאעדא ללנאס פירצודו כ[ל] יקע

time and [24] his recovery will be fast depending on his [i]ll[ness.] If an illness lasts for a longer period and his injury [25] lasts a long t[ime, he nee]ds a long time, to be put in order and to be brought back to normal. [26] And he demonstrates the spee[d of the recovery by the phrase] *And we will live before Him*, i.e. as we have been before [27] Him in [...].

Hosea 6:3: Then he shows that by being in His sanctuary, they will acknowledge [28] (and) understand what is their obligation. Therefore they will be eager and keen to | [1] [know the Lord ... . With the phrase *Like the*] *dawn* he demonstrates their drawing near. Then he shows [2] [by the phrase *And He will come like the rain for us*] that He will make them grow and multiply them like [the rain] does [...] [3] [... in this] book that [the early rain] precedes the late rain [...] [4] [... the] late rain. If it delays because [5] [... by] *For behold the winter is past* (Song of Songs 2:11).

14a

Hosea 6:4: The verse thereafter [6] [...] their [return] in the [...] he was from them [7] [...].

Hosea 6:5: [It is said] that [the phrase *I have*] *he*[*wn by*] *the prophets* alludes [8] [to ...] this word [*I have k*]*il*[*led*] *them by the wor*[*ds of my mouth* refers to those wh]o were [9] [... they com]manded to kill them or [they] pro[phesized ... to] kill. [10] [The phrase *And your judgements go forth as light* means that ...] was clear as light. Others say that the phrase [11] [*And your judgements go forth as light*] refers to pro[phecy. Then] he shows that He used to kill them with His decree.

Hosea 6:6: [12] The phrase *For I desire kindness* is closely related to *And your kindness is like a morning cloud* (Hosea 6:4), and the phrase *And knowledge of God* [13] corresponds to *To know* YWHW (Hosea 6:3).

Hosea 6:7: Some say that the meaning of the phrase *like Adam* [is an equivalent for] the gene[ral] human being; [14] others say that He refers to the First Adam who disobeyed. The word *There* is an allusion to [15] the place where the pious deeds should be performed; they, however, did the opposite, [16] as we have said in the verse *Do not come to Gilgal! And do not ascend to Beth-Awen!* (Hosea 4:15).

Hosea 6:8: *Gilead* is the name [17] of a city, as it is said in the Law *Moses gave Gilead to Makhir, the son of Manasseh, and he settled* [18] *there* (Numbers 32:40). He shows that, after they had reached the utmost degree of righteousness, [19] these people of Gilead became corrupted [...] *evildoers*, and they [20] deceived the people, shed their blood and took their properties.

Hosea 6:9–10: Some say that וּכְחַכֵּי אִישׁ [21] is to be understood as the fishhooks with which they catch schools of fish; others say [22] that it [is derived from (the imperative) הַכֵּה and] belongs to the lexical class of 'waiting'. It is said [that those] who are in wait for a man are *gangs*, [23] i.e. as the gangs are

24	[בידיהם] ליקתלוה פיא[כדו] מאל כדלך גמע אלכהנים קד חצלו
25	מתל אלגדודים עלי אלנאס קו' כי זמה עשו יכון משאר אלי
26	אלכהנים פוצף קובח פיעלהם ויגוז י[..כ]ון [..][כאי.] ענה באנהם

14b

1	באנהם יקולו ען אלנאס אלדי [......................................]
2	עמילו. קו' גם יהודה שת קציר [לך ....]
3	מצאף אלי מא כאן קד פעלו פיה[..............................]
4	בהדא אלקציר אלי מא בעת א[............................]
5	שוחד פסאלה אן יפסד אלעאהד אלד[...................]י
6	מא כאן קד טל[...][עשא וחא.................] וישמע[
7	בן הדד אל ה[מלך] אסא [..................................]
8	ישראל פקאל [ויך את] עיון ואת דן ואת [אבל בית מעכה ....]
9	ויך [......]ל[..........] אלסנה אלסתה ותלאתינייה [................]
10	עלי טאה[ר ......] קד קאמת אלדלאלה א[............]
11	מולך אסא ואנגמא אצאף אליהא [.]ל[..........] אלדי כאן [..........]
12	אבויה רחבעאם ואב[..................]ד מונתהי אלי מות שלמה
13	פבאן כאן קד [..........] עלי אלאומה לאגל מא גרי עלי יד שלמה
14	באן תנקסם סתה ותלתין סנה פאן אגתמעו בע[ד ד]אך ותוולפו
15	תנצלח קלובהם בעצהם לבעץ פלמא כאן פי דאך אלעצר גרי מן
16	יהודה אלפיעאל אלמדכור פאזדאדו ישראל נפור מנהם וחצל
17	בינהם בועד ומונאפרה פיכון קו' הונא בש[ו]בי שבות עמי
18	[י]ענו ענד וַמַלת אן יכון רגועי מע סבי קומי פיתולפו כמא
19	כאנו. כרפאי: ע[נד] אישפאיי לאל אסראיל אנכשף דנב אפרים
20	ובלייא שמרון אד פעלו בא[ט]ל וסארק אדא מא כאן יגי יגאר
21	עלי גוק כארג. ובל: ולם יקולו פי קלובהם באן כל בלי[יתהם]
22	קד דכרת פי אלסאעתה אלדי אסתדארו בהא ש[מ][אי][לה]ם וליס יקולו א[ן] חדא
23	וגהי כאנו: ברעתם: בבלייתהם יופר[חו מל]ך ובגוח[ד]אתהם ר[ווסא:]
24	כלם: כלהם פגאר מתל תנור מ[שתע]ל מן גהה כב[אז] מא
25	יעטול אלפגור מן אלקריה מן לת אלעגן אל[ו]י כְּמְרָתה: יום: יום
26	--- מלכנא [אמרצֿו ר]ווסא ללמְלֶךְ חומיה מן במר

15a

1	חתי גָדַב ידה מע [אלטנאזין: כי: לאן קד קרבו כאלתנור]
2	קלבהם באיכמאנהם [כל אלליל נאים כבאזהם צובח הו] מ[ש]תעל
3	כנאר מותלהבה: כלם: [כלהם יוחמו כאלתנור ואכלו מע] חכאמהם

groups of the enemies against the people and lie in wait for anybody who falls [24] [into their hands] in order to murder him and to take his property, likewise the company of the priests were [25] like the gangs against the people. The phrase *For they did obscenity* is possibly an allusion to [26] the priests and a description of their shameful deed; or it is possibly a [...] about them, since they | [1] said about the people who [...] [2] they did. 14b

Hosea 6:11: The phrase *Judah, also—He has put a harvest [for you ... is]* [3] an addition to what they had done in [... He refers] [4] through this harvest to what he sent [...] [5] bribe. And he asked him to nullify the covenant which [...] [6] what was [... And [7] Ben Hadad [heeded] king Asa [and he sent the officers of his soldiers against cities of] [8] Israel* (1 Kings 15:20); and: *And he struck Iyon, Dan and [Abel Beth Maacah ...* (1 Kings 15:20) ...] [9] *And he struck [...* (1 Kings 15:20) ...] the thirty-sixth year [...] [10] against [...] the sign arose [...] [11] the kingship of Asa. And when he added to it [...] which was [...] [12] his paternal [...] Rehobeam, and [...] the end until the death of Solomon. [13] And [...] he was [...] against the people because of what had happened through Solomon, [14] in that they were divided for thirty-six years. When they will have gathered after that and be united, [15] their heart will be at peace with each other. And after [16] the mentioned deed of Judah has happened in this period, Israel has increased antipathy against them and [17] a distance and alienation between them was established, His word will be here *When I will return the captivity of my people,* [18] i.e. when I have regarded it to be convenient to return with the captivity of my people, they will be united as [19] they have been.

Translation

Hosea 7:1: When I gave a remedy to the people of Israel, the sin of Ephraim was uncovered [20] and the decline of Samaria, for they acted false[ly]. And when a thief is wont to come in, he attacks [21] a group outdoors.

Hosea 7:2: They did not say in their hearts that [22] I remembered all their wicked d[eeds] by the time when their d[eed]s have surrounded them. And they do not say that [23] they were [before] My face.

Hosea 7:3: With their wicked deeds they make rejoice a king and with their ingratitudes chiefs.

Hosea 7:4: [24] They are all adulterers like an oven heat[ed] by a bak[er,] [25] as long as the adultery ceases from the town, from the kneading of th[e dough] unt[il] it is fermented.

Hosea 7:5: (On) the day [26] of our king, chiefs [made ill] the king with the heat of wine | [1] until he stretched out his hand with [the mockers]. 15a

Hosea 7:6: [For they have drawn near] [2] their heart [like the oven] while they lie in wait. [All the night their baker sleeps; in the morning it] bu[rn]s [3] like a blazing fire.

4	כל מלוכהם קד סקטו [לאן ליס יכון נאדי פיהם] אליי: אפרים:
5	אפרים פי אלשעוב [הו יסקוט אל אפרים כאן] בקורצה
6	גיר מקלובה: א[כלו: אכלו אלגרבא קואה והו לא] עאלם איצֿא
7	שיבה נָזְּחַ֫[ת בה והו לא עאלם: וענה: פסא יש]הד איקתדאר
8	אל אסראיל [פי וגהה ולא רגעו אלי אלרב א]לאההם ולא
9	טלבוה פי כ]ל הדה: ויהי: וכאן] אפרים [כחמ]אמה גֿאפלה
10	ליס להא תחצ]יל מצר קד נאדו] אלי אשור קד סלכו: כאשר:
11	פענד מא יסל]וכו אבסוט עליהם [שבכיי כטאיר אלסמא אחדרהם
12	אוודבהם [.................................]: הדא אלפצל מנתסק
13	אלי אלפצל אלדי [קבלה לאנה קו׳ ....]ה [.........] קו׳ בשובי
14	שבות עמי [..................................] פקאל ברפאי לישראל יעני ענד
15	מא ארדת נ[..................................]הם ינשפו ממא הום וינגברו ויעודו
16	אלי מא כאנו אלצלאח פזאדו מעאצי פבכו׳ ונגֿלה אורא
17	אנהם קבל דאך כאנו מתסתרין באלמעאצי פענד דלך אטהרוהא
18	ו[תטא]הרו בהא וקו׳ ורעו]ת ש]מרון ישיר אלי מא אחדתו פי שמרון
19	וזא[.........]מר אלבעל ואלאשירה וגֿיר דלך תום אורא אן קד כאן קבל
20	הדא אלדא[.... מ]נהם יתלצו פי] אל[סר] ואלאן פקד צֿארו יגֿארו עלי
21	אלנאס טֿאהר מכשוף פי אלשוארע לאנה כל כאנו לילין צארו
22	נהארין [צ]א[ר] אמרהם פ]י] אלבלא תום אורא קסאה קלובהם
23	ואנהם אדא אמתחנו במחנה מן גהתה ליס יקולו אן אללה קד
24	[דכר]נא ואן הודא יונבהנא בל יקולו הדא עארץֿ ואתפאק לאנהם
25	ליס יעתקדו אן אפעאלהם חדא נטר]י ב]ל ענדהם אני גֿאפל ענהם

15b

1	[.................................. מל]וכהם ורווסאהם ואורא אן
2	[..................................] עגבהם בכ׳ ישמחו מלך
3	תום אורא [אן ....] דלך פמתל אמרהם פי
4	דלך באלתנ[ור אלמשתעל מן אלכבאז אלדי כאן ח]אמי לא יברוד לאנה פי
5	ען הדא אלאמר תום באלגֿ [.............]א [..................]

Hosea 7:7: [They all are hot like the oven, and ate with] their judges; [4] all their kings are fallen. [For no one among them cries out] to Me.

Hosea 7:8: [5] Ephraim among the nations, [he will fall; the people of Ephraim were] a round cake of bread [6] (that has) not been turned over.

Hosea 7:9: [The strangers have devoured his strength, and he did no]t know; also [7] old age was sprinkled [on him, and he did not know].

Hosea 7:10: [And] the strength [8] of the people of Israel will testify [against him; but they did not return to the Lord], their God, and they did not [9] seek him in a[ll this].

Hosea 7:11: [And] Ephraim [was] like a foolish dove, [10] which has no understand[ing. They called to Egypt;] they went to Assur.

Hosea 7:12: [11] And even as they go, [I will spread] My nets [upon them]; like the birds of the sky [12] I will bring them down. I will discipline them according to [the report of] their [congregation].

Exegesis

This section is closely related [13] to what [precedes it since ...] to *When I return* [14] *the captivity of My people* (Hosea 6:11) [...].

Hosea 7:1: The verse *When I heal Israel* means: as soon as [15] I wanted [... to] their [...], they will be healed from their present state, and they will be restored and return [16] to their previous righteousness; however, they increased sins. He shows by the phrase *It is uncovered* [17] that earlier, they did their sins secretly, but then they brought them to light [18] and made them ma[nif]est. The phrase *The ev[il of Sa]maria* alludes to what they established in Samaria [19] [and they ad]de[d ...] the Baal, the Ashera and similar. Then he shows that [20] previously there was [...] of them, and they robbed s[ecretly], but now they attacked [21] the people visibly (and) openly in the streets, for all what happened during the nights, took place [22] during the days, [and] their affairs were in distress.

Hosea 7:2: Then he shows the hardness of their hearts [23] and that, (even) when being subject to a severe trial of His, they did not say, 'God [24] has [remembered] us and, behold, He observes us', rather they say, 'This is something accidental and it happened by chance.' For they [25] do not believe that their deeds are before [My eyes; rat]her, in their opinion, I do not pay attention to them | [1] [...]

Hosea 7:3: [...] their kings and their chiefs. And he shows that [2] [...] their astonishment, as it is said *They make glad a king*.

Hosea 7:4: [3] Then he shows [...] that, and he compares their situation in [4] that respect with the oven [lit by a baker which was h]eated (and) it does not cool off, for he is in [5] [...] because of this matter. Then he exaggerates

15b

6	פי אלבׄלא[א] .... א]לקריה פאנמא מקדארה
7	מא בין לת אל]עגין ובין כמרתה ....]למא מׇתׅלהם הום
8	באלתנור חסון [.............................] בדלך אלי תדבירהם
9	עלי חורם אל]פגור ....]לה כמא יוׄגׇמר
10	אלעגין: אלהי א]להי [אל]די פי בוׅעׇ]רה זאיד והו בוער] דכר ולו כאן
11	אלהי אצלי כאן [מו]נתׅ ו].................]ר: מתל ושחטה
12	שטים אלדי אלהי פיהא [מ]ופכׅ] .... פהי ושחׇט:
13	קיל אן קו׳ יום מלכנו משאר אלי [.............] הדא אלתפסיר
14	[מלכנו] משאר אלי אל]חא]ל] ....]ין קד כצה
15	מלכנא ומולאנא קד געלוה [..........................] פי שי מן
16	אלעילם ומן אלואגבאת וקיל אן אלא] .... י]מ]לכו מלך
17	עליהא יגׄוׅ יכון קו׳ החלו שרים מרצׄו פי [......]הם מן כתרה שורב
18	אלכמר ויכון קו׳ משך ידו ראגע אלי כל ואחד מנהם ויגוׄ יכון קו׳
19	החלו יעני אמרצׄו אלמׅלׅך אלרווסא ממא חאפו עליה באלכמר חתי מד
20	ידה מע אלטנאזין פאגאבהם אלי מא [.]ין] .[. פאורא בהדא אל]קו[ל
21	אנהם אדא אקעדו מלך מא ינטורו [כל] אלמטׅאלם ולא] .... [
22	אלרעׅאייה בל פי אלאכל ואלשורב ואל]ל] ....]עב. למא מתל] הדא
23	פגורהם באלתנור חסון אן ימתל בא] ...] ל] ... [ל]ל] .... [הם באלתנור
24	פי מעני] ..... [פקו׳ כי קׅרׅבו יעני מא יוקדם אל]ח]טב אלי אלתנור
25	חתי יוקד [כׄ]דלך הום יוקדימו אלי קלובהם אלתד]ביר ואלת]כמין
26	עלי [..]ד אל]נאס] ואכד אמואלהם פטול אלליל ליס להם פיעל בל תדביר
27	מתל אלתנור אלדי הו טול אלליל יוקד ואלבבאז נאים מא לה פיעל
28	פאדא כאן בוכרה קד אנתהא אלוקוד חאן ללבבז ונטיר

16a

1	הדא אלבלאם. [................................ קו׳ הוי חשבי]
2	און ופועלי רע על מ]שכבותם באור הבקר יעשוה תום]
3	שבה טולמהם ותעדי]הם [...........................]
4	וצעובתה כדלך שבה אל] [.............................]
5	יוחמא אלתנור [.....]ל] [.............................]
6	אלי קתלהם לכל [..................................]
7	יכון בדנובה] .... [
8	כל מלכיהם נפל]ו .... [
9	פיקתלה כמ]א .... קו׳ אין קרא בהם אלי ... [
10	אן לם יכון פיה] .... [
11	עלי אלבלא. אור]א .... [
12	תום נדבהם ונאח ע]ליהם .... תום שבההם[
13	באלקורצה אלדי ק]ד .... [
14	פיהא מן תחת אל] .... קו׳ אכלו זרים כוח]ו[

[6] in the [...] the town. As for the time [7] between kneading the [dough and its fermentation, ...]. After comparing them [8] with the oven, it is appropriate [...] by that for their planning [9] of the sin of [adultery ...], as [10] the dough is fermented.

Grammatical Note
The *he* in בּוֹעֵרָה [is an added letter, since תַּנּוּר is] masculine. If [11] the *he* were to belong to the morphological base, it would be feminine and [...], like וְשָׂחֲטָה 12] שֵׂטִים] (Hosea 5:2) where the *he* in it is [...], and it is וְשַׂחַט.

Hosea 7:5: [13] Some say that *The day of our king* alludes to [.... According to] this explanation, [14] *Our king* alludes to the sit[uation ...]. He specified him as [15] 'Our king and our lord'. They appointed him [...] in some [16] knowledge and duties. Others hold that the [day (?) ... whom] they appointed king [17] over them. It is possible that the phrase הֶחֱלוּ שָׂרִים means: they fell ill in their [...] from the great amount of drinking [18] wine; and the phrase *He stretched out his hand* refers to each of them. It is possible that [19] הֶחֱלוּ means: the chiefs made ill the king because they harmed him with the wine until he stretched out [20] his hand with the mockers, and he answered them to what [...]. He shows with this verse [21] that, when they had paralysed a king, he will not see [all] the wrongdoings and [he will] not [...] [22] the flock, rather in food, drinks and amusement.

Hosea 7:6: After comparing [...] this [23] their harlotry with the oven, it is appropriate that he compares [...] in the oven [24] in a different sense. The phrase *For they drew near* means: as one draws near the firewood to the oven [25] until it burns, likewise they draw near the plan [and the esti]mation to their hearts [26] to [...] the p[eople] and to seize their possessions. And throughout the night they are inactive, rather planning, [27] like the oven which burns throughout the night while the baker sleeps (and) is inactive [28]. And when morning comes, the burning has stopped (and) time for baking has come. Like | [1] this verse [... Woe to those who] [2] consider iniquity and do evil upon [their beds. When the morning comes, they do it (Micah 2:1).

Hosea 7:7: [Then] [3] he compares their iniquity and [their] transgressions [with ...] [4] and his difficulty. Likewise he compares the [...] [5] he heats the oven [...] [6] to kill them for all [...] [7] he is in his sins [... . The phrase] [8] *All their kings have fal*[*len* ...] [9] and He kills him, as [... . The phrase *There is none among them who calls Me* ...] [10] that there was not among [them ...] [11] because of the distress.

Hosea 7:8: He shows [that ...]. [12] Then he bewails them and bemoans th[em .... Then he compares them] [13] with the round cake of bread which [was ...] [14] in it from under the [...].

16a

15	קו׳ גם שבה זר[קה בו ישיר ב]ה אלי צַעְפַּהם ואיכתלאל ממלכתה[ם]
16	וליס יחו[ן................] עוגבהם ובלאהם ומע דלך פלם ינכסרו
17	וירגעו אלי רבהם תום שבההם באלחמאמה אלבלהאה אלמתחיירה
18	אלדי מא תדרי אין תקצד ובין דלך בקו׳ מצרים קראו פָאנָה
19	אורא [אנ]הם כאנו ידב[רו אן] ימורו יסתעינו באלמצריין פינאדו
20	ב[................גי]ירו ראי אן ימורו אלי אשור
21	יטר[חו................ אלחמ]אמה אלבלהאה אלדי תקצד מוצע
22	תום יב[..] לה[................] לאן ליס להא ת[ח]צ[י]ל צחיח פלמא
23	מתלהם ב[................]ר והו פיעל מ[ן ד]מום ל[אנהם] יתכלו
24	עלי [אלמ]דמ[ומין] אן ינצרוהם מתל אלעקובה אלוארדה עליהם
25	[בשבכה] אלטאיר פקאל אין מא סלכו אן סלכו אלי מצרים או אלי
26	אשור אנא אבסוט להם אלשבכה ואצטאדהם יעני בדלך לא
27	יתם להם אמר ולא ראי וקו׳ איסירם יעני אוודבהם וקו׳ כשמע

16b

1	[................ל[...]ל[...]אהם והי]ה אם שמע
2	תשמעו .... תח[ת אשר לא עבדת. ועבדת
3	את איביך ....] אימנת יגעלה אֶיחָם יֵחַם
4	[................]: אוֹרַב אסם אלכמן פענד
5	[אלאצאפה צאר בארבם .... יתבול]ל מן התבוֹלֵל: והי ל[.....]
6	[................] אֶי]סִירֵם מן הַיֵסֵר
7	[מתל השמד .... פאדא רכבה אימנת יגעלה אייסר] יַיסֵר מַיִיסִּיר
8	[................]ן לגה אלזיואל
9	[................]בה אימנת יגעלה
10	[................ הֵיֶס]ֵר פאדא רכבהא
11	[................].ַ. יר ואלדליל עלי
12	[................יקול אן הדה אליוד
13	[................] או: אלויל חצ]ל להם אד קד נפרו
14	מני נהב חצל על[יה]ם אד [גרמו בי ואנא פכו]נת אפדיהם והום
15	[פ]תכלמו עליי כדב: ולא: ומא צרכו [אליי פי קלב]הם אדא מא
16	יוולולו עלי מצאגעהם בסבב אלדגן ואלמסטאר [לאג]ל אן יתקווהו
17	בה מן גהתי והום יזולו מן טאעתי: ואני: ואנא למא אדבתהם
18	שדדת [א]דרעתהם ובסבבי כאן יפכרו רדא: ישובו: אן כאן פי

Hosea 7:9: The phrases *Strangers have eaten his strength* (and) [15] *Old age was sprinkled [upon him* are allusions] to their weakness and the deficiency of their kingdom [16] and [...] not [...] their conceit and their affliction.

Hosea 7:10: And despite that, they were not broken [17] and did not return to their Lord.

Hosea 7:11: Then he compares them with a foolish (and) confused dove [18] which does not know where to go. He explains that by the phrase *They have called Egypt*, and [19] he shows [that] they plan[ned to] go (and) ask the Egyptians for help. Then they call [20] [... they changed their] mind to go to Assur [21] to rem[ove ...] the foolish do[ve] which goes to a place; [22] then it [...] for she had no proper lea[rning].

Hosea 7:12: After [23] comparing them [with a dove ...], i.e. a blameworthy deed for they rely [24] on [the b]lamewo[rthy ones] to deliver them—, he compares the punishment that will come upon them [25] with the bird's [net], and He said that wherever they travel, be it they travel to Egypt or to [26] Assur, I will spread the net over them and I will hunt them; that means that no [27] deed or plan of theirs will be materialized. The phrase *I will afflict them* means: I will discipline them. *Like the hearing* | [1] [*for their congregation* ...] *their* [...]. *And* 16b *it will be if you* [2] [*hearken* ... (Deuteronomy 11:13) ... *because*] *you did not serve* (Deuteronomy 28:47); *you will serve* [3] [*your enemies* (Deuteronomy 28:48) ...].

Grammatical Notes

[יֵחַמּוּ (Hosea 7:7) ...] (the prefix letters) אימנ״ת, it will make it אֵיחַם, יֵחַם [4] [...]. אוֹרֵב (Hosea 7:6) is a noun (meaning) 'lying in wait'. And in [5] [the construct it becomes יִתְבּוֹלָל] .[... בְּאָרְבָּם] (Hosea 7:8) is (derived) from (the imperative) הִתְבּוֹלָל, that is [...] [6] [...]. אֲיִסְרֵם (Hosea 7:12) is (derived) from (the imperative) הַיְסֵר [7] [like הַיְצֵא. If you attach (the prefix letters) אימנ״ת, you say [,אֵייְסֵר מַיְסִיר, יֵיְסֵר [8] [...] of the lexical class 'abandoning' [9] [... If you attach] (the prefix letters) אימנ״ת, it will make it [10] [...]. If you attach to them [11] [...] and the proof for [12] [...] he says that this *Yod* [13] [...]

Translation

Hosea 7:13: [The Woe happen]ed to them, for they have turned away [14] from Me. Plunder befell them, for [they committed an offense against Me. And I] redeemed them, and they [15] have spoken lie(s) against Me.

Hosea 7:14: They have not cried [to Me in] their [heart] when [16] they wailed upon their beds because of the grain and the new wine [with whic]h they would be fed [17] by Me. And they cease to obey Me.

Hosea 7:15: And I after I disciplined them, [18] I strengthened their arms, but they considered evil against Me.

19 וקת ירגעו מן מא הום עליה פליס אלי אלעאלי ירגעו בל [צארו]
20 בכוס מכרה פלדלך יסקוטו באלסיף [רווסאהם] מן זעם [לסאנה]ם פענד
21 תמאם הדה אלבליה עליהם יחצ̇ולו מטנזה פי ארץ מצר: אל: אלי
22 חֲנַכְךָ יָא נבי ארפע בוק ב[ס]ב[ב .... כא]לנסר עלי בית
23 אלרב גזא אנהם [עב]רו עהדי ועל[י שריעתי גר]מו בי: לי: אלי
24 יצרוכו ויקולו יא אלאהנא קד ערפנאך [ל[אנה]ם א]ל אסראיל אלמכתצין
25 בי: זנח: כָּדַ̇ל אל אסר' אלכיר פלדלך אלעדו י[כלב]ה: ה[ם]ום
26 מלכו וליס מן גהתי רַוְסוּ ומא עלימת פצתהם ודהבהם עמילו
27 להם בהא אותאן לאגל ינקטע: זנח: כַ̇דלך עגלך יא שמרון לאן
28 אשתד גצ̇בי בהם מתי ליס יטיקו אלתברי מן מא הום

17a
1 פיה: כי: אן אֲצָ̇לָה מן אל אסר' והו פצאנע עמילה וליס הו אלאה
2 לאן שֲׁרָאר יכון עגל שמרון: כי: לאן ריח יזרעו וזובעה יחצ̇דו
3 קאמה ליס לה בל נבאת ליס יעמל דקיק פעל יעמל יסיר אלגרבא
4 י[ב]לעוה: נבלע: הלך אל אסר' אלסאעה צארו פי אלאחזאב כאינא ליס
5 [פיה מר]אד: כי: לאנהם טלעו אלי אשור פחצלו כחמאר אלוחש אלדי
6 [הו מון]פרד בראיה שעב אפרים קד חצלו מְגַאדַרִין במחבאת:
7 גם: איצ̇[א אדא מא יוגאדרו פי אלאחזאב אלסאעה אגמעהם עליהם
8 [ואבת]דו קליל מן חֲמַל מלך מע רווסא: כי: לאן קד כתר אפרים
9 [מדאבח לי]כטי עליהא תום צארו לה מדא[בח] ליכטי עליהא: אכתוב:
10 [כנת אכתוב] לה איכתַ̇אר ש[ריעתי מת]ל [א]לגריב חסיבו לה: זבחי:
11 [דבאיח עטאיאי ידבחו לח]ם פ[יאכלו אלרב מא ירצ̇י ע]נהם בל אלסאעה
12 יד[כר דנבהם ויפתקד כטאיאהם] פהם אלי מצ[ר יר]געו: וַיִשְׁכַּח: פנסי
13 אל אס[ראיל כאלקה ובנא היאכ]ל [ו]יהודה כתר קורי חצינאת פסא
14 אוסרח [נאר פי קוריה ותאכל ק]צורה: הדא אלפצ̇ל מנתסק אלי מא קבלה

Hosea 7:16: Whenever [19] they returned from where they (were), they do not return to The High, rather [they were] [20] like a deceitful bow. Therefore [their chiefs] will fall by the sword because of the anger of their [tongue]. And when [21] this tribulation will be completed against them, they will be [a mockery in the land of Egypt].

Hosea 8:1: To [22] your gum, prophet, lift up a trumpet be[cause ... like t]he eagle onto the house [23] of the Lord because they have [transgres]sed My covenant and against [my Law they have sinned, against Me].

Hosea 8:2: To Me [24] they cry out and say, 'Our God, we have acknowledged You'. For they are the people of Israel who are special [25] to Me.

Hosea 8:3: The people of Israel have forsaken the Good One, and therefore the enemy will pursue him.

Hosea 8:4: They [26] have made kings, but not with Me (being involved). They have appointed chiefs, and I did not know. Their silver and their gold they made [27] idols with it for themselves, so that it will be cut off.

Hosea 8:5: Your calf has forsaken you, Samaria. For [28] My anger became severe against them. How long will they not be able to be free from what they are | [1] in?

17a

Hosea 8:6: For its origin (is) from the people of Israel, and a craftsman made it, and it is not a god. [2] For sparks will be the calf of Samaria.

Hosea 8:7: For they sow wind, and they will harvest storm. [3] It has no standing corn, rather sprouts which produce no flour. And even if He does produce, the foreigners [4] will de[vo]ur it.

Hosea 8:8: The people of Israel are perished. Now they have become among the nations like a vessel [5] which is of no value.

Hosea 8:9: For they went up to Assur, and they were like the wild ass which [6] [was se]parated in his view. The nation of Ephraim paid for love affairs.

Hosea 8:10: [7] Also, though they paid among the nations, I will now gather them against them, [8] [and] they began a little from the burden of a king with chiefs.

Hosea 8:11: For Ephraim has multiplied [9] [altars to] sin on them. Then he had altars to sin on them.

Hosea 8:12: [10] [I wrote] for him numerous things of [my Law; like the writings of] the stranger they were regarded by him.

Hosea 8:13: [11] [(As for) the sacrifices of My presents they slaughter meat and they eat. The Lord does not accept from] them; rather now [12] He will rem[ember their sins and visit their wrongdoings], and they will retu[rn] to Egy[pt].

Hosea 8:14: [13] The people of Israel have forgotten [his creator and built build]ings, [and] Judah has multiplied fortified cities. And I [14] will send [fire into his cities, and it will consume] his palaces.

15 לאנה וצף דנוב[הם ומא אלדי] אסתחקוה עליה[א מן] אלגזא פלמא [כ]ת[ם]
16 דלך אלפצל פקאל אי[סירם צדר הד]א אלפצל פקאל אוי להם יעני אלויל חצל
17 להם מן גהה אפאת אל[סמא ונה]ב חצל עליהם מן גהה אלעדו ואלסבב פי
18 דלך לאני קד כונת אפד[יהם מן] אלאעדא ואפוכהם והום פקאבלוני עלי
19 דלך באלכלאם אלכדיב ואל[.... תו]ם אורא אנהם ליס ינכסרו תחת אלתאדיב
20 וקו׳ בלבם יעני מא צרכ[ו ....] פי קלובהם לם ידכרוני בל יולולו
21 וינוחו [עלי מצׄאעהא [ס]ם ב[סבב אלכיר] אלדי זאל מנהם: יתגוררו משתקה מן
22 קו׳ אשר אני מ[תגורר עמה וחקי]קתהא תגרור ל[................] הו
23 אלתקווׄת יענ[י ....]ם עליהם ואקותהם והום זאילין מן
24 טאעתי פלדלך מנעתהם אלקות תום אורא בקו׳ יסרתי חזקתי אנה למא
25 ודבהם צברהם עלי [.].[ל.....................]ע דאך פכאן יצכרו אליה
26 דלך עלי טריק אלד[...... ו]הֻמא דברו עלי כזבים תום קאל ואלי יחשבו
27 [ר]ע ליעוֹם אלטאהר ואלבאטן אורא בקו׳ ישובו לא על אנהם אן
28 [...] פי וקת ואנכסרו פליס אלא אללה ירגעו ואנמא אלסבב מן

17b
1 אלאסבאב ומתלהם באלקוס אלמכרה פי דלך אלדי יוקׄדר פיהא
2 אנהא תנפע והי צׄרר תום אורא אן לאגל אלסכט אלדי חצל עליהא
3 מן גהה כלאמהם אסתחקו רוׄסֹאהם אן יוסֹלמו ביד אלעדו פיקתלוהם
4 באלסיף ככ׳ מזעם לשונם. ואורא בקו׳ זו אן ענד תמאם הדה אלבלייה
5 פיהם יחצלו מטנזה פי ארץׄ מצר ענד אעדאהם: קו׳ ללנבי [אל חכד]
6 שופר יעני ארפע צותך מתל אלבוק לאן אלנבי קד לוקׄב בצ[...ות לאן קד]
7 גרת עאדה אל[צׄוף]ה באן יצרב באלבוק וינדׄר אלקום וקו׳ כנשר [ישיר בה]
8 אלי מא קאל צ[אח]ב אלשריעה כאשר ידאה הנשר ואלאשאר[ה אלי]
9 [נב]ו[כ]דנצׄ[ר וכשד]ים תום אורא אלסבב פי דלך בקו׳ יען כי [לי יזעקו]

Exegesis

This section is closely related to what precedes it, [15] for he described [their] sins [and] the punishment they deserved for them.

Hosea 7:13: After completing [16] that section by saying *I will af[flict them* (Hosea 7:12), he begins thi]s section with *Woe to them*, i.e. woe should occur [17] upon them by (the) damages of [the heaven, and plund]er should occur upon them by the enemy. The reason for [18] that is that I redeemed [them from] the enemies and liberated them; they, however, requited Me for [19] that with the mendacious and [...] speech.

Hosea 7:14: Then he shows that they did not break under the chastisement. [20] The phrase *In their heart* means: they did not scream [...] in their hearts. They did not remember Me rather they wail [21] and lament [on the]ir [beds] be[cause of the benefit,] which have been removed from them.

Grammatical Note

יִתְגּוֹרָרוּ is derived from [22] the verse *With whom I d[well* (1 Kings 17:20); but] its true me[aning] is 'Being neighbours' [...].

[...] is [23] food, i.e. [...] on them and I will feed them; they, however, ceased [24] to obey Me. Therefore I have deprived them of the food.

Hosea 7:15: Then he shows by the phrase *I have afflicted, I have strengthened* that after [25] disciplining them, He comforted them on [...] this and they cried to Him. [26] That is by way of [...] *they have spoken lies about Me* (Hosea 7:13). Then he says *And they think* [27] *evil of Me* to include the visible and the hidden.

Hosea 7:16: He shows by the phrase *They return not (to The) High* that they [28] [...] at a time and were defeated, they did not return to God. One of | [1] the reasons that he compares them with a deceitful bow is that it is believed [2] to bring benefit but it is damaging. Then he shows that because of the anger which came upon them, [3] caused by their word, their chiefs deserved to be delivered into the hand of the enemy, so that they should kill them [4] by the sword, as it is said *Because of the fury of their tongue*. He shows by the word *This* that when this their tribulation [5] has come to an end, they will be a derision in the land of Egypt among their enemies.

17b

Hosea 8:1: The phrase, addressed to the prophet, *To your palate* [6] *a shofar* means: raise your voice like a trumpet. For the prophet had the by-name the voi[ce of the watchman, since] [7] it was the practice of [the watchman] to blow the trumpet and to warn the people. The phrase *Like an eagle* [alludes] [8] to what the master of the Law said *As an eagle will swoop* (Deuteronomy 28:49), and the allusio[n refers to] [9] [Neb]uka[dnezza]r and the Chald[eans]. Then he shows the reason for that by the phrase *Because*.

10 [......] חל בהם אלבלא דאך [......] אראד בה אן פי
11 [......] צחו קול [......] ויקולו קד ערפ[נא]ך
12 [......] כקו׳ אלהי [......] יפעלו הדא
13 [......]ני. ידענוך. קו׳ זנח ישראל טוב יע[נ]י
14 בסמך אדא כאן ישירו [......] עדו [......]כלבה א[ל] וכ[ס]רה אסתחק אן [י]
15 קו׳ למען יִכָּרֵת [......] רווס וא[דא כאן] בשין יכון ת[יכון אזאלה]
16 אלדי הדה אלעצבים [אלדי עמ]לו זהב וא[ל] משאר אלי אלכס[ף] אלמדכור
17 אלדי בעץ אלעגלים [יחתמל אנהם עמ]לו שמרון עגלך לשומהם לפקרהם קו׳
18 ש]מרון עגל אלדי כאן עמל ירבעם אלי שמרון וי[חתמל לאן ח]מלו פי
19 בקו׳ [בעל ואלאשירה] בלאיא [אלעגל ואל] תאלת פקד חצל פי שמרון ג׳
20 יעני אצל הדא אלעגל קו׳ כי [מישראל] וגם האשרה עמדה בשמרון.
21 [ואלא]ן רגעו הונא טרוה והו הום כאן קד אנסוה קדים פי אלמדבר
22 לקבוה אללקב אלדי קד [......]ל[......] איצא עמל צאנע מתל דאך
23 וחרק כמא [......]בבים כי ש[תום אורא בקו׳ ל[....] גמי[עהם]
24 וישרף אשר עשו [ויקח אל העגל] אוחרק דאך לאן כדי קאל ען דאך
25 אורא בה אנהם מא יתעבו פיה ויוקרבו באש: קו׳ כי רוח יזרעו.
26 בין ידי אלעגל ואלבעל פמא יחצול להם מנה פאידה בל ובאל
27 יעטיהם יפעל אולי יעש]ני לעל אללה והדא תשביב כלאם וקו׳ אולי י[
28 קו׳ נבלע ישראל אלגר[בא והום] יאכלוה: שי מן אלגלה פיוסלט עליהם אלהים
29 [......] עלי טריק אלונוח עליהם וקו׳ ככלי אין חפץ בו ישיר בה אלי
30 [......]הא אלה כֹזף אלדי יסתעמלהא אלמחַזִין לאנה אדא רמא ב

18a 1 [.......] לא יושרב בהא מא ולא יוכד פיהא נאר כך׳ לחתות אש מיקוד
2 [ולחשוף] מים מגבא: תום אורא אלסבב בקו׳ כי המה עלו אשור יעני הום
3 [חבו] מכאלטה אלגוים וקו׳ התנו אהבים יעני כאלטוהם פי מעבודאתהם
4 [......]ם מחבאת ואורא בקו׳ התנו יעני הום אלדי ארשוהם ללגוים
5 [......] לקב דלך בגועל וגדר לאנה בסבב אלמעבודאת אלדי
6 [......] מנהם קו׳ גם מצאף אלי פיעלהם יעני כמא אבתדו הום

Hosea 8:2: By the phrase [*They will cry to Me*] [10] he intends that in [...] the misfortune befell them. This [...]. [11] And they say, We know [you ...] it became clear [...] [12] they do this [... as it is said *God,*] [13] *we know you.*

Hosea 8:3: The verse *Israel has rejected (The) Good (One)* me[ans: ...] [14] and he defeated him, he deserved that the [enemy will persue him].

Hosea 8:4: [**Grammatical Note**: When הֵשִׂירוּ is (written)] with *samekh*, [15] it means 'removing'. When it is (written) with *sin*, it means ['appointing for leader'].

The phrase *So that it will be cut off* [16] alludes to *silver* and *gold*, mentioned [before, which they ma]de into idols, [17] so that they became their calamity and their destitution.

Hosea 8:5: The phrase *Your calf, Samaria* [may indicate that they transferred] one of the calves [18] which Jeroboam had made, to Samaria; or [it may be that they] made a [19] third calf in Samaria. And there have been three afflictions in Samaria: [the calf, the] Baal and the Asherah, as it is said [20] *And also the Asherah stood in Samaria* (2 Kings 13:6).

Hosea 8:6: The phrase *For* [*from Israel*] means: the origin of this calf. [21] They made it once in the wilderness [and n]ow they returned there to restore it, and [22] also a craftsman made (it) like this [...] the name, which they called it [23] [...] all [of them]. Then he shows by *For sp*[*linters*] that ...] and it was burned, as [24] that one was burned, for thus it is said about that one [*He took the calf*] *they had made and burned* (*it*) [25] *in fire* (Exodus 32:20).

Hosea 8:7: He shows with the phrase *For they sow wind* that whatever they toil and offer [26] before the calf and the Baal, they will not have benefit from it rather harm, [27] and this (is) a figure of speech. The phrase *Perhaps* [*He will make* me]ans: perhaps God will act (and) give them [28] something of the crops; however, He will impose the forei[gners] as rulers over them [and they] will devour it.

Hosea 8:8: The phrase *Israel is swallowed up* [29] (is said) by way of lamenting them. The phrase *Like a vessel in which is no pleasure* alludes to [...] [30] a vessel of pottery the decorator uses, for when he has thrown in [it ...] | [1] [...]   18a
one does not drink water out of it and takes no fire in it, as it is said *To scrape a burning coal from a fire* [2] [*and to scoop*] *water from a cistern* (Isaiah 30:14).

Hosea 8:9: Then he shows the reason by the phrase *For they ascended to Assur*, i.e. they [3] [loved] the association with the nations. The phrase *They paid* (*for*) *love* means: they associated with them in their idols [4] [...] love. He shows by the phrase *They paid*, i.e. who gave them as a tribute to the nations [5] [...] called that a payment and a fee, for it is because of the idols which [6] [...] from them.

7 וכ[אלט]ו אלגוים [כ]ד[ל]ך איצֹא אנא אול[...] אלי מא בינהם פ[......]ה[.]
8 אלאכתלאט בהם זעם בעץֹ אלמפ[סר]ין אן עתה אקבצם הונא מחמוד
9 פילזמה יגעל יָתְנוּ איצֹא מחמוד פיגעלה [... ז]כאיה ו[ת]ובה והדא
10 בעיד לאן אלכלאם כלה מונתטֹם עלי אלדם פקו' עתה אקבצם משאר
11 אלי אלגוים יעני אגמעהם עליהם חתי יגלוהם וקו' ויחל[ו] מעט מא יקוי
12 דלך לאנה משאר אלי מא אבתדא פול א[ג]ל[י]הם ומ[ן] וגד פהם קליל מן
13 אלכתרה וקו' ממשא מלך שרים [ ] יגוז ישיר בה] אלי אלמלוך ואלרוסא
14 ליסתמלכוהם ויסתעבדוהם ויגוז יקאל מן חַ[מַ]ל אלמלך ואלרוסא להם
15 וקד קיל אנה אראד בהדא איבתדא חמלתהם [א]להדאיא אלי מלוך אשור
16 וארוסאהם לינכפו ענהם קאל כי הרבה אפרים מזבחות יושאר בדלך
17 אלי אלמדאבח אלדי אנשוהום וקו' היו לו מזבחות ישיר אלי מדאבח
18 קד בנוהא גירהם והום יכְּטוּ יַדְּנְבוּ עלי הדה ועלי הדה ואתבע דלך
19 בקו' אכתב לו לאנה כאן קד נהאהם פי יום סיני בקו' לא תשתחוה להם
20 ולא תעבדם. קיל קו' אכתב לו רובי תורתי אנה משאר אלי גמלה
21 אלתורה פיכון הדא משאר אלי מא אַמַר אלנבי משה בכתבתהא כקו'
22 ויכתוב משה את התורה הזאת וקיל אן אכתב לו ראגע אלי אלעשר דברות
23 אלדי קיל ענהא ויכתבם על שני לחות אבנים פעלי אלתפסיר אלאול יכון
24 קו' רוּבֵּי איכתאר ועלי הדא אלתפסיר יכון קו' רובי אַגֻל שראיעי
25 ואעלאהא והי אלעשר דברות לאנה קד אסמא אלי' דברות תורה כך'
26 ואתנה לך את לחות האבן והתורה והמצוה: אשר כתבתי: וקד קאמת
27 אלדלאלה אנה לם ידפע אליה גיר אללוחות פקט: קו' כמו זר נחשבו: [יחתמל
28 יורד אלי אלתורות אנהם קד חצלו ענדהם מקאם כותב אלגֹרבא אל[די]

18b
1 ינתפעו בהא ויחתמל יכון ראגע אליהם הום כאנהם קד [...............]
2 גרבא מן שריעתהם פליס ינתפעו בהא כמא ליס ינתפעו[...............]
3 אל[די] הום גרבא מנהא יוכאל הבהבי אנה אסם ואליוד פי[ה זיאד ....]
4 ואלאשאר בדלך אלי אלדבאיח אלדי ידבחוהא ללאות[אן] יוקאל אן

Hosea 8:10: The word *Also* (means:) in connection with their deed, i.e. just as they began [7] to as[sociate with] the nations, [li]kewi[se] I also [...] to what is among them [... I cancel] [8] the association with them. Some commentators hold that the phrase *Now I will gather them* is to be taken as praiseworthy in this context, [9] and the phrase *They pay* as well must be praiseworthy. And he holds it to be his [justice] and his repentance. However, this [10] is unlikely, because the speech is entirely presented as a chastisement. The phrase *Now I will gather them* alludes [11] to the nations, i.e. I will gather them against them to exile them. The phrase *They began a little* does not support [12] that, for it alludes to what [Tiglatpil]eser started: [he exiled them and whoever] was found, they were little [13] in number. The phrase *From the burden of a king (and) chiefs* [possibly refers] to the kings and the chiefs [14] to rule over them and to enslave them. It it also possible that the meaning is: 'From the burden of their king and of their chiefs'. [15] Some interpret that he referred with this to the beginning of their bringing [t]he [gif]ts to the kings of Assur [16] and their chiefs with the intention that they should refrain from them.

Hosea 8:11: The phrase *For Ephraim has increased altars* alludes [17] to the altars they had erected. The phrase *He had altars* alludes to altars [18] others had built; and they trespassed and sinned on both of them.

Hosea 8:12: He makes that follow [19] by the phrase *I write for him*, for He had prohibited them on the day of Sinai saying *You shall not prostrate yourself to them* [20] *nor worship them* (Exodus 20:5). Some commentators say that the phrase *I will write for him myriads of My Torah* alludes to the [21] entire Torah, and this is an allusion to the decree of the Prophet Moses when writing it, as it is said [22] *And Moses wrote this Torah* (Deuteronomy 31:9). Other commentators say that *I will write for him* refers to the Ten Commandments [23] about which it is said *And he wrote them on two stone tablets* (Deuteronomy 4:13 = 5:18). According to the first interpretation, [24] רֻבֵּי is a great number, and according to this (latter) interpretation, רֻבֵּי are the most significant [25] and the most important of My laws, namely the Ten Commandments, for the Ten Commandments are called 'Torah', as it is said [26] *And I shall give you the stone tablets and the Torah and the commandment that I have written* (Exodus 24:12). [27] This indicates that He did not hand over to him anything else but the tablets alone. [It may be that he intended] the phrase *They were regarded as alien* [28] to mean that they regarded the laws as the writings of foreigners [from] | [1] which they gained benefit. Or it may refer to them, as if they had [...] [2] foreigners from their law, and they did not gain benefit from them, as they did not gain benefit [from ...] [3] which are more alien than them.

Hosea 8:13: **Grammatical Note:** Some commentators hold that הַבְהָבַי is a noun and the *yod* in it [is pleonastic ...], [4] and the allusion by that (is) to

5 הַבְהָב עֲטַא משתק מן הב ויגוז יכון אליוד פיהא נסב [..................]
6 קאל אלדבאיח אלדי כאן יגב אן תכון ל[...............]ל[..................]ת
7 ומא שאכל דלך קד צארו ידבחוהא בין ידי אלאותאן ויא[כלוהא] פלדלך
8 ליס הי מרציה בל ובאלהא עליהם וקו׳ המה מ[צרי]ם ישובו ישיר בה אלי
9 מא אלתגו אן ירגעו אלי מצר האולי והאולי כמא הו מדכור פי אַבְּבּאַרהם
10 אן כל מן בקי מן [ס]איר אלאסבאט אגתמעו ורגעו אלי מצר קו׳ ויבן היכלות
11 יוקאל אן משאר [א]לי אלבמות אלדי כאן קד בנו לעבודה זרה ויקאל אנה
12 משאר אלי אלקצו[ר] אלדי קד בנו מלוכהם ליתחצנו בהא ומתלה קאל ען
13 יהודה הרבה ער[י]ם בצורות לית[חצן בהא אלואחד מן שְׁבָבִים יגב יכון
14 שֶׁבֶב לאן גמע שָׁבּ]יב הו שָׁבִי[בִים אלתיו פי סופתהָ תפכים ואנמא הו
15 סופה: התְנו מן התנה ואלאצל מנה אֶתְנָה׳ הֵמה: לאן לִלגַדֶר אסמין
16 ואחד בנונין ואחד והו את פאלדי בנון ואחד הו אֶתְנָה ואלדי
17 בנונין הו אתנן וגמע רֵבֵה רֵבִים ואלמצאף מן רֵבִים רבֵי תורתי:
18 מתל אשה ואשֵׁי אלדי הו מצאף אשים: אל: לא תפרח יא אסראיל
19 אלי טרב כאלשעוב לאנך קד טגית ען טאעה אלאהך אחבת
20 גועל מע כל אנאדר דְגַן: גורֶן: פלדלך אלאנדר ואלמעצרה לא ירעאהם
21 כל ואחד מנהא ואלמוסטאר פינכתם מנהא: לא: ליס יגלסו פי ארץ
22 אלרב בל ירגע אפרים אלי מצר ופי בלד אשור נגס יאכלו: לא: לאן
23 ליס הודא ירושו ללרב כּמר וליס הודא יערבו לה אפעאלהם
24 לאן דבאיחהם כטעאם כופאר להם פכל פכל אַיכְלַיה יתנגסו לאן
25 טעאמהם לאנפוסהם ליס ידכול אלי בית אלרב: מה: מא דא תעמלו
26 פי יום מוֹעֵד ופי יום צחייה אלרב: כי: אן הודא קד סלכו מן בעד

the offerings they used to offer to the idols. [Another opinion is that] [5] הַבְהָב 'gift' is derived from הַב (Proverbs 30:15 = Daniel 5:17) and the *yod* in it could be a gentilic [...] [6] he said the offerings which had to be [...] [7] and similar cases.

They used to offer them before the idols and ate them, and therefore [8] they were not acceptable, rather they brought calamity upon them. He alludes by the phrase *They returned to E[gyp]t* to [9] where they sought refuge: that they both return to Egypt, as it is mentioned in their annals [10] that each of the [rem]aining tribes, which was left behind, gathered together and returned to Egypt.

Hosea 8:14: Some say that *He built temples* [11] alludes to the high places which they had built for idolatry. Others say that [12] it alludes to the castles which their kings had built to fortify themselves in them. And likewise it is said about [13] Judah *It has multiplied [fortified] cities* [to forti]fy himself in them.

Grammatical Notes

The singular of שְׁבָבִים (Hosea 8:6) should be [14] שֶׁבֶב because the plural of שָׁבִיב (Daniel 3:22) is שְׁבִיבִים. The *taw* in סוּפָתָה (Hosea 8:7) is an emphatic element, yet it is [15] סוּפָה. הִתְנוּ (Hosea 8:9) is (derived) from (the imperative) הַתְנָה; its morphological base is אֶתְנָה הֵמָּה (Hosea 2:14); for two nouns belong to the root, [16] one with two *nun*s and one with one *nun* (only). The one with one *nun* is אֶתְנָה (Hosea 2:14), and the one [17] with two *nun*s is אֶתְנָן (Hosea 9:1). The plural of רַבֵּה (Hosea 8:12) is רַבִּים and the conjoined form of רַבִּים is רַבֵּי תוֹרָתִי (Hosea 8:12), [18] like אִשֶּׁה and אִשֵּׁי which is the conjoined form of אִשִּׁים.

Translation

Hosea 9:1: Do not rejoice, Israel, [19] unto a joy like the nations! For you have committed harlotry away from obeying your God. You loved [20] payment with all threshing-floors of grain.

Hosea 9:2: And therefore the threshing-floor and the wine press will not feed them [21] each of them—, and the new wine will be concealed from it (= the land).

Hosea 9:3: They will not stay in the land [22] of the Lord, rather Ephraim will return to Egypt, and they will eat unclean (food) in the land of Assur.

Hosea 9:4: For [23] behold, they will not pour out wine to the Lord and, behold, their deeds will not be pleasing to Him. [24] For their sacrifices (will be) to them like the food of unbelievers, and all who eat it will become unclean. For [25] their food is for themselves; it will not enter the house of the Lord.

Hosea 9:5: What will you do [26] on the day of the appointed time and on the day of the sacrifice of the Lord?

27 נהב פמצר תגמעהם תום מֻףּ תַקְבְּרֵהם פאלמואצֵּע פאלמתמנאה
28 [לא]מואלהם {שוךּ} חַרְשַׁףּ יִרְתָהֵ֑ם: ואיצֹא שוךּ ינבות פי אכבייתהם:
29 באו ואפו איאם אלאפתקאד קד ואפו איאם אלמכאפאה סא יעלמו

19a
1 יש[ר]אל גֹאיל [............] ל[...]ל[.........]ל[............]
2 מווסוס ו[מגנו]ן [עלי כתרה דנבך וכתרה מחאקדה: צופה:
3 דידבאן אנצב לה א[פרים מע אלאהי נבי פך יוהק עלי כל טֹ]ורקהֵֻ
4 מחאקדה פי בית אל[אהה: ה[עמיקו: גמקו אפסדו כאיאם
5 אלגבעה פל[ד[ד]ל[ך ... יד[כ[ר ד]נבהם ת[ום יפתקד כטאיאהם: הדא אלפצֹ]ל מנתסק
6 אלי מא ק[בלה ל[אן פיה איצֹא דכר מעאציה[ם ....]
7 אלעקובאת כמא חט פי אכר אלפצֹל אלמותקד[ם .... כקוֹ ושלחתיֹ
8 אש בעריו נהאהם אדא חצֹלו פי מא בין אלאות[אן ....]
9 ולמא כאן הדא תכליף מא לא יוטאק לאן ליס יכפף [............]
10 אלפרח כאלכסב ואלמרה ואלולד ומא שאכל דלך פקאל אל [תשמח ישראל]
11 לא תפרחו אלפרח אלדי יוודי אלי אלטרב ואלי אלכרוג [מן טאעתה תום]
12 קיידה באמר תאלת פקאל כעמים מן גנס מא יעמלו [..............]
13 חצלתהם פי מא [בינהם] תום אורא אלעל[ה] בקוֹ כי זנ[ית ....]
14 [ת]כונו בין אלשעוב מונכסרין לאנכם קד ע[................]
15 [ש]רח פי קוֹ כי זנית יעני אחבתם מכאלטה אלאו[תאן ......]ע[......]
16 מ[............] ויעטאהם אלגֹדור ואלעטאיא כקֹ קבל הדא אפרים
17 [התנו אהבים קוֹ ע]ל כל גרנות דגן יעני אנמא חמלהם עלי הדא כתרה
18 אל[דגן ....] פלדלך הודא אסלובכם הדה אלכ[יראֹ]ת כקֹ בעדה
19 גרן [ויקב לא ירעם ק]וֹ יכחש בה משאר אלי אלארץ יעני יוֹעַדַם
20 פיה[א ....] כ[חֵשׁ פִיבַָחֵשׁ יפעל יעני יכתום נפסה פיהא
21 [..............] לא ישבו [בארץ ייי אור[א] אנהם לא יסתחקו אן יגלסו
22 פי אלב[לד אלכאץ ....]ם קסמין פאורא אן בעצֹהם יֹ[גלס
23 במצר ובע[צֹהם יגלס באשור קוֹ] טמא יאכלו יעני ילתגו אלי אֲכָל

Hosea 9:6: For, behold, they have walked away from [27] plunder. And Egypt will gather them, then Memphis will bury them. As for the desirable places [28] [of] their wealth, {thorns} thistles will inherit them; and also thorns will grow in their tents.

Hosea 9:7: The days of visitation have come; the days of retribution have come. | [1] Israel will know: A fool [...] [2] foolish [... because of the multitude of your sin, and great is hatred]. 19a

Hosea 9:8: [3] As a watchman, Ephraim has been set up for him [with my God. A prophet a snare is thrown on all] his ways; [4] hatred (is) in the house of [his] God.

Hosea 9:9: [They deepened and they corrupted as in the days of] [5] Gibeah. And therefore [He will remember] their sin, th[en he will punish their iniquities].

Exegesis
This section is closely related [6] to what precedes it, for he mentioned in it also their sins [...] [7] the punishments, as he placed it at the end of the preceding section, [as it is said *I will send*] [8] *fire in his cities* (Hosea 8:14). He prohibited them when being in front of the ido[ls to ...]. [9] When this was disobedience against what He cannot bear, for he did not [...] [10] the joy, e.g. the gaining of profit, a woman and a the child and similar cases.

Hosea 9:1: He says *Do not [rejoice, Israel*, i.e.] [11] do not rejoice in joy, which leads to the amusement and to the walking away [from obeying them. Then] [12] he links it with a third matter and says *Like the people* because of the category they do [...] [13] you have been in what [is between them]. Then he demonstrates the reason by the phrase *For [you have] whored* [...] [14] you will be defeated among the nations, for you have [...]. [15] He provides and explanation with the phrase *For you have whored*, i.e. you loved to associate with the ido[ls ...] [16] [...] he gave them the payment and the presents, as it is said before that *Ephraim* [17] [*hired lovers* (Hosea 8:9) ...]. The phrase *On all the threshing-floors of grain* means: when He induced them to this, the abundance [18] of the [grain ...].

Hosea 9:2: And therefore, behold, I will take these blessings away from you, as it is said afterwards [19] *Threshing-floor [and wine-press will not graze them]*. The phrase *It will deceive in it* alludes to the land, i.e. there will be missing [20] in it [... dec]eive and it forms *it will deceive*, i.e. it will conceal itself in it [21] [...].

Hosea 9:3: [The verse *They will not dwell*] *in the land of YHWH* demonstrates that they do not deserve to dwell [22] in the [special] land [...] two allotments. He shows that some of them [will live] [23] in Egypt and some [of them will

24	אלאשיא אלנגס[ה ....מכאלטין ללגוים קו׳ לא יסכו יקאל
25	אנה ראגע ע[לי ......]ת כאנה ק[אל.. אג]לו פי אלגלות פלא יתמכנו אן
26	יקרבו ואלאק[רב אן] יכון וצף אפעאלהם והום פי ב[לד]הם פכאנה ק[אל]
27	מא כאן מנה[ם ....]פוע חית כאנו פי אלבלד אלכאץ לאנהם ליס כאנו
28	יקימו באלואגבאת ליס [ירו]שו ללרב אל[יין] אל[.די .[ל]...] פי כל יום ול[א]

19b	1	תרציה גמיע א[פעא]ל[הם .... אלקראבין אלדי קרבו] בין ידי אלאותאן
	2	[...........................טעאמהם] לאנפוסהם ליס
	3	[ידכול בית אלרב ....] פאורא אנה טמ[י] לאן כל
	4	[............] א[ל]ט[עאם אלדי יצלחוה
	5	[ה.............] קו׳ [מה תעשו ל]י[׳ום מועד יעני
	6	[............] אי[ש תעמלו פי אליום אלדי [הו א]ל[מוע]ד
	7	[............] אלעדו יק[תול פיכם וקו׳ [צ]ח]י׳ אלרב פי
	8	[............] מן אלאפאת באזא מא לם תקימו באלואגבאת
	9	[............]חגוג פתוק̇רבו פיהא אלקראבין אלואגבאת תוגעלו
	10	[............] בסאיר אלאפאת. קו׳ הלכו משו̇ד יעני מרו אלי מצרים
	11	[...........]קרי בעד אן קד נוהבו וסוביו פאורא אן תם יגתמעו
	12	[............] אסם [א]ל[סוקע .....] ואיצא נוף וקו׳ מחמד לכספם
	13	[ראגע אלי אלמואצ̇ע א[ל]די] כאן פיהא אלאיגל ואל[......] תציר כלהא
	14	[מנא]בת [אלחר]ש̇[ו]ף כ[ראב יב]א[.]ב קו׳ באו ימי הפקדה יעני איאם
	15	אלאיפתקאד עלי יד אלעדו וקו׳ ימי השלום יעני איאם אלמוכאפא[ה]
	16	באפאת אלסמא פאנה קאל מוה̇[יל .....]יל[תם זמאן ....]
	17	אלוקת וקו׳ יד̇עו ישראל עלי טריק אלתשפי מנה[...........] אן
	18	הדא אלדי נזל בהם ת̇מרה מא כאן יתענתו [קו׳ אויל הנביא יעני
	19	אלנבי אלמוכאט̇ב סמוה אויל ואלדי יולהם ב[אלריח סמוה] משוגע
	20	[אמא] אויל פכמא קאלו ען ירמיה בכי׳ לה ג̇[ם המה קראו אחריד] מלא
	21	לאן מעני מ̇לא ומעני אויל ואחד ו[...............]ליהוא
	22	מדוע בא המשגע הזה אליך וכדל[ך קאל שמעיה הנחלמי] אלי צפניה
	23	פי כתאבה לכל איש משגע ומת[נבא ....] בינהם מסתפיץ̇
	24	פקאל יא ישראל הדא חלבד [עלי כתר]ה [דנבך.............] גיר הדא
	25	אלמעני ואיצא לאגל כתרה מחאקדה נביא ש[קר עלי] נביאי צדק:

live in Assur. The phrase *And in Assur*] *they will eat unclean (food)* means: they will be forced to eat [24] unclean food [...] mixed with the nations.

Hosea 9:4: Some commentators hold that the phrase *They will not pour out* is [25] to refer to [...] as if he s[aid, They were exiled] in the exile, and they are not able to [26] bring an offering. It is more [likely that] he describes their deeds while they were in their land, and as if he said, [27] it was not from them [...] because they were in the special land, since they did not [28] fulfil the obligations; they did not [pour] out to the Lord [the wine which they were obliged to] every day and there is no | [1] acceptance of all [... the sacrifices which they sacrificed] before the idols [2] [... their food is] for themselves; it will not [3] [come into the house of the Lord]. And he shows that he was thirs[ty] because all [...] [4] [...] the food which they make suitable [5] [...]. 19b

Hosea 9:5: The phrase *What will you do for the day of the appointment?* means: [6] [... What] will you do on the day which [is an appointed time] [7] [... the enemy] will k[ill] among you. The phrase *And for the day of the feast of YHWH?*, the day of the offering of the Lord on [...] [8] [...] from the calamities corresponds to the obligations they did not fulfil [9] [... the] festivals and you offer the required offerings on them, you will be taken [10] [...] by all the calamities.

Hosea 9:6: The phrase *They went from plunder* means: they went to Egypt [11] [... ci]ties, after they had been robbed and captured. And he shows that then they gathered [12] [...] the name of the country [...] and also Memphis. The phrase *Treasure for their silver* [13] [refers to the places] where there were the assets [...] it will all be [14] [the planta]tion [of th]or[ns], desolated (and) devastated.

Hosea 9:7: The phrase *The days of visitation have come* means: the days [15] of the visitation by the enemy, and the phrase *The days of retribution* means: the days of the recompense [16] by the plagues of Heaven. And He said: You have been given time [...] [17] the time. The phrase *Israel will know* (is said) by way of revenge on him [...] that [18] this which befell upon them, is the result of their obstinance. [The phrase *The prophet is a fool* means:] [19] the prophet who gave a speech they called him *a fool*, and who is inspired with [the spirit they called him] *mad*. [20] As for a fool, as they said about Jeremiah, as it is said to him [*Even they called behind you*] *full* (Jeremiah 12:6) [21] because the meaning of *full* and the meaning of *fool* is identical. [...] to Yehu [22] *Why did this mad (man) come to you* (2 Kings 9:11); and likew[ise ...] to Zephaniah [23] in his book *For every man who is mad and prophesies* (Jeremiah 29:26) [...] between them extensive. [24] And he said, Oh Israel, this is your tax [for the multit]ude [of your sins ...] except this [25] meaning; and also because of the multitude of hatred of the prophets of false[hood against] the prophets of righteousness.

26	צופה אפרים עם אלֹהַי קול הושע למא דכר [.............]ה ביין
27	[למן] הי פקאל ד[יד]ב[א]ן אן [...] ל[.].[א]פרי[ס מע אלאהי אלדי אכתצני

20a

1	באלנבוה תום ביין אן [..............] תום ביין
2	[...] מא [...] מנה פאורה [..............] ומתלה באל[פך] אלמנצוב
3	אלדי יֻזהק תום ביין אן [..............] בית אלהיו
4	פי בית ביות מעבודא[ת ....] א[ג]תמעו נביאי
5	שקר פי אלבמות [ית]לובו [..............] מ[ן] בינהם ובינהם
6	[.......] קו' העמיקו יעני כ[.......]ל[.............]
7	[קו' שחתו יעני אפ]סדו פי כתרה [אלאותאן] [............]
8	[............] מ[עבודאת לא].[............]
9	[י]באב אלפרוג ואלמ[אל ....] וקו' [יזכור עונם ישיר בה אלי]
10	פסל מיכה אלדי תטאהרו שבט[י ישראל ....]
11	בדאך פאסתחקו יהלכו האולי מ[נהם ....]
12	אלמ[....]ל[.].[.] וקו' יפקד [חט]אותם [יעני ....]
13	וַרְבָה חקיקתהא וכתירה. וכדלך משטַ[ ]מה חקיקתהא מחאקדה: כענבים:
14	כעינב פי אלבר אצבת אל אסראיל אל כבכי[רה פי אלתין פי אבתדאהא]
15	ראית אבאכם הום דכלו אלי בעל [פ]עור פתנגבו מן [אלכזי]
16	פצארו ארגאס ענד מחב[תהם] דלך: אפרים: [כאלטאיר יתטאיר]
17	כר[מ]הם מן ולאדה ומן א[ן]חשא ומן חב]ל: כי: בְאָן אָן כאן [ירבו ב]ניהם
18	פאני אַתְכְלהם מן [בני אלאנסא]ן לאן אי[צֹּא אלויל ק]ד חצל להם ענד
19	זואלי מנהם: אפרים: אפרים קד כאן [כמא] ראית צור משתולה פי
20	אלוטן ואפרים אלאן קד אלתגא אן יכרג אלי קאתל בניה: תן: אועטיהם
21	יא רב מא יסתחקו תועטיהם אועטיהם רחם מותכל ותדאיא מְכַמַשֶה:
22	כל: כל בלייתהם פי אלגלגל דכרת לאן תם שניתהם ואיצא עלי
23	[רדא] שמאילהם מן ביתי אט[ר]ודהם ליס אעאוד למחבתהם לאן כל
24	רו[וסא]הם זאִגִ֫ין: הוכה: קד צֻורב אפרים לאן אצלהם קד חצל יאבס
25	תֹ֫מרה ליס יעמלו איצֹא א[ד]א מא ילדון אנא אקתול מתמנאאת
26	אח[ש]אהם: ימאסֵם: סא יַזְהַדהם אלאהי לאן מא סמיעו מנה פיכונו

Hosea 9:8: [26] The phrase *A watchman (is) Ephraim with my God* is the word of Hosea. After mentioning [...], he explains [27] [for whom it is], and the watchman said and [...] to him [...], Ep[hraim] is with my God who has specially favoured me | [1] with the prophecy. Then he explains that [...]. Then he explains [2] [...] what [...] from him. And he shows [... and he compares him with] the snare which is set up [3] (and) thrown. Then he explains that [...] *in the house of his god* [4] in one of the houses of the idol[s ...] the prophets [5] of lie gathered together on the high places who defame [...] between them and between them [6] [...]

20a

Hosea 9:9: [The phrase] *They deepened* means: [...]. [7] [The phrase *They corrupted* means:] they [corr]upted in large number [the idols ...] [8] [...] the idols (did) not [...] [9] devastated of the emptiness and the [... . The phrase *He will remember their iniquity* refers to] [10] the idol of Micah which the tribes [of Israel] displayed [...] [11] by this. And those of them deserved to be destroyed [...] [12] ... . The phrase *He will visit their sins* [means: ...]

Grammatical Notes
[13] וְרַבָּה (Hosea 9:7): its basic meaning is 'and much'. Likewise מַשְׂטֵמָה (Hosea 9:7): [its basic meaning is 'hatred'].

Translation
Hosea 9:10: [14] Like grapes in the desert, I obtained the people of Israel; like the early fru[it on a fig-tree at its beginning] [15] I saw your fathers. They came to Baal-Peor and devoted themselves to [the shame], [16] and they became objects of filth, when [lo]ving that.

Hosea 9:11: Ephraim [like the bird] [17] their hon[our will fly away]: from birth and from the wo[mb and from pregn]ancy.

Hosea 9:12: For even if [they bring up] their sons [18], I will make bereave them from [... a man]. For also [the woe] has been to them when [19] I abandoned them.

Hosea 9:13: Ephraim was, [like as] I saw Tyre, planted in [20] the homeland. And now Ephraim had been forced to bring his sons out to a slayer.

Hosea 9:14: Give to them, [21] Lord, whatever they deserve, you will give to them, give them a childless womb and shrivelled breasts!

Hosea 9:15: [22] All their wickedness in Gilgal I have remembered, for I hated them there. And also because of [23] [the evil] of their deeds I will drive them from My house. I will not love them any more, for all [24] their chi[efs] wander astray.

Hosea 9:16: Ephraim is stricken, for their root is dried up, [25] they will not produce fruit. Even i[f] they give birth, I will slay the delights [26] of their intestines.

27	מצ'טרבין פי אלאחזאב: הדא אלפצל איצ'א מנתסק אלי מא קבלה לאן
28	פיה וצף מעאצי אלקום ודכר מא יסתחקוה עלי דלך פכאנה למא חט

20b

1	עלי דכר איאם אל[.............ו] פי הדא אלוקת מ[עת]קין
2	אלי דלך דכר בעל פעור [.............] ללסיף
3	פי הד[א] אלוקת יסתחקו אל [.............] אלדי טג'ו
4	ד כאנו הום מ[כא]לפין [.............] אמרין אל
5	נטיר קול [............] ממרים הייתם] עם ייי מיו[ם] דעתי [א]תכם: פקאל
6	חסנין [............] כעינב פי אלבר [............] ל[...]ל[......]
7	ל[............] קו' כבכורה בתאנה בר[אשיתה ישיר אלי
8	[............] ז] מן וגהין [............]
9	[............] לה אל[............]
10	[............] ק[............] ו' והיו שקוצים יעני בעכס מא כאנו
11	[............] פי עהד יהושע יקול פינחס המעט לנו
12	את עון פעור אשר לא הטהרנו ממנו עד] היום ה[זה] למא דכר מא פעלוה
13	[............] ע עליה אל[.].בא ויתנאקצו אעדאדה]ם ואצ'[אף
14	[............לו]ן[...] ואל[...] אן וכתרה אלאפאת פדכר פי הדא
15	[............]אס[תחקוהא פתתנאקץ אעדאדהם בהא קו' כעוף יתעופף
16	[............] ועגלה וקו' כבודם משאר בה אלי אלנסל אלדי להם בה
17	[............] קו' מלדה ישיר בה אלי ו[לד ... ואנ]ה פי וקת כרוגה מן
18	אלאחשא יהלך וקו' ומ[בטן יש]יר בה אלי ו[לד ....] בעד פי אלשחשא
19	פיוסקט וקו' ומהריון יחתמל יכון עדם אלחמל ויחתמל יכון אראד בה מא
20	יחל באלגין מן אלאפאת קבל יתצוור ויסתכמל יהלך תום אורא באן אן
21	סלם להם ולד ורבוה חתי יתרערע פאני אתכלהם איאה וקו' מאדם
22	ליורי סלאמה גירהם מן דלך ליבין אנהם מקצודין בהדה אלצ'רב[את]
23	וקו' כי גם אוי להם מצ'אף אלי מא קד חצל להם מן אלמאתה מן [גיר]
24	אלאולאד פיחצול להם איצ'א ויל ונדב רפע אלענאיה מנהם ויחתמל
25	יכון קו' כי גם אוי להם מוקאבל קו' פי צדר אלפצל אלמותקדם אוי להם
26	כי נדדו ממנו כאנה קד קאל פי דאך אליול קד חצל להם אד קד
27	בעדו מן טאעתי פקאבלה בהדא פקאל איצ'א ויל קד חצל להם

Hosea 9:17: My God will forsake them, because they have not obeyed Him; so they will [27] become fugitives among the nations.

Exegesis
This section is closely related to what precedes it since [28] he describes the sins of the people in it and mentions what they deserved for that. And when he mentions | [1] the days of the [...] in this time ... (?) [2] to the sword [... in addition] to that, he mentions Baal Peor [3] [where] they committed crimes [...] in this time they deserve [4] the two [...] things [...] they were transgressors, [5] similar to the word [... *You have been rebels*] *against* YHWH *since the day I know you* (Deuteronomy 9:24).

Hosea 9:10: And he says [6] [...] *like grapes in the desert* [...] the good ones [7] [...]. [The phrase *Like a ripe fruit on a fig tree*] *in its beginning* alludes to [...] [8] [...] from two ways [...] [9] [...] [10] [...]. The phrase *And they were detestable* means: the opposite of what they have been [11] [...] in the covenant of Joshua, Pinhas says *Is* [12] [*the sin of Baal-Peor*] *not enough for us* [*from which we have not become cleansed*] *until this day?* (Joshua 22:17). After mentioning what they had done [13] [...] to him the [...], and they were decimated in their numbers, [he ad]ds [14] [...] and the multitude of the plagues. And he mentions in this [15] [...] they [des]erved it, so that their number was decimated by it.

Hosea 9:11: The phrase *Like the bird he flies* [16] [...] and his speed. The phrase *Their honour* alludes to the offsprings they had [17] [... . The phrase] *From birth* alludes to a t[ime ... and] that, when leaving [18] the womb, it will perish. The phrase *And from the womb* alludes to [...] in the womb, [19] and He causes a miscarriage. The phrase *And from the pregnancy* may be interpreted as that there is no pregnancy, or it may interpreted, that [20] he meant the misfortunes that befall the foetuses; before it develops and is completed, it perishes.

Hosea 9:12: Then he shows that even if [21] a child would be given to them and they would raise it until it comes into the prime of life, I will bereave them of it. The phrase *From man* [22] is to demonstrate a state of well-being from which He changed them, to make clear that they are meant by these plague[s]. [23] The phrase *For woe is to them, as well* is an addition to the suffering that happened to them apart from [24] the children. And it will be for them 'Woe', as well, and he mourned when he removed the care from them. Another interpretation is [25] that *For woe is to them, as well* is an equivalent to the word at the beginning of the preceding section *Woe to them* [26] *for they have moved away from Me* (Hosea 7:13). He said that that Woe occurred to them when [27] they stopped obeying Me. He compares it with this by

20b

21a

1 בזואלי א[י]אי] מנ[ה]ם פחצל קו' בשורי מהם מקאבל קו' נדדו ממ[ני ....]ן
2 מכת[ו]ב בשין פאן מתלה כתיר ממא תסתכדם אללגה אלש[י]ן מוצֹ[ע א]לסמך
3 ואלסמך מוצֹע אלשין מתל שְׂעָרה בשין וסערה בסמ[ך .... כד]לך כתיר:
4 וְ[אִפְ]הֶם אנהם כאנו [משתולין] פי דולתהם ופי [מדינ]תהם [כמא ראי]ת צור
5 פי זמאנהא [............] לאגל [............ א]ור[א ... א]נעכאס א[חואל]הם
6 ואנהם בעד אלמנ[ע] ואלתחצון קד [.........] יצֹאנעו ען אנפסהם באולאדהם
7 באן יסלמוהם אלי מן יקתלהם: [............ אן קו' תן להם ייי]
8 דועא להם למא אורא אנהם קד אחתאגו אן יסלמו אולאדהם אלי מן יקתלהם
9 פלא תרזוקהם ולד בל תן להם רחם משכיל ותמאם אלקול [......]ב[....]
10 ואן כאן קד עארץֹ בקו' תן להם פקאל לא יגוז מן אלנבי [אלדי ד]עא [ענ]הם בהדא
11 אלדועא אלא עלי וגה מ[תל] קלנא ליס אלקול מן אלד[ו]עא עליהם ואנמא
12 הו צפה כאנה קאל אעטא [............] יארב מא יסתחקוה יעני הודא
13 תפעל בהם הדא פדכר עילתין אלו[ן אח]ד[ה [בא]טנה ואלאוכרי טאהרה
14 רחם משכיל הו אלבאטן יעני תחצול אלאלה לא תקבל ולד פאן סלם
15 להם ולד לא יגי מא ירצֹע לאגל אלעילה אלטאהרה פי אלתדאיא פיהלך
16 ורד אלגואב פקאל כל רעתם בגלגל כאנה קאל יסתחקו מא קד וצפתה לאגל
17 מא פעלו פי אלגלגל אלמוצֹע אלשריף תום קאל וכמא טרדתהם מן אלגלגל
18 כדלך אטרודהם מן ביתי וקו' לא אוסֵף אהבתם יעני לא אעאוד
19 ללענאיה בהם בל אכליהם ען ידי תום [נ]אח עליהם אלנבי פקאל הֻכָּה
20 אפרים יעני קד צֹורבו בהדה אלצַֹרַבַאת אלאוכָר וצֹף פי אלפסוק אלמתקדם
21 צֹרבאת אלנסא וצף פי הדא צֹרבאת אלרגאל פקאל קו[ם] מנהם שרשם יָבֵשׁ
22 יעני קד צֹורבו באלעיקרות קום אוכר פְּרִי בל יעשון פתכון
23 עילתין פי אלרגאל [כמא וצֹ]ף עלתין פי אלנסא תום אורא אנה ואן ולדו
24 פי אלתד[...] יוּבְתָסר וקו' מחמדי בטנם ידל אנהם יופְקְדו
25 אעז אולאדה[ם] וייבקא להם מא יגֹתמו בה פתכון מציבתין. קול אלנבי

saying, Woe was to them also | [1] when I withdraw Myself from them. **Grammatical Note:** The phrase בְּשׂוּרִי מֵהֶם ('When I turn away from them') is parallel with the phrase נָדְדוּ מִמֶּנִּי ('They have moved away from Me') (Hosea 7:13) [...]. It has been [2] written with *sin* and there are a lot of instances where the language uses the *si*[*n* is instead of] the *samekh*, [3] and the *samekh* is instead of the *sin*, like שְׂעָרָה with *sin* and סְעָרָה with *samekh* [and many] more examples.

Hosea 9:13: [4] And notice that they have been [planted] in their state and in their [province as I have see]n Tyrus [5] in its time [...] to the most important [...], he shows the reverse [of] their si[tuation] [6] and that they after the preve[ntion] and the protection [...] they will bribe with their children for their advantage [7] in that they deliver them to someone to kill them.

Hosea 9:14: Some commentators [hold] that *Give to them, YHWH* is [8] a prayer in favour of them. After showing that they had to hand over their children to someone to kill them—, [9] do not give them a child, rather *Give them a bereaving womb* etc.! And this ... (?) [10] and he raised objections by saying *Give them*. Another interpretation is: It is impossible that a prophet curses them in this [11] prayer, rather in the way of a metaphor. We said, the word is not a prayer for their disadvantage, but [12] a description, as if he said, Give [...], Lord, what they deserve, i.e. behold, [13] You will do this to them. He mentions two defects: the first is hidden, the second is visible. [14] *A bereaving womb* is the hidden one, i.e. she is sterile and does not conceive a child. And if He gives [15] them a child, there will be nothing to suck from because of the visible disease on the breasts, and it will perish.

Hosea 9:15: [16] He gives the response and says *All their evil (is) in Gilgal*, as if He says: they deserve what you described, because of [17] what they did in Gilgal, the illustrious place. Then He says: And as I have driven them from Gilgal [18], likewise I will drive them away from My house. The phrase *I will not continue to love them* means: I will not [19] take care of them any more, rather I will remove them from my hand.

Hosea 9:16: Then the prophet [be]wails them and says [20] *Ephraim has been smitten*, i.e. they have been smitten by these latest plagues. Whereas in the previous verse he describes [21] the afflictions to the women, in this one, he describes the afflictions to the men. Some people say, *Their root is withered* [22] means they are smitten by sterility; other people (say), *They will not produce a fruit*. Hence [23] the two defects in the men are [like] the two defects in the women [he described]. Then he shows that even if they have given birth [24] in the [...], he will be damaged. The phrase *The treasures of their womb* refers to (the fact) that they will lose [25] their dearest children and will continue grieving about him. Hence there will be two misfortunes.

26 ימאסם אלהי ה[.......] כך׳ פי אלפצל אלמותקדם עם אלהָי תום אורא
27 אלסבב פי דלך בקו׳ כי לא שמעו. וקו׳ ויהיו נדדים בגוים ישיר בה אלי
28 אלגלות פכאנה קאל אן לאגל [..............] ע[...] נַדְדִים בגוים.

21b
1 [כאהבם]: מתל בְעָבְרָם ומא שַאכלהא מצַדר: צְמֻקִים אלואחד
2 מ[...........] ואלאצל מנה צמוק הי משתקה מן צימוקים יעני בה
3 אלגפ[נה ....]: גפן באיר קד כאן אל [אי]סראל תָמַר כאן יוסווי
4 ל[ה מ]תל כַתְרַה תַ[מרה] כדלך כתֹר פיעל [א][ל][מדאב]ח מתל חוסן ארצֹה
5 כדלך חַסַן מצאטב]: חָ[לק: לדלך: אנק]סם ק[לבהם אלסאעה
6 [יואכו]דו הו יַקפְיהם מ[ע מדאבחם]הם ינהב מ[צא]טבהם: כי: לאן
7 אלסאע[ה] יקולו ליס לנא מלך לא[ן מא] כשינא אלרב ואלמְלִך פמא דא יפעל
8 בנא: דְבָרו: [ד]נב מא תכלמו בכטוב פהי חֻורג גזאף קטע עהד פסא
9 ינפ[ר]ע כאלסם פיהם חוכם עלי אתלאם אלצחרא: לעגלות: מע
10 עוגול בית א[ון] תורי יגאורו סוכאן שמרון אי הָאת לאן קד חזן
11 עליה שעבה ו[כ]מארהٓ אלדי עליה כאן [יט]רבו אלאן הודא יחזנו
12 עלי כרמה אד [ק]ד אנגלא מ[נה: גם:] איצ̇א איאה אלי אשור
13 יוגִלַב ואיצ̇א הד[י]ה למְלֶך יָרֵב כְזָיה אפרים יאבוֹד וְיָבֹזא אל
14 אסראיל מן משוורתה: נדמֶה: קד שָבה שעב שמרון מע מְלִכהא כְזָבֹד
15 עלי וגה מא: ונשמדו: לאן סא יוסתאצלו [בי]ע גל אלדי כאנת
16 סבב כטייה אל אסראיל שוך ודרדר יטלע עלי מדאבחהם
17 פיקולו ללגבאל גֹטונא וללרואבי אסקוטו עלינא: הדא אלפצל
18 איצ̇א מנתסק אלי מא דכר מן דנוב אלקום פקו׳ גפן בוקק ישיר בה

Hosea 9:17: The word of the prophet [26] *My God will reject them* [...] as the word in the preceding section *With my God* (Hosea 9:8). Then he shows [27] the reason for that by the phrase *They did not listen*. The phrase *They will wander about among the nations* alludes to the exile, as if he said that because of [... *They will*] *wander about among the nations*.

[1] Grammatical Notes

כְּאָהֲבָם ('as they loved') (Hosea 9:10) is like כְּעָבְרָם ('as they crossed') (2 Kings 2:9); the infinitive is similar to it. צִמְקִים (Hosea 9:14): the singular [2] of [it ...] and its basic form is צָמוֹק which is derived from צִימוּקִים, i.e. in it (is) [3] the gra[pe ...].

Translation

Hosea 10:1: An uncultivated grapevine was Israel; fruit was similar [4] to it. Like the multitude of [its] fr[uit, s]o it multiplied the work of [the al]tars; like the goodness of its land, [5] so it ameliorates pillars.

Hosea 10:2: [Therefore] their heart is div[ided]; now [6] they will be [puni]shed. He will break them down together with their altars; He will plunder their m[as]tabas.

Hosea 10:3: For [7] now they will say, We have no king, fo[r] we did [not] fear the Lord. And the king what will he do [8] among us?

Hosea 10:4: [S]in (is) what they have spoken in speech, namely swearing falsely, making a covenant, and [9] judgement will sprout among them like the poisonous herb upon the furrows of the field.

Hosea 10:5: With [10] the calves of [Beth-Awen] do you think the inhabitants of Samaria will be in immediate vicinity? That is to say: Come, for [11] its people will mourn over it, and its priests who were overjoyed by it now, behold, they are mourning [12] over its glory because it has been removed from it.

Hosea 10:6: It, too, to Assur [13] it will be brought and also a gift to the king of Yareb. Ephraim will receive shame, and the people of [14] Israel will be ashamed of its counsel.

Hosea 10:7: The people of Samaria together with their king were similar to foam [15] on the surface of water.

Hosea 10:8: For the temples of wickedness which have been [16] the reason for the sin of the people of Israel, will be destroyed; thorn and thistle will grow up on their altars [17] and they will say to the mountains, Cover us!, and to the hills, Fall upon us!

Exegesis

This section [18] is also closely related to the sin of the people that he mentioned.

19 אלי מא כאנו פי מצרים קלה בכו' להם בשבעים נפש ירדו אבתיך
20 מצרימה פקו' פרי ישוה לו ישיר בה אלי אלכתרה אלדי כתרהם
21 כק' להא רבבה כצמח השדה נתתיך. והדא נטיר קול אלולי ען
22 אלאומה גפן ממצרים תסיע פקד לוקבו בגפן והום פי מצרים:
23 אורא מכאפאתהם לה עלי מ[א אנ]א פק[אל פקאל מן אלגמיל
24 באזא אלכתרה אלדי כַּתַרהם הו כָּתרו הום מד[אבח] אלאצנאם
25 נטיר קו' להם כי מספר עריך היו אלהיך יהודה ומספר חוצות ירוש'
26 שמתם מזבחות לבושת. ובאזא מא [אחס]ן ארצהם וזיינהא וכַּתַר
27 [כירה]א [חַסַנ]ו הום אל[מצאטב] ללאותאן פקאל אלנבי ענהם

22a
1 חָלק לבם ישיר בדלך אלי אינקסאם [.........................]
2 [...]ל[.................] ען ענד מא [.............] קו' עתה]
3 יאשמו [...........]י אלמאע[....]. קו' [הוא יערף מזבחותם
4 [...........]על הו סבב [....]ל[.................]
5 [.]י[.] [...........] יכון עלי טריק [.................]
6 עלי טֹ[.....]הו יקפיהם א[.........................]
7 דיך ל[..........] תעודה אל[................] בה [.] ק[ו' ו]נת[תי את פגריכם
8 {על} פגרי גלוליכם. וק[ו' י'][שדד] מצבותם יש[י']ר אלי נהב מא עליה[א] מן
9 אלתיאב ואלחלי ומא [שא]כ[ל דלך. ביין בק]ו' כי עתה יאמר[ו אי]ן מלך לנו
10 אן הדה אלאי[...........][מאן אינקסאמהם (....]ל[......]ק[ד קאל]ו מן תחת
11 אמר אלמלך וקד [........] מן אל[........] יקולו ל[א יר]אנ'ו את יי'
12 קד זולנא ען טא[עתה ....]א ואלמל[ך ....]א פמא [.....] ל[...]א אמר:
13 קו' דברו דבר[ים] ישיר בה מא כאן יגי להם פי אוקאת מן
14 אלכלאם אלגמיל פיתבעו דלך ב[...] [אמאת ועהד יקטעוה לרבה[ם]
15 ל[......] אלות שוא לא יפו בה פיכון דלך סבב הלאכהם לאן אללה
16 יַטָהר פיהם אח[כ.]אמ[ה] כאלסם אלמור טאהרה מכש[ופה וקו'] לעגלות
17 בית און יגורו שכן שמרון עלי טריק אלתימה ויגוז יכון [עלי טריק]
18 אלתהדדוד כְּאָנהֹ קאל קד גאן[ורו זמ]ן טויל. יגאוורו א[הל שמרון
19 באן [קב]ל הדא קד קאל זנח עגלך שמרון ולם יועלם ה[..............]
20 מן אין נוקל אלי שמרון פביין הונא באן אלדי כאן פי ב[ית און נקלו]ה
21 אלי שמרון לאן בית און הי און אל פביין אלסבב אלדי יוגב אן לא יגאוורו

Hosea 10:1: The phrase *A barren vine* alludes to [19] the small number they have been in Egypt, as it is said *With seventy souls your ancestors descended* [20] *to Egypt* (Deuteronomy 10:22). The phrase *He made fruit for it* alludes to the great number to which He increased them, [21] as it is said *I made you as numerous as the plants of the field* (Ezekiel 16:7). This is like the word of the psalmist about [22] the people, *You cause a vine to journey from Egypt* (Psalms 80:9); they were called *a vine* while they were in Egypt. [23] He shows their requitals to Him for the good [He gave to them] and says, [24] Corresponding to the great number to which He increased them, they multiplied the al[tars] of the idols, [25] like the word addressed to them *For the number of your cities were your gods and the number of the streets in Jerusalem* [26] *you have put altars to the shame* (Jeremiah 11:13). And corresponding to Him doing good to their land, making it beautiful and multiplying [27] its [goods], they [improved] the [*mastaba*s] for the idols.

Hosea 10:2: The prophet says concerning them | [1] *Their heart is divided*, alluding to the division [of their heart ...] [2] [...] with what [... . The phrase *Now*] [3] *they bear punishment* [...] the meaning [... . The phrase *He will destroy their altars* ...]. [4] [...] it is the reason [...] [5] [...] it is in the way [of ...] [6] upon [...]. He will break them down [...] [7] of your owner [...] threat [...] in it, as it is said *I will give your carcasses* [8] *upon the carcasses of your idols* (Leviticus 26:30). The phrase *He* [*will plunder*] *their pillars* alludes to the plunder of [9] their garments, the jewellery and [sim]ilar.

22a

Hosea 10:3: He explains by the phrase *For now they say: We have no king* [10] that this [...] their division [... they said] from under [11] the authority of the king. And [...] from the [...] they say *We did n[ot fear] YHWH*. [12] We have abandoned obe[ying Him ...] and the king [...] and not [...] a command.

Hosea 10:4: [13] The phrase *They have spoken words* alludes to [14] the pleasant speech which was said sometimes to them. They let follow that by [...] and a covenant they make with their Lord, [15] [...] *False oaths* which they do not fulfil. That is the reason that they perish, for God [16] will reveal His judgements over them like the bitter poison, visible (and) open.

Hosea 10:5: The verse *Because of the calves* [17] *of Beth-Awen the inhabitants of Samaria will be neighbours* is said as a question; or it is possible [that it is said as] [18] a threat, as if he said, They have been neighbours for a long time. They will be neighbours [of the people of Samaria] [19] since before this he said *Your calf has forsaken, Samaria* (Hosea 8:5). And it was not known [...] [20] from where it had been moved to Samaria. And he explains here that the one which had been in B[eth-Awen, they moved] [21] to Samaria, since Beth-Awen is (identical with) Beth-El. He explains the reason which made it necessary that

22 פקאל כי אָבַל עליו עמו. וכמריו איצֿא קד חזנו עליה בעד פְרָחֹהֹם
23 וטרבהם והדא אלחזן עלי כבודו וקו׳ גם אותו ידל אן אלדי כאן פי [ד]ן
24 כאן קד חומֹל קבל הדא פקאל איצֿא הו יוגלב אלי אשור אלי בלד אשור
25 יוחמל הדייה אלי מלך יכאצֹם ענהם וינאטֹר פלדלך קאל בעדה בשנה
26 אפרים יקח לאן הו אלדי אָנֻשָׂא הדה אלעגלים בָשנה אסם מקאם בושה.
27 גמעה בְשָנות. קו׳ נדמֶה בְשָנות יכון עלי מא קלנא מן לגה אלתשביה

22b
1 [ויחתמל יכון] מענאה הָדוּנָהם מן אלסלטאן ואלממלכה
2 [.....................] מ[.]ז [.........]ל[.....]א[.]ל מא יכון
3 [.....................] ע[...............]הם ונהיה כאן לאאצל
4 [.........................] ת[ום אורא אן [.....] זואל
5 [.........................] יכטו פיהא ו[..........]
6 [.........................] למזבחות כתם [ב]קו׳ קוץ
7 ודר[דר] יעלה מ[ן]זבחותם [...............] כסונו עלי [טריק] אלמבאלגה
8 ואנמ[א ...] מענאה קון[...]ל[...] ילחקהם[: מ]ימי: מן איא[ם] אלגבעה
9 קד א[כטאת] יא אל אסראיל אלדי חֲמָה תְֹהבתו [לא] כאן תלחקהם פי אלגבעה
10 מלחמה [עלי] דוי גור: בָאַוֹתִי: אלאן בשה[וֹתי] אסֹלמהם וארבטהם
11 חתי יוחש[רו] עליהם שעוב בסבב רבט[הם] לְמַעֲנָיָיתֵיהֶם: ואפרים:
12 ואפרים פ[כאן מ]תל עגלה [מועלמה מחבה ללד]יָאס ואנא פעברת
13 עלי גוד עונקהא פקלת אורכב אלניר עלי אפ[ר]ים פיחרות יהודה
14 תום יכרוב לה יעקב: זרעו: וכדי קלת להם אזרעו לכם חסב
15 אלעדאלה פאנכם תחצודו ח[ס]ב אלאחסאן אלדי תעמלו ליכן
16 אחר[תו לכ]ם חרתֿ ואגעל וקת לאילתמאס אלרב מהמא הודא
17 [יגי וי]עַלמכם עדל: חרשתם: פמא קבלתום בל חרתֿתם טֹולם
18 [............]ה אלגור חצדתום תום אכלתום תָמר גח[ו]ד לאנך אתכלת
19 [עלי טריק]ד אלסו עלי כתרה גבאברתך: וקם: פסא יתסות רהג

they will not be neighbours [22] and says *For its people mourned over it and its priests* also mourned over it after their joy [23] and their delight; this is the mourning over *its glory*.

Hosea 10:6: The phrase *It, too* shows that the one which has been in Dan, [24] had been transported before this. And it is said, 'It also will be brought to Assur': to the land of Assur. [25] A gift will be transported to a king who brings legal action and trial against them. Therefore it is said thereafter [26] *Ephraim will take shame*, for he is the one who has made these calves.

Grammatical Note: בָּשְׁנָה is a noun in the place of of 27] בּוּשָׁה], its plural being בָּשְׁנוֹת.

Hosea 10:7: **Grammatical Note:** נִדְמֶה may, according to what we have said, belong to the lexical class of 'comparing' | [1] [or] its meaning [may be] 'their quietness', partaining to the ruler and the kingdom.

[2] [...] what will be [3] [...] their [...] and the prohibition of it [...] was the origin [4] [...].

Hosea 10:8: Then he shows that [...] the end [5] [...] they sinned on them and [...] [6] [... He began the section with *He will multiply] for the altars* (Hosea 10:1); he concludes with the phrase *Thorn* [7] *and thi[stle] will sprout on [their altars ... .] Cover us* (is said) by way of exaggeration [8] and as for [...] its meaning is [...] it will afflict them.

22b

Translation

Hosea 10:9: Since the days of Gibeah [9] you [have sinned], people of Israel, who stood there. [10] War did not afflict them in Gibeah [against] the wicked ones.

Hosea 10:10: Now by [my] desire, I will hand them over and I will bind them [11] until nations will be gathe[red] against them because they are bound to their two furrows.

Hosea 10:11: [12] And Ephraim is like a [trained] calf, [that loved th]reshing. And I have passed over [13] upon the goodness of her neck. And I said, I will fasten the yoke on Ephraim, and Judah will plough. [14] Then Jacob will harrow for himself.

Hosea 10:12: Thus I said to them, Sow for yourselves in accordance with [15] the righteousness, and you will harvest in accordance with the kindness you do, but [16] plough [for your]selves a ploughing and set a time to seek the Lord whenever, behold, [17] [he comes and] teaches you righteousness.

Hosea 10:13: And you have not obeyed rather you have ploughed wickedness; [18] [after this] you have harvested wrong-doing; then you have consumed the fruit of deceit. For you trusted [19] [in your] evil [way], in the multitude of your mighty men.

20 פי ק[ומ]ך וגמיע חצונך ינהב כל ואחד מנהא כנהב שַׁלְמַן בית
21 ארבל פי יום מלחמה אלדי אום מע בנין פוקיסַת: ככוה: כדלך
22 קד פעל בכם אלעגל אלדי אנצבתום פי בית אל מן קיבל רְדָאה
23 רְדַאתכם פלדלך פי {ב}אלפַגר אינבכאם אנבכם מֶלֶך אל אסראיל:
24 כִּי: לאן חְדָת כאן אל אסראיל פאחבתהֹ ומן מצר נאדית באבני:
25 קראו: פלמא נאדו בהם אלַיְי כדלך סלכו מן קודאמהם פללאותאן
26 כאן יוַדַבחו וללאצנאם כאן יוקתרן: ואנכי: ואנא פָדֵדִית
27 לאפרים פאכדְתֻהם אלנבי עלי דראעיה ומא עֳרפו אני קד

23a
1 [אשפיתהם: בחבלי: בחבאל אלנאס] כונת אגדֹבהם במוקט
2 מַחְ[נה וצ]רת [להם כמרפע]י ניר [עלי] כַּדֵיהם ת[ום] מַיָלַת אליה
3 ואנא אַ[טְי]ק: לא: לי[ס יר]גע אלי ארץ מצר וא[ל]י ארץ] אשור הו
4 מֶלֶכֹה לאנהם אבו ללרגוע: וחל]ה: ותבתדי סיף פי] קוראה תום
5 תַפְנִי דהוקה לאנה]א תאכל מן משווראתהם: ועמי: ושעב]י
6 פמועלקין לאיגל ר]געתי ואלי אלעאלי ינאדוה] והם
7 גמיעא ליס פיהם [ירפע]י: איך: כ[יף אגעלך יא אל אפרים] כיף אגֹעלך
8 יא אל אסראיל כ[יף] אגעל]ך מתל אדמה [כיף אגעלך מ]תל צבויים קד
9 אנקלב עלי קלבי גמיעא הא[גת] תעָ]אזי: לא]: ליס אעמל שדה
10 גצבי ליס ארגע לא[פסאד] אפרים לאן ט]איק אנא] ולא אימר פי וסטך
11 אכון קדוס וליס אדכול פי קרי]ה אוכרי] א]לא פי ירושל]ם: אחרי: ליכן פי
12 אלוקת אלדי ורא אלרב יסלוכו כאלאסד אלדי י]זיר לא]נה הו אלדי יזיר
13 אליהם פינזעגו בנין מן גהה אלגֹרב: יחרדו: ינזעגו כעצפור מן
14 גהה מצר וכחמאמה מן ארץ אשור פאוגֹלסהם פי ביותהם זועם
15 אלרב: הדא אלפצל מנתסק אלי אלפצל אלדי קבלה לאנה מגאנס להא פי
16 דכר מעאצי אלקום דיכר מא אסתחקוה עליהא מן [א]ל]גזא] אלא אנה למא

TEXT AND TRANSLATION 87

Hosea 10:14: And the sound of tumult will arise [20] among your p[eop]les and all your fortresses will be plundered every single of them like Shalman's plundering of Beth- [21] Arbel on the day of war when a mother together with (her) children was torn asunder.

Hosea 10:15: Thus [22] the calf, which you had established in Beth-El, acted among you because of the evil [23] of your evil. And therefore at dawn, the king of the people of Israel has been utterly silenced.

Hosea 11:1: [24] For a young man was the people of Israel, and I loved him, and from Egypt I called my son.

Hosea 11:2: [25] And when they called them to Me, likewise they went away from them, and [26] they sacrificed to the idols and burnt incense to the images.

Hosea 11:3: And I pampered [27] Ephraim, and the prophet took them upon his arms, and they did not know that I | [1] [healed them]. 23a

Hosea 11:4: [With the cords of man] I pulled them, with the rope [2] of love, [and] I was [for them like those who lif]t a yoke [upon] their two jaws; [then] I bent down to him, [3] and I will prevail.

Hosea 11:5: He will not [re]turn to the land of Egypt and [to the land of] Assur—, he (is) [4] his king, because they refused to return.

Hosea 11:6: [A sword will begin in] his cities. Then [5] it will destroy his branches, for it [will devour because of their teachings].

Hosea 11:7: [And] my [people] [6] they are in suspense about re[turning to Me; and to the Most High they call him], and they [7] altogether there is no one among them [who exalts] Me.

Hosea 11:8: H[ow can I treat you, people of Ephraim]? How can I treat you, [8] people of Israel? How can I treat you like Admah? H[ow can I treat you] like Zeboim? [9] My heart has been turned around against Me. Together [My] conso[lations] have been arou[sed].

Hosea 11:9: I will not carry out the vehemence [10] of My wrath. I will not return to de[stroy] Ephraim. For [I am The All-powerful] and not a man. In your midst [11] I will be holy, and I will not enter a cit[y other] th[an Jerusale]m.

Hosea 11:10: However, at [12] the time when they will go after the Lord, He (is) like the lion which [roars. Fo]r He is the one who roars [13] towards them, and sons will be stirred up from the west.

Hosea 11:11: They will be stirred up like a sparrow from [14] Egypt and like a dove from the land of Assur. And I will make them dwell in their houses—declaration of [15] the Lord.

Exegesis
This section is closely related to the sections before it, because it is similar to them in [16] mentioning the sins of the people, (and) mentioning the pun-

17 כאן קבל הדא קד דכר אלגבעה בקו׳ מימי הגבעה [...]א אליה פקאל
18 מימי הגבעה יעני אן איבתדא אלבלא וכמירתה [כאנו] מן [א]יאם
19 אלגבעה אלדי כאנו גמיעא ישראל ובנימן מתטאב[קי]ן ע[ל]י אלבטא עלי
20 מא קלנא אן ישראל כאן פי וסטהם פסל מיכה ואל[....] דלך וכדלך
21 סבט בנימן כאן פי מא בינהם אהל אלגבעה ולם יכונו ינכרו עליהם
22 מא יטׄהירוה מן פיעׄל אלקביח וקו׳ שָׁם עָמְדוּ ישיר בה אלי אלמוצׄע
23 אלדי וקפו פיה אלתקו האולי מע האולי ואכרג דלך בעמידה לתבאתהם
24 יום בעד יום /בׄקו׳ ענהם ויוסיפו לערוך מלחמה במקום אשר ערכו שם
25 ביום הראשון וקו׳ לא תשיגם כְּאֵנָה קאל תׄבתו ולם יוטׄפרו לאן מא
26 כאנת תלחקהם יעני לאהל אלגבעה מלחמה מן גהתהם מע מא כאנו

23b

1 גאירין וטׄאלמין לאנהם [..........................]
2 אלקול אלוג[.. קו׳ ו]א[ס]פו עליה[ם ע]מים [...]
3 [.ק]...[מ].................[יעני .... וא]ל[ז]ימהֻם ה]דה אל[בלאיא
4 וקו׳ [באסרם לשתי עינתם יעני ..... אלש]נ]י עגלים אנצבו ואחד פי
5 דן ו[אחד פי בית אל ....ל[..]ושד עליהא פתחרות
6 פי מ[עניתין כקו׳ הנשבעים באשמת קמרון] ואמרו חי אלהיך דן וחי דרך
7 באר [שבע ונפלו ולא יקומו עוד................ א]ולא מתל אלעגלה
8 אלמועׄלמה [אלתי ..] יגי ענהם פי [.... וקו׳ א]והבתי ליורי ניהא תפכים
9 ואנמא אראד [....... קו׳] לדוש יעני מ[........ ט]אעתי אלא ו[ה]ום ה][...]בין
10 מ[ו]ן[ח]יבין וקו׳ וא]נ]י עברתי על ט[וב] צוא[רה י]עני לם אולפהם מא לא יטיקו
11 ולא אלזמתהם אמ[רי ונהי. וקו׳ ארכי]ב אפר[ים יחרש יהודה יעני מלת
12 מנהם ורגית באנהם א[דא חַ]צ[ֹ]ל[ו ....] ותעאצׄדו עלי פיעׄל
13 אלטאעה לאני רגבתהם. קו׳ זרעו לכם לצדקה ישיר בה אלי אלאיגל
14 כאנה קאל אעמלו אעמאל צאלחה חסב אלתואב אלדי אוגבת[ה] לכם
15 ולא תקולו אן לאגל אלאיגל אנקוצכם פי אלעאגל בל אחצודו פי אלעאגל
16 חסב אלאחסאן אלדי תעמלו מע בעצׄהם בעץׄ יעני כאני אבלף
17 עליכם וקו׳ נירו לכם ניר נציחה להם יעני ותרו אעמלו שי
18 יבקא [ב]קו׳ ועת לדרוש את ייי ישיר בה אלי אלנואפל אלדי געל להם

ishments they deserved for them, except that, after [17] it was before this, he mentions Gibeah by saying *Since the days of Gibeah.*

Hosea 10:9: [18] [...] to him and says Since the days of Gibeah, i.e. that the beginning of the affliction and its origin [were] since the days [19] of Gibeah when Israel and Benjamin together agreed to the sin, according to what [20] we said: that in the midst of Israel was the idol of Micah (Judges 18:31), and the [like], and likewise [21] the nation of Gibeah was among the tribe of Benjamin, and they did not disapprove of them [22] with regard to the disgraceful deed they would reveal. The phrase *There they stood* alludes to the place [23] where they stood (and) where they encountered each other. And he expresses that by standing permanently [24] day after day, as it is said *And they continued to array themselves for war in the place where they had arrayed* [25] *on the first day* (Judges 20:22). The phrase *It did not reach them* (is) as if he says: they resisted and they did not grant victory because [26] it did not reach them, i.e. war did not reach the people of Gibeah from them although they were | [1] unjust and sinners, since they [...] 23b

Hosea 10:10: [...] [2] the word [...] [The phrase *And* the nations shall be gathered against them [...] [3] [...] means: [And I] im[p]ose misfortunes on them. [4] [*When they are bound to the two burrows*] means [...] the two calves which they set up, one in [5] Dan and [one in Beth-El ...] and they were harnessed that they should plough [6] in [two furrows, as it is said *They who swear by the sin of Samaria,*] *and say, By the life of your God, Dan, and By the life of the way* [7] *of Beersheva,* [*even they will fall and never rise up again*] (Amos 8:14).

Hosea 10:11: [...] first like the [8] trained calf [which ...] comes from them in [.... The phrase] *Who loves* is to show the end of the consideration, [9] and he wanted [...]. The phrase *To thresh* means [... ob]eying Me, rather: and they [...] [10] those who love. The phrase *And I* [*passed over*] *the goodness of her neck* means: I did not domesticate them something they will not endure [11], and I did not impose on them [my] de[cree and my prohibition]. The phase *I made* [*Ephr*]*aim ride and Judah ploughs* means: I felt sympathy [12] for them, and I hoped that when [they] re[cei]ved [...], they would support one another in the deed [13] of obedience, because I have asked them.

Hosea 10:12: With the phrase *Sow for yourselves according to righteousness* he alludes to the future reward, [14] as if he would say, Do good deeds according to the reward which I have assigned to you [15] and do not say that because of the future reward, I will diminish (your reward) in the present, rather harvest in the present [16] according to the performing of good deeds you do to each other, i.e. as I will compensate [17] you. The phrase *Till for yourselves a tilling* is an advice for them, meaning: do abundantly something [18] that will last. With the phrase *A time to seek YHWH* he alludes to the supererogatory acts He

19	טריק אלי [.....]א וקו' עד יבוא משתק מן קו' עד היותי על אדמתי.
20	יעני מהמא [הודא] יְגִי יריד בדלך מהמא אלאנביא פי וסטכם
21	אורא בעד דלך בקו' חרשתם רשע אנהם מא אנְתַפעו מן
22	נציחתה להם בל עמילו בצֻדְ[הַ]א פלדלך אסתחקו אלהלאך קו'
23	כשׂד שלמַן יוקאל אנה שלמנאסר וקיל אנה אסם מלך נָהָב
24	קריה יוקאל להא בית ארבֵל וכאן מלך משהור מערוף קו'
25	להם מפני רעת רעתכם כְּאן רָעתם הי אלעגלים אלדי אחדתוהא
26	פי בית אל ופי גִירה פהום מדמומין עלי פיעלהא ואלרְעה אלתאניה
27	אלדי להא הי אלקראבין ואלעבאדאת אלדי כאנו יפעלוהא בחצֻרתהא

24a

1	פהי אלדי סבבת עליהם אלבّ[לא ....ני באכרהֿ]
2	אלבלא ואסרע אליה אלי מלך ישראל [.............]י נטיר קו'
3	פי אלפצّל אלמתקדם נדמֶה שמרון מלכה [קו' כי נער ישרא]ל יעני אנהם
4	חית כאנו פי מצרים כאנו [א]ופייא כ[..............פע פיה]
5	אלתרגّיב ואלתרהיב פלדלך ענ[ית] בהם ו[..............ל]אן מן
6	[מצרי]ם יעני מן איבתדא אמורהם אל[די] א[..........] נאדית
7	ב[הם] באלמולאטפה כמא יונאדי אלאנסן [אולאדה..........] תום ביין
8	[.....] קאל קראתי אנה עלי יד וסאיט וא[נביא......] אלי משה ואהרן
9	כקו' ויבא משה ויקרא לזקני העם. וכ[די קא]ל [............]ים פלדלך
10	קאל הונא קראו להם פערפנא הונא [א]נהם פי מצרים קד כאן פיהם
11	מן ידבח ללאותאן ויבבّר להא וכדי קאל ליחזקאל ואת גלולי מצרים לא עזב[ו]
12	פקו' כן הלכו מפניהם ישיר בה אלי אינצראפהם מן קודאם אלאנביא
13	וקו' בעדה ואנכי תרגלתי לאפרים יעני מא ואכדתהם על[י'] דלך
14	וכדי קאל ליחזקאל [וא]עשה למען שמי לבלתי החל לעיני הגוים אשר המה בתוכם
15	תרגל[תי..................ל].........ה ואנמא תופסר מן אלמעני. וקד
16	[...............................] גַסֻתַ והו מן אללגה מומתנע
17	[...............................]י]עני פמומתנע לאן הדא אלכלאם
18	[...............................אנכ]י תרגלתי הי אלמלאטפה
19	[..........] אלצבי ויו[רבי..............]ל מנהא תַרגֶל פאדא רכבהא
20	[אימנת] תקול אֲתַרגֶל יתרג[ל] מתרגל קו' קח[ّ]ם [על זר]עתיו משאר אלי אלנבי

did for them [19], a way to [...]. The phrase *Until he comes* is derived from *Until I was in my country* (Jonah 4:2), [20] i.e. with 'whenever, behold, he comes' he wants to say: whenever the prophets are in your midst.

Hosea 10:13: [21] With the following phrase *You have ploughed wickedness* he demonstrates that they did not make use of [22] His advice to them, rather they did just the opposite, and therefore they deserved the annihilation.

Hosea 10:14: [23] Some interpret the phrase *Like the plundering of Salman* as to be Shalmaneser; others, however, hold that it is the name of a king who plundered [24] a city which is called *Beth-Arbel* and who was a famous (and) well-known king.

Hosea 10:15: The word to [25] them, *Because of the evil of your evil* (is) as if their evil are the calves which they had established [26] in Beth-El and in other places, and they are to be blamed for making them. And the second evil, [27] which was related to them (= the calves), are the offerings and the services which they held in their presence | [1] and they are those which caused the [afflictions ...] against them [...] in the last [2] affliction. And Elijah ran to the king of Israel [...] like the verse [3] in the preceding section *The king of Samaria is silenced* (Hosea 10:7).

24a

Hosea 11:1: [The phrase *When Israel was a child*] means: while [4] being in Egypt, they were [fa]ithful [...] in it [5] the temptation and the threats. And therefore I was worried about them and [... be]cause from [6] [*Egypt*] means: from the beginning of their affairs whi[ch ...] I called [7] [them] in friendliness, as a man calls [his sons]. Then he explains [8] [...] he said *I called*, that he [...] by mediators and [prophets ...] to Moses and Aaron, [9] as it is said *Moses came and called the elders of the people* (Exodus 19:7).

Hosea 11:2: And [likewise] he said [...], and therefore [10] he says here *They called them*. We learn here that there were among them in Egypt [11] those who offered to the idols and gave incense to them. In the same way He said to Ezekiel *They did not forsake the idols of Egypt* (Ezekiel 20:8). [12] With the phrase *So they went away from them* he alludes to them abandoning the prophets.

Hosea 11:3: [13] The following verse *And I taught Ephraim to walk* means: whenever I reproached them for that, [14] and likewise He said to Ezekiel *And I acted for the sake of My name that it not be desecrated in the eyes of the nations in whose midst they were* (Ezekiel 20:9). [15] *I taught to walk* [...], for it has to be explained from the meaning.

Grammatical Note: And [16] [...] 'I tested' and it is from the lexical class 'abstaining' [17] [...] i.e. and abstaining, for this speech [18] [...] *I taught to walk* is friendliness [19] [...] the boy and he g[rows ... .] from it תַּרְגֵּל and when you attach to it [20] [(the prefix letters) אימנ״ת] you say [מְתַרְגֵּל, יְתַרְגֵּל, אֲתַרְגֵּל, etc].

21	[אלדי אבדהם] עלי [דראעיה כקו׳] כי תאמר אלי שאהו בחיקך פאתבע
22	[...][מ][... פה].................[.................] חסב מא ישאכל אלמעני וקו׳
23	ולא ידעו [כי ר]פאתים יעני הם יעת[רפו .....]כי אני אשפיתהם מן עבודיה
24	אלמצריין וקו׳ בחבלי אדם אמשכם ישיר בה אלי אלמלאטפה באלכלאם
25	לאן חבאל אלבהאים הי אלחבאל עלי חקיק[תהא וח]באל אלנאס אלדי [י]גדבו
26	בהא הו אלכלאם אללטיף תום אורא אנה מ[.......]לך במחבה וענאיה בקו׳
27	בעבותות אהבה. ישיר בדלך אלי מא תלא עליהם אלנבי בקו׳ והייתם

24b
1	לי סגלה וקו׳ [ואתם תהיו לי מ]מלכת כהנים. וקו׳ ואהיה להם כמרימי
2	עול יעני [...................ס] אולאיך אלדי כאן להם אלניר עלי אענאקהם
3	אראד ב[ה אן כמא כלצתה]ם מן תחת עבודיה אלמצריין ואדכלתהם תחת
4	עבודיה [אשור כדלך] אדכלהם תחת נירי בגיר פאידה בל ואט אליו
5	[...][ל...] א[טהרת אחסאני עליהם ידכול תחת הדא מא
6	עאמ[להם בה מן ....] ומא אועדהם בה מן אמר אלבלד ואיצ׳א
7	תמבע[ה............] קו׳ אוכי[ל] יעני גמיע מא וׂעדתהם בה אנא אקדר
8	עליה מא [.................] וקו׳ ל[א] ישוב אל ארץ מצרים ידל אן כאן קד
9	געלו פי מ[צר .... א][ן יר]געו] אלי מצר פקאל ליס אובלגהם דאך באן ירגעו
10	אלי אלמוצ׳ע אלדי אכרגתהם [מנ]ה בל אנמא אגליהם אלי אשור פיסתעבדוהם
11	ואלסבב פי דלך לאנהם קד אבו ירגעו אלי טאעתי תום אורא בקו׳ וחלה חרב
12	אן הודא קד אבתדת סיף מלך אשור פיהם פקד אפנת כוׂבראהם
13	ואגילאהם והודא הי עלי ממ[ר] אלזמאן תפני וקת בעד וקת וכל מא
14	חל בהם מן סבב מ[ד]אהבתהם אלדי אנגצבוהא ומן אפעאלהם אלקביחה
15	תום אורא אן [גמיע]הם מועלק[ין ב]אלרגעה יעני לו רגעו מן קבל הום עליה
16	לאנצלחת אחואלהם תום אורא [......................]ביה הום
17	ויסתדעיהם עלי אידי אנביא[ה ....]ה [אלי]
18	אלעאלי אלדי אמרה יל[אטפהם ....] כקו׳ ונאם
19	הגבר הוקם על וקד קא[ל.....................]
20	אן ליס פיהם ולא וא[חד.......קו׳ ...ה ב]ר[.] קו׳ איד[]
21	אתנך אפרים עלי טריק אלאי[......... אורא אנ]ה [.........]
22	אן ינזל בהם כמא נזל באדמ[ה וצבאים .... אלמ[ע]אצ[י] [.........]
23	לאיבקא פקו׳ נהפך עלי לבי [ישיר בה אלי ....קד או]ן[...]
24	חיכמתה אן ירעד להם וקו׳ יחד נכמרו ניחומי ישיר בה [אל]י מא קד ועד

The phrase *He took them on] his arms* alludes to the prophet [21] [who took them] on [his arms, as it is said] *For you say to me, Carry him in your bosom* (Numbers 11:12). He lets it follow [22] [...] according to what has a similar meaning. [23] The phrase *And they did not know that I healed them* means: They acknowledge [...] that I healed them from the slavery [24] of the Egyptians.

Hosea 11:4: With the phrase *With the cords of a man I drew them* he alludes to the friendliness in speech, [25] since 'cords of animals' are cords in their basic meaning, and 'the cords of the man' [26] with whom they are drawn, is the friendly speech. Then he shows that he [...] with love [and care]. With the phrase [27] *With bonds of love*, he alludes to what the prophet recited about them when saying *And you shall be* | [1] *to Me a peculiar treasure* (Exodus 19:5) and [*And you shall be to Me a*] *kingdom of priests* (Exodus 19:6). The phrase *And I was to them like those who lift up* [2] *a yoke* means: [...] these who had the yoke on their necks [3]. He intends by this [that as I deliver]ed them from the slavery of the Egyptians and brought them under [4] the slavery [of Assur, likewese] I will bring them under My yoke without benefit, rather *And I bent down to him* (5) (וְאַט אֵלָיו) [...] I have shown My benificence for them. He includes therein [6] [the ...] He did [to them ...] and the matter of the land He promised them, and also [7] [... . The phrase *I will feed*] means: all I have promised them, I will be able to do [8] [...].

24b

Hosea 11:5: The phrase *He will not return to the land of Egypt* indicates that they [9] made in Eg[ypt ... th]at they re[turn] to Egypt, and He said, I will not notify them about this that they will return [10] to the place from where I have brought them forth, rather I will exile them to Assur, so that they will subjugate them. [11] The reason for that is that they refused to return to my obedience.

Hosea 11:6: Then he shows by *A sword will begin* [12] that when the sword of the king of Assur began among them, it annihilated their distinguished (people) [13] and honourable personalities. And, behold, in cou[rse] of time, it destroys time after time. And all that [14] happened to them, (was) because of their doctrins which they established, and because of their evil deeds.

Hosea 11:7: [15] Then he shows that all of them are undecided to return, i.e. if they would return from their actual state, [16] their situation would improve. Then he shows [...] they, [17] and He calls them through [His] prophets [... to] [18] the Most High who ordered him [to treat them kindly ..., as it is said *And the speech*] [19] *of the man who was raised (on) high* (2 Samuel 23:1). And he said [...] [20] that there is among them not a single [one who ...] the phrase.

Hosea 11:8: [The phrase *How*] [21] *can I hand you over, Ephraim* (is said) in the way of [...]. [...] he shows that [...] [22] that it will befall them, as it befell Ad[mah and Zeboim ...] the sins [...] [23] that I remain. And the phrase *My heart has been overturned on Me* [refers to ...] [24] his wisdom, that he appalls

25 עלי איאדי אלאנביא וליס יג[וז] מן טריק אלחכמה אן לא [.....] מא ועד.
26 למא כאן קד מַתַל יהודה [בסד]ום ועמורה פי אעמאלהם חסן אן יוקאבל
27 ישראל באדמה וצבויים [לאנ]ה דל מן הדא אלקול אן אפעאל האולי
28 כאנת דון אפעאל אולאיך לאן אולאיך כאנו פי אלקודס פי אכץ

25a
1 מוצע [......][ל][..........] יעמלו [....] וקד זאדו עלי אולאיך פי אלקבאיח
2 בכׄ ענהם כי [מ]את נ[ב]יאי [ירושלם] יצאה חנופה לכל הארץ פכתם הדא
3 אלפצל בא[שאר]ה [...א ל]מא דכר נ[חומ]י אקרן אליהא פקאל לא אעשה חרון
4 א[פי לא אשוב לשחת אפרים] כי אל אנכי פלא בוד מן תמאם אלמואעיד
5 [בקוׄ ולא איש אורא] אנה ליס יכתאר באומה גירהם בך בקרבך
6 קד[וש ..] אור[א אנה ליס יכתא]ר בבלד גיר אלבלד אלבאץ לקוׄ ולא אבוא בעיר:
7 פכׄאן אלקאיל יקול [.......] הדה אלמואעיד פאגאב ען דלך בקוׄ אחרי ייי
8 ילכו: יעני פי אלוקת [..... ירג]עו אלי טאעתה ויסלוכו וראה יעני ינקאדו
9 אלי מרצאתה וקוׄ [כאריה יש]אג משאר אלי כל ואחד מנהם נטיר קוׄ ויקרא
10 אריה על מצפה [תום אור]א בקוׄ כי הוא ישאג פאן הו יזיר אליהם יעני
11 באלעלאמאת [אלתי ..]..ר בהא פאורא אן אול תחריך יכון מן גהה אלגרב
12 בקוׄ ויחרדו בנים מים תום אורא בקוׄ יחרדו כצפור ממצׄ אנהם אדא צארו
13 מן אלגַׄרב אלי חד מצרים פקד סהול עליהם מא בקי אלטריק לאנהם
14 יַסְרעו כמא יַסְרע אלעצפור אלי וכרה ובעד דלך קאל וכיונה מארץ אש
15 אורא אן האולי בעד אולאיך והם אבטא מנהם איצא. עַלְוָה ועוׄלָה ואחד
16 הי מן אלמותבדלה מתל שַמלה ושלמה: ואסׁרֶם מן סזׁר לאן לו כאן
17 מן אאסור לי[כו]ן אאסרם: פיכון סזׁר ארבט מקאם אסור ויגוז תוגעל
18 מן לגה אלתאדיב לאנה גיר מומתנע ל[א פי] אללפט ולא פי אלמעני.
19 פכאן חקהא עלי הדא תכון אסׁוׄרֶם ליכן אלאצאפאת כדי יסתעמלה
20 אלכתאב: עוׄנָה אסם אלמעניה גמעהא עוׄנות ומתלהא מַעֲנָה
21 כך כבחצי מענה גמעהא מַעֲנות: ומתלהא מַעֲנית כך הארכו למעניתם:

them. The phrase *My mercies have been kindled together* alludes to what He promised [25] through the prophets. And it is not conceivable in the way of wisdom that he [does] not [fulfil] what he has promised. [26] After comparing Judah with Sodom and Gomorrah concerning their deeds, it is appropriate to compare [27] Israel with Admah and Zeboim, for he demonstrates with this phrase that their deeds [28] were not as their deeds, for these were in the sanctuary, at the most distinguished | [1] place [...] they do [...]. They excelled these by (the) shameful deeds, [2] as it is said about them *For deceit has spread out over all the land from the prophets of Jerusalem* (Jeremiah 23:15).

25a

Hosea 11:9: He concludes this [3] section [by ...] after [mentioning] *My mercies* (Hosea 11:8). he connects with it by saying *I will not carry out My* [4] *wrath, [I will not return to destroy Ephraim] for I am God*. There is no doubt about the fulfillment of the promises. [5] [He shows by the phrase *And not a man*] that he will not choose another nation than them. With the phrase *In your midst* [6] *the Ho[ly One ...]* he shows [that he will not choose] another land than the special land, as it is said *I will not enter a city*.

Hosea 11:10: [7] And as if the narrator says [...] these promises, and he responds to that with the phrase [8] *They will go after YHWH*, i.e. at the [...] time [they will return] to obey Him and go after Him, i.e. they will obey [9] his requests. The phrase [*Like a lion He will r]oar* alludes to each of them, corresponding to the verse *And* [10] *a lion called out, On the lookout* (Isaiah 21:8). [Then] he shows by *For He will roar* that He roars towards them, i.e. [11] with the signs by which [...]. He shows that the first stirring up will be from the west [12] by the phrase *And sons will tremble from the west*.

Hosea 11:11: Then he shows by the phrase *They will tremble like a bird from Egypt* that, when they went [13] from the west to the border of Egypt, the rest of the journey was easy for them because [14] they hurried as the sparrow hurries to its nest. The following phrase *And like a dove from the land of Assur* [15] demonstrates that these are after those, and also: they are slower than they are.

Grammatical Notes

עַלְוָה (Hosea 10:9) and עוֹלָה are identical [16] by metathesis, like שִׂמְלָה and שַׂלְמָה. וְאֶסְרֵם (Hosea 10:10) is (derived) from (the imperative) סֹר, since if it would be (derived) [17] from (the imperative) אֱסוֹר, it should be אֲאָסְרֵם; and סוֹר 'tie up!' (is used) in the place of אֱסֹר. It may be that it is formed [18] from the lexical class 'discipline', for it is not impossible neither regarding the linguistic expression nor regarding the meaning. [19] According to rule it should be אֲסוֹרֵם; however, [20] the Book uses conjoined forms in this way. עוֹנָה (Hosea 10:10) is a noun (meaning) 'furrow'; its plural being עוֹנוֹת. An equivalent for it is מַעֲנָה [21] as in כְּבַחֲצִי מַעֲנָה (1 Samuel 14:14); its plural is מַעֲנוֹת. And (another) equivalent

22	גמעהא מַעֲנִיתוֹת: ויגוז תכון מן אלאסמא אלדי ליס תתְכַתֵּר מתל
23	חֲפָשִׁיֹת ומא שאכלהא: וְאַט יחתמל יכון מורכם הי פיכון מן הַטֶה ויחתמל
24	יכון מן הַט פיכון אמר בראסה: מתל צַ[וֹ] אלדי הו אמר בראסֹה עלי ראִי
25	בעץ אשלמתכלמין פי אללגה: אוֹבִיל מן הוֹבִיל משתק מן יוֹבַל ומא שאכלה:
26	וחלָה מן חֻול אלמאצִי חָל ואלמונת חָלָה והדה מתל וְשָׁבָה חקיקתה פאעלה יעני
27	תחצול מובתדייה: אמגֻנך: תופסר כסֻר משתקה מן אשר מָגֵן ותופסר

25b

1	תסלים: סבבוני: אסתדארו בי ב[גחוד אל א]פרים [ובמכר אל א]סראיל
2	ואל יהודה זאדה אסתולא מע אל[טאיק] ומע אלקו[ן דוס תא]ב[ת]: אפרים:
3	אפרים רעאי ריח וכאכל ריח שרקי כל אליום כ[דב] ונהב יוכ[ת]ר ועהד
4	מע מלך אשור יקטעו ודוהו אלי מצ[ר] יוגלב: וריב: ונטר ללרב: מע
5	אל יהודה איצא וסיף תקד עלי אל יע[קב בטורקה כשמאילה יר]וֹד
6	לה: בבטן: אלדי פי אלאחשא אעתק[ב עלי אכיה ובקותה]
7	תראוס מע מלך: וַיָּשַׂר: פלמא תרא[וס מע] מָלַך קדר עליה
8	חתי בכא תום תחנן אליה תום פי ב[ית אל] יציבה וְתָם איצא
9	כאן יוכאטב מענא: ויי: ואלרב פ[הו אללה א]לגיוש אלרב דכרה:
10	ואתה: ואנת פאלי אלאהך תרגע פאיחס[ן] וחוכ[ם] אחפט וארגו
11	אלי אלאהך דאים: כנען: לאן אלתאגר [פבידה] מואזין מכר
12	[פ]לל גֻשׁם הו מוחב: ויאמר: פקאל אפרים {כאץ קד א[ס]תגנית}
13	כאץ קד איסרת קד אצבת מָנאל לי כל אתעאבי ליס
14	יציבו לי דנב אלדי הו כְטא: ואנכי: ואנא אלרב אלאהך מן ארץ
15	מצר זאדה סא אגל[ס]ך פי אלאכביה כאיאם מַועד: ודברתי:
16	וקד תכלמת עלי איְדי אלאנביא ואנא פווחי קד כתרת ועלי יד
17	אלאנביא אושבה: אם: אן כאן אהל גלעד אסתעמל גֵיל פכאץ

for it is מַעֲנִית as in הֶאֱרִיכוּ לְמַעֲנִיתָם (Psalms 129:3), [22] its plural being מַעֲנִיתוֹת. It is possible that it (belongs to such) nouns which cannot form a plural, as [23] חָפְשִׁית and similar cases. וְאַט (Hosea 11:4) has possibly its *he* apocopated and (is derived) from (the imperative) הַטֵּה; or it is possible [24] that it is (derived) from (the imperative) הַט and is an imperative in its primary form, as צַו which is an imperative in its primary form according to the opinion [25] of some scholars of the language. אוֹכִיל (Hosea 11:4) (is derived) from (the imperative) הוֹכִיל which is derived from יוּכַל and similar cases. [26] וְחָלָה (Hosea 11:6) is (derived) from (the imperative) חוּל, the past tense is חָל, the feminine is חָלָה. This is like וְשָׁבָה whose basic meaning is an active participle feminine, i.e. [27] 'she is beginning'. אֲמַגֶּנְךָ (Hosea 11:8) can be translated with 'breaking', if derived from אֲשֶׁר מִגֵּן 'Who has delivered' (Genesis 14:20); it can be translated | [1] with 'handing over'.

25b

Translation

Hosea 12:1: The people of Ephraim have surrounded Me with re[jection, and with deception the people of] Israel. [2] And the people of Judah are still rulers with the [Powerful One] and are faith[ful] to the Hol[y One].

Hosea 12:2: [3] Ephraim grazes wind and seizes east wind. All the day he multiplies falsehood and destruction; [4] they make a covenant with the king of Assur, and oil [is carried] to Egypt.

Hosea 12:3: [The Lord has a lawsuit] against [5] the people of Judah, too, and He will visit the people of Jaco[b according to his ways; in accordance with his deed, He will re]pay [6] him.

Hosea 12:4: Who in the intestines grasped the heel of [his brother, and in his strength] [7] he gained mastery over an angel.

Hosea 12:5: And after he had gained mast[ery] over an angel, he overpowered him [8] until he wept. Then he implored him for a favour. Then he will find him in B[eth-El]. And there also [9] he used to speak with us.

Hosea 12:6: And the Lord is [the God of] the legions. The Lord is His name.

Hosea 12:7: [10] As for you—, you will return to your God: [ob]serve kind[ness and just]ice, and have hope [11] in your God always!

Hosea 12:8: For the trader [in his hand] (are) scales of deceit, [12] and he loves to act unjustly.

Hosea 12:9: And Ephraim said, {Indeed, I have become wealthy} [13] Indeed, I have become rich; I have gained a fortune for me. All my property [14] they will not establish in me an iniquity that is sin.

Hosea 12:10: And I am the Lord your God from the land of [15] Egypt. I will yet again make you d[we]ll in the tents as (in) the days of a festival.

Hosea 12:11: [16] I have spoken through the prophets and have multiplied a vision. And through [17] the prophets I give parables.

18 גזאף קד צארו לאן פי אלגלגל תִּירְאַן דְּבָחוּ איצֿא מדאבחהם
19 צארת כתלול עלי אתְלָאם צחרא: ויברח: פהרב יעקב אלי צִּיעַה
20 ארם תום כְּדַם ישראל באימראה ובאימראה אוכּרי חֲפַט אלגַֿנֶם:
21 ובנביא: ובנבי אצעד אלרב אל אסר' מן מצר ובנבי אנְחֲפַּט:
22 הִכְעִיס: אגֿאיֿ אפרים [ר]בה פחצל פי מראראת ודמאה עליה
23 יוסַיִּב ומעייִרתֿה ירוד אליה מולאה: כדבר: ענד תכלום אפרים
24 כאן יאכוד אלנאס רעדה לאנה כאן שריף פי אל אסראיל
25 פלמא אתַֿם בעבאדה אלותן עוקב: ועתה: ואלסאעה פהודא
26 יזידו פי אלכטא לאן קד עמלו להם מסבוכה מן פצֿתהם
27 כבניתהם אצנאם עמל צונאע כולה להם הום קאילין דאבחי

26a
1 [אלאנסאן] תון[ם] ללעגול יֻקַב[לון]: לְכֵן: פלדלך יכונו כגֿמאם צובח
2 וכאל[נד]א אלדי הו מודֿלג [ס]אלךֿ כמוץ יועצף מן אנְדַּר וכדֿכאן
3 י[כר]וגֿ מן רוזנה: ואנכי: ו[א]נא אלרב אלאהך מן ארץֿ מצר ואלאה
4 [סוא]י פליס תערף ומוגֿע פליס לך גֿירי: אני: אנא אלדי עֲרַפְתְּךֿ
5 פי [אלבר] פי אַ[ר]ץֿ קפֿאר: כמרעיתם: ענד רעאיתהם פְּשַבְעוּ
6 לַמָּא שָבְעוּ ארתפע [ק]לבהם עלי דלך נסיוני: ואהי: פלדלך צרת
7 להם מתֿל אלאסד כאלב[בר] עלי טריק אלמַח: אפגשם: אפאגיהם
8 כדוב תכול פאשוק [אגֿלא]ק קלבהם תום אכולהם תַֿם כאללבוה וחוש
9 אלצחרא [תושקקהם]: שחתך: אנמא אפסדך יא אל אסראיל {אל} לאן בי
10 כאנת תסתעין פציֿרת פי עַוְנך: אֶהִי: אין אלדי כאן יקול לך
11 אנא אכון מליכך אלאן חתי יגֿיתֿך פי כל קוראך ואין חוכאמך
12 אלדי קולת איגֿאאל אגעל לנפסי מְלִיךְ ורווסא: אתן: ואנא פכונת
13 אגעל לך מלך בגֿצבי ואכודֿ בחלטתי: הדא אלפצֿל ישתמל עלי

Hosea 12:12: If the people of Gilead used wickedness, they became only [18] vanity. For in Gilgal they slaughtered bulls; also their altars [19] became like hills upon the furrows of a field.

Hosea 12:13: And Jacob fled to the domain of [20] Aram. Then Israel served for a woman, and for another woman he guarded the sheep.

Hosea 12:14: [21] And by a prophet the Lord brought the people of Israel up from Egypt, and by a prophet it was safeguarded.

Hosea 12:15: [22] Ephraim has angered his Lord, and He became bitter. And his blood [23] will be poured upon him, and his Master will repay him his disgrace.

Hosea 13:1: When Ephraim spoke, [24] trembling seized the people, for he was honoured among the people of Israel. [25] When he sinned by worshipping the idols, he had been punished.

Hosea 13:2: And now, behold, [26] they increase the sin, for they have made for themselves a molten (image) out of their silver, [27] according to their pattern, idols all of them the work of craftsmen. They say to them(selves), Those who have slaughtered | [1] [the men], shall then kiss the calves.

26a

Hosea 13:3: And therefore they will be like the morning cloud [2] and like the dew that disappears before day-break, like chaff that is blown away from a threshing-floor, and like smoke [3] that evades from a window.

Hosea 13:4: And I am the Lord your God from the land of Egypt. And gods [4] [beside] Me you are not to know; and a helper there is no one except Me.

Hosea 13:5: It was I who knew you [5] in [the wilderness], in the la[n]d of dried-out regions.

Hosea 13:6: When being pastured, they were satisfied. [6] After they were satisfied, their heart became arrogant; therefore they forgot Me.

Hosea 13:7: Therefore I became [7] like the lion to them; like the t[iger] I will lurk by a road.

Hosea 13:8: I will come suddenly upon them [8] like a bear, bereaved (of its cubs), and I will tear open the enclosure of their heart. Then I will devour them there like the lioness, and the wild beasts [9] of the desert will tear them open.

Hosea 13:9: Indeed, it has destroyed you, people of Israel. For [10] you turned to Me for help, and I became your help.

Hosea 13:10: Where is the one who said to you, [11] 'I will now be your king', so that he may help you in all your cities? And where are your judges [12] of whom you said, 'Please, appoint for me a king and officers'?

Hosea 13:11: And I [13] appointed a king for you in My wrath, and I will take (him) away in My anger.

14	מעאני כתיר והו פמונתסק אלי מא קבלה לאנה וצף אפעאל אלקום איצّא
15	וצף מא אחסָן אליהם פלם יעתרפו בה ומא אסתחקוה עלי דלך מן
16	אלגזא קו' סבבוני בכחש יעני בגחוד אלניעם ואלכירّאת אלדי אנעמת
17	עליהם לאנהם יסובוהא אלי גّירי וקו' ובמרמה ידל עלי ממאכרה
18	ומוראיאה וקו' ויהודה עוד רד מצّא אלי פיעל אולאיך כאנה קאל
19	מא כפא מא פّעלוה ישראל חתי יהודה איצّא קד תאסّא בהם
20	וקו' רָד יעני אסתאוולו צארו ברוסא יעני אסתגّנו עני מע מא
21	אנא קאדר ומע מא אנא מכצוץ ותאבת אסתגّנו עני באלאצנאם
22	אלמוחّדתה אלדי הי גّיר קאדרה וגّיר תאבתה פאורא אן אשתגّאלהם
23	בהדה אלמעאני כאנסן יוראעי אלריח ויכלוב ריח אלשרקי אלדי
24	הי צَרَר בגّיר מנפוע וקו' כָזָב וָשׁוד יַרבּה: ישיר בה אלי
25	טולמה/ם/ ותעדיהם בעצّהם עלי [ב]עّץ תום דכר תוכّלאנהם עלי

26b
1	מלך אשור ומלך מצרים פדכר [עّן] אשור ברית ואכתצר ד[לך פّי
2	אבَّאר מצרים וכדלך דכר אלה[דאי]א אלדי תוחْמَל אלי מ[צר יעני]
3	דוהן וגּّירה' ואכתّצר ידכור דלך פי אבَّבאר אשור וקו' ו[ריב] לייי עם
4	יהודה: מצّאף אלי מא דَכר מן אבَّבאר [א]פّרים: לَمَا צّדّר בّדَכר
5	אפّّעאל אפרים ואקרן אליה יהודה בקו' [ו]יהודה עוד רד אקר[נה א]ליה
6	איצّא פי אלמטאלّבة פכאנה קאל וריב לייי איצّא ע[ם] יהודה [כמא פَّעَ]ל
7	באפרים: קו' בבטן עקב את אחיו בעד דלך ליור[י'] אנה [ישיר ל]הם
8	עלי מא לם יעתרפו לה באחסאנה אליה[ם] ואיחסאנה אלי אבוהם
9	קבّלהם פלמא כאנת אלאסמין אלדי סומי'[...]ל[...]ב מע[...]פّה מן מועّגّיז
10	פّועّילת מעה חסון אן ידכורהא פי תעّ[...] אלאיחסאן וק[ד]ס אלמוקדّם
11	פّקו' עקב א' אחיו ידל עלי אנה הו מכנّה מנ[ה ל]יّסתדל בדלך עלי אן
12	יכון הו אלגّאלב ואלّטّאפּר וקו' ובאונו יעני עّנד מא אשّתד וקוי וביّן
13	הונא מא לם יביّן פי אלתורה לאן תّם קאל עّן אלמלאך באנה קאל לה שّלחّני
14	כי עלה השחר זאד הונא שרח בקו' בכה ויתחנן לו וקו' הונא שרה את א'ים

Exegesis
This section includes [14] a lot of thoughts and is closely related to what precedes it because he describes also the deeds of the people [15] and describes the favours He bestowed upon them though they did not acknowledge Him, and [16] the punishment they deserved for that.

Hosea 12:1: The phrase *They surrounded Me with falsehood* means: by denying the benefits and the blessings I bestowed [17] upon them, since they ascribe them to somebody else than Me. The phrase *And with deceit* points out the deception [18] and the hypocrisy. The verse *And Judah still ruled* continues the action of those, as if he would say, [19] It was not enough what Israel had done, until also Judah had been established among them. [20] The phrase *He ruled* means 'they made themselves masters', 'they became chiefs', i.e. they had no need of Me. Though [21] I am powerful and though I am special and reliable, they had no need of Me because of the [22] manufactured idols who have no power and are not reliable.

Hosea 12:2: He shows that their devotion [23] to these ideas is like a man who tends the wind and seizes the east wind which [24] damages disadvantageously. With the phrase *He increases lie and plunder* he alludes to [25] their iniquity and their hostilities against each other. Then he mentions that they relied on | [1] the king of Assur and the king of Egypt. He mentions a covenant [with] Assur; that is briefly mentioned in [2] the historical narratives of Egypt. He also mentions the pre[sents], which were carried to Egypt: [i.e.] [3] oil etc.; that is briefly mentioned in the historical narratives of Assur.

26b

Hosea 12:3: The phrase *YHWH has a dispute with* [4] *Judah* is linked to what he mentions in the historical narratives of Ephraim. After firstly mentioning [5] the deeds of Ephraim and connecting Judah with it by saying *And Judah still ruled* (Hosea 12:1), he connects [it w]ith it [6] also in the claims, as if he would say, YHWH *has a dispute also with Judah*, [as He had] [7] with Ephraim.

Hosea 12:4: The following verse *In the womb he grasped the heel of his brother* is to demonstrate that he [refers to] them [8] in that they did not appreciate Him, as far as His beneficence toward the[m] is concerned and His beneficence toward their father [9] before them. Since the two names which [were given to him] are k[no]wn from two miracles, [10] which were performed to him, it is appropriate to mention them in [...] the benefit and he overtook the one who was first. [11] The phrase *He grasped the heel of his brother* implies that He made him stronger than him so that it can be inferred by that, that [12] he will get the upper hand and be victorious. The phrase *With his strength* means: when he became strong and vigorous.

Hosea 12:5: [13] Here he explains what is not explained in the Torah. For there it was said that the angel said to him (Jacob), *Let me go* [14] *for dawn has broken*

15	באזא קו' לה תַם כי שרית עם א"ים. וקו' בית אֵל ימצאנו ישיר בה
16	אלי מכאטבתה פי בית אֵל בעד רגועה כך וירא א"ים אל יעקב עוד בבאו
17	מפדן ארם וקו' ושם ידבר עמנו יומי הושע אלקול אלי נפסה
18	ואלי גֿירה מן אלאנביא פאורא שרף אלמוצע ואנה מַוֹצֵע מַאהל
19	ללנבווה כך' ענה פי אלאצל אֵין זה כי אם בית אל"ים. וקו' בעד הדא
20	וייי אלהי הצבאות יעני הו אל[קא]דר עלי אן יקוי מן ישא ויצעף מן ישא וקו'
21	ואתה באלהיך תשוב מוקא[ל] לה לאומה איכבאר במא יָתָארוה פי
22	אבֿר אלגלות כקו' להם ושב[ת] עד ייי אלהיך וקאל כי תשוב אל ייי אלהיך פכאן
23	אלנבי הושע יקול להם לא תקדרו אן בהדה אלאפעאל אלדי קד
24	פעלתם קד זאלת אלכצוצ[ה] ענכם בל אלכצוצה מובקאה עליכם
25	ולא בוד לכם מן רגעה: ק[ו'] חסד ישיר בה אלי מא בינהם ובין
26	אלנאס וקו' ומשפט ישיר בה אלי אלואגבאת אלדי עליהם לרבהם וקו' אל
27	אלהיך יעני ארגוה אן יְגִיתך כמא אַגַֿאת אבאך: פלמא קאל באלהיך תשוב
28	ביין מן איש ירגעו פדכר אלמטאלם אלדי הום עליהא כך' כנען

27a

1	וקו' תמיד ידל על[י] טול אלמכת פי אלגלות תום וצף ען א[...]
2	ב[אן] קד א[........]רה ומא קד אכתסבה מן [א]לטולם ואלגשם:
3	קו' כל יְגִיעַי יחתמל יורד אלי אלאמואל אלדי קד [...]הא פאורא באן
4	כאן ענדה אן מא עליה פיהא דנב ולא כטא ויח[תמל א]ן קו' כל יגיעי
5	ראגע אלי אלמעבודאת אלדי קד תעב פי גמעהא [פאורא] אן [מא]
6	עליה פי עבאדתהא דנב ולא כטא קו' ואנכי ייי אלהי[ך ראגע אלי] קו'
7	וקוה אל אלהיך וקו' עוד אושיבך באהלים ישיר ב[ה א]ל[י] ואחד] אלחגוג
8	אלדי כאנת להם וזאלת לאנהם כאן יגי מן [בעד ולד]ל[ד] צרבו כיים
9	לאן ירושלם מא כאנת תחמלהם וקו' [כימי מו]עד [יחתמ]ל יקאל מתל איאם

(Genesis 32:27), here an explanation is added: *He wept and he asked a favour of him*. Here it is said *He struggled with God* [15] corresponding to what has been said to him (Jacob) there, *For you have struggled with God* (Genesis 32:29). The phrase *(In) Beth-El He will find him* alludes [16] to His speech in Beth-El after his return, as it is said *And God appeared to Jacob again when he came* [17] *from Paddan Aram* (Genesis 35:9). In the phrase *And there He will speak with us*, Hosea points to himself [18] and to the other prophets and shows the nobility of the place and that it is a place suited [19] for (the) prophecy, as it is said about it in Genesis *This is none other than the house of God* (Genesis 28:17).

Hosea 12:6: [20] The following phrase *And YHWH is the God of the legions* means: He is the Powerful One in that He strengthens whom He wants and weakens whom He wants.

Hosea 12:7: The phrase [21] *And you will return by your God* is one of his addresses to the people and a notification of what they will choose at [22] the end of the exile, as it is said to them *You will return to YHWH your God* (Deuteronomy 4:30); and it is said *For you will return to YHWH your God* (Deuteronomy 30:10). [23] The prophet Hosea used to say to them, Do not presume that because of these deeds which [24] you have done, the special status has been withdrawn from you, rather the special status will stay with you, [25] and there is no doubt that you will return. The term *Kindness* alludes to the relationship between them and [26] the people. The term *And justice* alludes to their obligations toward their Lord. The phrase *And hope to* [27] *your God* means: Hope that He will help you as He helped your fathers. After saying *You will return by your God*, [28] he points out from what they should refrain, and he mentions the iniquities which they are involved in, as it is said *A trader* (Hosea 12:8). | [1] The term *Always* alludes to the length of the sojourn in the exile.

Hosea 12:8: Then he describes [...] [2] [...] and what he gained through iniquity and oppression.

Hosea 12:9: [3] The phrase *All my efforts* may refer to the property they had [purchased] and shows [4] that in his opinion, there was no sin and no wrongdoing attributed to him. Alternatively, the phrase *All my efforts* may [5] re[fer] to all the idols of whom he had become tired, [and shows that] there was no [6] sin and no wrongdoing on his part in worshipping them.

Hosea 12:10: The phrase *And I am YHWH your God* [refers to the phrase] [7] *And hope to your God* (Hosea 12:7). The phrase *I will yet settle you in tents* alludes to [one of] [8] their festivals which came to an end because they came from [far away; therefo]re they pitched tents [9] because Jerusalem did not harbour them. [The phrase *As the days of appoint*]*ment* may mean 'as the

27a

10	עמארה אלקודס לאנה מועֵד אסם אלקוד[ס ...]ׁן שח[......] ויחתמל יכון
11	ראגע אלי איאם אלאעיאד תום שַׁד ד[]לך] בקו׳ [ודברתי] על הנבאים
12	יעני קד בשרת בהדא וקד אַכְתַּרְתִּ [מ]ׁן אלבשאראת [ק]ׁו׳ בעד דלך אם
13	גלעד און ראגע אלי קו׳ כל יגיעי לא [י]ׁמצאו לי לאן כאן [ק]ׁד קאל קבל
14	הדא גלעד קרית פועלי און פקאל אהל גלעד לאגל אלמטלם אלדי
15	פעלו הלכו ואיצא לאגל מא דבחו פי אלגלגל אלדבאיח ללאותאן
16	[......................]ׁל[.]ׁל[.]ׁל[...] דלך [סו]ׁלבד אנת [אהל א]ׁפרים פידהב
17	[..............................] קו׳ בעד ה[..........] ויברח יעקב
18	[שדה ארם ....] ובאונו שרה את [אלהים ...]ׁא[.] בדלך
19	[......................] יעקב [...]ׁל[......]ׁא[.....]ׁן הַמָה ונסק
20	[.............] קו׳ ובנביא העלה: ליסאוי [אלנבי] באלאב אל[מ]ׁכְתָּסַב
21	[..........] קד תסאוו פי הדא אלמע[נ]ׁי [.................]ׁתסאוו באן [כ]ׁמא
22	[הרב יעקב] מן בין עשו כדלך הרב משה מן בין ידי פרעה בכו׳
23	[ויברח משה מפ]ׁני פרעה וכמא חצל יעקב ענד [כ]ׁאלה פתזווג אליה וכאן
24	ירעא גֻנמה כדלך משה חצל ענד [י]ׁתרו פתזווג אליה וכאן ירעא גֻנמה
25	פלדלך קאל ובנביא קאנה בנבי ישאכל אלאב אלדי הו איצֻא [נבי]
26	וקו׳ ובנביא נשמר קיל אנה ראגע אלי אהרן אלדי אנחפטו עלי
27	ידה מן אלמגפה בכק׳ ענה ויעמד בין החיים ובין המתים ותעצר המגפה
28	וקיל אן ובנביא נשמר ראגע אלי אליהו אלדי הו מחפוט לִיָבֵרג ישראל

27b

1	מן [הד]ׁא אלגלות כמא אכרגהם משה מן מצרים. עאד אלי כלאמה פקאל
2	הכעיס אפרים פאו[רא]ׁ מא חל בהם לאגל [דנו]בהם [וקו׳] ו[י]ׁאשם ב[על וי]ׁמֹת
3	משאר אלי מא ג[... מ]ׁעהם פי שמרון מן [.........] אלבע[ל ......] אחד[הם]
4	מע אלעגלים אל[מתק]ׁדמה פלדלך עוקבו תום אורא אנהם קד עמילו [לה]ׁם
5	איצא מצ[טבא]ׁת מן פֻצה עגול ובקו׳ ועתה יֹדל אן הדא אמר אמר אוחדת
6	קר[יב פימכן] אן למא אוגליית אלעגול אלדהב וחומילת אלי אשור לם
7	י[מכן אן פעל]ׁו בדלהא מן דהב פעמלו מן פֻצה וקו׳ להם הם אומרים
8	ישיר בה אלי [מא אמר] אלנאס להום בדלך לאנהם הודא ידבחו אולאדהם

days of [10] building of the sanctuary', since [**Grammatical Note**]: מוֹעֵד is a noun (meaning) 'sanctuary' [...]; or it may [11] refer to the days of the festivals.

Hosea 12:11: Then he emphasizes th[is] by saying [*I spoke*] *through the prophets*, [12] i.e. I heralded this and promoted abundant good tidings.

Hosea 12:12: The following phrase *If* [13] *Gilead (was) wickedness* refers to the phrase *All my efforts they will not find for Me* (Hosea 12:9), since [14] it is said earlier *Gilead is a city of those who do wickedness* (Hosea 6:8). He says: the people of Gilead [15] perished because of the iniquity they did and also because of the offerings they offered to the idols in Gilgal [16] [...] that [...] in you; you [...] Ephraim and he will go [17] [...].

Hosea 12:13: The following phrase *Jacob* [*fled*] [18] [*to the field of Aram* ...] *And with his strength he struggled wi*[*th God* (Hosea 12:4)]. By that [19] [...] Jacob [...] there and he put in good order [20] [...].

Hosea 12:14: The phrase *And by a prophet He brought up* is to position [the prophet] on the same level with the patriarch who acquired [21] [...] they were similar in this res[pect ...] they were similar in that, as [22] [Jacob fled] from Esau, likewise Moses fled from Pharaoh, as it is said [23] [*And Moses fled fro*]*m Pharaoh* (Exodus 2:15). And as Jacob was with his uncle and was linked to him by marriage and [24] grazed his sheep, likewise Moses was with Jethro and was linked to him by marriage and grazed his sheep. [25] Therefore he says *And by a prophet*, as if the patriarch who is also [a prophet], is similar to a prophet. [26] Some hold that *And by a prophet he was safeguarded* refers to Aaron through whose good offices they were safeguarded [27] from the plague, as it is said *He stood between the living and the dead* [sic!] *and the plague was restrained* (Numbers 17:13). [28] Others hold that *And by a prophet he was safeguarded* refers to Elijah who was safeguarded to bring out Israel | [1] of [this] the exile, as Moses brought them out of Egypt.

Hosea 12:15: He resumes his speech and says [2] *Ephraim has angered*. Then he shows what befell them because of their [sins].

Hosea 13:1: The phrase *He became guilty through Baal and died* [3] alludes to what he [did together wi]th them in Samaria through [...] the Baa[l ...] one [of them] [4] with the [...] calves; therefore they were punished.

Hosea 13:2: Then he shows that they made for themselves [5] also ma[stabas] from the silver of calves. The phrase *And now* indicates that this is a very [6] recent matter and, probably, that after the golden calves had been removed and brought to Assur, [7] they could not make a replacement of them from gold, and so they made (them) from silver. The phrase *They say to them* [8] alludes to [what] the people [said] to themselves in this matter: For, behold, they sacri-

9 אלדי הום [כאנו יד[ב]חו[ן] אלגמאדאת ואלדי מן שאן אלנאס אן יוקבילו
10 אולאדהם [.... יו[קבלו[ן] ......] הדה אלעגול אלמוצטנעה וְיָעְטָּמוּהַ.
11 אטבק עלי [דלך ב]קו' לכן י]הי[ו כענן בקר פי הדא אלפסוק ד' אמתאל
12 כענן בקר [כטל] כמוץ וכעשן באזא אלד' גואלי אלדי אוגליו עשרת
13 שבטים: למא דכר חצולהם פי אלגלות אתבע דלך פקאל ואנכי יי' אלהיך
14 מארץ מצרים יעני אנא אלדי אכרגת אבאכם מן מצר ואנא
15 אכרגכם מן הדה אלגלות לאנה קאל פי אכר אלפסוק ומושיע אין בלתי
16 ליס ל[כם] מן יגיתכם מן הדה אלגלות גירי: וקו' א[ני יד]עתיך במדבר
17 ליורי אנ]ה קד ד[עא אבאהם [פי אלבר ....[ל...]
18 קו' כמ[רעיתם רא]גע אלי אלדי [...................]
19 אנה[ם] ענד מא חצל]ת[ל[.................]
20 אלעו[ן ...] ונסיו [...............[גא נצחהם אלנבי במא ק......] ורם
21 לבבך ושכחת את [יי' פלד]לך קאל הונא וירם לבם על [כן שכחוני]
22 פאתבע דלך בד' אמתאל והו קו' כמו שחל כנמר [כדב כלביא]
23 ישיר בדלך אלי ארבע]ת שפט[יו הרעים וביין פי אלראבע[..........]
24 בדנהא עלי טאהרהא בקו' חית השדה תבקעם קו' שחתך ישראל
25 עלי טריק אלתאסוף עליהם יעני מא אפסדכם ואהלככם אלא
26 מא כונת אנתצר לכם ואגיתכם אבדא קו' להם אהי מלכך עלי
27 טריק אלתהדוד יעני אין אלמלוך אלדי כאנת תתגלב בעצהא

28a
1 [..]
2 [..]
3 [..]
4 [..]
5 ימלוך כל ואחד [...]א יריד ית[בעו] אלואחד עלי [..............]
6 מלך [...] כקו' באפי ואלמקתול פקד אובד מן אלמולך ב[............]
7 דאך[:] רָד משתקה מן אמרו עמי רדנו הו רֶד פיכון רֶ[............]
8 אסתולי: קו' ועם קדושים נטיר קול יהושע כי אלהים קדו[שים הוא יקאל]

fice their children. [9] Who [...] the inanimate bodies and who it is man's nature that they kiss [10] their children, [...] they kiss these manufactured calves and glorify them.

Hosea 13:3: [11] He concludes this by saying *Therefore they will be like a morning cloud*. He mentions four similes in this verse: [12] *Like a morning cloud, [like the dew,] like chaff, and like smoke*, corresponding to the four exiles into which the ten [13] tribes have been exiled.

Hosea 13:4: After mentioning them being in the exiles, he let that to be followed by the phrase *And I am YHWH your God* [14] *from the land of Egypt*, i.e. I am the One who has brought your fathers out of Egypt and I [15] will bring you out of this exile, for at the end of the verse he says *There is no saviour but Me*: [16] there is nobody for you who will deliver you from this exile but Me.

Hosea 13:5: The phrase *I knew you in the wilderness* [17] is to show that [He ca]lled their fathers [in the wilderness ...].

Hosea 13:6: [18] The phrase *According to their pasture* refers to those who [...] [19] that they whenever it happened to [...] [20] [...] and they forgot [...] the prophet admonished them by that [He said in the Torah *And*] [21] *your heart will become haughty and you will forget YHWH* (Deuteronomy 8:14). Therefore he says here *And their heart became haughty; therefore they forgot Me*.

Hosea 13:7–8: [22] This is followed by four similes, namely *Like a lion, like a leopard, [like a bear, like a lion]*. [23] That alludes to 'His four evil judgments', and he explains in the four [...] [24] according to its appearance by the phrase *The beast of the field will tear them*.

Hosea 13:9: The phrase *It has destroyed you, Israel* [25] (is said) by way of regret for them, i.e. he would not have destroyed and annihilated you, if [26] I had helped you and given you support.

Hosea 13:10: The word (addressed) to them *Where is your king?* (is said) by [27] way of intimidation, i.e. where are the kings some of them achieved supremacy (over)

[1] ...
[2] ...
[3] ...
[4] [Hosea 13:11: ...]
[5] every single one will be king [... as] he wishes and they follow in succession one upon [the other ...] [6] a king [...] as it is said *In my anger* and the killed one. He has been taken from the kings [...] [7] this.

28a

Grammatical Notes

רָד (Hosea 12:1) is derived from אָמְרוּ עַמִּי רַדְנוּ (Jeremiah 2:31); it is (derived) from (the imperative) רְד, and רֵד can be [...] [8] 'to get the mastery over'. The phrase

9	ענה קדוש ויקאל ענה קדושים: שָׂרָה את א׳ים מן שָׂרָהּ [................]
10	הֻשֵׁר משתק מן הֻשִׁירו ולא ידעתי: כנען אסם [אלתאגר ....]
11	כְּנַעֲנִי וקד יכון כנען ויכון גמעה כְּנַעֲנִים [................]
12	שֻׂוָרִים שׂוֹר והו מקאם שׂוֹר: רָתֵת אסם [אלרעדה ....]
13	רֶטֶט מקאם רְתֵת תלתהא תבדיא בר[עדה .... תבון אסם אלבנייה]
14	גמעה תְבוּנִים והו מדכר תַבְנִית פענד אלא[צ֗]אפ[ה הו] כְתֻבוּנָם: ת[לאוב]ה
15	אלואחדה מן תלאובות אסם ללקפאר: וָיָרֶם מן רום: סְגוֹר אֶסְם: חקיקתהא
16	מַגְלֶק קלבהם: יסוֹעֵר מן סוֹעֵר והו [...]ל[.]. אנה יועץ נפסה במא
17	יַנְחַמַל: צָרור: מַצְרור [דנוב אל אפרים] מַדְכּוּרָה בְּטִייתה: חבלי:
18	פלדלך אמכאץ֗ ואלדה [יגו לה ח]ית הו אבן ליס חכים פאן יגיה
19	וקת ליס יתבות פי מ[תבר בנין: מ]יד: בעד אן כונת [מ]ן מוצֹע
20	[אלתרא] אפדי]הם וכונת מן אלמו]ת אפוכהם אלאן אנא אכון
21	[ובאך אלי א]למות אנא אכון ח]תפך אל]י אלתֵּרא [אלצפ]ח ינסתר
22	מן חצרתי: [כי]: לאן הו בין אַ[גם יעני] א[כו]ה יַתָּמָ]ר] פלדלך
23	יואפי ריח שרקי הו ר[יח] אלרב [צאעד] מן אלבר פְיָיבַּס
24	מעדנה וְיָנֻשָף מְעִינָ]ה הו יסת]ביח כ]זא]נה כל אלה מותמנאה:
25	תאשם: תואכד שמרון אד כאלפת אלאההא באלסיף יסקטו
26	אטפאלהם יופקסו וחבאלאה יֻשַׁקק]ו]: הדא אלפצל מנתסק

28b

1	[................]
2	[................]
3	[................]
4	[................]

וְעַם קְדוֹשִׁים (Hosea 12:1) is like Joshua's word כִּי אֱלֹהִים קְדֹשִׁים הוּא (Joshua 24:19); [you can say] [9] referring to Him קָדוֹשׁ, and you can say referring to Him קְדוֹשִׁים. שָׂרָה אֶת אֱלֹהִים (Hosea 12:4) (is derived) from (the imperative) שְׂרֵה [...] [10] הָשֵׁר is derived from הֵשִׁירוּ וְלֹא יָדְעְתִּי (Hosea 8:4). כְּנַעַן (Hosea 12:8) is a noun [meaning 'trader' ...] [11] כְּנַעֲנִי; it may be כְּנָעַן, and its plural is כְּנַעֲנִים [...]. [The singular of] [12] שְׁוָרִים (Hosea 12:12) is שְׁוָר, and it (is used) in the place of of שׁוֹר. רְתֵת (Hosea 13:1) is a noun [meaning 'shudder' ...] [13] רֶטֶט (see Jeremiah 49:24) in the place of of רְתֵת; all three of them express (the meaning) 'tre[mbling' ... . תְּבוּן (see Hosea 13:2) is a noun meaning 'pattern']; [14] its plural is תְּבוּנִים; it is the masculine form of תַּבְנִית; in the conjoined state it is כְּתַבוּנָם. תַּלְאֻבָה (see Hosea 13:5) [15] is the singular of תַּלְאֻבוֹת, a noun meaning 'deserts'. וַיָּרָם (Hosea 13:6) (is derived) from (the imperative) רוּם. סְגוֹר (Hosea 13:8) is a noun; its basic meaning is [16] 'the enclosure of their heart'. יְסֹעֵר (Hosea 13:3) (is derived) from (the imperative) סֹעֵר, and it [is possible] that it (means) 'it blows in a gale itself' in that [17] it has been instigated.

Translation

Hosea 13:12: [The iniquity of the people of Ephraim] is wrapped up, his sin is stored up.

Hosea 13:13: [18] Therefore the labour pains of a woman giving birth [will come upon him, be]cause he is an unwise son. And when [19] time comes to him, he will not remain at [the birthstool of children].

Hosea 13:14: After I have delivered them from the place [20] of [the netherworld and] redeemed them from [the dea]th, now I will be [21] [your death for th]e death, I will be your death for the netherworld. Forgiveness will be hidden [22] from My presence.

Hosea 13:15: For he will bear fruit among r[eeds, i.e.] br[othe]rs. And therefore [23] an east wind will come, the wind of the Lord, [coming up] out of the desert; and [24] its fountain will become dry, and [its] spring will dry out; [he] will take as booty the treasure house, every costly item.

Hosea 14:1: [25] Samaria will be punished, for she has disobeyed her God. They will fall by the sword; [26] their infants will be dashed in pieces, and its pregnant women will be ripped open.

Exegesis

Hosea 13:12: This section is closely related
   [1] [to what precedes it since ...]   28b
   [2] ....
   [3] ....
   [4] ....

5	[.................. י]כון פי אל[.................] ו[י]תבות ב[ד]לך פי וקת
6	[.................. קו' מ]י[ ]ד שאול אפדם יעני מן יד אלאעדא [וקו'] ממות
7	[אגאלם יעני] מן אפאת אלסמא פלמא חט פי דכר אלמות [...] ע פיה
8	[.................. א]קצדך באפאת אלסמא נטיר קו' ויהפך להם לאויב הוא
9	[נלחם בם קו' א]הי קטבך שאול יעני עלי יד אלעדו וקו' נחם יסתר
10	[מעיני ....] בל פיכם שפאעה בכ' וינחם יי על הרעה וקאל
11	[..................] היה. קו' כי הוא משאר אלי אפרים אלמדכור
12	[קו' בין אחים יפרא י]עני בין אלגוים אלדי כאנו חואליהם פמתל
13	[..................]הם בריח אלשרקי והו אלעדו אלדי קצדהם
14	[פיכ]רב[..........] אליה משאר בק' הוא ישסה פמתל איקבאלהם
15	ודולתהם כמעין גארי פנשף ויב[ס] ואנקטע תום דכר מדינה
16	אלמולך והי שמרן פא[ורא] אן רגאלהם יסקוטו באלסיף ואטפאלהם
17	יופקסו חדאהם וקו' והריות[יו ישאר בה אלי] אפרים: נחם אסם
18	אלצפה גמעה נחמים אחים [אסם מ]קאם חחים אסם ללשוך
19	פיכון א[ח] אסם מקאם חא [...] ל חחים ויגוז יכון אח
20	מקאם אחו אסם ללב[ן] ג[מעה ...] ן [... יח]תמל
21	אל[...] מ[... יפרי]א מן [...] פ[אד]א [רכ]בה אי[מנת יגעל] יפריא
22	יפר[א מפרי]א [...ש]...]ה: אלואחדה מן[ן ה]ריות הריה:
23	והו אסם מקאם הר[ה שובה: אר]גע] יא אל אסראיל אלי אלרב
24	אלאהך לאנך ק[ד תעתר]ת בדנב[ד:] קחו: כדו מעכם כטוב
25	וארגעו אלי אלרב פקולו לה כל דנב לנא תגפר ואקבל מנא
26	הדא אלביר פנחן נופי בדל אלרתות כלאם שפתינא: אשור:

1	[אשור לא יגיתנא עלי ....]ם ליס נרכ[ב ולים נקול זאדה]
2	[אלאנא לעמל איד]י[נא פ]י[מא] אלדי בך [י]ורחם [.................]
3	[יתים: אר]פא: אשפי עותו[הם] /תום\ [א]חבהם לאיגל ה[ד]יה

[5] [...] it will be in the [...] he stands [... likewi]se in the time [6] [of the ...] Hosea 13:13: [...].

Hosea 13:14: The phrase *From the hand of the Sheol I will deliver them* means: from the hand of the enemies. The phrase *From the death* [7] [*I will redeem* them means:] from the evils of the heaven. After focussing on (the) death [...] in it [8] [... I] seek you in the evils of the heaven, like *And he changed toward them into an enemy; he* [9] [*fought them* (Isaiah 63:10). The phrase *I am*] *the one who decrees the Sheol upon you* means: through the enemy. The phrase *Remorse will be hidden* [10] [*from My eyes* means: ...], rather there is intercession for you, as it is said *And YHWH was sorry about the evil* (Exodus 32:14), and he said [11] [...].

Hosea 13:15: *For he* refers to Ephraim who was mentioned. [12] [The phrase *He will be fruitful between the marshes* mea]ns: among the nations who surrounded them, and he compares [13] [their ... and] their [...] with the east wind, i.e. the enemy who pursued them, [14] [will distress them ...]. He alludes to it by the phrase *He will plunder*. And he compares their welfare [15] and their city with a streaming well, then it dried out and became dry and stopped.

Hosea 14:1: Then he mentions the city [16] of the kings, namely *Samaria*. And [he shows] that their men will fall by the sword, and their infants [17] are dashed in pieces before them. The phrase *And their pregnant women* [alludes to] Ephraim.

Grammatical Notes

נֹחַם (Hosea 13:14) is a noun [18] meaning 'forgiveness', its plural being נְחָמִים. אַחִים (Hosea 13:15) is [a noun] in the place of חַחִים, a noun (meaning) 'thorns', [19] and אָח is a noun in the place of חָח [...] חַחִים; it is possible that אָח stands [20] in the place of אָחוּ, a noun meaning [..., its] plu[ral is ...]; or it is possible [21] [...]. [יַפְרִיא‎]א (Hosea 13:15) [is derived] from [(the imperative) הַפְרֵא. And wh]en [you att]ach (the prefix letters) אימנ״ת [it forms] 22 [אַפְרִיאט | יַפְרִיא, [מַפְרִיא].—[...]. [...] The singular of הָרִיּוֹת (see Hosea 14:1) is [23] הָרִיָה; it is a noun in the place of הָרָה.

Translation

Hosea 14:2: Ret[urn], people of Israel, to the Lord, [24] your God, for you [have stumbled] in your sin.

Hosea 14:3: Take words with you [25] and return to the Lord! And say to Him, May You forgive us all iniquity, and accept from us [26] this good! And we will fulfil the speech of our lips instead of bulls.

Hosea 14:4: [1] [Assur will not save us; upon a hor]se we will not ri[de and we will no longer say] [2] ['Our gods' to the wor]k of our hands. [And] what is in you, he finds mercy [...] [3] [—an orphan].

29a

4 לאן [קד רגע גצ̇]בי מ[נה: אה]יה: אכון כאלטל לאל [א]סראיל פינפרח
5 כאל[ס]ו[]סנה ויצ̇רב אצולה כא[]ללובנאן: יֵלְכוּ: תום יסלוכו רואצ̇עה
6 פיכון כאלזית [בהאי]ה וי[]כון ל[]ה ריחה כאללובנאן: ישובו: ירגעו
7 אלגולאס פי פייוה [י][בַ]קוּ דגן וינפרעו כאלגפן לאן דכרה יכון ככמר
8 לובנאן: אפרים: אפרים אדא קאל מא לי זאדה וללאותאן אנא
9 יכון קד אגבתה וְאֲלְמָחָה אנא אכון לה כברות ג̇י יא באיס מני
10 תָמַרך קד וגד: מי: מן הו אל[]חכים[] פיפה[ם] [האול]י אלכטוב פהם
11 ויע[]ל[]מה לאן מוסתקימין טו[]רק א[]לרב ועאדלין פהום יסלוכו
12 ב[]הם ומוגרמין פהום יתע[]תרו[ן] בהם: כתם אלנבי ספרה בהדא
13 א[ל]פצ̇[ל] יסתצלח בה אלאומה [ואלמ]עאצ̇י אלדי קד וצפהא פיהא
14 [.........]ל[]...[א].[]ה פקא[ב]ל[אלאו]מה בגומלתהא בקו' שובה ישראל
15 והדא אלרגוע רגוע ען אלאפעאל אלקביחה לאן אול מא [.].[]ל[.]
16 אלתאיב אן יפארק מא הי עליה מן אלקבאיח. קו' [עד] יי אלהיך
17 יעני [א]רגע אלי כאלקך א[]לדי קד כצך ע[.... ס]איר אלבלק תום
18 אורא אן אלמצלחה ל[..]
19 אן גמיע [אלחק]הם [..] אל[..................] שובה
20 תום קאל קחו: ליעום אֲלָאַחַ[.........] ק[ו']קחו עמכם דברים:
21 יעני [כ]ל[א]ס לטיף בטוב מו[.....] קו' ושובו אל יי יעני ארגעו
22 אלי פ[יע]ל מא אוגבה עליכם תום שרח אלדברים פקאל אמרו אליו
23 קו' כל תשא עון כל עָון תשא פרתב אלכלאם אורא אן אולא
24 יגב אן יוסל פי אלצפח ען אלדנוב אלמותקדמה ובעד דלך
25 וקח טוב ואלאשארה בה אלי מא קד פעלוה מן אלכיר תום

29b

1 [קאל ונשלמה פרים] שפתנו פביין [..................]
2 [....................ב] פאורא ב[.................] בין
3 [..........]ים דון ג[]פרת[א] ל[......... א][ל][מ]שהורה ב[..] ת[].... אל[
4 הונא שובה ואלאשארה בה אל[]י אל[....]למעא[.............] ע[]מכם
5 דברים ותחתה אלאיקראר ואלא[.................] אלרגוע
6 אלי פיעל אלואגב פחצלת ג' מנאזל ב[]זמן] אלר[גוע אל]י אלצ̇[מ]אן אן
7 לא יכון עודה לאן הדה אלד' שרוט שרוט [תובה] פלמא כאן

Hosea 14:5: I will heal their impertinence. Then I will love them because of [their presents], [4] for my [ang]er [has turned away] from [him].

Hosea 14:6: I will be like the dew to the people of Israel. And he will blossom [5] like the lily, [and he will strike out his roots like t]he Lebanon.

Hosea 14:7: Then his tender shoots will spread out, [6] and his [splendour] will be like the olive tree. And his scent will be like the Lebanon.

Hosea 14:8: [7] Those who sit in his shades will return; they will keep grain; and they will branch out like the vine, for his remembrance will be like the wine [8] of the Lebanon.

Hosea 14:9: When Ephraim will say 'What need have I any more of the idols?', I [9] will answer him and I will glance at him. I will be for him like a tender cypress. Oh miserable man, from Me [10] your fruit will be found.

Hosea 14:10: Who is the wise? He will understand these words. (Who is) understanding? [11] He will know them. For righteous (are) the ways of the Lord and just (persons) they will walk [12] on them, but sinners will stumb[le] on them.

Exegesis

Hosea 14:2: The prophet concludes his book with this [13] [sectio]n in which the people are reconciled [and the] sins which he had described among them [14] [...] and he addressed [the peo]ple altogether by saying *Return, Israel*. [15] This return is a return from the evil deeds, for the first (action) [16] a person who returns [has to do, is] that he leaves his evil things. The phrase *Un[to] YHWH, your God* [17] means: Return to your Creator [who] has given to you [... all] the creation! Then [18] he shows that the benefit [...] [19] that all their [...] the [...] *return*.

Hosea 14:3: [20] Then he says *Take!* in order to include the [...]. The phrase *Take words with you!* [21] means: a friendly speech, words [...]. The phrase *And return to YHWH* means: return [22] to a deed that He has not made obligatory for you. Then he explains the *words* by stating *Say to Him* [23]. The phrase *All may you forgive iniquity* means: *May you forgive all iniquity*, and he puts the speech in a proper order. He demonstrates that firstly [24] he has to be asked for forgiveness of the aforementioned sins, and after that [25] *And accept good!* This alludes to the good (deeds) they have done. Then | [1] [he says *And we will pay*] *our lips* [*for bulls*], and he explains [...] [2] [...]. He demonstrates [...] between [3] [...] instead of [...] the famous [...] [4] [here] *Return*. This alludes to [... *take with*] *you* [5] *words* and instead of this the confirmation and [...] the return [6] to the obligatory deed. There have been three stages [...] the guarantee: that [7] there will be no return, for these four conditions are conditions [...].

29b

8	עציאנהם קד וציף באנהם קצדו מלכי אשור ל[י]סתעינו בהם
9	ואתכלו עליהם באן יגיתוהם [.] קד קבל הדא וילך אפ[ר]ים אל אשור וקאל איצ'
10	גם אותו לאשו[ר יוב]ל וקאל וברית עם אשור יכרותו. חסון אן יצדר
11	פי אלצמאן פיקול אשור לא [יוש]ענו ולמא כאן איצ'א ק[ד ו]צף ענהם
12	פי מוצ'ע גיר הדא באנהם [כאן] יתכלו עלי אלכיל באן ינג]ו ע[ליהא
13	בקו' להם ותאמרו לא כי אל ס[ו]ס ננוס וקאל איצ'א ועל קל נרכב
14	חסון אן יקול הונא ענהם על ס[ו]ס ל[]א נרכב תום דכר אלצ[מאן
15	פי אמר אלמעבודאת אלדי כאן [יעבדוה]א בקר' ולא נאמר עוד אלנו
16	למ[ע]שה ידינו. וקו' עוד איחכאם כאנה אורא אן הדא אלאמר
17	לא יכון [אלצמאן] וקו' אשר בך ירוחם יתום תלטוף. לקב ישראל
18	ביתום לאגל אנ[...]עה אלי רבה [.][.]לה אחד גירה כמא אן ליס
19	[...........] אלולי יתום אתה היית
20	עוזר [......] יתומים היינו [........] ואין אב אורא [אלנ]בי אנהם
21	אדא [פעל] הדה [........]קו אלגואב עליה[ם] מן אלכאלק
22	בהדה אלאוצאף אלמדכורה [........] מא קדם ד[כר] אל
23	[מש[או]פה] עלי אלתובה בקו' ארפא משובתם יעני אדא פעלו
24	הדה אלאוצאף אסתחקו מני ה[דא] וקו' אהבם נדבה יעני אע[...]
25	[...]ם לאגל הדה אלתובה אלדי קד תסאכו בהא ואורא אלסבב
26	ל[]דלך כאנה רגוע אלגצ'ב כך' כי שב אפי וקו' אהיה כטל ליש'

30a
1	[.................................]
2	[.................................]
3	[.................................]
4	[.................................]
5	[.................................]
6	[.................................]
7	[.................................]
8	ור] [.................................]
9	[.................................]
10	רע] [.................................]
11	[.................................]
12	[.................................]
13	[.................................]
14	[.................................]

Hosea 14:4: After [8] their disobedience had already been described since they called the kings of Assur to help them [9] and they trusted them to rescue them, and already before this: *And Ephraim went to Assur* (Hosea 5:13), and also: [10] *It, too, will be brought to Assur* (Hosea 10:6), and: *They make a covenant with Assur* (Hosea 12:2), it is appropriate that he commences [11] with the guarantee: *Assur will not save us*. After describing them [12] in a different context that they trusted the horses in that they will be saved on them [13] by addressing them *And you say: Not so, we will flee on a horse* (Isaiah 30:16) and also *We will ride on light (animals)* (Isaiah 30:16), [14] it is appropriate to say here about them *We will not ride on a horse*. Then he mentions the guarantee [15] concerning the idols which [they worshipped], as it is said *And we will no longer say: Our gods,* [16] *to the work of our hands*. The word *Longer* is a confirmation as if he shows that this matter [17] is not [a guarantee]. The phrase *For it is with you that an orphan finds mercy* is friendliness. Israel is called [18] an *orphan* because of [...] to his Lord, [and they have no] one apart from him, as there is no [19] [... as] the friend (of God) [says] *An orphan you was* [20] *a helper* (Psalms 10:14) [...]; and: *We have become orphans] and there is no father* (Lamentations 5:3). [The prophet shows] that they [21] when he did these [...] the answer of the Creator to them [22] in these mentioned attributes [...].

Hosea 14:5: He mentions first the [23] [healing of] the repentance by saying *I will heal their returning*, i.e. when they performed [24] these attributes, they deserved this from Me. The phrase *I love them gratuitously* means: I will [...] [25] [...] because of this repentance by which they showed themselves generous. He demonstrates the reason [26] for that, that it is the turning away of the wrath, as it is said *For My anger has turned away*.

Hosea 14:6: The phrase I will be for Israel like the dew

[1] [...]
[2] [...]
[3] [...]
[4] [...]
[5] [...]
[6] [...]
[7] [...]
[8] [...]
[9] [...]
[10] [...]
[11] [...]
[12] [...]
[13] [...]
[14] [...]

30a

15	[.............][יהם אי]צֿא [................................]
16	אלוצֿף ישיר בדלך אלי ד[...................................]
17	לכל מן אסתעמלה מ[.].[ל].................. קו׳ מה לי]
18	עֿ[ו]ד לעצבים אשארה [.......................................]
19	דהב תעבנא פיהא [...]
20	פאנהם יסתחקו מן [..]
21	אלמחהם באלעאלאיה ו[.....................................]
22	אלדי יוגלל מן הו[..]
23	פקאל יא [...]
24	אשתגׁאלו [..]
25	אלי׳ אצנאף [..]
26	גהתי אנא תֿ[..]
27	אעדאדכם [..]

30b

1	[...]
2	[...]
3	[...]
4	[...]
5	[...]
6	[...]
7	[...]
8	[...]
9	[...]
10	[...]
11	[...]
12	[...]
13	[...]
14	[...]
15	[....................] גמע אלעלום: קָטָבְדּ
16	[...] יגי קָטָבְדּ פתחצל אסר [......................]
17	[................] א[רוחָם [יְ]רוחָם מרוחם נרוחם
18	[................] כמא קלנא כי צֿו: תם
19	[...]
20	[...............................] שמעו: אסמעו הדה
21	[................] ה]ל כאנת הדה פי איאמכם
22	[................] בהא קיצו לבניכם חתי
23	[................]לה [א]ל[ק]נדב
24	[................] א[כ]ל [אלקמ]ל:
25	[................] שוראב כמר
26	[................] כ]י: לאן [...] קד
27	[................] אסנאן אסד ואניאב

TEXT AND TRANSLATION

[15] [Hosea: 14:8: ... to] them al[so ...] [16]; he alludes with this description to [...] [17] for everybody who has used it [...]

Hosea 14:9: [... The phrase *What more need have I*] [18] *of idols* alludes [to ...] [19] gold on which we worked hard [...] [20] and they deserve from [...] [21] He glanced at them in the height and [...] [22] what he esteems higher than [...] [23] and he said, Oh [...] [24] occupation and [...] [25] the ten species [...] [26] My side

[...] [27] your numbers [...]
[1] [...]
[2] [...]
[3] [...]
[4] [...]
[5] [...]
[6] [...]
[7] [...]
[8] [...]
[9] [...]
[10] [...]
[11] [...]
[12] [...]
[13] [...]
[14] [...]

30b

Grammatical Notes

[15] plural (?) is 'information' (?)

קְטָבְדּ (Hosea 13:14) [16] [...] is derived קְטָבְדּ and it is[...] [17] [...]. [יְרַחַם (Hosea 14:4) ...] [18] רוֹחָם, יְרוֹחָם, מרוחם, ארוחם [... ...], as we have said כִּי צַו (Isaiah 28:10).

[19] (empty)

Translation

Joel 1:1: [20] [...]

Joel 1:2: Hear this [21] [...] Has this happened in your days? [22] [...]

Joel 1:3: [...] about it [say] to your sons until [23] [...]

Joel 1:4: [...] the locust [24] [...] the [...] has eaten.

Joel 1:5: [25] [. ...] wine drinkers [26] [...]

Joel 1:6: For a nation has [27] [...] lion's teeth ... and the molars

Textual Notes

Hosea 1:4

Only a part of the biblical quotation וּפָקַדְתִּי אֶת־דְּמֵי יִזְרְעֶאל and some words of the commentary, including the phrase 'house of Ahab' are preserved (3a:1–3).

Hosea 1:8

The reconstruction in the commentary אלא אנה 'except that' (3a:16) is based on the almost identical phrase in 3a:5–6: מן דאך [...] ידל אנהם אטהר פיעל אלא אנה.

Hosea 2:1

The orthography סא יכון 'he will be' (3a:19) with the particle of future written separately is characteristic of the commentator (see also Hosea 5:5, 9; 8:14; 9:7, 17; 10:4, 8, 14; 12:10; 4a:4). On the other hand, Yefet/Cod. Hunt. 206 join the particle with the verb, as is their regular practice: וסיכון (ed. Birnbaum 24:11, ed. Polliack and Schlossberg 151)/وسيكون (ed. Schroeter 30:19).

The rendition of מִסְפַּר (only here in Hosea) by אחצא 'number' (3a:19) is distinct from Yefet/Cod. Hunt. 206: עדד (ed. Birnbaum 24:11, ed. Polliack and Schlossberg 151)/عدد (ed. Schroeter 30:19), however, it occurs also in T-S Ar.24.165 fol. 9 recto 24. The noun אחצא anticipates the translation of the following verb יִסָּפֵר with יחצי 'it will be counted' (3a:20); see T-S Ar.24.165 fol. 9 recto 25 (יוחצא).

The phrase בְּנֵי יִשְׂרָאֵל has been translated literally as בני ישראל 'sons of Israel' (3a:20), whereas usually in connection with 'Israel' or 'Judah', the translator adds אל 'clan', 'people' (Hosea 2:2 [2×]; 3:1, 4, 5; 4:1). In the following phrase בְּנֵי אֵל חָי, he has chosen again בני 'sons' (3a:21); also in the phrase בְּנֵי זְנוּנִים (Hosea 2:6) he retains 'sons': בני טגיאנאת (3b:3). On the other hand בְּנֵי עַוְלָה (Hosea 10:9) is rendered with דוי גור, literally 'the owners of injustice' (22b:10). Yefet/Cod. Hunt. 206 render בני אסראיל (ed. Birnbaum 24:11, ed. Polliack and Schlossberg 151)/بنى اسرائل (ed. Schroeter 30:19).

The translator usually uses the identical Arabic preposition כ for rendering the Hebrew particle of comparison כ (3a:20: כרמל; see also: Hosea 2:5 [2×], 17; 4:4, 7, 9 [2×]; 5:10, 12; 6:3 [3×], 4, 7, 9; 7:6, 11 [reconstr.], 12, 16; 8:8; 9:1, 4, 10 [2×]; 10:4, 7, 14; 11:10, 11; 12:10, 12; 13:2, 3 [3×], 7, 8 [2×]; 14:6 [3×], 7, 8 [2×], 9; missing

TEXTUAL NOTES 119

text: Hosea 2:5; 3:1; 4:16; 5:10, 14; 7:6, 7, 12; 8:1; 9:9, 11; 11:4; 12:3). Only sporadically does he render it with מתל (Hosea 10:1 [2×]; 11:8 [2×]), which is usually his equivalent of כְּמוֹ (Hosea 7:4; 8:12 [reconstr.]; 13:7); כ + infinitive is rendered with ענד (Hosea 7:1; 9:10, 12; 13:1, 6). Whereas Cod. Hunt. 206 shares the translator's rendering: كمل (ed. Schroeter 30:19), Yefet prefers the preposition מתל (ed. Birnbaum 24:11, ed. Polliack and Schlossberg 151).

The literal translation of בְּמָקוֹם with פי אלמוצע 'at the place' (3a:20–21) can also be found in T-S Ar.24.165 fol. 9 recto 25–26. Very similar is the rendering in Cod. Hunt. 206: موضع (ed. Schroeter 30:20), whereas Yefet prefers בדל מא 'instead' (ed. Birnbaum 24:12, ed. Polliack and Schlossberg 151). Stuart 1987:35 n. 10: 'in the place where', or simply 'where.'

The word עַמִּי is rendered with שעבי 'my people'; see also Yefet: שעבי (ed. Birnbaum 24:13, ed. Polliack and Schlossberg 151), whereas Cod. Hunt. 206 renders it with قومي (ed. Schroeter 30:20); see also Hosea 2:3, 25; 4:4, 6, 8, 12; 6:11; 7:8; 9:1; 10:5, 10 [text missing: Hosea 1:9; 11:7], only Hosea 10:14 seems to have the alternative rendering קום 'people'.

אֵל is rendered with טאיק 'Powerful One' (3b:22). The same rendering of אֵל can be found throughout Saadiah's translations (e.g. Genesis 14:20, 22; 16:13; 17:1; 33:20; Isaiah 9:5; 10:21; Job 5:8; 8:5). The author uses the root קדר, which occurs in the translation of Yefet/Cod. Hunt. 206: אלקאדר (ed. Birnbaum 24:13; see also: 26:3, 8; ed. Polliack and Schlossberg 151)/القادر (ed. Schroeter 31:1) and T-S Ar.24.165 fol. 9 verso 1 (אלקאדר) 'the Powerful', in his exegesis: הו אלדי קדר עלי כלאצהם lit. 'He is the One who is able to deliver them' (4a:17).

חט (3b:21), which appears to belong to the author's favourite vocabulary (see 4a:21, 23 [2×]; 5b:26; 19:7; 20:28; 29b:3), is used as a synonym of געל (see Munk 249:21). Kazimirski gives the meaning 'appliquer son esprit, la réflexion à quelque chose' (1:450a).

כאן גרת (4a:12): There is no agreement between the masculine auxiliary verb 'to be' and the feminine form of the verb; see also כאן תוכאל (4a:12), כאן קד אקדמת (7a:11), כאן תלחקהם (22b:9).

For the phrase 'it will be said, So and so many qafiz' (4a:13) see Yefet: פיקאל פיה כדי וכדי קפיז (ed. Birnbaum 25:3).

Hosea 2:2

The author renders רֹאשׁ literally with רייס 'head' (3b:23); see also Yefet: ריסא (ed. Birnbaum 24:15, ed. Polliack and Schlossberg 151). He avoids the word מלך 'king', which is the translation found in Cod. Hunt. 206: ملك 'king' (ed. Schroeter 31:2).

The translator renders כִּי גָדוֹל יוֹם יִזְרְעֶאל literally with לאן כביר יום יזרעאל 'for great is the day of Jezreel' (3a:23–24), whereas Yefet/Cod. Hunt. 206 paraphrase with the almost identical phrase לאן יום פרג׳ יזרעאל יכון עטים (ed. Birnbaum 24:15– 16, ed. Polliack and Schlossberg 151)/لان يوم فرج يزرعال يوما عظيما (ed. Schroeter 32:2–3) 'for the day of Jezreel's relief will be great/a great day'.

The usual translation of the conjunction כִּי when indicating the reason is לאן 'for' (3a:23); see also: Hosea 2:6 (3b:3), 7 (3b:4), 9 (3b:9); 3:4 (6b:21); 4:1 [2×] (8b:10, 11), 6 (8b:18: לאנך), 10 (8b:25), 12 (8b:27), (text missing: Hosea 4:13, 14, 16); 5:1 (11a:27), 4 (11b:4), 7 (11b:9), but otherwise in Hosea 2:10 (באן); 5:3 (באן).

Hosea 2:3

The translator understands רֻחָמָה as 3rd person feminine singular perfect since he renders קד רוחימת 'she has been pitied' (3a:25), whereas Yefet/Cod. Hunt. 206 interpret the verb as a participle (*qal* passive?): מרחומה (ed. Birnbaum 24:18, ed. Polliack and Schlossberg 151)/مرحومة (ed. Schroeter 31:4); see also Hosea 2:25.

Hosea 2:4

רִיבוּ is rendered with כאצמו 'bring legal action!' (3a:25, 26). Saadiah's translation of רִיב is from the same root: כצומה (e.g. Genesis 13:7, ed. Derenbourg I, 20:17); see also Cod. Hunt. 206: خاصموا (ed. Schroeter 31:4), whereas Yefet translates with נאטרו (ed. Birnbaum 29:8, ed. Polliack and Schlossberg 153).

The combination of ליס with the feminine subject (3a:26) indicates that the translator regards ליס as a fossilized particle of negation, almost identical with the negator לא. See also the combination of כאן + feminine verb in Hosea 2:1. Yefet/Cod. Hunt. 206, however, have the feminine form: ליסת (ed. Birnbaum 29:8, ed. Polliack and Schlossberg 153)/ليست (ed. Schroeter 31:4).

The translator prefers the simple במרה 'as a wife' (3a:26) for אִשְׁתִּי instead of Yefet/Cod. Hunt. 206: צאחבתי (ed. Birnbaum 29:8, ed. Polliack and Schlossberg 153)/بصاحبتي (ed. Schroeter 31:5) and ברגול 'as a man' for אִישָׁהּ instead Yefet/Cod. Hunt. 206: צאחבהא (ed. Birnbaum 29:9, ed. Polliack and Schlossberg 153)/صاحب (ed. Schroeter 31:5); see also Hosea 2:9, 18. The suffix pronouns in אִשְׁתִּי and אִישָׁהּ are replaced by a preceding ל + suffix pronoun: לי 'for me', להא 'for her' (3a:26). Yefet adds two explanatory phrases אד ליסת צאחבתי עלי מא ינבגי וכד׳אך לא אכון אנא צאחבהא עלי מתל מא כנת 'for she is not my wife as it should be and therefore I am not her husband as I used to be' (ed. Birnbaum 29:8–9, ed. Polliack and Schlossberg 153), apparently to indicate the unusual deviation from the norm.

The reconstruction וּתָזִיל 'and let her remove' (3a:27) seems to be justified since the root סור is generally translated with the root زيل (see Hosea 2:19; 7:14; text missing: Hosea 4:18). See also Yefet/Cod. Hunt. 206 תזיל (ed. Birnbaum 29:10, ed. Polliack and Schlossberg 153)/تَزِيل (ed. Schroeter 31:5).

The translator uses the (artificial) plural טגיאנאתהא 'her harlotries' (3a:27) of a feminine variant of طغيان for the abstract plural זְנוּנֶיהָ, 'obviously to make this noun correspond more closely to the Hebrew equivalent' (Birnbaum 1941:xxxv); the same noun appears also in the translation of Hosea 4:12; 5:4. Yefet has the identical translation: טגיאנאתהא (Birnbaum 29:10, ed. Polliack and Schlossberg 153), whereas Cod. Hunt. 206 prefers the masculine noun: طغيانها (ed. Schroeter 31:5).

The translator imitates the abstract plural וְנַאֲפוּפֶיהָ by rendering it with the plural feminine noun ופגוראתהא 'and her adulteries' (3a:27), whereas Yefet has the singular masculine equivalent: ופגורהא (ed. Birnbaum 29:10, ed. Polliack and Schlossberg 153) and Cod. Hunt. translates with وزناها (ed. Schroeter 31:6).

Hosea 2:5

The reconstruction of the text כילא אסלכהא 'lest I will strip her' (3b:1) as the rendering of פֶּן־אַפְשִׁיטֶנָּה is based on Yefet/Cod. Hunt. 206: כילא אסלכהא (ed. Birnbaum 29:12)/ كَلا أسلخها ed. Schroeter 31:6), but Yefet, ed. Polliack and Schlossberg 153, כילא אסלבהא 'lest I will take away from her'.

Though the root שׂים was rendered by געל in Hosea 2:2, 14 (text missing: 11:8), it appears that here the author rendered וְשַׂמְתִּיהָ by אצירהא 'I will make her' (3b:2). Since he chose ואגעלהא 'and I will make her' (3b:2) as the rendering of the following וְשַׁתָּהּ, he may have preferred a variation of the verb. Yefet/Cod. Hunt. 206 translated with: ואצירהא (ed. Birnbaum 29:13, ed. Polliack and Schlossberg 153)/وأصيرها (ed. Schroeter 31:7).

The reconstruction כאלבר 'like the wilderness' (3b:2) is justified since this is the author's usual rendering; see Hosea 2:16 (5b:16), 9:10 (20a:14), 13:15 (28a:23); text missing: 13:5. Yefet/Cod. Hunt. 206 have the feminine equivalent: מתל אלבריה (ed. Birnbaum 29:13, ed. Polliack and Schlossberg 153)/كالبرية (ed. Schroeter 31:7).

The reconstructed מפאזה 'desert' (3b:2) as the translation of צִיָּה can also be found in Yefet/Cod. Hunt. 206: מפאזה (ed. Birnbaum 29:14, ed. Polliack and Schlossberg 153)/مفازة (ed. Schroeter 31:7).

Hosea 2:6

The reconstruction of the verb ארחם 'I will have mercy' (3b:3) is based on the usual rendering of the Hebrew root רחם with the Arabic cognate رحم (see Hosea 2:3, 25; 14:4; text missing: Hosea 1:6, 7); see also Yefet/Cod. Hunt/ 206: ארחם (ed. Birnbaum 29:15, ed. Polliack and Schlossberg 153)/ارحم (ed. Schroeter 31:7).

טגיאנאת 'harlotry' (3b:3), of which only the last letter ת has been preserved, has been reconstructed according to Hosea 2:4 and the similar phrase ריח טגיאנאת 'spirit of harlotry' (Hosea 4:12; 5:4). Yefet/Cod. Hunt. 206 have the definite masculine noun: אלטגיאן (ed. Birnbaum 29:15, ed. Polliack and Schlossberg 153)/الطغيان (ed. Schroeter 31:8).

The translation בניהא פלא ארחם, literally 'and her sons I will not have mercy (on them)' (3b:3) imitates the Hebrew word order וְאֶת־בָּנֶיהָ לֹא אֲרַחֵם by retaining the direct object in topicalized position, followed by the rest of the phrase which is introduced by the connective conjunction פ. Yefet/Cod. Hunt. 206 follow the usual Arabic word order: verb—object: ולא ארחם בניהא (ed. Birnbaum 29:15, ed. Polliack and Schlossberg 153)/ولا ارحم بنيها (ed. Schroeter 31:7–8). The same structure of topicalisation can be observed throughout the translation and is one of the distinctive syntactical features of the author's style, e.g. Hosea 2:8 (ודהב פעמלוה ללותן) 10, (והי פמא ערפת) 10, (וסובלהא פלא תגד).

Hosea 2:7

Throughout his translation, the author provides two options for rendering the Hebrew root זנה, either the Arabic root طغى, as here (3b:4; also Hosea 5:3; 9:1; text missing: Hosea 1:2 [2×]; 4:13, 14 [2×], 15, 18; see also the noun طغيان in Hosea 2:4; 4:12; 5:4), or the homonymous root زنى (Hosea 3:3; 4:10). Saadiah usually renders זנה by the root טגי (e.g. Exodus 34:15, 16; Leviticus 20:6; Isaiah 1:21; 57:3), which corresponds to Aramaic טעא in the Targums. The orthography טגת 'she whored' (3b:4) is identical with Cod. Hunt. 206: طغت (ed. Schroeter 31:8), but differs from Yefet: טגית (ed. Birnbaum 29:16, ed. Polliack and Schlossberg 153 [with the variant reading טגת in some manuscripts]).

The reconstruction חאבלתהם 'who has conceived them' (3b:4) as an equivalent for הוֹרָתָם has been preferred because of the author's rendition of וְהֹרִיּוֹתָיו with וחבאלבה in Hosea 14:1. See also Yefet: חאבלתהם (ed. Birnbaum 29:16, ed. Polliack and Schlossberg 153) vs. Cod. Hunt. 206: حاملتهم (ed. Schroeter 31:8).

The translator renders the conjunction כִּי with לאן 'for' (3b:4), whereas Yefet/Cod. Hunt. 296 have: אד (ed. Birnbaum 29:16, ed. Polliack and Schlossberg 153)/اذ (ed. Schroeter 31:9).

For אסלוך ורא 'I will go after' (3b:4) see the phrase סלך ורא (Hosea 5:11; 11:10), though the translator renders הלך אחרי also with מר חדא (Hosea 2:15 = 3b:20). Yefet and Cod. Hunt. 206 have אסיר כלף (ed. Birnbaum 29:16–17, ed. Polliack and Schlossberg 153) and اسير تبع (ed. Schroeter 31:9), respectively.

Only here (3b:5) the translator chooses כובזי 'my bread' as a translation for לַחְמִי, whereas in Hosea 9:4 (2×), he has the more general equivalent טעאם 'food', which Yefet/Cod. Hunt. 206 prefer here: טעאמי (ed. Birnbaum 29:17, ed. Polliack and Schlossberg 153)/طعامى (ed. Schroeter 31:9) and throughout their translation.

The author prefers the rendering of מֵימַי with the plural noun ומיאי 'and my waters' (3b:5) against Yefet/Cod. Hunt. 206, who have the singular: ומאי (ed. Birnbaum 29:17, ed. Polliack and Schlossberg 153)/وماىُ (ed. Schroeter 31:9).

The reconstruction דוהני 'my oil' (3b:5) has been chosen because of the author's usual orthography of the noun with *mater lectionis* (see: 3b:11; 6b:23; 25b:4; 26b:3), whereas Yefet/Cod. Hunt. 206 prefer the defective writing: דהני (ed. Birnbaum 29:17, ed. Polliack and Schlossberg 153)/دهنى (ed. Schroeter 31:10).

The translator imitates the Hebrew plural וְשִׁקּוּיָי by his literal rendering ומשרובאתי 'and my drinks' (3b:6) vs. Yefet: ומשרובי (ed. Birnbaum 29:18, ed. Polliack and Schlossberg 153) and Cod. Hunt. 206: وشراىِ (ed. Schroeter 31:8), Aquila: ποτισμόν; Vulgate: *potum meum*. Some versions replace the concrete noun by more generalizing circumlocutions, e.g. LXX: πάντα ὅσα μοι καθήκει 'all that is appropriate to me'; Peshitta: ܡܕܡ ܕܡܬܚܫܚ ('all that is necessary [for me]'); Targum: כל פרנוסי 'all my provisions'.

It is noteworthy that in his grammatical notes, the commentator derives שקוי/שקוו from different morphological bases (5b:7–8). This understanding is in line with Ibn Nūḥ (*Diqduq* on Psalms 102:10, ed. Khan 2000:316–317), whereas e.g. Ḥayyūj regards both nouns as deriving from the same root with *yod* and *waw* interchangeable (Jastrow p. 217: وقد ابدلت هذه الياء بواو).

Hosea 2:8

The presentative particle הִנֵּה is usually rendered with הודא 'behold' (3b:6; see also Hosea 2:16; 9:6; text missing: Hosea 4:17). Several times, it has been added to the translation (Hosea 9:4 [2×]; 10:5, 12; 13:2). It is a distinct feature of the commentator's style and appears often in his exegesis (5a:13; 8a:12; 11b:12; 15a:24; 19a:18; 21a:12; 23b:20; 24b:12, 13; 27b:8). See Cod. Hunt. 206: ها (ed. Schroeter 31:10).

As the translation מסייג, literally 'hedging' (3b:6) demonstrates, the author derives Hebrew שָׂךְ from the imperative שׂוּךְ 'hedge up!', 'fence about!' (= סוך

11); see also Yefet/Cod. Hunt. 206: מסיג (ed. Birnbaum 29:19, ed. Polliack and Schlossberg 153)/مسيج (ed. Schroeter 31:10); LXX: ἀνοικοδομήσω 'I will wall up'; Ḥayyūj (ed. Jastrow p. 127). In his grammatical notes, the author mentions also the alternative derivation from the imperative סוך I 'pour in anointing!', 'anoint (with oil)!' (5b:9–10).

The reconstruction באלאשואך 'with the thorns' (3b:6) draws on the letters preserved and the author's exegetical remark סיאג שוך 'a fence of thorn(s)' (5a:13), Yefet: באלאשואך (ed. Birnbaum 29:19, ed. Polliack and Schlossberg 153) and Cod. Hunt. 206: بالاشواك (ed. Schroeter 31:10).

The author prefers a literal rendering of the Hebrew source text לֹא תִמְצָא with פלא תגד 'and she will not find' (3b:7), whereas Yefet/Cod. Hunt. 206: ולא תגד סבלהא (ed. Birnbaum 29:20, ed. Polliack and Schlossberg 153)/ولا تجد سبلها (ed. Schroeter 31:11), as well as LXX (τὴν τρίβον αὐτῆς 'her way'), provide a direct object.

Hosea 2:9

The translator chooses פתכלב 'and she will pounce on' as rendering of וְרִדְּפָה (3b:7); see also his translations of Hosea 8:3; 12:2. Yefet/Cod. Hunt. 206 also have תכלב (ed. Brinbaum 29:21, ed. Polliack and Schlossberg 153)/تكلب (ed. Schroeter 31:11). Also Saadiah renders the Hebrew root רדף by using the root كلب, e.g. Genesis 14:14 (וכלבהם), 31:23 (וכלבה), Exodus 14:8 (וכלב).

The translator renders תַּשִּׂיג with תלחקהם 'she reaches them' (3b:8); he uses the same root to translate כְּמַסִּיגֵי (Hosea 5:10) and תַּשִּׂיגֵם (Hosea 10:9); see also in the exegesis (22b:8; 23a:26; 29a:19); vs. Yefet/Cod. Hunt. 206: תדרכהם (ed. Birnbaum 29:21, ed. Polliack and Schlossberg 153)/تدركهم (ed. Schroeter 31:11).

By adding תום 'then' before 'she will seek them' (3b:8), the author creates a temporal sequence of the events. This is a characteristic of his translation technique (see also Hosea 2:9, 11, 14, 15 [2×], 16, 21, 25; 4:5; 5:5, 8; 8:11; 9:6; 10:11, 13; 11:6; 12:5 [2×], 13; 13:8; 14:5, 7).

Instead of translating וְלֹא תִמְצָא literally, the author supplies the object suffix and renders לא תגדהום 'she will not find *them*' (3b:8), obviously to harmonise this phrase with the preceding ולא תלחקהם 'and he will not reach them,' which corresponds to וְלֹא־תַשִּׂיג אֹתָם. See also LXX (αὐτούς) and Yefet/Cod. Hunt. 206: לא תגדהם (ed. Birnbaum 20:22, ed. Polliack and Schlossberg 153)/ولا تجدهم (ed. Schroeter 31:12). Vulgate, however, has not added an object.

The form אֵלְכָה has been rephrased: אלצואב אן אסלוך 'it is right that I go' (3b:8).

The translator prefers רגולי 'my man' as a translation of אִישִׁי, possibly to avoid any connotation with 'Baal'. Cod. Hunt. 206, however, renders with: بعلي (ed.

Schroeter 31:12), whereas Yefet prefers צֿאחבי 'my husband' (ed. Birnbaum 29:23, ed. Polliack and Schlossberg 153); see also Hosea 2:4.

Instead of rendering כִּי טוֹב לִי אָז literally, the translator chooses a more interpretative style: לאן קד כאן חאלי גייד חין אדן 'because my situation was better then' (3b:9). Yefet/Cod. Hunt. 206 have almost the same paraphrase: פאן קד כאן חיניד אצלח לי (ed. Birnbaum 29:23 ת ed. Polliack and Schlossberg 253)/فقد كان حينئذ اصلح لى (ed. Schroeter 31:12–13) 'for it was then better for me'.

It is noteworthy that the author writes חין אדן 'then' as two separate words (3b:9) instead of the standard orthography which can be found in Yefet/Cod. Hunt. 206: חיניד (ed. Birnbaum 29:23, ed. Polliack and Schlossberg 153)/حينئذ (ed. Schroeter 31:13).

Hebrew עַתָּה is rendered with אלסאעה 'now' (3b:10), the adverbial form of ساعة 'hour'; see also Hosea 2:12; 5:3; 7:2; 8:8, 10, 13; 10:2, 3; 13:2 (text missing: Hosea 4:16; 5:7). Yefet/Cod. Hunt 206 prefer the adverb: אלאן (ed. Birnbaum 29:24, ed. Polliack and Schlossberg 153)/الآن (ed. Schroeter 31:13).

Hosea 2:10

The reconstruction of the text אלדגן 'the grain' (3b:10) reflects the usual rendering of Hebrew הַדָּגָן (see Hosea 2:11, 24; 7:14; 9:1; 14:8). See also Cod. Hunt. 206: الدجن (ed. Schroeter 31:14), whereas Yefet prefers אלחב (ed. Birnbaum 30:1, ed. Polliack and Schlossberg 153).

The rendering אלמסטאר 'the new wine' (3b:11) for הַתִּירוֹשׁ is distinct from Yefet/Cod. Hunt. 206: ואלעציר (ed. Birnbaum 30:1, ed. Polliack and Schlossberg 153)/العصير (ed. Schroeter 31:14); see also Hosea 2:11, 24; 4:11; 7:14; 9:2.

The translation of the triad *corn*, *wine*, *oil* with דגן, מסטאר, דוהן is distinct from Saadiah's rendering of this traditional formula: בר, עציר, דהן (Deuteronomy 7:13; 11:14; 12:17; 14:23; 18:4; 28:51).

הִרְבֵּיתִי has been rendered with כתרת 'I have multiplied' from كثر II, whereas Yefet/Cod. Hunt. 206 prefer كثر IV: ואכתרת (ed. Birnbaum 30:2, ed. Polliack and Schlossberg 153)/واكثرت (ed. Schroeter 31:14).

וְכֶסֶף has been rendered literally ופצה 'and silver', whereas Yefet/Cod. Hunt. 206 specify the meaning as 'silver coinage': אלורק (ed. Birnbaum 30:2, ed. Polliack and Schlossberg 153)/الورق (ed. Schroeter 31:14).

The same applies to the rendering of וְזָהָב: the literal translation ודהב 'and gold' of our translator (3b:11), which can also be found in Cod. Hunt. 206: والذهب (ed. Schroeter 31:14) vs. Yefet: אלעין (ed. Birnbaum 30:2; ed. Polliack and Schlossberg 153) 'cash'.

Whereas the Hebrew source text has the verb עָשׂוּ (without a direct object), the translator adds an enclitic pronoun and renders פעמלוה 'and they made it'

(3b:11), referring to the topicalized וְהַזָּהָב 'and the gold'. Yefet offers a different solution by rendering: פעמלו מנהמא (ed. Birnbaum 30:2) 'and they made from both of them', מנהא 'from them' (ed. Polliack and Schlossberg 153), similarly Cod. Hunt. 206: فصنعوا منه (ed. Schroeter 31:14) who links the noun 'gold' with the preceding verb واكثرت.

בַּעַל/בְּעָלִים, when referring to idol(s), is rendered ותן/אותאן 'idols'/'idols' (3b:11; see also Hosea 2:15, 19; 11:2; 13:1); see also Yefet/Cod. Hunt 206 here: אותאנא (ed. Birnbaum 30:2, ed. Polliack and Schlossberg 153)/اوثانا (ed. Schroeter 31:15). The reconstruction ללותן 'for the idol' (3b:11) reflects the article in לַבַּעַל.

Hosea 2:11

The author renders אָשׁוּב וְלָקַחְתִּי with ארגע פאכוד 'I will return and I will take' (3b:12), thus indicating that he understands both verbs as parallel; see also Cod. Hunt. 206: ارجع وآخذ (ed. Schroeter 31:15) whereas some versions interpret שׁוּב as a *verbum relativum* ('I will take back').

For the translation of the elliptical construction לְכַסּוֹת אֶת־עֶרְוָתָהּ the translator expands *ad sensum* and introduces a syndetic relative clause, including an additional finite verb with the resumptive pronoun: וכתאני אלדי געלתה 'and My flax which I made ...' (3b:13), thus indicating that God is the creator of the flax which he made for the purpose of covering her nakedness. A similar syntax, using the verb 'to give', is exhibited by the Targum (דיהבית לה לכסאה 'that I gave her to cover') and Ibn Ezra (שנתתי לה 'that I gave her'); see also Qimḥi's interpretation (צמרי שנתתי לה לכסות את ערותה אציל אותם ממנה 'My wool etc. which I have given to her for covering her shame, I will take it from her'). Modern commentators, e.g. Macintosh 1997:57 render: 'which I gave her to cover her nakedness' (also: Vielhauer 2007:143, 145). Yefet renders אלתי כנת אגטי בהא 'with which I used to cover' (ed. Birnbaum 30:4, ed. Polliack and Schlossberg 154). LXX, which consider לְכַסּוֹת to be a purpose clause linked with the verb, had to add a negation: τοῦ μὴ καλύπτειν 'so as not to cover'. The same solution is offered by Cod. Hunt. 206: من ان يغطي 'so that it will not cover' (ed. Schroeter 31:16). Rashi indicates a possessive relationship (אשר היה לה).

The orthography סוותהא 'nakedness' is noteworthy, whereas Yefet/Cod. Hunt. 206 have the usual: סואתהא (ed. Birnbaum 30:6, ed. Polliack and Schlossberg 154)/سوءتها (ed. Schroeter 31:16).

Hosea 2:12

The translation סקאטהא for the *hapax legomenon* נַבְלֻתָהּ indicates 'shameless behaviour' (3b:14), literally: 'rubbish', 'waste' (سقاطة or سقاط, Hava p. 326).

The versions suggest various derivations:

(1) נבל II 'senseless folly', 'disgraceful deed': Vulgate: *stultitiam* 'folly'; Ibn Ezra: 'when nakedness is uncovered, there is senseless folly' (נבלה), i.e. disgraceful behaviour.

(2) נבל III 'to sink', 'to drop down', 'to languish'. Ibn Janāḥ (Neubauer p. 402) explains פמעני נבלה ומעני מפלת ואחד יריד בה אלגתה אלואקעה אלסאקטה אלמנצרעה 'The meaning of נְבֵלָה and מַפֶּלֶת is the same, the intention being a fallen carcass, which has dropped or been thrown down' and links the verse with Nahum 3:6 (וְנִבַּלְתִּיךְ parallel to 'I will cast loathsome filth over you') and Job 42:8.

LXX renders: ἀκαθαρσίαν ('impurity'); Targum: קלנה ('shame'); Peshitta: ܦܘܪܣܝܗ ('her nakedness', 'her pudenda'); Yefet/Cod. Hunt. 206 use the same noun as in Hosea 2:11 (for עֶרְוָתָהּ): סואתהא (ed. Birnbaum, 30:6), סותהא (ed. Polliack and Schlossberg 154)/سوءتها (ed. Schroeter 31:17).

לְעֵינֵי has been rendered by חדא 'opposite', 'face to face with', whereas Yefet prefers קדאם 'before' (ed. Birnbaum 30:7, ed. Polliack and Schlossberg 154) and Cod. Hunt. 206: بحضرة 'in the presence' (ed. Schroeter 31:17).

Hosea 2:13

וְהִשְׁבַּתִּי has been rendered with פאעטל 'and I will stop'; see also Yefet/Cod. Hunt. 206: אעטל (ed. Birnbaum 30:8, ed. Polliack and Schlossberg 154)/واعطل (not: واغطل ed. Schroeter 31:17).

The reconstruction of שהרהא 'her month' (3b:15) is based on the author's usual rendering of the singular. He specifies חָדְשָׁהּ as רוס שהרהא 'her New moon'. Yefet expands: וסרור מגיהא פי זמאן שהרהא (ed. Birnbaum 30:8–9, ed. Polliack and Schlossberg 154) and Cod. Hunt. 206 has the plural: وشهورها (ed. Schroeter 31:18) 'and her months'; see also and T-S Ar.21.182: שהורהא (fol. 1 recto 2).

The translator renders the singular מוֹעֲדָהּ with the plural form אעיאדהא 'her festive seasons'; see also Cod. Hunt. 206: اعيادها (ed. Schroeter 31:18), whereas Yefet prefers the expanded translation: וכל עיד להא (ed. Birnbaum 30:9, ed. Polliack and Schlossberg 154). A plural form can also be found in 4QpHos[a]: מועדיה (III:15). LXX translates all nouns as plural, and Peshitta has all nouns in the plural except 'her rejoicing,' which is in the singular.

Hosea 2:14

The translator renders the collective singulars גֶּפְנָהּ וּתְאֵנָתָהּ with plural nouns: גפאנהא ותיאנהא 'her vines and her figs' (3b:16); cf. also Targum: פירי גופנה ותינה 'the fruits of her vine and her fig'. Yefet/Cod. Hunt. 206 prefer the singular: גפנהא ותינתהא (ed. Birnbaum 30:10, ed. Polliack and Schlossberg 154)/جفنها وتينها (ed. Schroeter 31:19).

The translator renders the *hapax legomenon* אֶתְנָה with גֻעל 'pay' (3b:17). The same word appears with the spelling גועל as the translation of אֶתְנַן 'the prostitute's fee' in Hosea 9:1 (18b:20); see also Yefet: גֻעל (ed. Birnbaum 30:10) גֻעלי (ed. Polliack and Schlossberg 154). Cod. Hunt. 206 employs in both cases the root جدر: جدروني (ed. Schroeter 31:19) and الجدر (ed. Schroeter 40:5). In his grammatical notes, the author only clarifies that אֶתְנָה belongs to the category 'noun' (5b:13) without referring to the usual equivalent אֶתְנַן (Hosea 9:1; see also Deuteronomy 23:19; Micah 1:7). Cod. Hunt 206 derives אֶתְנָה and אֶתְנַן from the same root אתן to which *he* and *nun* have been added as an affix, respectively (Schroeter 25:4–7).

The suffix pronoun הם- in the reconstruction of פאגעלהם 'and I will make them' (3b:17) as the translation of וְשַׂמְתִּים has been suggested because of the following rendering of וַאֲכָלָתַם with לתאכלהם 'so that she will eat them' (3b:18). Yefet has the dual suffix pronoun in the translation of וְשַׂמְתִּים in some manuscripts (ותאכלהמא) and also in the translation וַאֲכָלָתַם (ותאכלהמא) (ed. Polliack and Schlossberg, 154). Cod. Hunt. 206 has the 3rd singular feminine suffix: واجعلها (ed. Schroeter 31:20).

For the translation שערא 'scrub country' (3b:18) of לְיַעַר 'for a forest' see Ibn Janaḥ (الشعراء). Yefet renders with לוחש אלצחרא (ed. Birnbaum 30:11, ed. Polliack and Schlossberg 154) and Cod. Hunt. 206 with دهلا 'forest' (ed. Schroeter 31:20).

Instead of the paratactic syntax וְשַׂמְתִּים ... וַאֲכָלָתַם, the author prefers a subordinate clause: פאגעלהא ... לתאכלהם (3b:17–18).

חַיַּת coll. 'beasts' has been rendered with וחוש 'animals' (3b:18); see also Cod. Hunt. 206: وحوش (ed Schroeter 31:20) vs. Yefet: חיואן (ed. Birnbaum 30:12, ed. Polliack and Schlossberg 154).

Hosea 2:15

The translation אפתקד 'I will visit' (3b:18) is another example of the author's preference of Arabic cognates. See also Hosea 4:9 (text missing: Hosea 1:4; 4:14; 9:9) and the rendering of פְּקֻדָּה with אלאפתקאד (Hosea 9:7). Also Yefet: ואפתקד (ed. Birnbaum 30:15; Polliack and Schlossberg 154) vs. Cod. Hunt. 206: واطالبها (ed. Schroeter 31:20).

The author renders יְמֵי literally with איאם 'days' (3b:19), whereas Yefet/Cod. Hunt. 206 prefer the noun זמאן (ed. Birnbaum 30:13)/زمان (ed. Schroeter 31:21, ed. Polliack and Schlossberg 154) 'time'.

The phrase הַבְּעָלִים אֲשֶׁר is represented in the translation with the masculine relative marker אלדי and the antecedent אלאותאן 'the idols'. According to the rules of Classical Arabic the feminine form אלתי is required, as is found in Yefet (ed. Birnbaum 30:13, ed. Polliack and Schlossberg 154).

The reconstruction תקתר 'you will burn incense' (3b:19) as translation of תַּקְטִיר seems to be justified since the author uses the same root in Hosea 11:2 (יוקתרו for יְקַטֵּרוּן); see also Cod. Hunt. 206: تقتّر (ed. Schroeter 31:21) vs. Yefet: תבכר (ed. Birnbaum 30:14, ed. Polliack and Schlossberg 154) and T-S Ar.21.182: וכאנת תבכר (fol. 1 line 10). The root בכר appears in the author's exegesis on Hosea 4:17 (11a:12).

נִזְמָהּ has been rendered with the plural בשנופהא 'with her earrings' (3b:19); see also Cod. Hunt. 206: بشنوفها (ed. Schroeter 31:21), whereas Yefet translates literally with שנפהא (ed. Birnbaum 30:14, ed. Polliack and Schlossberg 154).

The preposition אַחֲרֵי has been rendered with ורא 'after' (3b:20), whereas Yefet/Cod. Hunt. 206 have כלף (ed. Birnbaum 30:14, ed. Polliack and Schlossberg 154)/خلف (ed. Schroeter 31:22) with the same meaning.

The translator imitates the Hebrew accusative marker וְאוֹתִי by translating ואיאיי 'and me' (3b:20); for the morphology see also the form איאה (20b:21; 21b:12). The pronominal object particle إيّا ['iyyā], which in Arabic usually supports the second of two pronominal enclitic objects, is here used, as in Qurānic Arabic, as a carrier for a pronoun that has been separated from the verb to express emphasis.

In his grammatical notes, the author states that the masculine noun חֳלִי for which no biblical reference exists, is the absolute state of the construct חֲלִי (Proverbs 25:12) (5b:15). The translation of the *hapax legomenon* חֲלִיָתָהּ with وبشرها in Cod. Hunt. 206 (ed. Schroeter 31:22) reveals that he derived the noun from חֳלִי 'disease'.

The rendering of the phrase נְאֻם יהוה with זועם אלרב 'declaration of the Lord' (3b:20) is a characteristic feature of the translation (see also Hosea 2:18, 23; 11:11) vs. Yefet: קול קאל אללה 'a word that God spoke' (ed. Birnbaum 30:15, ed. Polliack and Schlossberg 154) and Cod. Hunt. 206: يقول الله 'God speaks' (ed. Schroeter 31:22).

The translator adopts the translation אלרב 'the Lord' (3b:20) for the tetragrammaton throughout his work, whereas Yefet/Cod. Hunt. 206, here and elsewhere, prefer אללה (ed. Birnbaum 30:15, ed. Polliack and Schlossberg 154)/الله (ed. Birnbaum 30:15) 'God'.

Hosea 2:16

The translator renders מְפַתֶּיהָ literally with the participle מוכדעהא 'deceiving her' (5b:16), whereas Cod. Hunt. 206 prefers the imperfect: انا اخادعها (ed. Schroeter 32:1) and Yefet translates with האנא אלטף בהא (ed. Birnbaum 41:10, ed. Polliack and Schlossberg 158). By choosing this translation, the author joins those commentators who interpret the phrase *in malam partem*, as T-S Ar.21.182: האנה מכדעהא (fol. 2 recto 16), LXX: ἐγὼ πλανῶ αὐτήν, Rashi: שהוא לה והולכתיה בגולה כמדבר וציה ('And I bring them into the exile which is for her like a desert and dry place'). Yefet: מנכדעה (ed. Birnbaum 114:18, ed. Polliack and Schlossberg 195) and Cod. Hunt. 206: مخدوعة (ed. Schroeter 38:5) use the root כדע for rendering פֹּתָה (Hosea 7:11); see also Saadiah's translation of Exodus 22:15: ואן כדע רגל גאריה. Qimḥi, however, understands it *in bonam partem*: הענין אתן בלבה לשוב בתשובה בעודה בגלות וזה כענין פתוי כי המפתה את חבירו מעבירו מדעתו שהיה בו לדעת אחר ('the meaning is: I will give in her heart that she will return while she is still in the exile; and this has the meaning of persuading; for he who persuades his companion leads him away from the opinion that he has to another opinion').

The quotation from Ezekiel 20:35 (5b:24) has והוצאתי instead of MT וְהֵבֵאתִי, probably due to the preceding verb ויכרגו (5b:23) which is equivalent to the Hebrew root יצא.

Hosea 2:17

The translator provides a literal translation of וְאֶת־עֵמֶק עָכוֹר לְפֶתַח תִּקְוָה by rendering ומרג עכור לפתח רגא 'and the valley of Akhor into a gate of hope' (5b:17–18), whereas Yefet/Cod. Hunt. 206 supply the finite verb ואגעל (ed. Birnbaum 41:12, ed. Polliack and Schlossberg 158)/واجعل (ed. Schroeter 32:2) 'and I will make'.

Because of the wide range of meanings of the root ענה, the reconstruction of the translation is problematic.

(1) Usually וְעָנְתָה is derived from ענה I 'to answer', 'to respond', e.g. Theodotion (ἀποκριθήσεται); Ḥayyūj (ed. Jastrow p. 196); Cod. Hunt. 206: فتجاوب (ed. Schroeter 32:2); T-S Ar.21.182: ותגיב (fol. 2 verso 2).
(2) ענה II 'to be occupied', 'to be busy', 'to be attentive', e.g. Aquila (καὶ ὑπακούσει) and Targum ('they will heed').
(3) ענה III 'to be bowed down', 'to be afflicted', e.g. LXX (ταπεινωθήσεται), Symmachus (κακωθήσεται) and Peshitta (ܘܢܬܡܟܟܢ).
(4) The commentator understands the verb as being derived from ענה IV 'to sing', thus indicating the merging of the two Arabic roots عنى and غنى into the Hebrew ענה and suggesting the opposition to Hosea 2:13. There-

TEXTUAL NOTES   131

fore the reconstruction פתגני 'and she will sing' (5b:11) appears to be more likely than a possible verb פתגאוב 'and she will answer'. Also some versions prefer the interpretation of the verb as 'to sing': Ibn 'Ali: תגני, Yefet: פתרגע תגני (ed. Birnbaum 41:13, ed. Polliack and Schlossberg 158), Ibn Ezra and Qimḥi: תגנן ותשיר ('she will play and sing'), Saadiah (according to Qimḥi): וישירו לאל יתברך על הנפלאות וזהו שאמר וענתה שמה מן תען להם מרים ;Vulgate: et canet; and Jerome. See also D. Stuart 1987:60 who combines option (1) and (4) in his translation: 'I will respond/sing'.

Hosea 2:18

The reconstruction פיכון 'and it will be' (6a:8) as rendering of וְהָיָה is based on the author's translation of Hosea 2:23 (6b:21) and 4:9 (8b:22) vs. Yefet/Cod. Hunt. 206: ויכון (ed. Birnbaum 41:15, ed. Polliack and Schlossberg 259)/ويكون (ed. Schroeter 32:3).

תִּקְרְאִי has been rendered with תנאדי 'you will call' (6a:9), whereas Yefet/Cod. Hunt 206 and Yefet use the root סמי and add the enclitic pronoun 1. person singular: תסמיני (ed. Birnbaum 41:15, ed. Polliack and Schlossberg 159)/تسميني (ed. Schroeter 32:4) 'you will call me'.

The adverb עוֹד is rendered with זאדה 'still' (6a:9; see also Hosea 2:19; 3:1; 12:1, 10; 14:9; text missing Hosea 1:4, 6; 14:4]) from the root زاد 'to become greater', 'to increase', whereas Yefet prefers איצא (ed. Birnbaum 41:16 ned. Polliack and Schlossberg 159) and Cod. Hunt. 206 ابدا (ed. Schroeter 32:4).

Hosea 2:19

וַהֲסִרֹתִי has been rendered with פאזיל 'and I will remove' (6a:10); the same root can be found in Yefet: לאני אזיל (ed. Birnbaum 41:17, ed. Polliack and Schlossberg 159), whereas Cod. Hunt. 206 has ثم اقطع (ed. Schroeter 32:4), which he uses also as translation of וְכָרַתִּי in the following verse: واقطع (ed. Schroeter 32:5).

The author renders מִפִּיהָ with מן פמהא 'from her mouth'; see also Yefet: מן פמהא (ed. Birnbaum 41:17) vs. Yefet מן פאהא (ed. Polliack and Schlossberg, 159) and Cod. Hunt. 206: من فيها (ed. Schroeter 32:5).

The plural translation באסמאהם 'by their names' (6a:11) of the Hebrew singular בִּשְׁמָם 'by their name' harmonises the verse with the plural of the preceding sentence ('the *names* of the idols'); see also Cod. Hunt. 206: باسمائهم (ed. Schroeter 32:5) and LXX: τὰ ὀνόματα αὐτῶν, whereas Yefet retains the singular באסמהם (ed. Birnbaum 41:18, ed. Polliack and Schlossberg 159).

Hosea 2:20

The translator imitates the Hebrew phrase וְכָרַתִּי לָהֶם בְּרִית by providing a literal rendition ואקטע להם עהד 'and I will make a covenant for them', i.e. 'in their interest', 'for their benefit' (6a:11); see also Cod. Hunt. 206: واقطع لهم عهدا (ed. Schroeter 32:5) vs. Yefet: תם אקטע מעהם עהד 'then I will make a covenant with them' (ed. Birnbaum 41:19, ed. Polliack and Schlossberg 259). The term 'to cut a covenant' occurs also in Hosea 10:4; 12:2.

The Hebrew singular phrase חַיַּת־הַשָּׂדֶה has been rendered with the plural וחוש אלצחרא 'the beasts of the field' (6a:11–12), whereas Yefet/Cod. Hunt. 206 retain the collective singular noun וחש (ed. Birnbaum 41:19, ed. Polliack and Schlossberg 159)/وحش (ed. Schroeter 32:6).

The translator adds another ומע 'and with' before *the reptiles of the earth* (6a:12), possibly to show that he regards the three partners of the covenant as equal.

It is noteworthy that the author retains the Hebrew הָאֲדָמָה as a loanword in his translation and combines it with the Arabic article: אלאדמה 'the earth' (6a:12), whereas Yefet/Cod. Hunt. 206 have the Arabic equivalent אלארץ (ed. Birnbaum 41:20, ed. Polliack and Schlossberg 159)/الارض (ed. Schroeter 32:6).

The translator also retains the Hebrew וּמִלְחָמָה/ומלחמה 'and warfare' (6a:13; see also his translation of Hosea 10:9). His intention was probably to retain the rhyme of the Hebrew אדמה/מלחמה and to connect them with the preceding Arabic אלצחרא. Yefet renders with וסאיר אלאת אלחרב (ed. Birnbaum 41:21, ed. Polliack and Schlossberg 159); similar Cod. Hunt. 206: وجميع الات الحرب (ed. Schroeter 32:7) 'and all the weapons of the war'; see also Qimḥi and modern commentators (Wolff, Mays).

The rendering אכסר מן אלארץ 'I will break from the earth' (6a:13) retains the *constructio praegnans* of the Hebrew source text אֶשְׁבּוֹר מִן־הָאָרֶץ.

The literal rendition of וְהִשְׁכַּבְתִּים with פאצגעהם 'and I will make them lie down' (6a:13) see also Aquila: κοιμήσω αὐτούς is distinct from Yefet (ואנימהם, ed. Birnbaum 41:21, ed. Polliack and Schlossberg 159) and Cod. Hunt. 206 (وأسكنهم, ed. Schroeter 32:7). However, a similar translation can be found in T-S Ar.22.127: ואצגעתהם (fol. 1 recto 13). See the versions: LXX: κατοικιῶ σε; Symmachus: κατοικίσω αὐτούς; Theodotion: κατοικιῶ αὐτούς.

The Hebrew לָבֶטַח is reflected in the phrase באטמאניה 'in peace' (6a:13). A similar translation (with the article) can be found in Yefet: באלאטמאניה 'in the tranquility' (ed. Birnbaum 41:22, ed. Polliack and Schlossberg 159), whereas Cod. Hunt. 206 prefers a participle in the adverbial accusative واثقين 'being safe' (ed. Schroeter 32:7).

TEXTUAL NOTES

Hosea 2:21

The translator renders וְאֵרַשְׂתִּיךְ with the term פאמליכך, literally 'and I will acquire you' (6a:14), which reflects the acquisition of the bride by the groom's payment of the bride-price to her father, vs. Yefet/Cod. Hunt. 206: ואערסך (ed. Birnbaum 41:23; ed. Polliack and Schlossberg 159)/واعرسك, (ed. Schroeter 32:8); however, the second time Cod. Hunt. 206 has: واملكك.

לְעוֹלָם has been rendered אלי אלאבד 'forever' (6a:14), whereas Yefet prefers ללדהר (ed. Birnbaum 41:23; ed. Polliack and Schlossberg 159); similar Cod. Hunt. 206: الى الدهر (ed. Schroeter 32:8).

The author imitates the Hebrew plural וּבְרַחֲמִים by rendering וברחמאת 'and with mercies' (6a:15), whereas Cod. Hunt. 206 prefers the singular ورحمة (ed. Schroeter 32:8); see also the definite singular noun in Yefet: ואלרחמה (ed. Birnbaum 41:24; ed. Polliack and Schlossberg 159).

וּבְחֶסֶד has been rendered with ובאחסאן 'and with kindness' (6a:15), whereas Yefet choses the equivalent ואלפצׄל (ed. Birnbaum 41:24; ed. Polliack and Schlossberg 159); similar the indefinite وفضل in Cod. Hunt. 206 (ed. Schroeter 32:8).

Yefet qualifies the term אלמוקף (see 6b:7) in another context with the relative clause אלדׄי אגתמעו פי ערבות מואב 'where they gathered in the wilderness of Moab' (ed. Birnbaum 84:21–22).

Hosea 2:22

The translator renders בֶּאֱמוּנָה with the Arabic cognate באמאנה 'and with fidelity' (6a:15); Yefet/Cod. Hunt. 206 add the article: באלאמאנה (ed. Birnbaum 42:1)/بالأمانة (ed. Schroeter 32:9; ed. Polliack and Schlossberg 159).

The tetragrammaton has been rendered with אלרב 'the Lord' (6a:16), whereas Yefet/Cod. Hunt. 206 have אללה (ed. Birnbaum 42:1; ed. Polliack and Schlossberg 159)/الله (ed. Schroeter 32:9). See already Hosea 2:15.

Hosea 2:23

Whereas the translator renders the phrase בַּיּוֹם־הַהוּא literally with פי דלך אליום 'on that day' in Hosea 2:18 (6a:8–9) and Hosea 2:20 (6a:11), he varies his translation here by choosing פי דלך אלזמאן 'in that time' (6b:21), the usual rendering of Yefet/Cod. Hunt. 206: פי דׄלך אלזמאן (ed. Birnbaum 46:2; Polliack and Schlossberg 161)/فى ذلك الزمان (ed. Schroeter 32:9).

The translator imitates the plural of Hebrew הַשָּׁמַיִם by rendering with אלסמואת 'the heavens' (6b:22), whereas Yefet/Cod. Hunt. 206 prefer the singular אלסמא (ed. Birnbaum 46:3; ed. Polliack and Schlossberg 161)/السماء (ed. Schroeter 32:10).

Hosea 2:25

The translator prefers the Arabic cognate زرع when rendering וּזְרַעְתִּיהָ with פאזרעהא 'and I will sow her' (6b:24); see also Yefet: ואזרעהא (ed. Birnbaum 46:6; ed. Polliack and Schlossberg 161), whereas Cod. Hunt. 206 has واغرسها 'and I will plant her' (ed. Schroeter 32:11).

The translator renders the phrase וְרִחַמְתִּי אֶת־לֹא רֻחָמָה literally with תום ארחם אלדי מא רוחימת 'then I will have mercy with who has not been pitied' (6b:24), whereas Yefet/Cod. Hunt. 206 expand by clarifying: וארחם אלדי סמיתהא לם תרחם (ed. Birnbaum 46:6–7; ed. Polliack and Schlossberg 161)/وارحم الذي سميتها لا ترحم (ed. Schroeter 32:12) 'I will have mercy on the one whom I named "She-has-not-been-pitied"'.

The translator changes the paratactic syntax of the second half of the verse *And I will say ..., and he will say ...* into a temporal sequence: בעד אן אקול ... והו יקול 'after I will have said ..., he will say' (6b:24–25) and introduces an asyndetic relative clause: 'to the one who was Not-my-people' (6b:24) instead of 'to Not-my-people'. By introducing a negation of the past, the translator makes it clear from the outset that the status of 'Not-my-people' is a fact of the past (לם יכון שעבי) as was the characterisation of 'She-has-not-been-pitied'.

Hosea 3:1

Taking into consideration his exegesis (7b:5: מר איצא: 'go again!'; see Zechariah 11:15), it may be assumed that the translator understands עוֹד to be connected with the following imperative ('go again!') (7a:16) rather with the divine address ('the Lord said again'). See LXX, Vulgate, Peshitta; also modern commentators are in favour of this interpretation (Harper, Wolff, Qyl, Macintosh).

The reconstruction of ופאגרה 'and an adulteress' (7a:17) reflects the author's rendering of the root נאף with פגר in Hosea 2:4 (3a:27), 4:2 (8b:12), 7:4 (14b:25); see also Yefet/Cod. Hunt. 206: והי פאגרה (ed. Birnbaum 48:15; ed. Polliack and Schlossberg 163)/فاجرة (ed. Schroeter 32:16).

The reconstruction כמחבה 'as the love of' (7a:17) as rendering of כְּאַהֲבַת reflects the author's usual rendering of the preposition כְּ (see commentary on

Hosea 2:1), whereas Yefet/Cod. Hunt. 206 have מתל מחבה (ed. Birnbaum 48:15; ed. Polliack and Schlossberg 163)/مثل محبة (ed. Schroeter 32:16).

The author either retains the Hebrew name יִשְׂרָאֵל (Hosea 2:1; 9:7; 12:13) which is the preferred name in his exegesis (13a:12; 14b:16; 19b:24; 23a:19, 20; 24a:2; 24b:27; 26a:19; 27a:28; 29b:17), or he uses, as here (7a:17), the Arabic name אסראיל (see also Hosea 3:5; 4:1; 5:1, 5, 9; 6:10 [2×]; 7:1, 10; 8:2; 9:1, 10; 10:6, 8, 9, 15; 11:1, 8; 13:9; 14:2).

The reconstruction ומוחבי 'and lovers of' (7a:18) as rendering of וְאֹהֲבֵי is based on the author's translations of מְאַהֲבַי in Hosea 2:7 (3b:5), 14 (3b:17); see also Yefet/Cod. Hunt. 206: ומחבין (ed. Birnbaum 48:16; ed. Polliack and Schlossberg 163)/ومحبي (ed. Schroeter 32:17).

The rendering of אֲשִׁישֵׁי is not preserved; the tentative reconstruction קנאני 'bottles of' (7a:18) relies on Yefet's rendering קנאני אלענב (ed. Birnbaum 48:16; ed. Polliack and Schlossberg 163) and Saadiah's translation of the phrase לַאֲשִׁישֵׁי קִיר־חֲרָשֶׂת (Isaiah 16:7) with אהל חרשת מן אלכמר בקנאני. See, however, the rendering in Cod. Hunt. 206: دساتيج الخمر (ed. Schroeter 32:17); the Persian loanword دستجة means 'bundle', 'handful', 'large glass-vessel' (Hava 1951:205).

Hosea 3:2

The reconstruction of the verb ואתבתתהא 'and I established her' (7a:18) is based on the author's phrase in his exegesis (7b:26: אתבת); see also Yefet/Cod. Hunt. 206: ואתבתתהא (ed. Birnbaum 48:17; ed. Polliack and Schlossberg 163)/فاثبتها (ed. Schroeter 32:17).

There are several options for the rendition of וָאֶכְּרֶהָ:

(1) Rashi derives the verb from כרה I 'to dig'; also Jerome, who compares Israel with a vine 'dug in', 'implanted' (see Isaiah 5); see also Aquila: καὶ ἔσκαψα αὐτήν 'I dug her in'; Vulgate: *et fodi eam*.

(2) The verb may be derived from the root כרה II 'to hire', 'to buy' (Qimḥi, Ibn Janāḥ); LXX: καὶ ἐμισθωσάμην ('I hired'), Peshitta: ܘܐܓܪܬܗ ('and I redeemed her'), Targum: ופרקתינון ('and I redeemed them').

(3) וָאֶכְּרֶהָ can be traced to the I *nun* root נכר 'to recognize'; this would explain the *dagesh*; see Ibn Ezra; Yefet, who borrowed from R. Yoḥanan (Pesikta, ed. Buber, Lyck 1868, p. 102a: ר׳ יוחנן פתח ואכרה לי ואבירה לי).

The translator with his rendering ואתבתתהא 'and I established her' (from ثبت IV) appears to prefer the second option. Saadiah also renders the root נכר with תבת (e.g. Genesis 27:23; 42:8; Deuteronomy 33:9). See R. Yoḥanan: ר׳ יוחנן פתח ואכרה לי ואבירה לי (Pesikta, ed. Buber, Lyck 1868, p. 102a).

The *lacuna* at the beginning of 7a:19 may be restored with בכמסה עשר 'for fifteen'. His literal translation of בַּחֲמִשָּׁה עָשָׂר כָּסֶף by rendering בכמסה עשר פי אלפצה 'for fifteen in silver' (7a:19) is distinct from others who add the monetary unit 'dirham', e.g. Yefet/Cod. Hunt. 206: בכמסה עשר דרהם (ed. Birnbaum 48:17; ed. Polliack and Schlossberg 163)/بـטו درهما (ed. Schroeter 32:17) and T-S Ar.22.127: כמסה אעשר דרהמא (fol. 1 verso 4). The author refers to 'the 15 dirham' (אלט״ו דרהם) in his exegesis (8a:8).

Unfortunately the translation of וְחֹמֶר is not clearly preserved (7a:19); however, from the remnants of the upper parts of the letters it may be assumed that the author used the term וגריב; the plural אלגראיב can be found in his commentary (7b:27); see also Yefet/Cod. Hunt. 206: וגריב (ed. Birnbaum 48:17; ed. Polliack and Schlossberg 163)/وجريب (ed. Schroeter 32:17).

The translator chooses as rendition of the *hapax legomenon* וְלֵתֶךְ the apparantly more familiar measurement ובכורי 'and for two *kurr*' (7a:19); a *kurr*, 'a certain measure of capacity' (Lane p. 2601), equals 60 *qafīz*. The measure כור equivalent of a *ḥomer* can be found in Targum Onqelos on Leviticus 27:16; Targum Isaiah 5:10; Targum Ezekiel 45:13, 14 and Jerome.

The passive verb אופיכו (7b:15) is derived from the root فكّ 'to ransom', 'to redeem', 'to liberate' (see also 17a:18: אפוכהם).

The text of the commentary [ומר]אלח 'the *ḥomer*' (8a:6) has been restored according to אלחומר in the following lines (8a:7, 8).

Hosea 3:3

The reconstruction כתיר 'many' (7a:20) as translation of רַבִּים is based on the same phrase in the next verse איאם כתיר 'many days' (7a:21), though the feminine form of the adjective would be expected; see Yefet: איאם כתירה (ed. Birnbaum 48:18; ed. Polliack and Schlossberg 163) vs. Cod. Hunt. 206: زمان طويل (ed. Schroeter 32:18).

The author renders לִי literally with לי 'for me' (7a:20), whereas Yefet: עלי אסמי (ed. Birnbaum 48:18; ed. Polliack and Schlossberg 163) and Cod. Hunt. 206: باسمى (ed. Schroeter 32:18) emphasise that the woman's 'sitting' happens 'in my name'.

The translator adds a finite verb between וְגַם־אֲנִי and אֵלָיִךְ and renders אנא אציר אליך 'I will come to you' (7a:21) probably for stylistic reasons, whereas Yefet mirrors the biblical text literally: ואיצֿא אנא אליך (ed. Birnbaum 48:19; ed. Polliack and Schlossberg 163); see also Cod. Hunt. 206: بل انا لك (ed. Schroeter 32:19).

Hosea 3:4

The Hebrew מַצֵּבָה is rendered with מצטבה 'mastaba' (7a:23) vs. Yefet: מנצבה (ed. Birnbaum 48:20; ed. Polliack and Schlossberg 163) and Cod. Hunt. 206: نصبة (ed. Schroeter 32:20) 'pillar'. Some versions thing of an 'altar': LXX: θυσιαστηρίου; Peshitta: ܡܕܒܚܐ; Vulgate: *altari*.

Whereas Yefet/Cod. Hunt. 206 render תְּרָפִים with אצטרלאב (ed. Birnbaum 48:22; ed. Polliack and Schlossberg 163)/اصطرلاب (ed. Schroeter 32:21) 'astrolabe', the translator prefers ציוור 'shapes', 'pictures', 'figures', 'statues', thus apparently confirming the interpretation of Judges 15:5 by R. Tanchum (ed. Theod. Haarbrücker Halle 1843): 'Some hold that תרפים (Genesis 31:34; 1 Samuel 15:23) are astrolabes. I do not approve this opinion, rather they are idols, either according to the shape of the stars, as these idolators thought them to be, or pictures which they imagined in their phantasy and whom they worshipped'.

The author provides a negative which is absent before the last word תְּרָפִים in the biblical text; however, instead of adding another ליס which is repeated five times, he chooses ולא 'and not' (7a:23), possibly in order to indicate that there is a closer link between צודרה 'ephod' and ציוור 'images' within the list. See also Cod. Hunt. 206: ولا اصطرلاب (ed. Schroeter 32:21).

The reconstruction of מדמונה (8a:22) in the exegesis is tentative; an attribute designating not only the negative/positive aspect, but the total rejection of these institutions would be preferable.

Hosea 3:5

וּפָחֲדוּ is translated with פיפזעו 'and they will be frightened'; see also Yefet/Cod. Hunt. 206: ויפזעון (ed. Birnbaum 49:1; ed. Polliack and Schlossberg 163)/ويفزعوا (ed. Schroeter 32:22). Also Ibn Barun refers to the semantic range of the Arabic root פזע when explaining the meaning of the verb פחד 'to fear' and 'to seek shelter in fear' (Wechter pp. 115, 185).

The author renders the *constructio praegnans* וּפָחֲדוּ אֶל־יְהֹוָה, literally *they (come) trembling to YHWH*, with פיפזעו פי גהה אלרב 'they will be frightened before the Lord' (7a:24–25). Yefet/Cod. Hunt. 206 prefer the prepostion 'in': ויפזעון מן אללה (ed. Birnbaum 49:1–2; ed. Polliack and Schlossberg 163)/ويفزعوا من الله (ed. Schroeter 32:22); see the versions, LXX: καὶ ἐκστήσονται ἐπί ('they will be amazed at'); Symmachus: καὶ ἐπαινέσωσι ('and they will praise'); Aquila: πτοηθήσονται ('they are passionately excited at'); Peshitta: ܢܕܥܘܢ ('and they will know'); Targum: ויתנהון לפולחנא דייי ('and they will present themselves for the worship of the Lord').

The translator renders וְאֶל-טוּבוֹ *and to His good* with ופי גהה בירה (7a:25), whereas Yefet/Cod. Hunt. 206 think specifically of God's 'dignity': ומן מסכן וקארה (ed. Birnbaum 49:2; ed. Polliack and Schlossberg 163 [one manuscript has חסר instead of מסכן])/ومن وقاره (ed. Schroeter 32:22); see also Saadiah (according to Qimḥi): ופירש רב סעדיה ז"ל ואל טובו אל כבודו כמו אעביר כל טובי על פניך ('R. Saadiah of blessed memory explains ואל טובו as "his honour" as in Exodus 33:19').

The phrase פי אכר אלאיאם 'at the end of the days' (7a:25) as rendition of בְּאַחֲרִית הַיָּמִים is distinct from Yefet/Cod. Hunt. 206: פי אכר אלזמאן (ed. Birnbaum 49:2; ed. Polliack and Schlossberg 163)/فى اخر الزمان (ed. Schroeter 32:22–23). Saadiah translates the same phrase either with פי אכר אלאיאם (Genesis 49:1; Numbers 24:14; see also Deuteronomy 4:30: פי אכר תלך אלאיאם) or with פי אכר אלזמאן (Isaiah 2:2).

Hosea 4:1

The translator chooses נטר 'seeing', 'vision', 'inspection', 'trial' (8b:10) as rendition of רִיב vs. Yefet/Cod. Hunt. 206: מנאטרה (ed. Birnbaum 56:8; ed. Polliack and Schlossberg 167)/مناظر (ed. Schroeter 33:2) 'debate', 'dispute'.

The plural יֹשְׁבֵי הָאָרֶץ has been rendered literally גלאס אלארץ 'the inhabitants of the land' (8b:10–11); see also Yefet: גלאס אלארץ (ed. Birnbaum 56:8; ed. Polliack and Schlossberg 167) vs. the singular collective in Cod. Hunt. 206: جالس الارض (ed. Schroeter 33:2).

חֶסֶד has been translated with איחסאן 'beneficience' (8b:11), whereas Yefet renders with אסתעמאל אלמערוף (ed. Birnbaum 56:9; ed. Polliack and Schlossberg 167) and Cod. Hunt. 206 offers a twofold translation: فضل and معروف (ed. Schroeter 33:3).

The phrase דַּעַת אֱלֹהִים has been rendered literally with מערפה אללה 'knowledge of God' (8b:11), whereas Yefet/Cod. Hunt. 206 emphasise the obligation to know God: מערפה מא יג׳ב ללה (ed. Birnbaum 56:9; ed. Polliack and Schlossberg 167)/معرفة ما يجب لله (ed. Schroeter 33:3) 'the knowledge that is owed to God'.

Hosea 4:2

By adding the particle בל 'rather' at the beginning of the verse (8b:12), the author emphasises the contrast between this verse and the preceding one: instead of truth, beneficence and knowledge of the Lord, instead swearing, lying etc. have gained influence. See also Yefet/Cod. Hunt. 206: בל (ed. Birnbaum 57:19; ed. Polliack and Schlossberg 167)/ بل (ed. Schroeter 33:4). The author adds בל also in his translation of Hosea 7:15; 8:7, 13; 9:3; 10:13.

The translator prefers the masculine noun וסרק 'and stealing' for Hebrew וְגָנֹב to the feminine noun which can be found in Yefet/Cod. Hunt. 206: וסרקה (ed. Birnbaum 57:19; ed. Polliack and Schlossberg 167)/وسرقة (ed. Schroeter 33:4).

The rendition of Hebrew פָּרָצוּ 'they have breached' with תגרו 'they increased' (8b:12) is similar to Yefet: ואתגרו (ed. Birnbaum 57:19; ed. Polliack and Schlossberg 167) vs. Cod. Hunt. 206: has كثروا (ed. Schroeter 33:4) 'they have increased'. All three translations share the same interpretative idea as R. Tanchum (Pocooke): نمت وزادت وانتشرت 'they grew, they increased and spread out'.

נָגָעוּ is rendered with קד אדנו 'they drew near' (8b:13), from the root دنى IV 'to be near', 'to draw near' vs. Yefet/Cod. Hunt. 206: אתצלו (ed. Birnbaum 57:20; ed. Polliack and Schlossberg 167)/اتصلوا (ed. Schroeter 33:5) 'they were joined', 'they were connected'; see also the similar renderings in LXX, Targum, Vulgate: *sanguines cum sanguinibus coniunguntur*.

Hosea 4:3

The translation תחזן אלארץ 'the land will mourn' (8b:13) indicates that the author derives תֶּאֱבַל from אבל I 'to mourn'; see also Yefet/Cod. Hunt. 206: תחזן (ed. Birnbaum 58:18; ed. Polliack and Schlossberg 168)/تحزن (ed. Schroeter 33:5) and LXX (πενθήσει); Peshitta (ܬܬܐܒܠ); Vulgate (*lugebit*) vs. deriving the verb from אבל II 'to wither', 'to dry up' as Targum: תחרוב ('it will dry up'), Rashi, Qimḥi.

The translator renders וְאֻמְלַל with a passive form of I: לאן קד קוטע 'because he will be cut off' (8b:13) vs. Yefet/Cod. Hunt. 206 refer to the root قصف 'to break', 'to shatter', 'to smash': וינקצף (ed. Birnbaum 58:18; ed. Polliack and Schlossberg 168)/وتقصف, ed. Schroeter 33:5). The addition of לאן 'for' (8b:13) to the biblical text is a characteristic feature of the translation; see also: Hosea 4:11; 5:8; 8:5; 9:4 [2×], 15, 16; 10:8; 12:8, 12; 13:2; 14:8; with suffix pronoun: לאנה (Hosea 13:1), לאנהא (Hosea 11:6), לאנהם (Hosea 8:2).

The rendition גאלס, literally 'sitting' (8b:13), imitates the Hebrew singular participle יוֹשֵׁב; see also Yefet: גֿאלס (ed. Birnbaum 58:18; ed. Polliack and Schlossberg 168), whereas Cod. Hunt. 206 chooses the plural participle with enclitic pronoun: جالسيها (ed. Schroeter 33:6).

Also the phrase בָּהּ has been rendered literally with בהא 'in her' (8b:13) vs. Yefet: פיהא (ed. Birnbaum 58:18; ed. Polliack and Schlossberg 168 [where one manuscript reads כל גאלסיהא).

The preposition בְּ ('*bet* of accompaniment') 'together with' in the phrase בְּחַיַּת הַשָּׂדֶה has been replaced with מן חתי 'including even', 'even from' (8b:14) to emphasise the climax: the total 'break-down' is not restricted to humans but includes all animals; see Yefet/Cod. Hunt. 206 who choose the preposition 'with': מע וחש אלצחרא (ed. Birnbaum 58:18; ed. Polliack and Schlossberg 168 [where one manuscript reads ויחשרו מע]/مع وحش الصحراء (ed. Schroeter 33:6).

The translator renders the collective חַיַּת with the plural וחוש 'wild animals' (8b:14), whereas Yefet/Cod. Hunt. 206 imitate the Hebrew by choosing the collective singular: וחש (ed. Birnbaum 58:19; ed. Polliack and Schlossberg 168)/وحش (ed. Schroeter 3:6).

The translator renders דְּגֵי with the plural סמאך 'fish' (8b:14) vs. Yefet/Cod. Hunt. 206 who choose the alternative plurals: אסמאך (ed. Birnbaum 58:19; ed. Polliack and Schlossberg 168) and وسموك (ed. Schroeter 33:6).

יֵאָסֵפוּ is an elliptical expression for 'they died' (see Genesis 25:8, 17; 35:29; Judges 2:10; 2 Kings 22:20). The author translates the verb in two different ways: firstly, he renders it literally with ינחשרו 'they will be gathered' and adds the place where the fish are gathered: אלי אליבס 'on dry land' (8b:15). Secondly, he offers the metaphorical translation פיהלכו 'they will perish' (8b:15). See Yefet: ינחשר (ed. Birnbaum 58:19; ed. Polliack and Schlossberg 168 [which reads תנחשר insead]); Ibn Ezra: ימותו ('they will die'); Qimḥi: יכלו וימותו ('they will perish and die'). Noteworthy is Ibn Ezra's remark: he concludes from the total devastation, including the fish of the sea, which were not killed during the time of the Flood, that the actual generation is more wicked than that generation (Genesis 6–8): אלה רעים מדור המבול כי דגי הים לא מתו ('these are worse than the generation of the Flood, for the fish of the sea did not die').

Hosea 4:4

The Hebrew introductory conjunction אַךְ 'indeed' at the beginning of the verse is rendered with כאץ 'only', 'especially', 'in particular', 'exclusively' (see also Hosea 12:9, 11), which functions as emphasis of the following word אימר 'man' (8b:15). Yefet has the identical translation כאץ (ed. Birnbaum 59:11; ed. Polliack and Schlossberg 168), whereas Cod. Hunt. 206 prefers the feminine equivalent وخاصة (ed. Schroeter 33:7). This is another example for the author's general preference of masculine forms to feminine ones (see e.g. البرة ألبר).

The author renders the verb יָרֵב with יכאצם 'he brings legal action' (8b:14) (see also Hosea 2:4) vs. Yefet/Cod. Hunt. 206: ינאטר (ed. Birnbaum 59:11; ed.

Polliack and Schlossberg 168 [where one manuscript reads אן ינאטׄר]/يناظر (ed. Schroeter 33:7).

The verb יוֹכַח is rendered with יוובך 'he will reprimand' (8b:15); see also Yefet: יובך (ed. Birnbaum 59:11; ed. Polliack and Schlossberg 168) vs. Cod. Hunt. 206: يعظ (ed. Schroeter 33:7).

The translator adds the copula פקד חצלו 'and they were' (8b:16) between וְעַמְּךָ and כִּמְרִיבֵי כֹהֵן and renders 'and your people were like those who bring legal action against a priest'. His intention is probably to locate the action in the past, thus establishing a temporal contrast between the two parts of the verse (see also Hosea 6:10; 7:13; 8:9 [2×]; 9:12, 16; 12:15); see also Yefet: בל צאר שעבך כמכאצמי אלאמם 'rather your people were like those who bring legal action against the priests' (ed. Birnbaum 59:11–12; ed. Polliack and Schlossberg 168) vs. the literal translation in Cod. Hunt. 206: وقومك لمخاصى الامام (ed. Schroeter 33:7–8). Most versions retain the Hebrew source text; see LXX: ὁ δὲ λαός μου ὡς ἀντιλεγόμενος ἱερεύς ('my people are like a contentious priest'), Aquila: ὡς ὁ ἀντιδικῶν ἱερεῖ; Symmachus: ὡς ἀντίρρησις ἡ πρὸς ἱερέα ('like contention with a priest'), Peshitta: ܘܥܡܟ ܐܝܟ ܟܗܢܐ ܕܚܪܝܢܐ ('and your people like contentious priests'), Vulgate: *populus enim tuus sicut hii qui contradicunt sacerdoti* ('like these who contend with the priest'). Only Targum adds a verb: ועמך נצן עם מלפיהון ('your people quarrel with their teachers').

Hosea 4:5

וְכָשַׁלְתָּ has been rendered with פתנעתר 'and you will stumble' from the root عثر VII which is not attested in Wehr, Hava, Kazimirski, whereas the author renders the following וְכָשַׁל with תום ויועתר 'then he will stumble' (IV). Yefet has in each case VII: תנעתׄר and וינעתׄר (ed. Birnbaum 60:13; ed. Polliack and Schlossberg 169), whereas Cod. Hunt. 206 translates with وتتعس/ويتعس 'and you/he will fall' (ed. Schroeter 33:8).

The translator renders לַיְלָה with the definite feminine noun אלליליה 'the night' (8b:17); he adds the article presumably to achieve a closer parallel to the complimentary אליום. The masculine noun אלליל can be found in Yefet (ed. Birnbaum 60:13; ed. Polliack and Schlossberg 169 [where some manuscripts have לילא]); see also Cod. Hunt. 206: لَيْل (ed. Schroeter 33:8).

The interpretation of the verb וְדָמִיתִי *and I will be silent* is controversial.

(1) Ibn Ezra and Qimḥi translate וְדָמִיתִי with the verb כרת 'to cut off', thus indicating that they derive it from דמה III 'to cease', 'to bring to an end', 'to destroy'; see Zephaniah 1:11 (parallel to כרת), Isaiah 15:1 (parallel to שדד). Ibn Janāḥ paraphrases the verb with 'destruction' (אלהלאך).

(2) LXX links the verb with דמה I 'to compare': νυκτὶ ὡμοίωσα τὴν μητέρα σου ('I have likened your mother to night'), thus obviously reading וְדִמִּיתִי.

(3) Some versions derive the verb from the root דמם 'to be silent', though they take the verb as intransitive; see Aquila and Theodotion: νυκτὸς ἐσιώπησα ('I have been silent in the night'), Symmachus: νυκτὸς σιωπήσω ('I will be silent in the night'), Peshitta: ܫܬܩܬ ('[your mother] was silent') and Rashi who comments 'like a man who sits in terror and no answer comes to his mouth'.

(4) Also the translator derives it from the root דום/דמם 'to be silent', but his rendering with אלם IV shows his understanding of the verb as transitive: פאבכם 'I will silence' (8b:17) (from אלם IV). This rendering has also been adopted by Yefet/Cod. Hunt. 206: אבכם (ed. Birnbaum 60:14; ed. Polliack and Schlossberg 169)/ابكِ (ed. Schroeter 33:9) and Vulgate: *nocte facere feci matrem tuam* ('in the night I made your mother silent'). See also the translation of Hosea 4:6; 10:15.

Hosea 4:6

Again, the translator derives נִדְמוּ from דמם 'to be silent', ni. passive, and renders אנבכמו 'they have been silenced' (8b:18) (אלם VII); see also Yefet: אנבכמו (ed. Birnbaum 61:3; ed. Polliack and Schlossberg 169) and Cod. Hunt. 206: حتى ينبكموا (ed. Schroeter 33:9); Aquila/Theodotion: ἐσιώπησεν; Symmachus: ἐφιμώθη; Peshitta: ܫܬܩ; Vulgate: *conticuit*. LXX refers again to דמה I, as is evident from the translation ὡμοιώθη 'he has been likened'.

The root מאס in מָאַסְתָּ and *qere* וְאֶמְאָסְךָ has been rendered in both cases with the root זהד 'to abstain', 'to reject' (8b:18, 19); see also Yefet: זהדת (ed. Birnbaum 62:2, 3; ed. Polliack and Schlossberg 169), whereas Cod. Hunt. 206 offers a twofold translation of the first verb: نسيت 'you have forgotten' (ed. Schroeter 33:10; see also Wolff 1965:98: '... "Weisung deines Gottes", die er "vergessen" hat') and وزهدتها 'and you have abandoned it' (ed. Schroeter 33:10) and continues with وزهدتك 'and I have abandoned you' for the second one.

By adding וכמא 'and as' and כדלך 'likewise' (8b:19–20), the translator creates a syntax of comparison which is not to be found in the biblical source text. His intention is obviously to achieve an exact congruence ('talio'): in the same way (כמא) as Israel forgets God's Torah, likewise (כדלך) He forgets Israel. Similarly Yefet/Cod. Hunt. 206 add פלדלך (ed. Birnbaum 61:5; ed. Polliack and Schlossberg 169)/ولذلك (ed. Schroeter 33:11) 'and therefore' before the last phrase of the verse.

מִכַּהֵן has been rendered with מן אלתאמום 'from the being a priest' (8b:19), denominative from امام 'priest'; see also Yefet/Cod. Hunt. 206: אלתאמם (ed. Birnbaum 61:4; ed. Polliack and Schlossberg 169)/تأمم (ed. Schroeter 33:10); the reading [ta'ammum] is preferable to Schroeter's suggestion تأمّ (Schroeter p. 33 note 1).

The translator copies the unusual word order of the Hebrew source text by placing איצא אנא 'also I' at the end of the sentence (8b:20) whereas Yefet adopts the usual syntax: פלדלך אנא איצא אנסא אולאדך (ed. Birnbaum 61:5; ed. Polliack and Schlossberg 169 [where one manuscript reads ולדלך איצא אנסא אנא]).

Hosea 4:7

The reconstruction כדלך 'likewise' (8b:20) for כֵּן is based on the translation of כֵּן in Hosea 11:2; similar Cod. Hunt. 206: كذاك (ed. Schroeter 33:12; ed. Polliack and Schlossberg 170) and Yefet: כדאך (ed. Birnbaum 62:5).

After the first sentence of the verse *like their multitude, likewise they sinned against Me*, the author inserts פלדלך 'and therefore' (8b:21), in order to indicate that the punishment which is described in the second sentence, is the consequence of Israel's sin. Additional פלדלך can also be found in the translation of Hosea 7:16; 8:3; 9:2; 10:15; 13:7, 13, 15. See also Yefet: פלדלך (ed. Birnbaum 62:5; ed. Polliack and Schlossberg 170); Cod. Hunt. 206: فلذلك (ed. Schroeter 33:12).

כְּבוֹדָם is rendered with כרמהם 'their honour' (8b:21), whereas Cod. Hunt. 206 and Yefet translate with وقارهم (ed. Schroeter 33:12)/וקארהם (ed. Birnbaum 62:6; ed. Polliack and Schlossberg 170).

When rendering בְּקָלוֹן *in shame*, the translator adds the 3rd person plural masculine suffix pronoun: בכזיהם 'in their shame' (8b:21), probably in order to harmonise this phrase with the preceding opposite כרמהם/כְּבוֹדָם *their honour*. Yefet and Cod. Hunt. 206 translate with באלאסתכפאף (ed. Birnbaum 62:6; ed. Polliack and Schlossberg 170)/باستخفاف 'with contempt' (ed. Schroeter 33:13)

אבדל 'I will exchange' (8b:21) as translation of Hebrew אָמִיר indicates that the author does not adopt the *tiqqun soferim* הֵמִירוּ 'they have exchanged', which is attested in Peshitta (ܫܠܚܘ) and Targum (חליפו), but retains MT; see also Yefet: אבדל (ed. Birnbaum 62:5; ed. Polliack and Schlossberg 170) and Cod. Hunt. 206 ابدل (ed. Schroeter 33:12).

Again, the author retains the Hebrew word order slavishly, whereas Yefet and Cod. Hunt. 206 change into פלדלך אבדל וקארהם (ed. Birnbaum 62:5–6; ed. Polliack and Schlossberg 170)/فلذلك ابدل وقارهم (ed. Schroeter 33:12).

Hosea 4:8

The reconstruction of קרבאן חטאה 'sin-offering' (8b:21) is not absolutely safe. Although the noun חַטָּאת has usually been rendered with כטייה (Hosea 10:8; 13:12; text missing: 8:13; 9:9), the translator appears to have adopted the Hebrew technical term קרבן חטאת, in order to specify the Hebrew noun which includes both meanings 'sin' and 'sin-offering'; see also Cod. Hunt. 206: قربان خطأة (ed. Schroeter 33:13). Yefet retains the Hebrew technical term קרבן חאטת (ed. Birnbaum 62:16; ed. Polliack and Schlossberg 170).

Since the first component of the phrase חַטַּאת עַמִּי had been replaced by the construct chain קרבאן חטאה, it had become necessary to rephrase the second component עַמִּי of the biblical text. The author introduces a relative clause: 'the sin-offering which belongs to My people' (8b:21–22); the meaning is identical: 'the sin-offering of My people'. See Yefet: חטאת אלדי לשעבי (ed. Birnbaum 62:16; ed. Polliack and Schlossberg 170). Cod. Hunt. 206 has a threefold construct chain: قربان خطأة قومي (ed. Schroeter 33:13).

Instead of a literal translation of נַפְשׁוֹ with נפסה 'his soul', the translator prefers the plural noun and changes the suffix pronoun from 3rd masculine singular into 3rd masculine plural: אנפוסהם 'their souls' (8b:22), presumably to achieve congruence with the preceding plural verb ירפעו 'they lift up'. See also LXX and Symmachus (τὰς ψυχὰς αὐτῶν), Theodotion (ἐν ταῖς ψυχαῖς αὐτῶν) and Vulgate (*animas eorum*). Yefet and Cod. Hunt. 206, obviously aware of the grammatical incongruence, chose a different option; they change the plural verb into singular, introduce an additional subject and retain the singular object of the Hebrew source text ירפע כל ואחד נפסה (ed. Birnbaum 62:17; ed. Polliack and Schlossberg 170)/يرفع كل واحد نفسه 'each one lifts up his soul' (ed. Schroeter 33:13–14). A singular noun with the suffix pronoun of the 3rd person plural masculine ('their soul') is attested in Peshitta (ܢܦܫܗܘܢ), Targum (נפשהון) and 9 Kennicott MSS (נפשם).

Hosea 4:9

The translator adopts the future meaning of the Hebrew verb וְהָיָה by rendering with פיכון 'and he will be' (8b:22), whereas Yefet and Cod. Hunt. 206 have a verb form in the past צאר (ed. Birnbaum 63:14; ed. Polliack and Schlossberg 170)/صار (ed. Schroeter 33:14).

The reconstruction of כאלשעב as rendition of כָעָם is very likely bearing in mind the imitative style of the translator. Yefet has מתל אלשעב (ed. Birnbaum 63:14; ed. Polliack and Schlossberg 170), whereas Cod. Hunt. 206 translates with صار الشعب كالامام (ed. Schroeter 33:14).

TEXTUAL NOTES   145

By adding the personal pronoun ואנא 'and I' (8b:23) before אפתקד, the author emphasises the subject: it is God Himself who is determined to visit/punish.

The author prefers the Arabic cognate אפתקד 'and I will punish' as translation of וּפָקַדְתִּי (8:23) to possible فاطالبه (Cod. Hunt. 206, ed. Schroeter 33:14); see also Yefet: אפתקד (ed. Birnbaum 63:14; ed. Polliack and Schlossberg 170).

וּמַעֲלָלָיו has been rendered with ושמאילה (see also Hosea 5:4; 7:2; 9:15; translation missing 12:3), as do Cod. Hunt. 206: شمائله (ed. Schroeter 33:15) and Yefet: שמאליה (ed. Birnbaum 63:15; ed. Polliack and Schlossberg 170).

Hosea 4:10

The author prefers the Arabic cognate זנו 'they whored' (8b:24) as rendition of הִזְנוּ instead of possible פגרו; the same root can be found in Cod. Hunt. 206 وينفجروا (ed. Schroeter 33:15), whereas prefers אטגו (ed. Birnbaum 64:21).

After rendering וְלֹא יִפְרֹצוּ with וליס יתסעו 'and they will not increase' (8b:24), the translator adds the explanatory note יעני יכתורו 'i.e. they multiply' (8b:25), which is identical with Yefet's rendering: יכתרון (ed. Birnbaum 64:21) and Cod. Hunt. 206: يكثروا (ed. Schroeter 33:15; ed. Polliack and Schlossberg 171). According to the author, the expectations of harlotry, i.e. fertility rites of the Baal cult which claim to result in multiplication of progeny, will have just the opposite effect. He emphasises his understanding by creating a different syntactical structure; he introduces the conjunction כמא 'just as' (8b:24) to indicate that their expectations to increase and multiply to the same extend as they whored, have not been fulfilled. Rashi interprets: לא יגדלו בנים ('they will not raise children'); Targum: לא יולדון בנין; Qimḥi: וכן שכבתם עם בנשים כיון שבזנות היא ולא ירבו כי לא יהיו להם מהן בנים ואם יהיו ימותו מן הבטן ('And also their sleeping with women as it happens in harlotry, they will not multiply, because they will not have children from them; and if they will have some, they will die from the womb').

As the infinitive לִשְׁמֹר *to keep* seems to lack a direct object in the biblical source text, some connect the verb with YHWH and suggest the meaning 'they have given up to keep YHWH'. In this sense, Ibn Ezra and Qimḥi supply objects for the verb *ad sensum*; Ibn Ezra: עזבו לשמר דרכו או תורתו ('they have given up to keep *His way and His Torah*'); Qimḥi: עזבו לשמר דרכיו כי שימם לפצים בו ובדרכיו שמר דרכיו עזבו ('they have given up to keep *His ways*; for they do not like Him and His ways; therefore they have given up to keep *His ways*'). Also Cod. Hunt. 206 apparently thinks of the people who have given up observing God's law when rendering لان [شريعة] الله تركوا من ان يحفظوا ('for they gave up to observe the law of God'. Schroeter 33:15–16), whereas Yefet slavishly translates the infinitive construct plus preposition with ללחפט 'to keep' (ed. Birnbaum 64:22; ed.

Polliack and Schlossberg 171 [where one manuscript reads מן אן יחפטו]). Saadiah (according to Qimḥi) provides an object by connecting the infinitive with the following verse Hosea 4:11: ורבי סעדיה ז"ל הדביקו עם הפסוק הבא אחריו ('Saadiah of blessed memory connects it with the following verse'), i.e. he interprets: they have left YHWH to keep harlotry etc. In this way, also modern commentators try to solve the problems of the text (e.g. Wolff 1965:87, 102; Rudolph). The translator prefers the first option ('they have forsaken the Lord'), but introduces a new aspect: instead of rendering the infinitive construct לִשְׁמֹר literally with ללחפט (see Yefet), he transforms the infinitive into the finite verb of a subordinate clause which is dependent on a relative clause with אלרב 'the Lord' as antecedent: אלדי וגב עליהם אן יחפטו 'the Lord whom they were obliged to keep' (8b:25); in other words, he does not only suggest a missing object, but also emphasises that 'keeping the Lord', i.e. 'retaining Him in one's memory and following Him', was a religious duty.

Hosea 4:11

By adding לאן 'for' at the beginning of the verse (8b:26; see Hosea 4:10), the translator emphasises that the trias of nouns *harlotry, wine, new wine* must not provide the missing object of Hosea 4:10, but has to be regarded as the collective subject of the verb יִקַּח. At the same time, he establishes a close connection between the two verses since he regards Hosea 4:11 as giving the reason for not keeping YHWH; since harlotry, wine and new wine take away the heart, there is place for YHWH because of their incompatibility.

יִקַּח is rendered here with יקבל 'it takes' (8b:26) instead of possible יאבד (Yefet, ed. Birnbaum 65:13; ed. Polliack and Schlossberg 171)/يأخذ (Cod. Hunt. 206, ed. Schroeter 33:17). The root לקח occurs in Hosea eight times: four times the translator renders it with the Arabic root אבד (Hosea 2:11; 10:6; 11:3; 14:3), whereas here and in Hosea 14:3 (ואקבל) he prefers the root קבל; in two instances, the translation is not preserved (Hosea 1:2, 3).

The translation אלקלב 'the heart' (8b:26), though with additional article, reflects the Hebrew לֵב, whereas Yefet changes the singular into a plural noun: קלובהם 'their hearts' (ed. Birnbaum 65:14) and Cod. Hunt. 206 chooses the different equivalent العقل 'the mind' (ed. Schroeter 33:17; ed. Polliack and Schlossberg 171 [which reads עקולהם])

Hosea 4:12

When rendering בְּעֵצוֹ, the translator changes the Hebrew preposition ב into מן, but he retains the noun: מן כשבה 'from his wood' (8b:27). The rendering خشب 'wood' can also be found in T-S Ar.1b.23 recto 1, whereas Yefet and Cod. Hunt. 206 who retain the preposition, prefer a more precise noun: בעודה (ed. Birnbaum 66:8; ed. Polliack and Schlossberg 172) and بعوده (ed. Schroeter 33:17) 'stick', 'rod'; see also LXX ἐν συμβόλοις ('in indications'). Philo calls the Asherot ῥάβδοι.

The reconstruction טגיאנאת 'impiety' (8b:27) is based on similar phrases in Hosea 2:6; 5:4; see Yefet: אלטגיאן (ed. Birnbaum 66:9; ed. Polliack and Schlossberg 172 [which reads אלאטגיאנאן]) and Cod. Hunt. 206: الزنا (ed. Schroeter 33:17).

Hosea 4:15

The missing noun after אלי הדה in the exegesis (11a:1) is probably אלמואצע 'the places' (11a:2); see also the similar phrase in Yefet: אלי הדה אלמואצע (ed. Birnbaum 70:5).

Hosea 4:17

The restored text of the exegesis קד צאר מולף ללעצבים 'he is attached to the idols' (11a:9) is based on the translation of the verse in Cod. Hunt. 206 وقد الف افرّم الاوثان (ed. Schroeter 34:9) and Yefet: מולף מע אלאותאן (ed. Birnbaum 71:11; ed. Polliack and Schlossberg 174).

Hosea 4:18

The restoration of אגלאהא 'her important people' in the exegesis (11a:19) is based on Yefet: אגלאהא (ed. Birnbaum 72:19; ed. Polliack and Schlossberg 175) and Cod. Hunt. 206: ءاجلا (ed. Schroeter 34:14) of Hebrew מָגִנֶּהָ.

Taking into consideration his grammatical explanation (11a:25–26), it can be assumed that the author regarded the verb הֵבוּ as perfect 'they gave', derived from 'the basic form', i.e. the imperative הַב; see also the phrase in the exegesis ואעטו 'they gave' (11a:18). Symmachus (ἠγάπησεν ἀγάπην) apparently interpreted הַב as an abbreviation of the first component of the *figura etymologica* אָהֹב אָהֲבוּ

to form a parallel phrase with the preceding הַזֹּנָה הַזֶּה. See Yefet: אעטו (ed. Birnbaum 72:18; ed. Polliack and Schlossberg 175).

Hosea 5:1

The translator specifies the vague direct object, which consists of the demonstrative pronoun singular feminine זאת only, by adding a noun: הדה אלנציחה 'this advice' (11a:26). Yefet chooses as means of specification the noun: הדה אלנבוה 'this prophecy' (ed. Birnbaum 74:13; ed. Polliack and Schlossberg 176 [one manuscript lacks this phrase]), whereas Cod. Hunt. 206, omitting the object, prefers the absolute imperative: اسمعوا يا أئمة 'hear, oh priests!' (ed. Schroeter 34:17).

The imperative וְהַקְשִׁיבוּ has been rendered with the equivalent ואצגו 'and listen!' (11a:27); see also Yefet: ואצגו (ed. Birnbaum 74:13; ed. Polliack and Schlossberg 176); Cod. Hunt. 206 translates both וְהַקְשִׁיבוּ and the following הַאֲזִינוּ with the same verb وأنصتوا (ed. Schroeter 34:17).

The translator renders the address וּבֵית הַמֶּלֶךְ with ויא אהל בית אלמלך 'and oh people of the house of the king' (11a:27); see also Yefet: ויא אל בית אלמלך (ed. Birnbaum 74:14; ed. Polliack and Schlossberg 176 [where one manuscript omits אלמלך]) and Cod. Hunt. 206: ويا اهل الملك ('and oh people of the king', ed. Schroeter 34:17).

The masculine noun הַמִּשְׁפָּט has been rendered with אלחוכם 'the judgement' (11a:27; Yefet has the defective orthography אלחכם, ed. Birnbaum 74:15; ed. Polliack and Schlossberg 176), as the author generally prefers the masculine noun to a feminine one. Cod. Hunt. 206, on the other hand, chooses the femininine abstract الحاكمة (ed. Schroeter 34:18).

The translator renders the noun פַּח with מקאם פך 'the place of a snare' (11a:28), whereas Yefet translates literally with פך (ed. Birnbaum 74:15; ed. Polliack and Schlossberg 176), Cod. Hunt. 206 creates a simile: كفخ (ed. Schroeter 34:18).

Instead of only repeating the names of the places Mizpah and Tabor, the translator paraphrases by referring to the geography of the two sites: אטואר מצפה 'the mountains of Mizpah' (11a:27) and גבל תבור 'the mount of Tabor' (11a:28–11b:1); see also Yefet: גבל תבור (ed. Birnbaum 74:16; ed. Polliack and Schlossberg 176), Cod. Hunt. 206: جبل تبور (ed. Schroeter 34:19), Symmachus (τὸ ὅριον 'the boundary'), Targum (טור רם 'high hill'). The translator emphasises the parallelism of the two toponyms and does not support an appellative interpretation of מִצְפָּה, as do LXX: τῇ σκοπιᾷ ('look-out', 'mountain-peak'), Vulgate: *speculationi*, Peshitta: ܕܘܩܐ ('look-out', 'observer'), Targum: למלפיכון ('to your

TEXTUAL NOTES 149

teacher'), Cod. Hunt. 206: مطلع ('look-out', ed. Schroeter 34:18), Yefet: אלשרף (ed. Birnbaum 74:15; ed. Polliack and Schlossberg 176).

The translator changes the biblical metaphor וְרֶשֶׁת פְּרוּשָׂה *and a net spread* into a simile by adding the preposition מתל: ומתל שבכה מבסוטה 'and *like* a net spread' (11a:28); see also Yefet: מתֹל שבכֹה מבסוטה (ed. Birnbaum 74:15–16; ed. Polliack and Schlossberg 176) and Cod. Hunt. 206: وكشبكة مبسوطة (ed. Schroeter 34:19).

The phrase in the exegesis אלטולם ואלתעדי 'the injustice and aggression' (11b:14) has been restored according to the similar phrase טולמהם ותעדיהם in 13a:15.

The reconstruction of the phrase טֹאהר מכשוף 'visible and open' (11b:17) is based on similar phrases in 13a:15; 15a:21; 22a:16.

Hosea 5:2

The translator renders וְשַׁחֲטָה with a definite noun ואלדבח 'and the slaughter' (11b:1); Yefet has the feminine noun ודביחה (ed. Birnbaum 77:9; ed. Polliack and Schlossberg 177), whereas Cod. Hunt. 206 interprets the word as a verb in imperfect 3rd person plural, as is evident from his translation يذبحون 'they slaughter' (ed. Schroeter 34:19).

The reconstruction of אלחאידין 'the deviants' (11b:1) as translation of שֵׂטִים is based on the author's phrase in his commentary האולי אלחאידין 'those who turn aside' (11b:25). His translation indicates that he derives שֵׂטִים from שׂוט/שׂטה 'to swerve', 'to fall away', 'to deviate'. See also the renderings of Yefet (אלחאידין, ed. Birnbaum 77:9; ed. Polliack and Schlossberg 177), Cod. Hunt. 206 (الحائدين, ed. Schroeter 34:19), T-S Ar.24.7 fol. 1 recto 1 (אלחאידין) and T-S Ar.28.174 recto 15–16 (אלחאידין). Also for Ibn Janāḥ the word denotes 'deviation'.

The literal translation of the verb הֶעְמִיקוּ with גמקו 'they deepened', 'they made deep' (11b:1) is in line with the author's general preference of Arabic cognate roots whenever possible; see also Yefet: גמקו (ed. Birnbaum 77:9; ed. Polliack and Schlossberg 177), whereas Cod. Hunt. 206 obviously reads בָּעֵמֶק and translates: فى العمق ('[the deviants bring offerings] in the valley', ed. Schroeter 34:19–20).

The conjecture ואנא אדב 'and I am a chastisement' (11b:1) is based on the author's phrase in his exegesis אנא איצא אכון אדב 'I am also a chastisement' (11b:23). This translation indicates that he regarded מוּסָר as an abstract noun, as do Yefet: ואנא אדב (ed. Birnbaum 77:9; ed. Polliack and Schlossberg 177) and Cod. Hunt. 206: وانا ادب (ed Schroeter 34:20), whereas LXX (παιδευτής) and Vulgate (*eruditor*) presuppose a *piʿel* participle מְיַסֵּר; see also Targum: ואנא מיתי

יסורין ('I am bringing discipline') and Peshitta: ܐܢܐ ܕܝܢ ܐܪܕܐ ('I will instruct/chastise them').

The Hebrew לְכֻלָּם has been rendered with מן גומלתהם, literally 'from their totality' (11b:2), instead of possible לכלהם (Yefet, ed. Birnbaum 77:9; ed. Polliack and Schlossberg 177); Cod. Hunt. 206 has the variant لجميعهم 'for them all' (ed. Schroeter 34:20).

The phrase פקיל אנה ראגע אלי 'some interpret that it refers to' in the exegesis (11a:18) has been restored according to the similar phrase in 11b:24 (וקיל אן ושחטה שטים ראגע אלי אלכהנים).

Hosea 5:3

The translator appears to have changed the statement *and Israel is not hidden from Me* of the biblical text into a direct address, since before 'Israel' he added the vocative particle אי (11b:3). Consequently, the rendition of the 3rd singular masculine verb לֹא נִכְחַד *he was not hidden* should be expected to be changed into מא אנכתמת (2nd singular masculine) instead of לם ינכתם (Yefet, ed. Birnbaum 78:4–5), لم ينكتم (Cod. Hunt. 206, ed. Schroeter 34:21; ed. Polliack and Schlossberg 177) and פמא אנכתם (T-S Ar.28.174 verso 3).

The author usually renders the negated perfect with מא + perfect instead of possible לם + apocopate; see Hosea 2:10 (לֹא יָדְעָה—פמא ערפת) vs. Yefet: פלם תעלם (ed. Birnbaum 30:10; ed. Polliack and Schlossberg 153) and Cod. Hunt. 206 لم تعل (ed. Schroeter 31:13); Hosea 5:4 (לֹא יָדְעוּ—פמא ערפו), also Yefet (ed. Birnbaum 78:20) and Cod. Hunt. 206: وما عرفوا (ed. Schroeter 35:1; ed. Polliack and Schlossberg 178); Hosea 9:17 (לֹא שָׁמְעוּ—מא סמיעו) also and Cod. Hunt. 206: اذ ما قبلوا (ed. Schroeter 41:13) vs. Yefet אד לם יקבלו (ed. Birnbaum 149:15; ed. Polliack and Schlossberg 213); translation incomplete or missing: Hosea 7:9; 8:13.

The reconstruction קד תנגס אל אסראיל 'the people of Israel have become unclean' (11b:3) is based on the almost identical phrase פתנגס אל אסראיל as translation of Hosea 6:10 (נִטְמָא יִשְׂרָאֵל); T-S Ar.28.174 verso 3 has ונגס; see also Yefet: נגס ישראל (ed. Birnbaum 78:5–6; ed. Polliack and Schlossberg 177) and Cod. Hunt. 206: وتنجّس اسرائل (ed. Schroeter 34:21).

The translator adds איצא 'also', 'too' before 'the people of Israel have been defiled' (11b:3), presumably in order to achieve a closer parallelism to the preceding *Ephraim has committed adultery* and to include Israel explicitly in the sinful actions.

Hosea 5:4

The translation of יִתְּנוּ 'they give' with יתרוכו 'they let be, leave, relinquish, give up' is distinguished from Yefet: יגעלו (ed. Birnbaum 78:19; ed. Polliack and Schlossberg 178) and Cod. Hunt. 206: يجعلوا (ed. Schroeter 34:22): 'they make, put'. See the versions, LXX: οὐκ ἔδωκαν τὰ διαβούλια αὐτῶν τοῦ ἐπιστρέψαι, Vulgate: *non dabunt cogitationes suas ut reverantur* ('they do not dispose their counsels/thoughts that they should return'), Peshitta: ܠܐ ܥܒܕܝܗܘܢ ܫܒܩܝܢ ܠܗܘܢ ܕܢܬܘܒܘܢ ('their deeds do not permit that they turn'), Targum (לא שבקין עובדיהון למתת).

רוח 'spirit' (11b:4) as translation of רוּחַ has been restored according to the translation of Hosea 4:12: ריח טגיאנאת (8b:27) vs. Yefet: עזם (ed. Birnbaum 78:20; ed. Polliack and Schlossberg 178)/Cod. Hunt. 206: عزم (ed. Schroeter 34:22).

בְּקִרְבָּם has been rendered with פי אחשאהם 'in their midst' (11b:5), whereas Cod. Hunt. 206 and Yefet translate with فى نفوسهم (ed. Schroeter 34:22–35:1)/פי נפוסהם (ed. Birnbaum 78:20; ed. Polliack and Schlossberg 178).

The reconstruction ערפו 'they knew' (11b:5) as rendition of יָדְעוּ is likely since the root ידע which occurs 15 times in Hosea, is rendered preferably with the root ערף (Hosea 2:10, 22; 5:3, 9; 6:3; 8:2; 11:3; 13:4, 5), only 4 times with the root עלם (Hosea 6:3; 7:9; 8:3; 9:7); text missing: Hosea 7:9. See also Yefet (ערפו, ed. Birnbaum 78:20; ed. Polliack and Schlossberg 178), Cod. Hunt. 206 (عرفوا, ed. Schroeter 35:1), T-S Ar.28.174 verso 6 (ערפו).

Hosea 5:5

The translation of וְעָנָה with פסא ישהד 'and he will testify (against)' (11b:5) uses the same root as Cod. Hunt. 206: فيشهد (ed. Schroeter 35:1). Yefet chooses: ויגיב 'and he answers', but adds also the other option: ויקאל וישהד (ed. Birnbaum 79:10 ed. Polliack and Schlossberg 178); see also Vulgate: *respondebit* 'he will answer/testify'. Whereas all these translations derive the verb from ענה I 'to respond', 'to answer', 'to testify' (BDB 772–773), rabbinic commentators like Rashi, Ibn Ezra, Qimḥi, think of ענה III 'to be bowed down', 'to be afflicted' (BDB 776); see also LXX: καὶ ταπεινωθήσεται; Peshitta: ܢܬܡܟܟ; Targum: וימאך ('he will be abased').

איקתדאר 'strength' (11b:5) as rendition of גְּאוֹן has been restored according to the identical phrase in Hosea 7:10, where the translator has chosen the same term; see also Yefet: אקתדאר (ed. Birnbaum 79:10; ed. Polliack and Schlossberg 178) and Cod. Hunt. 206: اقتدار (ed. Schroeter 35:1). A similar translation of גְּאוֹן provide Peshitta (ܐܘܚܕܢܐ) and Targum (יקר), whereas LXX/Symmachus interpret the pride in a pejorative sense as ἡ ὕβρις, also: Aquila/Theodotion: ἡ ὑπερ-φανία and Vulgate: *arrogantia*.

The reconstruction פי וגהה 'before' is based on the translator's rendering of פְּנֵי in Hosea 2:4; 7:2; 10:7; see also Yefet (פי וגהה, ed. Birnbaum 79:11; ed. Polliack and Schlossberg 178), Cod. Hunt. 206 (فى وجهه, ed. Schroeter 35:1–2) and T-S Ar.28.174 verso 7 (פי וגהה).

The reconstruction ואל ישראל ואל אפרים 'and the people of Israel and the people of Ephraim' (11b:6) is based on the author's usual rendering; see also T-S Ar.28.174 verso 7 (ואל ישראל ואל אפרים) vs. Yefet: וישראל ואפרים (ed. Birnbaum 79:11; ed. Polliack and Schlossberg 178)/Cod. Hunt. 206: اسرائل وافرٌم (ed. Schroeter 35:2).

The reconstruction of איצא 'also' (11b:7) as rendition of גַּם is based on the author's usual rendering (Hosea 3:3; 4:3, 5, 6; 6:11; 7:9; 8:10; 9:12; 9:16; 10:6; 12:12); see also T-S Ar.28.174 verso 8: איצא, Yefet: איצא (ed. Birnbaum 79:12; ed. Polliack and Schlossberg 178), Cod. Hunt. 206: ايضا (ed. Schroeter 35:2).

Hosea 5:6

The reconstruction יסלוכו 'they will go' (11b:8) as rendition of יֵלְכוּ is based on the author's translations in Hosea 7:12; 11:10; 14:7, 10; another option is represented by Yefet: יסירו (ed. Birnbaum 82:2; ed. Polliack and Schlossberg 179), T-S Ar.28.174 verso 9 and Cod. Hunt. 206: يسيروا (ed. Schroeter 35:3).

The restoration לטלב 'to seek' (11b:8) as rendition of לְבַקֵּשׁ is based on the author's usual translation of the Hebrew root (Hosea 2:9; 3:5; 7:10); see also T-S Ar.28.174 verso 10: לטלב, Yefet: לטלב (ed. Birnbaum 82:2; ed. Polliack and Schlossberg 179)/Cod. Hunt. 206: لطلب (ed. Schroeter 35:3).

לא יגדו 'they will not find' (11b:8) has been restored according to author's usual rendering of the root מצא with וגד; see also Cod. Hunt. 206: ولا يجدوا (ed. Schroeter 3:3), whereas Yefet adds a suffix pronoun: ולא יגדוה (ed. Birnbaum 82:3; ed. Polliack and Schlossberg 179).

The restoration לאנה 'for he' (11b:8) is tentative, though probable, because of the author's preference to link phrases of this kind by introducing a causal conjunction.

חָלַץ מֵהֶם has been rendered with כלע מנהם 'He has withdrawn Himself from them' (11b:8). The same verb can be found in Yefet: כלע (ed. Birnbaum 82:3; ed. Polliack and Schlossberg 179)/Cod. Hunt. 206: خلع (ed. Schroeter 35:4); see also LXX: ἐξέκλινεν ('he has turned away'), Vulgate: *ablatus est*; Peshitta: ܗܦܟ ('he has departed'). Ibn Barhūn (Wechter 85) refers to the Arabic cognate خلص 'to be free', 'to be liberated from', 'to be rid of'.

TEXTUAL NOTES 153

Hosea 5:7

The translator renders בֵּיהוָה בָּגָדוּ literally with באלרב קד גדרו (11b:8–9), whereas Cod. Hunt. 206 renders with بعهد الله غدروا (ed. Schroeter 35:4).

The reconstruction בנין 'sons' (11b:9) as rendition of בָּנִים is more likely than possible אולאד (see Yefet: אולאד, ed. Birnbaum 82:23 and Cod. Hunt. 206: واولاد, ed. Schroeter 35:4; ed. Polliack and Schlossberg 179), since this is the author's usual translation (see Hosea 10:14; 11:10; translation missing: 2:6; 4:6; 9:12, 13; 11:1; 13:13), if he does not prefer אל (Hosea 2:1, 2; 3:1, 4, 5; 4:1; translation missing: 2:6) or דיי (Hosea 10:9).

The reconstruction of גרבא 'foreign' (11b:9) as rendition of זָרִים is based on the author's translation of Hosea 8:7 (אלגרבא) and Hosea 8:12 (אלגריב for the singular זָר) instead of possible אגנביין 'foreign'; see Yefet: אגנביין (ed. Birnbaum 82:23; ed. Polliack and Schlossberg 179), Cod. Hunt. 206: اجنبيين (ed. Schroeter 35:5) and with article T-S Ar.28.174 verso 14: אלאגנביין.

The addition of the conjunction פלדלך 'and therefore' (11b:9) before *now the new moon will eat them* demonstrates that the translator understood this sentence as the consequent punishment for the actions mentioned before; similar also Cod. Hunt. 206: لذلك (ed. Schroeter 35:5).

The reconstruction of אלסאעה 'now' (11b:9) reflects the translator's usual rendering of עַתָּה (see on Hosea 2:9).

The rendition of יֹאכְלֵם with יפניהם 'he will devour them' (11b:9) instead with the Arabic cognate (see Yefet: יאכלהם, ed. Birnbaum 83:1; ed. Polliack and Schlossberg 179), Cod. Hunt. 206: يأكلهم, ed. Schroeter 35:5 is also attested in an explicatory note in T-S Ar.28.174 verso 15–16: אלאן יאכלהם יעני יפניהם.

The reconstruction אנצבתהם 'their shares' (11b:10) is based on the term in the author's exegesis באנצבה (12a:24) vs. Yefet: גלאת ציאעהם (ed. Birnbaum 83:1; ed. Polliack and Schlossberg 179)/Cod. Hunt. 206: غلات ضياعهم (ed. Schroeter 35:6).

The author regards the noun 'a month' as the subject of the sentence in accordance with the biblical text: יְפָנִיהֶם שָׁהֵר 'a month will devour them' (11b:9–10), whereas Cod. Hunt. 206 introduces a new subject: لذلك يأكلهم العدو ('therefore the enemy will eat them') and transforms 'a month' into a temporal sequence: فى كل رأس شهر 'on every New Month' (ed. Schroeter 35:5); similar Yefet: שהר ראס כל פי אלעדו יאכלהם אלאן (ed. Birnbaum 83:1; ed. Polliack and Schlossberg 179). The translation ἡ ἐρυσίβη 'the locust' (LXX) suggests החסיל.

Hosea 5:8

Usually in Judaeo-Arabic Bible translations, both Hebrew terms שׁוֹפָר and חֲצֹצְרָה are rendered with the same Arabic noun بوق 'trumpet'; see e.g. Saadiah's translation of שׁוֹפָר (Exodus 19:16, 19; 20:18; Leviticus 25:9 [2×]; Isaiah 18:3; 27:13; 58:1) and חֲצֹצְרָה (Numbers 10:2, 8, 9, 10; 31:6). When being challenged by the hendiadys, the author translated שׁוֹפָר with בוק as in Hosea 8:1; for חֲצֹצְרָה, however, he chose the onomatopoeic צפארה 'whistle', 'siren' with some phonological resemblance to שׁוֹפָר. Yefet and Cod. Hunt. 206 render שׁוֹפָר with אלסאפור/السافور and חֲצֹצְרָה with אלבוק/البوق respectively (ed. Schroeter 35:6/ed. Birnbaum 83:15; ed. Polliack and Schlossberg 180), in both cases adding the article, whereas the translator retains the indefiniteness of the noun as found in the Hebrew source text.

By adding ואיצא 'and also' before 'the siren' (12a:24), the author apparently understood the two nouns as names of two different musical instruments. This corresponds with his usual interpretation of the parallelism of members as referring to two distinct actions, events, commodities etc. rather than a characteristic of poetic style

Ramah is understood as a proper place name; see also Yefet's explanation: מדינה אלרמה אלתי הי פי בלדד (ed. Birnbaum 83:20), whereas LXX takes it as an appellative: ἐπὶ τῶν ὑψηλῶν ('upon the heights').

The translator adds the preposition פי 'in' before בית און (12a:25) to interpret the biblical local accusative (see GK §118g).

The translator explains the difficult short phrase אַחֲרֶיךָ בִּנְיָמִין, which is confirmed by Aquila, Symmachus and Theodotion (ὀπίσω μου), Peshitta (ܒܬܪܟ) and Vulgate (*post tergum tuum*), by using various additions: (1) he connects the phrase with the preceding sentence by adding the conjunction לאן 'for' (12a:25); (2) he introduces the vocative יא אפרים in order to indicate that the phrase has to be addressed to Ephraim presumably because of the masculine suffix pronoun of אַחֲרֶיךָ which cannot refer to the usually feminine town Beth-Awen (12a:25); (3) he adds the verb ינגלי and regards 'Benjamin' as the subject of the sentence: 'Benjamin will be exiled' (12a:26). See Cod. Hunt. 206: تبعك يا بنيمين (ed. Schroeter 35:7).

Hosea 5:9

The author interprets אֶפְרַיִם at the beginning of the verse as vocative, as indicated by the additional vocative particle יא (12a:26), and the verb תִּהְיֶה is understood as 2nd masculine singular (תציר) instead of possible 3rd feminine sin-

TEXTUAL NOTES

gular. In his view, the verse has to be regarded as a direct address to Ephraim which continues the direct speech of Hosea 5:8, rather than being a prophecy about Ephraim, i.e. 'Ephraim, you will be' rather than 'Ephraim will be'.

תּוֹכֵחָה is rendered with תוביכה 'rebuke' (12a:26). The feminine noun imitates the Hebrew תּוֹכֵחָה, whereas Yefet and Cod. Hunt. 206 prefer the masculine equivalent אלתוביך (ed. Birnbaum 84:11; ed. Polliack and Schlossberg 180) and التوبيخ respectively (ed. Schroeter 35:8).

The translator adopts the asyndetic syntax of the Hebrew source text, when rendering בְּשִׁבְטֵי with פי אסבאט 'among the tribes' (12a:27); see also Yefet: פי אסבאט (ed. Birnbaum 84:11–12; ed. Polliack and Schlossberg 180), whereas Cod. Hunt. 206 adds the connective conjunction و 'and': وفى اسباط (ed. Schroeter 35:8).

The translator prefers a literal rendition of the nifʿal participle נֶאֱמָנָה by using the participle תאבתה 'confirmed', 'what is sure', 'established' (12a:27), whereas the versions refer to 'sure things' (LXX: ἔδειξα πιστά) or 'the truth' (Peshitta: ܫܪܝܪܬܐ; Vulgate: fidem), also Cod. Hunt. 206: الامانة 'the reliability', 'the faithfulness' (ed. Schroeter 35:8); Yefet: אלותיקה 'the firm', 'the reliable' (ed. Birnbaum 84:12; ed. Polliack and Schlossberg 180); Targum: אוריתא 'the Law'.

The reconstruction of the text of the exegesis אלזמאן אלדי תחל בה אלתוכיחות 'the time when the rebukes will take place' (13a:8) is based on Yefet (ed. Birnbaum 84:18–19).

The reconstruction of the text of the exegesis עלי יד משה 'through Moses' (13a:13) is also based on Yefet's commentary: קד ערפתי עלי יד משה הדה אלתוכחה אלנאמנה (ed. Birnbaum 85:1–2; cf. ed. Polliack and Schlossberg 180).

Hosea 5:10

כְּמַסִּיגֵי גְּבוּל 'like those who remove a boundary' (from סוג hi.) is rendered with כמולחקי אלתכם 'like those who attach the boundary' (12b:1). The same root لحق IV 'to attach', 'to affix', 'to join' can be found in the vocabulary list T-S AS 141:47 recto line 3 where מַסִּיג (Deuteronomy 27:17) is rendered with מלחק. Yefet and Cod. Hunt. 206 translate the phrase with כמזיגי אלתכם/ (ed. Birnbaum 85:9; ed. Polliack and Schlossberg 180)/كمزيغى التخم 'like those who deviate the boundary' (ed. Schroeter 35:9).

אלתכם 'the boundary' (12b:1) as translation of גְּבוּל could be restored from the visible sublinear vocalization signs and the phrase in the exegesis: במולחקי אלתכום (13a:14–15).

The reconstruction אספוך 'I will pour out' (12b:1) for אֶשְׁפּוֹךְ is tentative, though it can refer to Yefet: אספך (ed. Birnbaum 85:10; ed. Polliack and Schlossberg 180) and Cod. Hunt. 206: اسفك (ed. Schroeter 35:9). However, this rendering seems to be more likely than possible ואצב, since the author generally prefers Arabic cognates.

The reconstruction כאלמא 'like the water' (12b:1) as rendering of כַּמַּיִם is likely; see Yefet: מתֹל אלמא (ed. Birnbaum 85:10; ed. Polliack and Schlossberg 180) and Cod. Hunt. 206: كالء (ed. Schroeter 35:9).

The reconstruction of חלטתי 'my anger' (12b:1) as translation of עֶבְרָתִי is based on the author's rendition of Hosea 13:12 (בְּעֶבְרָתִי for בחלטתי) where he also uses a feminine form of حلط 'anger', obviously to imitate the Hebrew feminine noun; Cod. Hunt. 206 has the Arabic cognate: عبرتي (ed. Schroeter 35:9), whereas Yefet has: חלטתי (ed. Birnbaum 85:10; ed. Polliack and Schlossberg 180). However, in his exegesis the author uses the synonym אלסכט (13a:16) which occurs also other contexts of his work (5b:24; 17b:2).

Hosea 5:11

The restoration of מְרצוּץ 'crushed' (12b:2) as rendering of רְצוּץ is based on Yefet: מרצוץ (ed. Birnbaum 86:2; ed. Polliack and Schlossberg 181) and Cod. Hunt. 206: ومرضوض (ed. Schroeter 35:10); see also Saadiah's translation of the word in Isaiah 42:2: חתי קצבה מרצוצה לא יכסרהא (Derenbourg III, p. 63). Instead of 'crushed (is) judgement' some versions interpret 'crushed *by* judgement'; Vulgate: *fractus iudicio* ('broken by judgement'), Peshitta: ܘܐܠܝܨ ܒܕܝܢܐ ('crushed by judgement') and Targum: כבישין בדינהון ('oppressed by their judgements').

The author added presumably a noun before 'Ephraim' in order to indicate that not Ephraim itself is oppressed. The first and last letter ח/ל suggest a restoration חמל 'carrying', 'foetus', חפל 'gathering', חקל 'field'. Also LXX understand the passive participle in an active sense and add the noun τὸν ἀντίδικον ('the opponent') at this place, parallel to the following מִשְׁפָּט (κρίμα).

The restoration of אמען 'he devoted all his efforts' (12b:3) is based on Saadiah's rendering of הוֹאִיל in Deuteronomy 1:5 (see Derenbourg I, p. 252; see also Genesis 18:27; 31; Exodus 2:21), whereas Yefet and Cod. Hunt. 206 render with גהל (ed. Birnbaum 86:3; ed. Polliack and Schlossberg 181)/ جهل (ed. Schroeter 35:10); see Saadiah's rendering of Numbers 12:11 [גהלנא] and Isaiah 19:13 [גהלו]. The translator imitates the asyndetic syntax of the complementary and the finite verb הוֹאִיל הָלַךְ by rendering אמען סלך 'he willingly went' (12b:3).

The reconstructed וציה 'commandment' (12b:3) is based on the phrase in the exegesis וצאיא אלאנביא (13a:18–19), where the plural noun occurs.

The restoration of the *lacuna* after וציה אלאנביא 'the commandment of the prophets' (12b:3) is uncertain, though an attribute, such as 'false', 'wicked', referring to the prophets, can be expected.

The translation of צָו is problematic:

(1) The translator renders the noun צָו probably with וציה 'direction', 'instruction', 'command', 'order' (12b:3), as do Yefet: אלוֹצִיהֿ (ed. Birnbaum 86:3; ed. Polliack and Schlossberg 181 [one manuscript adds צו יריד בה מצות אל]) and Cod. Hunt. 206: الوصية (ed. Schroeter 35:11), i.e. the noun is to be derived from the root צוה 'to command'. Also Rashi and Ibn Ezra interpret it in the sense of מצות 'commandments' given by other people; see Rashi: ולמה לו כל זאת כירצה והלך אחרי ציואות חדשות של נביאי הבעל ('And why does all this happen to him? Because he agreed to walk behind the new commandments of the prophets of Baal'); Ibn Ezra: כי הואיל שהלך אחרי מצות אנשים ('Because he liked to walk behind the commandments of people'). The sense would be: Ephraim was foolish in that he permitted himself to be guided by human commands rather than God's commandments. Qimḥi takes the noun צָו as an abbreviated form of מצוה, indicating a pejorative sense, i.e. a false commandment. A positive meaning of the word is indicated in Cod. Hunt. 206 where after the translation of Hosea 5:11, an explanatory note has been added: צו (יריד به מצות אל 'צו' refers to "the commandment(s) of God"'), though his gloss surprisingly contradicts his immediately preceeding translation.

(2) In BT Sanhedrin 56b צָו is interpreted as denoting idolatry, which points to a reading שָׁוְא 'vanity'. This interpretation is in line with LXX: ὀπίσω τῶν ματαίων ('after vanities'); Targum: בתר ממון דשקר ('after deceitful money') and Peshitta: ܒܬܪ ܣܪܝܩܘܬܐ ('vanity', 'idols').

(3) Vulgate: *post sordem* ('after filth') obviously identifies צָו with צֹאָה (Isaiah 28:8); see also Jerome, Osee II v 306f. (Sordes) who interprets it as *idola quae sordibus comparantur*.

The translator seems to understand the 'command' also in a negative sense, as is indicated by his exegesis (13a:18).

Hosea 5:12

The translation is only sporadically preserved. The restoration ואנא 'and I' (12b:3) for וַאֲנִי seems to be most likely.

The translator renders כָּעָשׁ with כאלעות 'like the moth' (12b:4) see also Targum: כעשא ('like the moth'); Yefet: מתֿל אלעתֿ (ed. Birnbaum 86:19; ed. Polliack and Schlossberg 181); Cod. Hunt. 206: كعث (ed. Schroeter 35:13) rather than deriving the noun from עשׁ II; Aquila: βρωστήρ; Symmachus: εὑρώς ('decay'); LXX: ὡς ταραχή ('like disturbance', 'uprising'); Peshitta: ܐܝܟ ܕܠܚܐ ('like trouble'); Vulgate: tinea;

The rendering of וְכָרָקָב cannot be restored since in his exegesis the author has retained the Hebrew noun אלרקב (13a:21) instead of an Arabic equivalent. Possible renderings are וכאלנכר (see Yefet: מתל אלנכר, ed. Birnbaum 86:19; ed. Polliack and Schlossberg 181 [one manuscript reads ובאל]) or וכאלעפן (according to Cod. Hunt. 206: وكالعفن, ed. Schroeter 35:13); see also Saadiah's translation of Proverbs 12:4: וכאלעפן (ed. Derenbourg VI, p. 67), Proverbs 14:30: סוס (ed. Derenbourg VI, p. 77). LXX: ὡς κέντρον ('like a sting, goad'); Peshitta: ܐܝܟ ܢܐ ('elephantiasis', 'leprosy'); Vulgate: putredo; Aquila/Symmachus: σῆψις ('rottenness', 'decay'); Targum: רקבא.

Hosea 5:13

The reconstruction וראי 'and he saw' (12b:4) as rendition of וַיַּרְא is based on the translation of Hosea 9:10, 13; vs. Yefet: ונטר (ed. Birnbaum 87:11; ed. Polliack and Schlossberg 181) and Cod. Hunt. 206: فنظر (ed. Schroeter 35:13).

The translator supplies the subject 'Judah' before 'he sent' ad sensum (also Rashi, Ibn Ezra, Qimḥi, Yefet, ed. Birnbaum 87:13; ed. Polliack and Schlossberg 181).

There are various interpretations of מֶלֶךְ יָרֵב:

(1) Some versions interpret יָרֵב as qualitative of the king and derive it from the verb ריב 'to contend'; Targum: ושלחו למלכא דייתי לאתפרע להון ('they sent to the king that he should come to take vengeance for them'), Symmachus: ἔνδικον, ἐνδίκηθεν, Theodotion: κρίτην; Jerome (referring to Judges 6:32), Aquila: δικασόμενον ('contending', 'judging'), Symmachus: φωνέα ('murderer'), Vulgate: ultorem ('avenger'), Targum: דייתי לאתפרעא להון ('who should come to take vengeance for them'), Cod. Hunt. 206: الى ملك يخاصم عنه ('to a king who will bring legal action against him', ed. Schroeter 35:13–14), Yefet: אלי מלך יכאצם ענה (ed. Birnbaum 87:13; ed. Polliack and Schlossberg 181). In his exegesis, the author mentions the interpretation מלך יכאצם ענהם 'a king who brings legal action against them' as second option (13a:25).

(2) As the name of an Egyptian king only Theodoret: ὅτι δὲ τὸν βασιλέα Ἰαρεὶβ τὸν Αἰγύπτου καλεῖ βασιλέα, ἐκ τὸν μετὰ ταῦτα ῥάδιον μαθεῖν, ἐγένετο γὰρ Ἐφραὶμ ὡς περιστερὰ ἄνους οὐκ ἔχουσα καρδίαν Αἴγυπτον ἐπεκαλεῖτο καὶ εἰς Ἀσσυρίους ἐπωρεύετο.

(3) Peshitta understands Yareb as a toponym: ܡܠܟܐ ܕܝܪܒ ('king of Yareb'). Also Ibn Ezra states that Yareb is the place name, but according to him, it refers to an Assyrian city: ירב שם מקום באשור ('Yareb is the name of a place in Assur'); see also Qimḥi: הוא שם עיר בארץ אשור ('it is the name of a city in the land of Assur').

(4) The author regards Yareb as an alternative name for Egypt.

(5) Modern exegetes understand the phrase מֶלֶךְ יָרֵב as northern Hebrew rendering of *šarru rabū*, the title of the king of Assur.

The reconstruction of והו פליס יטיק 'and he is unable' (12b:6) as translation for לֹא יוּכַל instead of possible והו פליס יקדר is based on the rendition of וְהוּא לֹא יוּכְלוּ with ליס יטיקו in Hosea 8:5; vs. Yefet: והו פליס יקדר (ed. Birnbaum 87:13; ed. Polliack and Schlossberg 181) and Cod. Hunt. 206: وهو فليس يقدر (ed. Schroeter 35:15).

The reconstruction ישפיכם 'he will heal you' (12b:6) as rendition of לִרְפֹּא לָהֶם is based on the author's rendition of the root רפא with the root שפי in Hosea 6:1; 7:1; 11:3; 14:5; see Cod. Hunt. 206: يشفيک (ed. Schroeter 35:15).

The rendition יוברי 'he will free' (12b:7) for the *hapax legomenon* יִגְהֶה the derived noun only occurs in Proverbs 17:22 has been reconstructed according to the translations of Yefet: יברי (ed. Birnbaum 87:14; ed. Polliack and Schlossberg 181) and Cod. Hunt 206: يبری (ed. Schroeter 35:15).

After מדר 'rottenness' which is the rendering of מָזוֹר, an explanatory note has been added: יעני גורח 'i.e. a wound' (12b:7), in order to clarify the preceding noun מדר. The author repeats this explanation in his grammatical notes (13b:4).

When explaining יִגְהֶה 'he will heal', the author quotes several options for its derivation:

(1) כהה 'to be dim', 'to grow faint' (BDB 462); (2) גהה 'to depart, i.e. to be cured, healed' (BDB 155), quoting Proverbs 17:22; see also Yefet (ed. Birnbaum 87:23–88:1; cf. ed. Polliack and Schlossberg 181); (3) נגה 'to shine' (BDB 618).

Hosea 5:14

The restored text לאן אנא 'For I am' (12b:7) is most likely; see also Yefet: לאן אנא (ed. Birnbaum 88:3; ed. Polliack and Schlossberg 181); Cod. Hunt. 206: لأن انا (ed. Schroeter 35:15).

For the restored names of the animals כאלשבל 'like the lion cub' (12b:7) and וכאלצרגאם 'and like a lion' (12b:8) see Yefet: מתל אלשחל/ומתל אלצרגאם (ed. Birnbaum 88:3; ed. Polliack and Schlossberg 181) and Cod. Hunt. 206: مثل الشحل/ومثل الضرغام (ed. Schroeter 35:16).

The restored אפתרס 'I will tear' (12b:8) for אֶטְרֹף is based on Yefet: אפתרס (ed. Birnbaum 88:4; ed. Polliack and Schlossberg 181) and Cod. Hunt. 206: افترس (ed. Schroeter 35:16).

The restoration of ואסלוך 'and I will go' (12b:8) for וְאֵלֵךְ is based on the frequency of this rendition in the author's translation vs. Yefet: ואמצי (ed. Birnbaum 88:4; ed. Polliack and Schlossberg 181) and Cod. Hunt. 206: وامضي (ed. Schroeter 35:17).

אחמל 'I will carry' (12b:9) as rendition of אֶשָּׂא is likely; see also Yefet: אחמל (ed. Birnbaum 88:5; ed. Polliack and Schlossberg 181).

The reconstruction וליס מוכלץ 'and there is no deliverer' (12b:9) is based on the usual rendition of אֵין with ליס (see Hosea 3:4; 4:1; 7:11; 8:7, 8; 10:3; 13:4; translation missing: 7:7) and the translation of the root נצל with the root خلص in Hosea 2:11; see also Cod. Hunt. 206 (وليس مخلص, ed. Schroeter 35:17), whereas Yefet renders with וליס מנגי (ed. Birnbaum 88:5; ed. Polliack and Schlossberg 181).

The restoration of the missing part of the opening formula תום אורא אלסבב) פי דלך) 'then he showed (the reason for that)' (13b:4–5) in the text of the exegesis has been suggested because of the identical phrase in 17b:9 (see also 13a:17–18: תום אורא אלסבב).

Hosea 5:15

The reconstruction of אסלוך 'and I will go' (12b:9) for אֵלֵךְ is based on the statistics (see Hosea 5:14), whereas Yefet and Cod. Hunt. 206 render אמצי (ed. Birnbaum 89:1; ed. Polliack and Schlossberg 182)/ امضي (ed. Schroeter 35:17).

The reconstucted rendering ארגע 'I will return' (12b:9) for אָשׁוּבָה is likely, since this is the author's usual rendering of the Hebrew root; see also Yefet: ארגע (ed. Birnbaum 89:1; ed. Polliack and Schlossberg 182); Cod. Hunt. 206: ارجع (ed. Schroeter 35:17).

The reconstruction of מוצעי 'my place' (12b:9) for מְקוֹמִי is based on the translation of Hosea 2:1; see also Yefet: מוצעי (ed. Birnbaum 89:1; ed. Polliack and Schlossberg 182), whereas Cod. Hunt. 206 has the noun مكاني (ed. Schroeter 35:17).

The reconstruction of אלי אן 'until' (12b:9) for עַד אֲשֶׁר reflects the author's tendency for a literal translation, whereas Yefet and Cod. Hunt. 206 have אלי וקת (ed. Birnbaum 89:1; ed. Polliack and Schlossberg 182)/ والى وقت (ed. Schroeter 35:17–18).

The rendering of יֶאְשָׁמוּ with ינדמו 'they will repent', i.e. 'they acknowledge their guilt' (12b:9), can be found in a similar way in Aquila/Theodotion: πλημμελήσωσι; Symmachus: πλημμελοῦντες; Peshitta: ܢܣܟܠܘܢ; Targum: ידעון רחבו ('to be guilty'). See also Yefet: ינדמון (ed. Birnbaum 89:1; ed. Polliack and Schlossberg 182) and Cod. Hunt. 206: يدمون (ed. Schroeter 35:18).

By rendering וּבִקְשׁוּ פָנָי with פיטלובו רחמתי 'and they will seek My mercy' (12b:9–10), the author obviously intends to eliminate the anthropomorphism; see also Targum: ויתבעון דחלתי ('they will seek the fear of Me'), Yefet: ויתגון נצרתי ('and they will seek My help', ed. Birnbaum 89:1–2; ed. Polliack and Schlossberg 182) and Cod. Hunt. 206: ويطلبون نصرتى (ed. Schroeter 35:18).

The completion of [רחמ]תי 'My mercy' (12b:10) for פָּנָי 'My face' has taken into consideration the translation of Cod. Hunt. 206: نصرتى 'My help' (ed. Schroeter 35:18) and Yefet: נצרתי (ed. Birnbaum 89:2; ed. Polliack and Schlossberg 182), as well as Yefet's explanatory note: וקיל וקארי (ed. Birnbaum 89:2; cf. ed. Polliack and Schlossberg 182–183).

The reconstruction of פי אלציק 'in the distress' (12b:10) for בַּצַּר reflects the author's tendency of a literal translation; see also Yefet: ענד אלצִיק (ed. Birnbaum 89:2; ed. Polliack and Schlossberg 182), whereas Cod. Hund. 206 renders the phrase with a subordinate clause واذا ضاقت 'when it became uneasy' (ed. Schroeter 35:18).

The reconstruction of ידאלגוני 'they will set out to me at dawn' (12b:10) for יְשַׁחֲרֻנְנִי reflects the author's rendition of the Hebrew root שכם in Hosea 6:4; 13:3, i.e. the author understands the verb as a denominative of שחר 'dawn'. In Hava only دلج IV 'to set out at night-fall', 'to begin a journey before daybreak' is attested (Hava p. 213; see Wehr p. 290). The translator, however, introduces دلج III with a transitive meaning (see Birnbaum xxxiv). See also Yefet: ידאלגוני (ed. Birnbaum 89:2; ed. Polliack and Schlossberg 182) and Cod. Hunt. 206: يدلّجون الى (ed. Schroeter 35:18–19). The sense seems to be: 'they set out to God like the dawn'; see also the versions: LXX: ὀρθριοῦσι πρός με ('they rise early to me'), Vulgate: *mane consurgunt ad me* ('they rise up early [and come] to me'), Peshitta: ܢܩܕܡܘܢ. Ibn Ezra interprets 'setting out at dawn' as 'eagerly'. For the verb שחר with God as object see Psalms 63:2; 78:34; Isaiah 26:9.

Hosea 6:1

Before the beginning of the direct speech, the translator inserts the introduction וכדי יקול בעצהם לבעץ 'thus they will say to each other' (12b:10–11). By this addition, he indicates that the verses Hosea 6:1–3 are not to be understood as part of the divine speech (so: LXX, Peshitta, Targum), but as a separate unit comprising the word of the people who express their penitence formally. A similar introduction has Qimḥi: יאמר איש לחבירו לכו וגו ('one says to the other: Come etc.'). See also the shorter phrases of Rashi: אמרו לכו ונשובה וגו', LXX: λέγοντες ('saying'), Peshitta: ܘܐܡܪܝܢ, Targum: יימרון ('they will say').

The translator renders the imperative לְכוּ with תעאלו בנא (12b:11), i.e. as imperative in combination with בנא [bi-nā] which calls for an action: 'come with us!', 'let us go!' By his rendering, the author apparently intends to emphasise the urgency of the repentance. Yefet: תעאלו (ed. Birnbaum 91:20; ed. Polliack and Schlossberg 184) and Cod. Hunt. 206: تعالوا (ed. Schroeter 36:2) have only the imperative.

The reconstruction of אלי אלרב 'to the Lord' (12b:11) for אֶל־יְהֹוָה reflects the author's usual rendering, whereas Yefet prefers the formula: אלי רב אלעאלמין (ed. Birnbaum 91:20; ed. Polliack and Schlossberg 184) and Cod. Hund. 206 has الى الله (ed. Schroeter 36:2).

The translator formulates two parallel relative clauses, introduced by the relative marker אלדי (12b:11, 12), apparently in order to avoid the paratactic syntax of the biblical text.

The verb טָרָף is rendered with אפתרסנא 'he has torn us' (12b:11), i.e. the translator adds the suffix pronoun 1. plural communis which in the biblical text only can be found in the conenction with the following verb וְיִחְבְּשֵׁנוּ 'and he will bandage us'; the same addition has been made in יצרבנא 'he will smite us' (12b:12), the rendition of Hebrew יַךְ; see also Cod. Hunt. 206: كسرنا and ضربنا (ed. Schroeter 36:2) and Peshitta: ܘܡܚܐ ܠܢ 'and he bruised us'. Yefet translates literally with אפתרס (ed. Birnbaum 91:21; ed. Polliack and Schlossberg 184).

The shortened imperfect יַךְ is rendered with כאן יצרבנא 'he used to smite us' (12b:12) to indicate a frequentative sense in the past; see also Yefet: כאן יצרב (ed. Birnbaum 91:21; ed. Polliack and Schlossberg 184). Also Ibn Ezra and Rashi interpret the verb יַךְ in a frequentative or present sense. It is noteworthy that the translator applies his changes of the verbs smoothly by echoing the Hebrew imperfect יַךְ in his rendition יצרבנא and transforming the latter into the past by adding כאן 'he was'.

The author emphasises the subject by adding the independent personal pronoun: והו יגברנא 'and *He* will heal us' (12b:12); see also Yefet: והו יצמדהא (ed. Birnbaum 91:21; ed. Polliack and Schlossberg 184), whereas Cod. Hunt. 206 translates ضمدنا (ed. Schroeter 36:2).

Hosea 6:2

The rendering of יְחַיֵּינוּ with יחיינא 'he will make us live' (12b:12) is another example for the translator's literal rendering using Arabic cognates; see also Aquila/Symmachus ἀναζωώσει, Peshitta: ܘܢܚܝܢ; Targum: יחיננא; Quinta: ὑγιεῖς

TEXTUAL NOTES 163

ἀποδείξει ('he will restore [us] to health'), whereas LXX (ὑγιάσει 'he will heal') echoes more the phrases in Hosea 6:1. See Cod. Hunt. 206: ويبرينا ('and he will heal us', ed. Schroeter 36:3) with reference to Isaiah 38:9 (ed. Schroeter 36:4) and Yefet: יברינא (ed. Birnbaum 93:4; ed. Polliack and Schlossberg 184); this form appears in the author's commentary (13b:19).

The translator retains the Hebrew preposition מן in the phrase מִיֹּמָיִם by rendering מן יומין literally 'from two days' (12b:13); see also Yefet: מן יומין (ed. Birnbaum 93:4; ed. Polliack and Schlossberg 184), whereas Cod. Hunt. 206 replaces it by في يومين (ed. Schroeter 36:3).

וְנִחְיֶה has been rendered by using the Arabic cognate: ונחיא 'and we will live' (12b:13), whereas Yefet and Cod. Hunt. 206 translate with ונעיש/ (ed. Birnbaum 93:5; ed. Polliack and Schlossberg 184)/ونعيش (ed. Schroeter 36:3).

Hosea 6:3

וְנֵדְעָה has been rendered with ונעלם 'and we know' (12b:13), whereas Yefet and Cod. Hunt. 206 translate with ונערף (ed. Birnbaum 94:3; ed. Polliack and Schlossberg 185)/ونعرف (ed. Schroeter 36:5).

נִרְדְּפָה is rendered with נכלוב 'we will seize' (12b:14); see Hosea 2:9; 12:2; 8:3 [reconstructed] and also Cod. Hunt. 206: نكلب (ed. Schroeter 36:5), whereas Yefet has נטלב (ed. Birnbaum 94:3; ed. Polliack and Schlossberg 185).

The translator replaces the asyndetic syntax וְנֵדְעָה נִרְדְּפָה by creating a subordinate clause using the conjunction כיף 'how' (12b:14); see also Yefet: כיף (ed. Birnbaum 94:3; ed. Polliack and Schlossberg 185) and Cod. Hunt. 206: كيف (ed. Schroeter 36:5).

נָכוֹן has been rendered with מסתוי; see also Yefet: מסתוי (ed. Birnbaum 94:4; ed. Polliack and Schlossberg 185) and Cod. Hunt. 206: مستوى (ed. Schroeter 36:5).

מכרגה 'his appearance', literally: 'the place of his going forth' (12b:14), like Hebrew מוֹצָאוֹ which is used for the rising of the sun (see also: Psalms 19:7); Yefet and Cod. Hunt. 206 have מוצע טהורה (ed. Birnbaum 94:4; ed. Polliack and Schlossberg 185 [which reads מוטע]) and موضع ظهوره (ed. Schroeter 36:6) respectively.

The root בוא occurs in Hosea ten times; three times it is rendered with the root وفي III, as here: פיואפי (see also Hosea 9:7; 13:15), three times with دخل (Hosea 9:4, 10; 11:9) and twice with جاء (Hosea 7:1; 10:12); in two cases the translation is not preserved.

The Hebrew phrase כַּגֶּשֶׁם has been rendered with כאלגית 'like abundant rain' (12b:15), whereas Yefet and Cod. Hunt. 206 have the more common מתל

אלמטר (ed. Birnbaum 94:4; ed. Polliack and Schlossberg 185)/مثل المطر (ed. Schroeter 36:6).

The translation of כְּמַלְקוֹשׁ with כאללקיש (12b:15) reflects the Aramaic לְקִישׁ 'late rain' (Jastrow p. 719); see also Yefet: ומתׄל אללקיש (ed. Birnbaum 94:4–5; ed. Polliack and Schlossberg 185) and Cod. Hunt. 206: ومثل اللقيس (ed. Schroeter 36:6).

יוֹרֶה can be interpreted as participle of the root ירה 'to fill', 'to satisfy', 'to water', so that the translation could be 'like late rain which waters the land'; see Targum: דמרוי ערעא ('which saturate the earth'). However, the translator understands יוֹרֶה as a noun: אלבכיר 'former rain' (12b:15) as opposed to לקיש 'late rain'; see also his exegesis (14a:3–4). Both Yefet: ואלבכיר אלדי ינחדר (ed. Birnbaum 94:5; ed. Polliack and Schlossberg 185) and Cod. Hunt. 206: والبكير الذى يخدر (ed. Schroeter 36:6–7) form an identical relative clause with 'late rain' as antecendent: 'and the late rain which falls down (to earth)'.

Hosea 6:4

The translator renders וְחַסְדְּכֶם with ואחסאנכם 'and your beneficience' (12b:16), whereas Yefet and Cod. Hunt. 206 have ודינכם (ed. Birnbaum 96:23; ed. Polliack and Schlossberg 186)/ودينكم (ed. Schroeter 36:8).

By adding ואנמא הו (12b:17) after ואחסאנכם, the translator emphasises the worthlessness of their piety: 'Your beneficience, truly, is like morning clouds'.

For the translation מודלג (12b:17) as rendering of מַשְׁכִּים see Hosea 5:15 (ידאלגוני); also Yefet: מדלג (ed. Birnbaum 97:1; ed. Polliack and Schlossberg 186) and Cod. Hunt. 206: مدلج (ed. Schroeter 36:8).

Hosea 6:5

The author imitates the Hebrew phrase עַל־כֵּן very closely by rendering עלי דלך 'therefore' (12b:18); see also Yefet: עלי דלך (ed. Birnbaum 98:6; ed. Polliack and Schlossberg 187), wherease Cod. Hunt. 206 prefers the more idiomatic ولذلك (ed. Schroeter 36:9).

The author retains the plural וּמִשְׁפָּטֶיךָ by rendering with ואחכאמך 'and your judgements' (12b:18) like Vulgate: *et iudicia tua*, Yefet: ואחכאמך (ed. Birnbaum 98:7; ed. Polliack and Schlossberg 187) and Cod. Hunt. 206: واحكامك (ed. Schroeter 36:9), whereas some versions read a singular noun with the 1st singular suffix pronoun (מִשְׁפָּטִי), e.g. LXX: καὶ τὸ κρίμα μου; Peshitta: ܘܕܝܢܝ; Targum: ודיני 'and my judgment', and combine the final ך as preposition with the following noun into כָּאוֹר, i.e. my judgment comes forth *like light*; see also modern commentators (e.g. Vielhauer 2007:46, 49).

Also the translator changes the metaphor אוֹר into a simile by introducing the inseparable preposition כ plus article: כאלנור 'like the light' (12b:19); similar Yefet: מתל אלנור (ed. Birnbaum 98:7; ed. Polliack and Schlossberg 187) and Cod. Hunt. 206: مثل النور (ed. Schroeter 36:10); see also LXX: ὡς φῶς ('like light'), Peshitta: ܐܝܟ ܢܘܗܪܐ and Targum: כניהר.

The verb יֵצֵא has been rendered literally with יכרג 'he will come forth' (12b:19), whereas Yefet and Cod. Hunt. 206 choose a verb more fitting with אוֹר: יטהר (ed. Birnbaum 98:7; ed. Polliack and Schlossberg 187)/يظهر 'it will appear' (ed. Schroeter 36:10).

Hosea 6:6

חֶסֶד has been rendered again with איחסאן 'beneficience' (12b:19; see Hosea 6:4), whereas Yefet and Cod. Hunt. 206 translate with אסתעמאל אלדין (ed. Birnbaum 100:3)/إستعمال الدين (ed. Schroeter 36:10; ed. Polliack and Schlossberg 187).

The translator does not interpret the preposition מן in מֵעֹלוֹת to have privative force, as do Vulgate: *et non*, Peshitta: ܘܠܐ 'and not', Yefet: ולא (ed. Birnbaum 100:3; ed. Polliack and Schlossberg 187) and modern commentators (e.g. Wolff 1965:153; Macintosh 1997:232; Vielhauer 2007:46), but as a particle of comparison, as do LXX: ἢ ('rather than'). By using the compound preposition אגל מן 'rather than' in both phrases (אגל מן צואעד and אגל מן דביחה), the author achieves a closer parallelism (12b:19–20); see also Cod. Hunt. 206: من اجل. (ed. Schroeter 36:11).

The rendition צואעד 'burnt offerings' (12b:20) imitates the Hebrew עֹלוֹת; see also Cod. Hunt. 206: تقريب الصواعد (ed. Schroeter 36:11), whereas Yefet retains the Hebrew technical term for holocaust: תקריב אלעולות (ed. Birnbaum 100:5; ed. Polliack and Schlossberg 187).

Hosea 6:7

The translator chooses the Arabic cognate עברו, literally 'they crossed' (12b:20) as rendering of עָבְרוּ, whereas Yefet and Cod. Hunt. 206 translate with גאזו (ed. Birnbaum 100:19; ed. Polliack and Schlossberg 188)/جاوزوا (ed. Schroeter 36:11).

The indefiniteness of the noun בְּרִית has been retained in the author's translation עהד, whereas Yefet and Cod. Hunt. 206 add the article: אלעהד (ed. Birnbaum 100:19; ed. Polliack and Schlossberg 188)/العهد (ed. Schroeter 36:12). Some versions add the 1st singular suffix pronoun, e.g. Peshitta: ܩܝܡܝ; Targum: קימי 'my covenant' (see Hosea 6:5 where both have 'and my judgement').

Hosea 6:8

The rendering of עֲקֻבָּה is not preserved, except for the final ה, which can be restored as גרבזה according to Yefet: וגרבזה (ed. Birnbaum 101:16; ed. Polliack and Schlossberg 188) or מגרבזה according to Cod. Hunt. 206: جريزة (ed. Schroeter 36:12). The form appears to be the feminine adjective 'deceitful', 'deceptive' rather than the abstract noun جريزة 'deception'. In any case, the author derives the word from the root עקב, as is also clear from the paraphrase in his exegesis 'they deceived the people' (14a:19–20). Yefet and Cod. Hunt. 206 refer to עָקֹב לֵב (Jeremiah 17:9) which is translated with with גרבז אלקלב (ed. Birnbaum 102:1–2; ed. Polliack and Schlossberg 188 [where one manuscript reads جريز القلب/[גרבזן]) (ed. Schroeter 36:15); see Aquila: περικαμπὴς ἀπὸ αἵματος ('bent round through blood') and Vulgate: *subplantata sanguine* ('tripped up through blood'). On the other hand, Theodotion (ἡ πτερνὰ αὐτῆς ἀφ' αἵματος 'her foodstep is from blood') obviously interpreted the word as a noun עָקֵב 'heel', 'footprint' plus suffix pronoun.

Whereas the biblical text has no copula (see also Yefet: בלד גלעד קריה, ed. Birnbaum 101:16; ed. Polliack and Schlossberg 188 [where one manuscript reads קריה גלעד]), the translator adds the verbal form קד צארת 'it was' (12b:21) after גלעד, in order to clarify that this statement refers to events in the past.

The translator specifies the ambiguous Hebrew מִדָּם 'from blood' by rendering מן גהה ספך אלדם 'because of the bloodshed' (12b:22); a similar translation can be found in Yefet: מן ספד אלדמי (ed. Birnbaum 101:16–17; ed. Polliack and Schlossberg 188 [where one manuscript reads אלדם]).

Hosea 6:9

וּכְחַכֵּי is rendered with וכצנאניר 'like fish-hooks' (12b:22), i.e. the translator derives the words from the root חנך (BDB 335); see also Yefet: ומתל שצוץ (ed. Birnbaum 102:3; ed. Polliack and Schlossberg 188) and also his exegesis: והי אלאת אלציאדין (ed. Birnbaum 103:1), Cod. Hunt. 206: ومثل شصوص (ed. Schroeter 36:16) and Isaiah 8:15; 19:8; Habakkuk 1:15. The translator expands the simile by adding a relative clause '(fish-hooks) with which schools of fish are caught', thus interpreting the noun גְּדוּדִים 'groups' as referring to fish סמך אגואק. Also according to Rashi and Saadiah חַכֵּי denotes 'fish-hooks'; Rashi: וכאסיפת איש ציד דגים

האוספים בחכה יחד כן חכי גדודים חבורות כהניהם המתחברים ללכת בדרך ירצחו שם כולם שכם אחד ('Like the assembling of a fisherman who collects them in the fish-hook together, likewise are the fish-hooks of their gangs, i.e. the groups of their priests, who gather together to walk on the road to murder there all of them unanimously'); Saadiah (according to Qimḥi): כמו שמשליכים ציידי הדגים החכה למשוך הדגים אשר ביאור והציידים בהשליכם החכה עומדים על גדות הנהר או היאור ומשם צדים בני מדם ('like the fishermen throw the fish-hook to pull the fish which are in the river, and the fishermen when throwing the fish-hook are standing at the bank of the river and hunt fish from there, likewise the gang of the priests hunt the people'). The alternative is to derive וּכְחַכֵּי from the root חכה 'to wait': 'and as those who wait' (14a:22). The author mentions this option in his exegesis (14a:21–22); see also Ibn Ezra and Qimḥi.

אִישׁ has been translated literally with אימר 'man' (12b:22), whereas Yefet and Cod. Hunt. 206 render with אלציאד (ed. Birnbaum 102:3; ed. Polliack and Schlossberg 188)/الصياد 'the fishermen' (ed. Schroeter 36:16), obviously to support their understanding of the simile.

The translator renders גְּדוּדִים with אגואק 'troups', 'groups' (12b:23), whereas Yefet and Cod. Hunt. 206 interpret the plural noun as עלי אלשטוט (ed. Birnbaum 102:3; ed. Polliack and Schlossberg 188)/على الشطوط 'on the river banks' (ed. Schroeter 36:16).

The translator adds כדלך 'likewise' (12b:23) after the simile to mark the beginning of the application of the *tertium comparationis*; see also Yefet: כדאך (ed. Birnbaum 102:3; ed. Polliack and Schlossberg 188) and Cod. Hunt. 206: كذالك (ed. Schroeter 36:16).

The addition of the preposition עלי 'upon' (12b:23) before אלטריק is due to improvement of the style; Yefet adds a different preposition: פי אלטריק (ed. Birnbaum 102:4; ed. Polliack and Schlossberg 188), whereas Cod. Hunt. 206 has Ø (ed. Schroeter 36:16).

The translator adds the direct object אלנאס 'the people' (12b:23) after יקתלון 'they kill', as do also Yefet: אלנאס (ed. Birnbaum 102:4; ed. Polliack and Schlossberg 188) and Cod. Hunt. 206: الناس (ed. Schroeter 36:17).

The anomalous vocalization שֶׁכְמָה instead of usual שְׁכֶמָה 'to Shechem' indicates that the term is not the city שְׁכֶם with the *he locale*, rather it is to be derived from the noun שְׁכֶם 'shoulder', i.e. 'with one shoulder', 'with one consent', 'unanimously', '*uno consensu*'. Also the translator interprets שֶׁכְמָה as מנכב 'shoulder' and adds ואחד (12b:23–24), in order to indicate the unanimous action, thus imitating the phrase in Zephaniah 3:9: שְׁכֶם אֶחָד '(to worship him) with a united resolve'. Similarly, Targum understands שְׁכְמָה in the sense of באורח חדא קטלין נפשן כתף חד ('in the same way they kill men with one consent'); also Aquila and Theodotion, according to Jerome, interpret the phrase as 'shoulder', 'back':

ὕμερος/*in dorso*; Qimḥi: בדרך ירצחו כלם שכם אחד 'they murder all of them on the road unanimously'. Yefet and Cod. Hunt. 206 have the phrase: כתף בגנב כתף (ed. Birnbaum 102:4; ed. Polliack and Schlossberg 188)/كتف بجنب كتف 'shoulder beside shoulder', i.e. 'closely packed', or 'approaching them closely' (see Schroeter 36:17, p. 164 n. 1). Rashi's interpretation points into the same direction: שְׁכְמָה ('שכמה לשון כת אחת means: one group').

By replacing כִּי with ומע דאך פאן (12b:24), the translator indicates that he understands the following phrase *they committed adultery* in an adversative sense, i.e. though they acted unanimously, what they did was nevertheless an atrocity. Yefet and Cod. Hunt. 206, on the other hand, translate לאנהם (ed. Birnbaum 102:5; ed. Polliack and Schlossberg 188)/لِأنّهُم (ed. Schroeter 36:17), giving the cause or reason.

The translator uses the indefinite feminine noun פאחשה 'abomination', 'atrocity', 'crime', 'adultery', 'fornication' (12b:24) for rendering זִמָּה; Yefet has a noun from the same root with the definite article אלפחשה (ed. Birnbaum 102:5; ed. Polliack and Schlossberg 188) and Cod. Hunt. 206 the definite plural الفواحش (ed. Schroeter 36:17).

The phrase באנהם erroneously appears twice in the exegesis, as the last word in 14a:26 and as the first word in 14b:1.

Hosea 6:10

The translator chooses פאקרה 'misfortune' (12b:25) as rendering of שַׁעֲרִירִיָּה; see also LXX: φρικώδη ('a horrible thing'), Vulgate: *horrendum*, Targum: שנו ('strangeness', 'deviation'), Peshitta: ܬܗܪܐ ('an amazing thing'); Yefet and Cod. Hunt. 206 use an identical or similar equivalent as for זִמָּה in the preceding verse: פחשה בשעה 'a hideous aborration' (ed. Birnbaum 103:5; ed. Polliack and Schlossberg 189)/فاحشة (Schroeter 36:22). Ibn Janāḥ, Ibn Ezra and Qimḥi compare שַׁעֲרִירִיָּה with Jeremiah 29:17: הַתְּאֵנִים הַשֹּׁעָרִים 'rotten figs'.

The translator adds the finite verb חצל 'it became' (12b:25) after תם 'there', thus transforming the nominal sentence into a verbal clause, literally 'there, harloteries were to Ephraim'.

The translator changes the asyndetic syntax of the Hebrew source text by introducing the verb 'she is defiled' with the connective conjunction פ 'and' (12b:25); see Yefet: ותם נגס (ed. Birnbaum 103:6; ed. Polliack and Schlossberg 189) and Cod. Hunt. 206: وتنجس (ed. Schroeter 37:1).

Hosea 6:11

בְּשׁוּבִי is paraphrased with ענד מא ארדת אן יכון רגועי 'when I wished that there would be My return' (12b:26), thus emphasising that God's return was no incidental event, but happened according to His 'intention', 'will', 'wish'.

The translator does not regard the second half of the verse as a unit (*when I restore the captivity of My people*), i.e. שְׁבוּת עַמִּי is not understood as direct object of a transitive שׁוּבִי, rather he interprets בְּשׁוּבִי as intransitive (*when I return*) and inserts the conjunction מע 'with' (12b:27), thus rendering 'My return together with the captivity of My people'; see Yefet and Cod. Hunt. 206 who provide the identical translation: ענד רגועי מע סבי שעבי (ed. Birnbaum 103:16; ed. Polliack and Schlossberg 189)/عند رجوعی مع سبی شعبی (ed. Schroeter 37:1–2).

ומלת in the exegesis (14b:18) appears to be derived from لم 'convenir', 'être opportun' (Dozy 850), probably II.

Hosea 7:1

Whereas Yefet and Cod. Hunt. 206 render כְּרָפְאִי with the infinitive I as שפאיי (ed. Birnbaum 104:15; ed. Polliack and Schlossberg 190)/شفائي (ed. Schroeter 37:7) 'to cure from disease', the translator appears to refer to the infinitive IV אישפאיי 'to give a medicine to' (14b:19); see Hava p. 370; Lane p. 1575.

The perfect with *waw* consecutive וְנִגְלָה has future meaning 'it will be revealed', as reflected in some of the versions: LXX: καὶ ἀποκαλυφθήσεται ἡ ἀδικία Ἐφραΐμ ('the iniquity of Ephraim will be revealed') and Targum: ויתגלין ('[then the guilt of Ephraim] will be revealed'). However, the translator renders it with a past tense: אנכשף 'it was uncovered', 'it was revealed' (14b:19); see also Peshitta: ܐܬܓܠܝ ('it was revealed'), Vulgate: *revelata est* ('it was revealed'), Rashi: כשאני חפץ להושיעם ולרפאותם עונותם נגלו לפני ('When I liked to help them and to heal them, their sins were revealed before Me') and Ibn Ezra: בעבור שאמרו כי הוא טרף וירפאנו אמר כאשר ארצה לרפאם עמד לפני רשעם בלבם שלא עזבוהו עד עתה ('Because of what they said *He ript us apart and he will heal us* (Hosea 6:1), he says now When I like to heal them, their wickedness in their heart stood before Me which they have not left until now'). Yefet and Cod. Hunt. 206 prefere the composed past כאן ינכשף (ed. Birnbaum 104:15; ed. Polliack and Schlossberg 190)/كان ينكشف 'it was uncovered' (ed. Schroeter 37:7).

וְרָעוֹת is rendered with ובלייא (see also Hosea 7:2; 9:15), whereas Yefet and Cod. Hunt. 206 both share the same translation: וקבאיח (ed. Birnbaum 104:16; ed. Polliack and Schlossberg 190)/وقبائح (ed. Schroeter 37:7).

The translator renders שֶׁקֶר with באטל 'lie', 'falsehood' (14b:20), whereas Yefet and Cod. Hunt. 206 have the eqivalent אלכדב (ed. Birnbaum 104:16; ed. Polliack and Schlossberg 190)/الكذب (ed. Schroeter 37:8).

פָּשַׁט is rendered with יגאר (14b:20), derived from the root غور IV 'to raid', 'to invade', 'to attack' (with على); see also LXX: ἐκδιδύσκων, Peshitta: ܡܚܠܨ, Vulgate: *spolians*; Targum: קפחין; Cod. Hunt. 206 translates with يسلخ 'he strips off' (ed. Schroeter 37:8), whereas in his grammatical notes, he refers to حط 'to put down', 'to descend'. Yefet renders יגי סלך (ed. Birnbaum 104:17; ed. Polliack and Schlossberg 190 [where one manuscript reads יסלך]).

The author chosses again גוק 'group' (14b:21; see Hosea 6:9) as translation of גְּדוּד, whereas Yefet and Cod. Hunt. 206 render with אלכרדוס (ed. Birnbaum 104:16; ed. Polliack and Schlossberg 190 [where one manuscript reads אלפרדוס])/الكردوس (ed. Schroeter 37:8).

בַּחוּץ is rendered with כארג 'outside' (14b:21), whereas Yefed and Cod. Hunt. 206 have ברא (ed. Birnbaum 104:16)/برا (ed. Schroeter 37:8); see also LXX: ἐν τῇ ὁδοῦ αὐτοῦ ('in his [i.e. Ephraim's] way'), Vulgate: *foris*, Peshitta: ܒܫܘܩܐ ('in the streets'), Targum: בדברא ('in the pasture').

Hosea 7:2

The translator has the plural noun פי קלובהם 'in their hearts' (14b:21) instead of the singular לִלְבָבָם 'to their heart'; see also his translation of Hosea 7:14 (16b:15). The phrase פי קלובהם can also be found in his exegesis (17a:20). Yefet and Cod. Hunt. 206 also prefer the plural noun: פי קלובהם (ed. Birnbaum 106:7; ed. Polliack and Schlossberg 190)/في قلوبهم (ed. Schroeter 37:13).

The restoration of בלייתהם 'their wicked deeds' (14b:21) for רָעָתָם is based on the translation of בְּרָעָתָם in Hosea 7:3 (14b:23), whereas Cod. Hunt 206 and Yefet have قبائحهم 'their shameful deeds' (ed. Schroeter 37:13)/קבאיחהם (ed. Birnbaum 106:7; ed. Polliack and Schlossberg 190).

The author renders עַתָּה with פי אלסאעתה 'at the time' (14b:22) which he uses as the antecendent of the following subordinate clause vs. Yefet: אלאן (ed. Birnbaum 106:8; ed. Polliack and Schlossberg 190) and Cod. Hunt. 206: الآن (ed. Schroeter 37:13).

The restoration שמאילהם 'their deeds' (14b:22) is based on the author's usual translation of מעלים (see Hosea 4:9; 5:4; 9:15; 12:3); see also Yefet: שמאילהם (ed. Birnbaum 106:8; ed. Polliack and Schlossberg 190) and Cod. Hunt. 206: شمائلهم (ed. Schroeter 37:14).

אן חדא 'that (they were) before' (14b:22) as rendition of נֶגֶד has been restored according to a phrase in the exegesis (15a:25), vs. Yefet (ed. Polliack and Schlossberg 191) and Cod. Hunt. 206: مقابل (ed. Schroeter 37:14).

TEXTUAL NOTES 171

By inserting וליס יקולו אן 'and they do not say that' (14b:22) before 'they were before My face', the translator suggests that the phrase is parallel to the preceeding: ולם יקולו 'they did not say' (14b:21), though they are distinct in their temporal stand (present/past).

Hosea 7:3

The author translates the abstract בְּרָעָתָם with a concrete plural noun בבלייתהם 'with their wicked deeds' (14b:23); see also LXX: ἐν ταῖς κακίαις αὐτῶν, whereas Yefet and Cod. Hunt. 206 choose here the singular noun בשרהם (ed. Birnbaum 107:1; ed. Polliack and Schlossberg 191)/بشرهم 'with their wickedness' (ed. Schroeter 37:14).

ובגחודאהם 'and with their ingratitudes' (14b:23) imitates the Hebrew plural וּבְכַחֲשֵׁיהֶם, whereas Yefet and Cod. Hunt. 206 have the singular: ובגחודהם (ed. Birnbaum 107:1; ed. Polliack and Schlossberg 191)/وبجحودهم (ed. Schroeter 37:15).

The reconstruction of רווסא 'chiefs' (14b:23) for שָׂרִים reflects the author's translation in Hosea 3:4; 5:10; 7:5; 8:10; see also Yefet: אלרוסא (ed. Birnbaum 107:1; ed. Polliack and Schlossberg 191) and Cod. Hunt. 206: الرؤساء (ed. Schroeter 37:15).

Hosea 7:4

The translator chooses the plural pattern *fuʿāl* פגאר 'adulterer' (14b:24) as rendition of מְנָאֲפִים, whereas Yefet and Cod. Hunt. 206 prefer the pattern *faʿala*: פגרה (ed. Birnbaum 107:17; ed. Polliack and Schlossberg 191)/فجرة (ed. Schroeter 37:15).

כְּמוֹ is rendered with מתל 'like' (14b:24); see Yefet: מתל (ed. Birnbaum 107:17; ed. Polliack and Schlossberg 191) and Cod. Hunt. 206 مثل (ed. Schroeter 37:15). The reconstruction of the masculine participle משתעל 'heated' (14b:24) as rendition of בֹּעֵרָה is based on the translation of Hosea 7:5 (15a:2); see also Yefet: אלמשתעל (ed. Birnbaum 107:17; ed. Polliack and Schlossberg 191) and Cod. Hunt. 206 المشتعل (ed. Schroeter 37:16).

The author explains the *he* in the participle בֹּעֵרָה as a supernumerary, added letter (זאיד). He comments claiming the form as masculine (15b:10–12); see also Yefet (ed. Birnbaum 229:8–9). Ibn Ezra notes that the Massoretes accented the participle on the *penultima* (*mil'el*) to harmonise it with the masculine noun תַּנּוּר 'oven': ותנור לשון זכר על כן מלת בוערה מלעיל כמו לילה מחלה עבר על נפשינו

is masculine, therefore the word בֹּעֵרָה [though feminine] is accentuated on the *penultima* as לַיְלָה and מַחֲלָה). See also Ibn Nuḥ: אלהי פיה זאיד והו בֹּעֵר לשון אלהי פיה זאיד והו אלאניד פי השפלה זאיד נטיר בֹּעֵרָה זכר נטיר השפלה הגבה ואלהי (92b) ('The *he* in it [i.e. in בֹּעֵרָה] is an added letter and it is the masculine, בֹּעֵר, like הַשְׁפָלָה הַגְּבֵהּ [Ezekiel 21:31] where the *he* in הַשְׁפָלָה is an added letter like בֹּעֵרָה'); see also the grammatical notes of Cod. Hunt. 206 (ed. Schroeter II, 26:8–9).

The reconstruction of כבאז 'baker' (14b:24) for מַאֲפֶה is based on a phrase in the exegesis: ואלכבאז 'and the baker' (15b:27); see also Cod. Hunt. 206: الخباز (ed. Schroeter 37:16).

The rendition of יָשְׁבוּת is יעטול 'it rests'; see also Yefet: יעטל (ed. Birnbaum 107:17; ed. Polliack and Schlossberg 191) and Cod. Hunt. 206: يعطل (ed. Schroeter 37:16); Quinta: ἐπαύσατο, Vulgate: *quievit paululum* ('[the city] rested a little'); Peshitta: ܢܒܗܠ ('he ceases').

The translator introduces the additional noun אלפגור 'the harlotry' (14b:25) as subject of the verb יעטול 'it rests', which he obviously regarded as missing in the biblical source text.

The translator interprets מֵעִיר as מן אלקריה 'from the town' (14b:25); see also Yefet: מן אלמדינה (ed. Birnbaum 107:18; ed. Polliack and Schlossberg 191), Cod. Hunt. 206: من القرية (ed. Schroeder 37:16), Jerome: *quasi clibanus succensus a coquente pistore, postquam quievit paululum civitas a commistione fermenti*, Targum: מקרויתון ('from their cities'), Peshitta: ܡܢ ܡܕܝܢܬܐ ('from the city'), Vulgate: (*quievit paululum*) *civitas*. Rashi rejects this rendition arguing י״ת מה שתירגם ואיני יכול ליישב בו לשון ימקרא ('Jonathan may translate what he translated, I myself cannot adjust it with the context'). Modern commenators understand מֵעִיר as verb from the root עור I 'to rouse oneself', hi. 'to rouse', 'to stir up' (BDB 734); see Arabic وغر 'to be hot'.

The reconstruction of אלעגין 'the dough' (14b:25) for בָּצֵק is based on the phrase in the exegesis אלעגין (15b:10); see also Yefet: אלעגִין (ed. Birnbaum 107:18; ed. Polliack and Schlossberg 191) and Cod. Hunt. 206 العجين (ed. Schroeter 37:16).

The conjecture of the text of the exegesis באלתנור אלמשתול מן אלכבאז אלדי כאן חאמי 'lit by a baker which was heated' (15b:4) is based on Yefet's interpretation תם מתלהם באלתנור אלמשתעל מן סגר אלכבאז אלדה יכון חאמי גדא (ed. Birnbaum 107:20–21; ed. Polliack and Schlossberg 191).

The text in 15b:10 can be reconstructed according to Ibn Nūḥ (*Diqduq*, ed. Khan 2011, 392): זאיד והו בֹּעֵר.

Hosea 7:5

The reconstruction of אמרצוּ 'they became ill' (14b:26) as rendition of הֶחֱלוּ is likely. Though the author refers in his exegesis to both options: מרצו 'they became ill' (15b:17) and אמרצו 'they made ill' (15b:19) and does not explicitly point out to which option he inclines, it may be assumed that he preferred the transitive interpretation אמרצוּ 'they made ill', since he suggests the transitive aspect of the verb by interpreting that 'they held back a king' (15b:21). This is also the preferred option of Yefet: אמרצוּ (ed. Birnbaum 108:9; ed. Polliack and Schlossberg 192) and Cod. Hunt. 206: امرضو (ed. Schroeter 37:17). See Ibn Nūḥ 92b.

The alternative interpretation of the phrase הֶחֱלוּ שָׂרִים by exegetes reflects the problem as to how to understand the verb: Is the verb intransitive or transitive? I.e. did the chiefs become ill, or did the chiefs make ill?

(1) The first option 'they became ill' is adopted by Rashi: נעשו שרינו חולים ('our chiefs became ill').

(2) However, according to Qimḥi, the verb is transitive and the chiefs are the subject who make ill the king: היה עסקם באכילה ושתייה עד שהחלו המלך מרוב שתות היין ('Their business was eating and drinking until they made ill the king from the amount of drinking wine'); זהו חמת מיין שהיה זה בא בנאדו מלא יין וזה בא בנאדו ומשקין המלך כד שמחלין אותו ('This is the meaning of heat of wine that one came with his flask of wine and the other came with his flask of wine and gave to drink to the king until they made him ill').

The conjecture of the translation אלטנאזין 'the mockers' (15a:1) as rendering of לֹצְצִים is based on the word in the exegesis (15b:20). The same noun appears in Yefet: אלטנאזין (ed. Birnbaum 108:10; ed. Polliack and Schlossberg 192) and Cod. Hunt. 206: الطنازين (ed. Schroeter 37:18). LXX: μετὰ λοιμῶν ('with pestilent fellows'); Aquila: χλευαστῶν ('scoffers'), Vulgate: *cum inlusoribus*; Peshitta: ܒܝ̈ܫܐ ('evil men'); Targum: סיעת שקרין ('a company of falsehood').

The addition לֹמלך (14b:26) to the biblical text indicates the direct object; see the phrase in the notes of Cod. Hunt. 206: امرضو الرؤساء للملك (ed. Schroeter II, 26:11–12) and Yefet's exegesis: אמרצוּ אלרוסא ללמלך (ed. Birnbaum 108:14; ed. Polliack and Schlossberg 192).

מָשַׁךְ has been rendered with גדב, literally 'he pulled' (15a:1); see also Yefet: גדב (ed. Birnbaum 108:9; ed. Polliack and Schlossberg 192), whereas Cod. Hunt. 206 translates with مد (ed. Schroeter 37:17). LXX: ἐξέτεινεν ('he stretched out'); Vulgate: *extendit*; Peshitta: ܢܓܕܘ (plural!); Targum: נגד.

Hosea 7:6

The restoration of the beginning of the verse with לאן קד קרבו כאלתנור קלבהם 'for they draw near like the oven to their heart' (15a:1–2) is tentative; see LXX: ἀνεκαύθησαν ('they are inflamed'); Peshitta: ܥܒܕ ܠܚܡܗ; Symmachus/Theodotion: ἤγγισαν ('they have brought near'); Vulgate: *applicuerunt* ('they have apppplied'); Yefet: לאנהם קדמו מתֿל אלתנור קלבהם (ed. Birnbaum 109:9; ed. Polliack and Schlossberg 192) and Cod. Hunt. 206: لا نهم قاربوا قلبهم كالتنور (ed. Schroeter 37:18); Targum: ארי אתקרבו לעצת חטאין ('for they draw near the convent of sinners'). Ibn Ezra ('to make close to', 'to approximate to'). Rashi takes the verb in the sense of 'to make ready', 'to prepare': הכינו והזמינו את לבם במעשה אורב שלהם כתנור זה שמכינים ומסיקין אותו לאפות ('they prepared and invited their heart with the deed of their ambush like an oven which they prepare and heat for baking'). Qimḥi: לבם שהוא בוער כתנור קרבו אותו בארבם כלומר קרבו אותו למעשה הרע כלומר שמו לבבם לחשוב מחשבות רעות שיעשו הרע אחר המחשבה ('their heart that burns like an oven, they draw it near in their ambush, means: they draw it near to the bad deed, i.e. they put their heart to think bad thoughts that they do the evil after the thought').

כל אלליל 'all night' (15a:2) for כָּל-הַלַּיְלָה is based on a phrase in the exegesis: טול אלליל (15b:27) which can slo be found in Yefet's translation: טול אלליל (ed. Birnbaum 109:9–10; ed. Polliack and Schlossberg 192 [where one manuscript lacks אלליל ראקד]) and Cod. Hunt. 206: طول الليل (ed. Schroeter 37:18).

נאים 'sleeping' and כבאזהם 'their baker' (15a:2) have been restored on the basis of 15b:27: ואלכבאז נאים vs. Yefet: ראקד כבאזהם (ed. Birnbaum 109:10; ed. Polliack and Schlossberg 192 [where one manuscript lacks ראקד]) and Cod. Hunt. 206: راقد ... خبازهم (ed. Schroeter 37:7).

Despite the use of בוכרה 'early morning' (بكرة) in the author's exegesis (15b: 28), the noun צובח has been chosen for the reconstruction of rendition of בֹּקֶר (15a:2), since this is the Arabic equivalent also in his translation of Hosea 6:4; 13:3 vs. Yefet: באלגדאה (ed. Birnbaum 109:10; ed. Polliack and Schlossberg 192) and Cod. Hunt. 206: بالغداة (ed. Schroeter 37:19).

The translation כאר מותלהבה 'like a *blazing* fire' (15a:3) for כְּאֵשׁ לֶהָבָה underlines the author's preference for Arabic cognates; see also Yefet: מתֿל נאר מלתהבה (ed. Birnbaum 109:10–11; ed. Polliack and Schlossberg 192), whereas Cod. Hunt. 206 renders مثل نار مشعولة (ed. Schroeter 37:19).

The reconstruction of the grammatical notes on Hosea 7:6 (16b:4–5) is based on the phrase פענד אלאצאפה צאר (5b:10–11).

Hosea 7:7

The reconstruction, including the orthography of יוחמו 'they are hot' (15a:3) as rendition of יֵחַמּוּ, is based on יוחמא (16a:5); see also Yefet: יחמו (ed. Birnbaum 110:23; ed. Polliack and Schlossberg 193) and Cod. Hunt. 206: يحمون (ed. Schroeter 37:20).

כאלתנור 'like the oven' (15a:3) has been reconstructed according to the author's usual rendition of Hebrew תַּנּוּר (see Hosea 7:4, 6); see also Yefet: מתל אלתנור (ed. Birnbaum 110:23; ed. Polliack and Schlossberg 193); Cod. Hunt. 206: مثل التنور (ed. Schroeter 37:20).

ואכלו 'and they ate' (15a:3) has been reconstructed according the author's usual rendering of the Hebrew root אכל (see Hosea 2:14; 4:8, 10; 9:3, 4; 13:8; translation missing: Hosea 8:13, 14; 7:9; 11:6; Hosea 5:7: יפניהם); see also Yefet: ואכלו (ed. Birnbaum 110:23; ed. Polliack and Schlossberg 193) and Cod. Hunt. 206: وأكلوا (ed. Schroeter 37:20).

The reconstruction מע חכאמהם 'with their judges' (15a:3) is tentative though the author sometimes renders אֶת with מע (e.g. Hosea 5:7); see also Yefet: מע חכאמהם (ed. Birnbaum 110:23; ed. Polliack and Schlossberg 193) and Cod. Hunt. 206: مع حكامهم (ed. Schroeter 37:20). The other option is to take חכאמהם as direct object: 'they eat their judges'.

ליס 'not to be' (15a:4) is the author's usual rendering of אֵין, see also: Hosea 3:4 (2×); 4:1; 7:7, 11; 8:7, 8; 10:3; text missing: 5:14; see Yefet: ליס (ed. Birnbaum 111:1; ed. Polliack and Schlossberg 193) and Cod. Hunt. 206: وليس (ed. Schroeter 37:21).

The root ندو/נדו appears to be the author's usual rendition of Hebrew קרא (see Hosea 2:18; 11:1, 7; text missing: Hosea 1:4, 6, 9; 7:7, 11), so that the reconstruction נאדי 'calling' (15a:4) may be justified. However, Yefet and Cod. Hunt. 206 have and דאעי (ed. Birnbaum 111:1; ed. Polliack and Schlossberg 193)/داعى (ed. Schroeter 37:21).

The reconstruction of פיהם 'among them' (15a:4) as rendition of בָּהֶם reflects the phrase אן לם יכון פיהם of the exegesis (16a:10); see also Yefet: פיהם (ed. Birnbaum 111:1; ed. Polliack and Schlossberg 193); Cod. Hunt. 206: فيهم (ed. Schroeter 37:21).

Hosea 7:8

The rendition of יִתְבּוֹלָל is not preserved (15a:5). The conjecture יסקוט 'he will fall' is likely when considering the translation of Yefet: יסקט (ed. Birnbaum 111:23; ed. Polliack and Schlossberg 194) and Cod. Hunt. 206: يسقط (ed. Schroeter 37:21); both Yefet and Cod. Hunt. 206 add an explanation of the verb: יעני יכס

מקדארה (ed. Birnbaum 111:23–112:1; ed. Polliack and Schlossberg 194)/يعني يُخسّ مقادره (ed. Schroeter 38:1). In his notes, Schroeter refers to R. Tanchum's explanation يفسد يتغير ويختلط 'it is corrupted, changed and mixed' (167 n. 1) three possible renditions of the verb. The versions think of 'to mingle oneself'; see LXX: συνεμίγνυτο; Vulgate: *commiscebatur*; Peshitta: ܐܬܚܠܛ ('it mingled together'); Targum: אתערבו ('it mingled itself with/it had dealings with').

The translation בקורצה 'in a round cake' (15a:5) as rendition of עֻגָה is distinct from Yefet: מלה (ed. Birnbaum 112:1; ed. Polliack and Schlossberg 194) and Cod. Hunt. 206: ملة ('cake', ed. Schroeter 38:1), but can be found in the Arabic translation of the Polyglotta. The preposition ב in the phrase בקורצה '*in* a round cake' (15a:5) is a variant of the usual accusative after כאן.

The rendition מקלובה 'turned over' (15a:6) for הֲפוּכָה, which can also be found in Yefet: מקלובה (ed. Birnbaum 112:1; ed. Polliack and Schlossberg 194), is preferable to Cod. Hunt. 206: مقبولة (ed. Schroeter 38:1), which seems to be erroneous for مقلوبة.

The length of the *lacuna* between אלשעוב and בקורצה (15a:5) suggests that the translator may have added an explanation of the verb יסקוט, similar to Yefet: יעני יבס מקדארה 'meaning his power will decrease' (ed. Birnbaum 111:23–112:1; ed. Polliack and Schlossberg 194) and Cod. Hunt. 206 (see above).

The reconstruction תום שבההם 'then he compares them' (16a:12) in the exegesis is tentative. The formula is based on the identical phrase in 16a:17; however, also תום מתלהם, as in 16a:23, is possible.

The reconstruction הַיְצֵא in the grammatical notes (16b:7) is based on Ibn Nuḥ's explanation: אמרה הַיְבֵר נטיר הַיְצֵא (92b).

Hosea 7:9

For the reconstruction אלגרבא 'the strangers' with article (15a:6) as translation of the indefinite זָרִים see Hosea 8:7, where the indefinite noun זָרִים is also renderd with the definite אלגרבא. Yefet and Cod. Hunt. 206 have also a definite, though different noun: אלאגנביין (ed. Birnbaum 113:1; ed. Polliack and Schlossberg 194)/الا جنبيين (ed. Schroeter 38:2).

The reconstruction קואה 'his strength' (15a:6) as rendering of כֹּחוֹ a *hapax legomenon* in Hosea is tentative, though likely; see Yefet: קואה (ed. Birnbaum 113:1; ed. Polliack and Schlossberg 194) and Cod. Hunt. 206: قواه (ed. Schroeter 38:2).

The second phrase והו לא עאלם 'and he does not know' (15a:7) has been reconstructed according to the first occurence in the same verse (15a:6).

The translator imitates the Hebrew feminine noun שֵׂיבָה by rendering it with the Arabic feminine cognate שיבה 'old age' (15a:7); see also Yefet who adds the article: אלשיבה (ed. Birnbaum 113:2; ed. Polliack and Schlossberg 194), whereas Cod. Hunt. 206 has the usual masculine noun الشيب (ed. Schroeter 38:3).

זָרְקָה has been rendered with נצחת 'she has been sprinkled' (15a:7); see also Yefet: נֻצְּחת (ed. Birnbaum 113:2; ed. Polliack and Schlossberg 194) and Cod. Hunt. 206: نضح (ed. Schroeter 38:3); Vulgate: *effusi sunt* ('they were poured out'); LXX: ἐξήνθησαν ('they have come out'); Targum: חלשותא מטיתנון. Ibn Janāḥ emphasises that the verb denotes 'to sprinkle' and explains 'old age has made him grey'.

Hosea 7:10

The reconstruction of פסא ישהד 'he will testify' (15a:7) as rendition of וְעָנָה is based on the identical phrase in Hosea 5:5 vs. Yefet: ושהד (ed. Birnbaum 114:5; ed. Polliack and Schlossberg 195 [which reads ישהד]) and Cod. Hunt. 206: وشهد (ed. Schroeter 38:3).

The reconstruction פי וגהה ולא רגעו אלי אלרב אלאההם (15a:8) is based on similar phrases in Hosea 5:4, 15; see also Yefet: פי וגהה ולא ירגעו אלי אלרב אלאההם (ed. Birnbaum 114:5–6) and Cod. Hunt. 206: فى وجهه ولم يرجعوا إلى الرب إلهم (ed. Schroeter 38:3–4; ed. Polliack and Schlossberg 195).

It is most likely that the translator rendered בְּכָל־זֹאת literally with פי כל הדה 'with respect to all this' (15a: 9), whereas Yefet and Cod. Hunt. 206 add a noun: בכל הדה אלשדאיד (ed. Birnbaum 114:6; ed. Polliack and Schlossberg 195)/فى كل هذه الشدايد 'in all these calamities' (ed. Schroeter 38:4–5).

Hosea 7:11

פוֹתָה is rendered with גאפלה 'negligent', 'careless', 'inadvertent' (15a:9), whereas both Yefet: מנכדעה (ed. Birnbaum 114:18; ed. Polliack and Schlossberg 195) and Cod. Hunt. 206: مخدوعة (ed. Schroeter 38:5) refer to the root خدر 'to be numb', VII 'to be deceived' (Hava p. 159). Vulgate: *seducta*; LXX: ἄνους; Peshitta: ܒܪܬܐ ('foolish'); Aquila: θελγομένη ('spell-bound'); Symmachus: ἀπατωμένη ('beguiled'); Targum: שריחתא דאתנסיבו ('a foolish [dove] whose young have been snatched away').

The translator renders the phrase אֵין לֵב 'there is no heart' with an asyndetic relative clause and an addition prepositional phrase: ליס להא תחציל 'she has no understanding' (15a:10); see also Yefet: ליס לה עקל (ed. Birnbaum 114:18–19;) and Cod. Hunt. 206: ليس لها عقل (ed. Schroeter 38:5; ed. Polliack and Schlossberg

195); Vulgate: *non habens cor*. The unique rendition תחציל is derived from the root حصل II 'to acquire (science)' (Hava p. 128).

Hosea 7:12

The reconstruction of the author's rendering אבסוט 'I will spread' (15a:11) as translation of אֶפְרוֹשׂ is taken from a phrase in his exegesis (16a:26); see also Yefet: אבסט (ed. Birnbaum 115:5; ed. Polliack and Schlossberg 195) and Cod. Hunt. 206: اسط (ed. Schroeter 38:6).

The metaphor 'spreading the net' occured already in Hosea 5:1. Whereas the translator renders רֶשֶׁת in Hosea 5:1 with the singular noun שבכה, he uses here the plural שבכיי 'my nets' (15a:11) as rendering of רִשְׁתִּי; see also Yefet: שרבי (sic) (ed. Birnbaum 115:5; ed. Polliack and Schlossberg 195) and Cod. Hunt. 206: شبكي (ed. Schroeter 38:7).

From the free space after אוודבהם 'I will chastise them' (15a:12), it can be assumed that the author must have rendered the phrase כְּשֵׁמַע לַעֲדָתָם *according to the hearing of their congregation* with a paraphrase rather than provioding a literal translation, probably similar to Yefet: באלכבר אלדי אבברתה לקאטבתהם (ed. Birnbaum 115:6–7; ed. Polliack and Schlossberg 195) or Cod. Hunt. 206: بما اسمعت قاطبتهم (ed. Schroeter 38:7–8). The versions demonstrate various attempts of paraphrasing the difficult biblical text: Aquila: κατὰ ἀκοῆς τῆς συναγωγῆς ('concerning the report of [their] meeting'); Peshitta: ܐܝܟ ܫܡܥܐ ܕܣܗܕܘܬܗܘܢ ('according to the report of their witness'); Vulgate: *secundum auditionem coetus eorum* ('according to the report of their meeting'); Targum: על דשמעו ליעיצתהון ('because they listened to their counsel').

In his grammatical notes, the author makes the remark that 'the second *yod* in אֲיִסְרֵם is superfluous' (16b:12–13); see: Rashi (referring to Dunash): ונוסף היוד השני באיסירם כאשר נוסף בייושירו ועפעפיך יישירו נגדך ('and the second *yod* in אֲיִסְרֵם has been added as it has been added in יַיְשִׁרוּ, *And your eyelashes look before you* [Proverbs 4:25]'); also Ibn Ezra refers to Proverbs 4:25. The imperative is הִיָּסֵר (16b:6), whereas Cod. Hunt. 206 has אֲיָסֵר امر ه (ed. Schroeter 26:13; see Schroeter 32 note 2). By mentioning the lexical class אלזיואל 'abandoning' (16b:8), the author reveils that he considers the derivation of the verb אֲיִסְרֵם from the imperative סור, which would correspond to Arabic زول.

The conjecture מתל השמד in the grammatical notes (16b:7) is based on the identical phrase in Yefet: מֹתֶל הַשְׁמֵד (ed. Birnbaum 229:15).

Hosea 7:13

The translation אלויל 'the woe' with article (16b:13) has been reconstructed from 17a:16; see also Yefet: אלויל (ed. Birnbaum 116:1; ed. Polliack and Schlossberg 196)/Cod. Hunt 206: الويل (ed. Schroeter 38:8) and the reconstruction of Hosea 9:12.

In the reconstructed translation, the verb חצל 'it happened' (16b:13) has been added to the biblical text to fill the *lacuna*, according to the following parallel phrase נהב חצל עליה (16b:14) and the phrase in the exegesis: אלויל חצל להם (17a:16–17).

גרמו 'they commited an offence' (16b:14) as rendition of פָּשְׁעוּ has been suggested because the author uses the same root in his translation of וּפְשָׁעִים in Hosea 14:10: ומוגרמין (29a:12; translation missing: Hosea 8:1) vs. Yefet: עצו (ed. Birnbaum 116:2; ed. Polliack and Schlossberg 196) and Cod. Hunt. 206: غدروا (ed. Schroeter 38:8).

The *plene* orthography of the reconstructed פכונת, literally 'and I was' (16b:14), is based on the author's phrase in his exegesis כונת אפדיהם (17a:18).

Hosea 7:14

The translator renders וְלֹא־זָעֲקוּ with מא + perfect: ומא צרכו 'they did not call' (16b:15) instead of possible לם + apocopate, as translate Yefet: ולם יצרבֹו (ed. Birnbaum 117:3; ed. Polliack and Schlossberg 196) and Cod. Hunt. 206: ولم يصرخوا (ed. Schroeter 38:9).

The meaning of יִתְגּוֹרָרוּ is a matter of controversy:

(1) Qimḥi points out: ('יתגוררו ענין אסיפה וחבור כמו גור יגורו עלי עזי) has the meaning of "assembly" and "coming together" as in Isaiah 54:15 and 29:4'); see also Targum: הוו כנשין ('[the grain and wine which] they were gathering'); Peshitta: ܡܬܟܬܫܝܢ ('they strove', 'they struggled'), Yefet: כאנו יגֿאורו (ed. Birnbaum 117:4; ed. Polliack and Schlossberg 196 [where some manuscripts read כאן]), Cod. Hunt. 206: يجاورو 'they are the neighbours' (ed. Schroeter 38:10),

(2) Vulgate: *ruminabant* and Symmachus: ἐμηρυκῶντο ('they ruminated') relate the verb to גרה 'cud'. Jerome argues that the verb 'to ruminate' is chosen here to emphasise that their preoccupation is identical to that of brute beasts.

(3) LXX translates κατετέμνοντο ('they cut themselves').

(4) Aquila: περιεσπῶντο ('they stripped themselves').

From his translation יתקוותו בה מן גהתי 'they are fed by Me' (16b:16–17) and his exegesis, one may conclude that the commentator also derives the verb from

גרר 'to drag', 'to drag away', 'to chew the cud'. This seems to be confirmed by the noun אלתקוות 'food' (17a:23) and ואקותהם 'and I will feed them' (17a:23). However, this understanding is to be questioned since in the grammatical explanation, he derives the verb from גור I 'to sojourn', 'to abide', hitpol. 'to seek hospitality with' (see BDB: 'dubious') and translates it with תגרור 'being neighbours' (17a:22); see also Cod. Hunt. 206 in his grammatical notes: يَجَاوِرُوا ('they are neighbours', ed. Schroeter II, 26:15).

The translator expands the phrase יָסוּרוּ בִי *they turn away from Me* by rendering והום יזולו מן טאעתי 'and they cease from obeying Me' (16b:17). This translation is echoed in his commentary: והום זאילין מן טאעתי 'and they are ceasing from obeying Me' (17a:23–24). An identical translation can be found in T-S Ar.24.7 fol. 2 verso 13: יזולו מן טאעתי; see also the similar rendering in Cod. Hunt. 206: ويجوزوا عن طاعتى ('they pass from obeying Me', ed. Schroeter 38:11), R. Tanchum: يزولون من طاعتى وامرى and Yefet: כאנו יגוזו מן טאעתי (ed. Birnbaum 117:5; ed. Polliack and Schlossberg 196: יזוגו).

Hosea 7:15

By adding למא 'when' before אדבתהם 'I disciplined them' (16b:17), the author establishes a temporal sequence; an additional למא can also be found in Hosea 11:2; 12:5; 13:1.

The author adds an enclitic pronoun to indicate the direct object: אדבתהם 'I disciplined *them*' (16b:17) to render יִסַּרְתִּי; see also the author's exegesis: 'after disciplining *them*' (17a:24–25) and Symmachus: ἐπαίδευον αὐτούς, whereas others render the biblical text literally without any additions: Yefet: אדבת (ed. Birnbaum 117:20; ed. Polliack and Schlossberg 197), Cod. Hunt. 206: ادبت (ed. Schroeter 38:11), Vulgate: *erudivit*, Peshitta: ܪܕܝܬ; Targum: מיתי יסורין; however, see the additional suffix pronoun in Yefet's exegesis: יעני אדבתהם (ed. Birnbaum 117:21; ed. Polliack and Schlossberg 197).

Hosea 7:16

The verse has provoked the translator to add major explanations. He rephrased the first sentence יָשׁוּבוּ לֹא עָל by introducing a temporal clause: אן כאן פי וקת ירגעו 'whenever they returned' (16b:18–19). Also modern exegetes emphasise the frequentative imperfect by translating 'Time and again' (Macintosh 1997:284). The author also added a remark about the situation from where they will return: מן מא הום עליה 'from where they were' (16b:19).

The rendition אלי אלעאלי 'to The High' (16b:19), i.e. the addition of the preposition and the definite article instead of biblical עַל, indicates that the translator understands 'high' to be a name of God: 'The Most High'; see also Qimḥi who takes עַל to be an adjective like עליון referring to God: 'when trouble comes, they revert to calling upon idols and not to Me who am higher than everything'. Cod. Hunt. 206 renders لا يعودوا الى نفع 'they do not return to benefit' (ed. Schroeter 38:12) and explains in his grammatical notes: יהועיל לא وقيل انه منفوع وهو مشتق יועילו ('some they that it means "benefit" and is a noun derived from Jeremiah 23:32', ed. Schroeter 26:18). Yefet renders similarly: לא ירגֿעון אלי נפע (ed. Birnbaum 118:7; ed. Polliack and Schlossberg 197) and refers to this translation in his exegesis: מצרים אלדֿי ליס להם נפע (ed. Birnbaum 118:11; ed. Polliack and Schlossberg 197).

The translator repeats the verb ירגעו 'they will return' (16b:19) after אלי אלעאלי to emphasise the returning of the people to God.

The phrase כְּקֶשֶׁת רְמִיָּה has been rendered with כקוס מכרה 'like a deceitful bow' (16b:20); see also Yefet: כקוס מכרהֿ (ed. Birnbaum 118:7; ed. Polliack and Schlossberg 197), whereas Cod. Hunt. 206 translates كقوس مكارة (ed. Schroeter 38:12). See also Vulgate: *dolosus*, Peshitta: ܢܟܝܠܐ, Targum: נכילא ('treacherous'); and the different concept in LXX: ἐντεταμένον ('strung for shooting') and Symmachus: ἀνεστραμμένον ('twisted backwards').

By introducing פלדֿלך 'therefore' (16b:20) before the phrase *their chiefs will fall by the sword*, the punishment is clearly labelled as the direct result of their actions. See also Cod. Hunt. 206: فلذلك (ed. Schroeter 38:13), whereas Yefet translates literally: יסקטו באלסיף רוסאהם (ed. Birnbaum 118:7–8; ed. Polliack and Schlossberg 197 [where one manuscript reads מן ריסאהם באלסיף יקעו זעם]).

The reconstruction of רווסאהם 'their chiefs' (16b:20) as rendition of שָׂרֵיהֶם is based on the author's usual translation; see also Yefet: רוסאהם (ed. Birnbaum 118:8; ed. Polliack and Schlossberg 197) and Cod. Hunt. 206 رُؤَسَاءَهم (ed. Schroeter 38:13).

The translator expands the vague demonstrative pronoun זוֹ into the phrase 'and when *this* misfortune will be completed upon them' (16b:20–21); see also his exegesis: ענד תמאם הדֿה אלבלייה פיהם (17b:4–5). Probably he intends to achieve a temporal sequence of the punishments: after the killing of the chiefs by the sword, they will be ridiculed in Egypt.

The last phrase of the verse מנטזה פי ארץ מצר 'a mockery in the land of Egypt' (16b:21) as rendition of לַעְגָּם בְּאֶרֶץ מִצְרָיִם is based on the author's phrase in his exegesis (17b:5).

The orthography אלא 'to' (17a:28) in the exegesis is obviously erroneous for אלי.

The conjecture מטנזה פי ארץ מצר '(they will be) a derision in the land of Egypt' (16b:21) is taken from a phrase of the exegesis (17b:5) vs. Yefet: הדה הזוהם פי ארץׄ מצר (ed. Birnbaum 118:8–9; ed. Polliack and Schlossberg 197) and Cod. Hunt. 206: وهوذا هزؤهم فى بلد مصر (ed. Schroeter 38:13–14).

Hosea 8:1

The addition of the vocative יא נבי 'oh prophet' after 'to your gum' (16b:22) indicates that the first phrase is understood as being addressed to the prophet, i.e. God is the speaker who ordered the prophet to raise his voice. Moreover, the translator rephrases the ellipsis 'to your gum a shofar' by adding the imperative אפרע 'lift up!' (16b:22). Also modern translators add a verb, e.g. Macintosh 1997:291: 'Put the ram's horn to your mouth!'; see also Yefet's exegesis: אמר אללה ללנבי אן ירפע צותה (ed. Birnbaum 119:23; ed. Polliack and Schlossberg 198). A similar understanding of the verse can be found in Targum including the vocative 'o prophet': נביא בחכך אכלי כד בשופרא אימר ('o prophet, shout with your palate as with a horn and say ...'); also in Rashi's view the verse is God's address to the prophet: שכינה אומרת לנביא השנע קול חכך וקרא בשופר ('the Shekhinah speaks to the prophet: Let hear the voice of your palate and call in the shofar') and Yefet (according to Ibn Ezra): דברי השם אל הנביא ('these are words of God to the prophet'), whereas Qimḥi, on the other hand, regards the words as an address of the prophet to the people. However, some versions retain the biblical elliptical style: Symmachus: ἐπὶ φάρυγγί σου κερατίνῃ ('upon your throat with a horn'), Vulgate adds a form of 'to be': *in gutture tuo sit tuba*; Peshitta does not represent MT אל when rendering: ܦܘܡܟܐ ܐܝܟ ܩܪܢܐ ('your mouth [is] like a horn').

After the first imperative ארפע בוק 'lift up a trumpet!' (16b:22), the translator adds the reason for the command, introduced by בסבב 'because of' (16b:22); unfortunately the following text is not preserved and could not be restored.

גזא, literally 'as compensation' (16b:23), is translation of יַעַן, which occurs only here in Hosea. The same rendering can be found both in Yefet: גזא (ed. Birnbaum 119:22; ed. Polliack and Schlossberg 198) and Cod. Hunt. 206: جزاء (ed. Schroeter 38:16). See also Saadiah who uses גזא as translation of עֵקֶב (Genesis 22:18; Numbers 14:24; Deuteronomy 7:12).

The reconstruction of עברו 'they transgressed' (16b:23) as rendering of עָבְרוּ is based on the author's preference for this Arabic cognate also in Hosea 6:7; 10:11, whereas Yefet and Cod. Hunt. 206 render with גאזו עהדי (ed. Birnbaum 119:22; ed. Polliack and Schlossberg 198) and جاوزوا عهدى (sic) (ed. Schroeter 38:16–17).

The reconstruction of שריעתי 'My law' (16b:23) as rendition of תּוֹרָתִי is based on the translation of Hosea 4:6 (שריעה) and 8:12 (ש[ר]יעתי); see Yefet: בשריעתי

(ed. Birnbaum 119:22; ed. Polliack and Schlossberg 198) and Cod. Hunt. 206: شَرِيعَتِي (ed. Schroeter 38:17).

For the reconstruction of גרמו 'they committed a crime' (16b:23) as rendering of פָּשְׁעוּ see Hosea 7:13 vs. Yefet: ועצו (ed. Birnbaum 119:22; ed. Polliack and Schlossberg 198)/Cod. Hunt. 206: وعصوا (ed. Schroeter 38:17).

The translator retains the unusual word order of MT, whereas Yefet/Cod/Hunt 206 create a verbal clause: وعصوا شريعتي (cf. ed. Polliack and Schlossberg 198 [which reads בשריעתי]).

Hosea 8:2

The translator adds ויקולו 'and they say' after 'they cry out to Me' (16b:24) probably for stylistic reasons to introduce the direct speech probably for stylistic reasons and/or to avoid the verb 'to scream' in close connection with addressing the name of God; see also Yefet: וכّדי יקולון (ed. Birnbaum 121:1; ed. Polliack and Schlossberg 198) and Cod. Hunt. 206: وكذى يقولون (ed. Schroeter 38:17).

The vocative יא אלאהנא 'our God' (16b:24) instead of MT אֱלֹהָי 'my God' harmonises the suffix pronoun with the plural verbs in this verse. The same harmonisation can be found in Peshitta: ܐܠܗܢ ('our God'), Cod. Hunt. 206: ربنا ('our lord', ed. Schroeter 38:17) and Targum: ארי לית לנא אלה בר מנך ('that there is for us no God except You'), whereas Yefet translates literally with: אלאהי (ed. Birnbaum 121:1; ed. Polliack and Schlossberg 198); see also Vulgate: *deus meus* ('my God').

The name 'Israel', which seems to be an isolated part of the phrase and could be interpreted as apposition to the subject, provoked the author to introduce a whole sentence, which gives the reason for the people's address: לאנהם אל אסראיל אלמכתצין בי 'for they are the people of Israel who are special to Me' (16b:24–25). Also Targum seems to emphasise the special relationship between God and Israel when explaining: ארי אנחנא עמך ישראל ('for we are your people Israel'); also modern commentators expand the text of their translation, e.g. Macintosh 1997:294: 'My God, we know you, we, your people Israel'. Cod. Hunt. 206 combines 'Israel' with an additional vocative 'God' and renders يا اله اسرائل ('o God of Israel', ed. Schroeter 38:18), whereas Yefet translates literally: יא אלאהי ערפנאך ישראל (ed. Birnbaum 121:1–2; ed. Polliack and Schlossberg 198).

Hosea 8:3

זָנַח has been rendered with כדל 'he has forsaken' (16b:25); see also Yefet: בّדל (ed. Birnbaum 121:12; ed. Polliack and Schlossberg 198) and Cod. Hunt. 206: خذلوا (ed. Schroeter 38:18). Ibn Janāḥ (on Hoses 8:5) understands the verb as denoting 'to be remote', 'to depart'.

The translator renders the indefinite טוב with אלכיר 'the good' (16b:25) which can be interpreted as 'the Good One', i.e. 'God'. Ibn Ezra clarifies: הוא השם הנכבד שהיה טוב לו ('It is the name of God who is good for Israel'), and also Qimḥi takes the phrase as a name of God: והוא האל ית׳ שאין טוב זולתו בלי מגרעת ('It is God Blessed, apart from Him is no good without deficiency'), whereas Yefet translates it with ללצואב ('that which is right', 'rightness', ed. Birnbaum 121:12; ed. Polliack and Schlossberg 198) or 'religious conduct' (Birnbaum p. xiv). The translation of Cod. Hunt. 206: الجيد is ambivalent (ed. Schroeter 38:18). Most of the versions take the adjective as neuter: LXX: ἀγαθά ('good things'), Peshitta: ܠܛܒܬܐ ('goodness'); Targum: טובא ('good'), Vulgate: *bonum* ('the good'); see also their translation of Hosea 14:3. Modern exegetes have either 'the Good One' (e.g. Stuart 1987:126, 128 n. 3a) or 'what is good' (e.g. Macintosh 1997:295).

The translator adds פלדלך 'therefore' (16b:25) before the second half of the verse, apparently to indicate the consequence of Israel's actions; since they have left God, the enemy will pursue them. See also Yefet Cod. Hunt. 206: ولذلك (ed. Schroeter 38:18; ed. Polliack and Schlossberg 198).

The reconstruction of יכלבה 'he will pursue him' (16b:25) as rendition of יִרְדְּפוֹ is based on Yefet: יכלבה (ed. Birnbaum 121:12; ed. Polliack and Schlossberg 198). With Yefet, the translator retains the 3rd masculine singular suffix pronoun, whereas Cod. Hunt. 206 changes it into plural: يكلبهم (ed. Schroeter 38:19).

Hosea 8:4

מִמֶּנִּי has been rendered with מן גהתי, literally 'from My side' (16b:28), indicating the source or author of the action, i.e. 'with Me being involved'; similar Yefet: מן קבלי (ed. Birnbaum 122:7; ed. Polliack and Schlossberg 199), whereas Cod. Hunt. 206 specifies: بامرى 'by My command' (ed. Schroeter 38:19).

Yefet (according to Ibn Ezra) explains the verb הֵשִׂירוּ 'they made princes' as הסירו 'they removed' (1 Kennicott MS and 2 de Rossi MSS read הסירו), so that the verbs are not parallel but antithetical: '*they appointed kings* without my prompting and *they removed them* without my knowledge'; ויפת אמר כמו סמך כמו בשורי מהם והטעם הפוך אם במליכו או אם השירו ('Yefet explains as if it was written with *samekh*, as Hosea 9:2, the phrase is therefore not parallel:

may they appoint kings or may they remove them'); similar Rashi: ד"א הסירו את זה ממלוכה והמליכו את זה ('another interpretation: They remove the one and appoint king the other'). Alternatively, the translator understands the verb to be derived from the root שׂרר (denominative of שַׂר) *hif'il* 'to make princes', as shows his rendering רווסו (16b:26); see also Yefet: רוסו (ed. Birnbaum 122:7; ed. Polliack and Schlossberg 199 [which reads רווס]) and Cod. Hunt. 206: رؤسوا (ed. Schroeter 38:19), LXX: ἦρξαν ('they ruled'), Vulgate: *principes extiterunt* ('they acted as princes'), Peshitta: ܐܫܬܠܛܘ ('they ruled') and Ḥayyūj (ed. Jastrow p. 130).

The translator renders יִכָּרֵת literally with a singular verb form ינקטע 'he will be cut off' (16b:27); also Yefet ינקטע (ed. Birnbaum 122:8; ed. Polliack and Schlossberg 199), whereas Cod. Hunt. 206 changes the verb into plural ينقطعوا (ed. Schroeter 38:20) and adds عن ذكرى ('they will be cut off from My memory'). Also the versions render with plural verbs suggesting that the subject are people or idols: LXX: ὅπως ἐξολεθρευθῶσιν ('in order that they may be destroyed'), Vulgate: *ut interirent* ('in order that they may perish'), Peshitta: ܢܬܒܛܠܘܢ ('that they will come to nought'), Targum: בדיל דישתיצון ('in order thay they will be consumed').

Hosea 8:5

In the phrase זָנַח עֶגְלֵךְ, the translator understands *your calf* as subject and supplies an object by adding a suffix pronoun to the verb form: כדלך '(the calf) has forsaken you' (16b:27); see also T-S 24.7 fol. 2 recto 9: כדלך. The author regards the name *Samaria* as vocative: יא שמרון 'oh Samaria' (16b:27). Ibn Ezra interprets the verb as מאס 'to reject' ('your calf, oh Samaria, has rejected you'). On the other hand, Yefet and Cod. Hunt 206 render the verb literally כׄדׄל עׄגׄלך (ed. Birnbaum 123:1; ed. Polliack and Schlossberg 199 [where one manuscript reads כׄדלך]/قد انخذل عجلك 'your calf is cast off' (ed. Schroeter 38:21). Ibn Janāḥ states that the verb in this verse has an intransitive meaning: 'your calf is remote', 'your calf has departed'. Qimḥi translates the verb with רחק 'to be distant' and gives a transitive and an intransitive option: (1) 'your calf has removed you afar off, o Samaria'; (2) 'your calf is far from you, o Samaria'. Rashi tries to introduce God as subject of the sentence: 'He, i.e. God, has rejected you, Samaria, because of the sin of the calves'. Some of the versions read an imperative: LXX: ἀπότριψαι ('reject!'); Theodition: ἀπόρριψαι ('get rid of!'), or a 3rd plural: Aquila: ἀπώθησαν ('they put aside [the calves]'); Peshitta: ܛܥܘ ('they have erred [through the calf]'); Targum: טעו בתר עגלא ('they have erred after the calf'), or a passive: Symmachus: ἀπεβλήθη ('he/it was rejected'); Vulgate: *proiectus est*.

The translator adds the conjunction לאן 'for' (16b:27) before the next phrase 'My anger became severe', which he regards as giving the reason for the preceding statement.

בָּם has been rendered literally with בהם 'among them' (16b:28), whereas Yefet and Cod. Hunt. 206 interpret the prepositional phrase as בישראל (ed. Birnbaum 123:2; ed. Polliack and Schlossberg 199). باسرائل (ed. Schroeter 38:21).

נְקָיֹן 'innocence', 'cleansing', 'purity' is rendered with the definite infinitive v אלתברי 'the freeing', 'the acquital' (16b:28); see also Yefet: אלתברי (ed. Birnbaum 123:3; ed. Polliack and Schlossberg 199) and Cod. Hunt. 206: التبرى (ed. Schroeter 38:22), whereas the versions prefer an infinitive without definite article, e.g. LXX: καθαρισθῆναι ('to become/be pure'); Aquila: ἀθῳωθῆναι; Symmachus: καθαρθῆναι; Vulgate: *emundari*; Peshitta: ܠܡܬܕܟܐ; Targum: לִמְזְכֵי. By adding the vague phrase מן מא הום פיה 'from what they were in' (16b:28–17a:1), the translator indicates the status from what they are cleansed, whereas Yefet and Cod. Hunt 206 refer directly to idolatry: מן עבאדה אלאותאן (ed. Birnbaum 123:3; ed. Polliack and Schlossberg 199)/من عبادة الاوثان (ed. Schroeter 38:22). Rashi also suggests that נְקָיֹן denotes 'innocence from that filth', i.e. from idolatry. Ibn Ezra comments: 'My anger will be against them until they become pure'.

Hosea 8:6

By adding אצלה 'its origin' (17a:1) at the beginning of the verse, the translator emphasises that Israel is the source and origin of the cult of the calves.

The author identifies the *hapax legomenon* שְׁבָבִים with שראר 'sparks' (17a:2); according to this view, the phrase would mean that the calf will be consigned to the flames, as Moses burnt the golden calf in the desert (Exodus 32:20). In his grammatical notes, the author derives the plural שְׁבָבִים from a *segholate* noun (*a*-type: *malk*) (18b:13–14), whereas he links the nominal pattern שָׁבִיב with the plural שְׁבִיבִים. Ibn Ezra compares the word שְׁבָבִים with שביבים 'sparks', 'flames' (see Job 18:5; Daniel 3:22; 7:9); BDB suggests the translation 'probably splinters'; see Targum: נסרי לוחין ('chips of boards'). Cod. Hunt. 206 renders فى الحقيقة عجل شومرون فى جملة المسبيين ('actually, the calf of Samaria is among the group of prisoners', ed. Schroeter 39:1–2), i.e. he derives שְׁבָבִים from שבי; see his grammatical note which includes three options (Schroeter 39:3–6). Abulwalid: ان مطرودا يكون صنم شمرين منقولا من بلده مسبيا مع عابديه ('the idol of Samaria should be exiled, carried from its land, lead into captivity with its worshippers'). Yefet gives three options: (1) Either the plural שְׁבָבִים has to be derived from a singular noun שָׁבָב in analogy with דְּבָר/דְּבָרִים (ed. Birnbaum 125:9–10;

cf. ed. Polliack and Schlossberg 200), (2) or from שְׁבִי (see: פקאל אנה יציר מן גמלה אלמסבאיין, ed. Birnbaum 124:17–18 and also his exegesis 125:7–8), (3) or has to be rendered with שראר אלנאר 'sparks of fire' (ed. Birnbaum 124:23). Some versions render with a participle/adjective: LXX: διότι πλανῶν ἦν ὁ μόσχος σου Σαμάρεια ('because your calf was deceiving, oh Samaria'); Symmachus: ἀκατάστατος ('unstable', 'unsettled'); or a noun: Peshitta: ܠܗܘܐ ܗܘܐ ܥܓܠܟܝ ('your calf, o Samaria, has become straying'); Vulgate: *aranearum telas* ('spiders' webs'). 4QpHos^b has שובבים.

Hosea 8:7

The translator adds בל 'rather' (17a:3) after 'it has no stalk' to create an antithesis between the stalk and the bud.

The translator renders the indefinite זָרִים with the definite noun אלגרבא 'the strangers' (17a:3); see Hosea 7:9. Yefet and Cod. Hunt. 206 prefer the equivalent אלאגנבײן (ed. Birnbaum 125:13; ed. Polliack and Schlossberg 201)/الاجنبيين (ed. Schroeter 39:8).

In his grammatical notes, the author explains the redundant *taw* in סוּפָתָה as a sign of emphasis, i.e. the form סוּפָתָה is an emphatic variant of סוּפָה (18b:14–15); see also Ibn Ezra: תיו סופתה נוסף כמו אימתה ('the *taw* is pleonastic as in Exodus 15:16'). Modern commentators (e.g. Vielhauer 2007:64) interpret the form as old accusative ending with reference to GK § 90 f.

Hosea 8:8

Whereas the translator has chosen the Arabic cognate יבלעוה for the rendition of יִבְלָעֻהוּ in Hosea 8:7, he prefers here for נִבְלַע the rendering הלך 'he perished' (17a:4), presumably in order to indicate Israel's total destruction; see also Yefet: הלך (ed. Birnbaum 126:12; ed. Polliack and Schlossberg 201). Cod. Hunt. 206 retains the Arabic cognate though in the passive voice: ابتلع (ed. Schroeter 39:9) 'it is swallowed down'; see also LXX: κατεπόθη; Vulgate: *devoratus est*; Peshitta: ܐܬܒܠܥ; Targum has אתבזיז 'it is plundered'.

בַּגּוֹיִם has been rendered with פי אלאחזאב 'among the groups' (17a:4), whereas Cod. Hunt. 206 and Yefet prefer بَيْنَ الأُمَم 'among the nations' (ed. Schroeter 39:9)/בין אלאמם (ed. Birnbaum 126:12; ed. Polliack and Schlossberg 201 [which reads בין אלאחזאב]).

The literal translation of כִּכְלִי with כאינא 'like a vessel' (17a:4) contrasts with the plural كآنِيَة in Cod. Hunt. 206 (ed. Schroeter 39:9) and Yefet's rendition with a different noun: מתל אלה (آلة) (ed. Birnbaum 126:13; ed. Polliack and Schlossberg 201).

For the rendition of אֵין חֵפֶץ בּוֹ with ליס פיה מראד '(a vessel) in which is no pleasure', 'value', 'worth', 'purpose' (17a:4–5) see LXX: σκεῦος ἄχρηστον ('useless vessel'). Yefet and Cod. Hunt. 206 render with לא מראד פיהא (ed. Birnbaum 126:13; ed. Polliack and Schlossberg 201 [which reads בה])/لا مراد فيها (ed. Schroeter 39:9). See Peshitta: ܡܐܢܐ ܕܠܐ ܚܫܚ; Targum: דלית צרוך ביה; Vulgate: *immundum* ('unclean').

Hosea 8:9

עָלוּ has been rendered with טלעו 'they ascended' (17a:5), whereas Yefet and Cod. Hunt. 206 prefer the verb צעדו (ed. Birnbaum 127:5; ed. Polliack and Schlossberg 201)/صعدوا (ed. Schroeter 39:10) with the same meaning; see also the versions: LXX: ἀνέβησαν; Vulgate: *ascenderunt*; Peshitta: ܣܠܩܘ, whereas Targum interprets ascending as גלו 'they were exiled'.

The author adopts the Hebrew name אַשּׁוּר *Assur* (17a:5); see also Yefet (ed. Birnbaum 125:5; ed. Polliack and Schlossberg 201), whereas Cod. Hunt. 206 has الموصل 'Mossul' (ed. Schroeter 39:10).

The translator adds the copula פחצלו 'and they were' (17a:5) and changes the metaphor פֶּרֶא into a simile by adding the inseparable preposition כּ: כחמאר אלוחש 'like a wild ass' (17a:5). A similar rephrasing can be found in Yefet: וצארו מתֿל חמאר אלוחש (ed. Birnbaum 127:5–6; ed. Polliack and Schlossberg 201) and Cod. Hunt. 206: وصاروا مثل حمار الوحش (ed. Schroeter 39:10); Peshitta adds ܐܝܟ, 'as [a wild ass]'. Targum paraphrases: על דהליכו ברעות נפשהון כערד מרוד ('since they went on their own accords like an ass running wild').

Instead of the participle בּוֹדֵד, the translator creates a relative clause: אלדי הו מונפרד. The reconstruction of מונפרד 'separated' (17a:6) is very likely; see also Yefet and Cod. Hunt. 206: אלמפתרד (ed. Birnbaum 127:6; ed. Polliack and Schlossberg 201)/المنفرد (ed. Schroeter 39:10). The additional הו 'he' (17a:6) would fill the existing *lacuna* at the beginning of the line and is based on the similar phrase אלדי הו מודלג, literally 'who is before daybreak' (26a:2), which is the translation of the participle מַשְׁכִּים in Hosea 13:3 and has a parallel structure: relative marker, independent personal pronoun functioning as copula, participle.

The translator paraphrases the לוֹ *for himself* by בראיה to indicate that the wild ass is not only alone by himself, but isolated 'in his opinion', 'view', 'thinking' (17a:5–6). A similar idea of isolated thinking can be found in R. Tanchum: منفرد برايه لنفسه (according to Schroeter p. 170 n. 4): 'separated in his view for himself', and Targum: עַל דהליכו ברעות נפשהון כערד מרוד ('since they went on their own accord like an ass running wild'). Ibn Ezra interprets בּוֹדֵד as referring to the various opinions which existed in Israel about the political situation: וטעם בודד כי לא היתה עצתם אחת ('the meaning of בּוֹדֵד is that their counsel was not only one'). Yefet and Cod. Hunt. 206 replace לוֹ by לנפסה (ed. Birnbaum 127:6; ed. Polliack and Schlossberg 201)/لنفسه (ed. Schroeter 39:10).

הִתְנוּ is rendered with קד חצלו מגאדרין 'they have paid' (17a:6), as in Hosea 8:10: יִתְנוּ which he translated with יוגאדרו. The translator derived the verb from the root נתן; see LXX: 'Ephraim loved gifts' (δῶρα ἠγάπησαν). Targum interprets the verb as passive: אתמסרו ביד עממיא דרחימו; see Schroeter pp. 51–52 note 3: 'Lohn'. The root גדר seems to be a dialectal variation for גדר. The sense is: they paid for their love-affair with Assur; see also Vulgate: *munera dederung amatoribus* ('they have given gifts to lovers'). It is noteworthy that Yefet and Cod. Hunt. 206 who translate אעאדו (ed. Birnbaum 127:6; ed. Polliack and Schlossberg 201) and اعادوا (ed. Schroeter 39:11) respectively, appear to have taken the Hebrew תנה 'to hire' (BDB) as derivative of Aramaic תני 'to repeat', 'to do again' (Hebrew שנה), i.e. 'they repeated friendships' (see Al-Fāsī, Uṣūl 806:5). This interpretation draws on BT Baba Batra 8a: אמר עולא פסוק זה בלשון ארמית נאמר (see Birnbaum p. xiv). In his grammatical notes, the author derives the verb הִתְנוּ from the imperative base הִתְנֵה, as does Ibn Nūḥ: מתל התנו אהבים אמרהא הִתְנֵה ('like הִתְנוּ אֲהָבִים, the imperative of which is הַתְנֵה', *Diqduq* on Psalms 78:41, ed. Khan 2000:300–301).

The translator imitates the abstract plural אֲהָבִים by rendering במחבאת 'love-affairs' (17a:6); see also Yefet: אלמחבאת (ed. Birnbaum 127:6; ed. Polliack and Schlossberg 201) and Cod. Hunt. 206: المحبات (ed. Schroeter 39:11)

Hosea 8:10

The rendering of יִתְנוּ with יוגאדרו 'they paid' (17a:7) leads to the conclusion that the translator interpreted the verb as *hifʿil* imperfect, whereas some versions understand the verb as passive, as is clear from their rendering: LXX: παραδοθή-σονται; Peshitta: ܢܫܬܠܡܘܢ ('they will be handed over'). As in Hosea 8:9, Yefet translates יִתְנוּ with יעודו (ed. Birnbaum 128:3; ed. Polliack and Schlossberg 202); see also Cod. Hunt. 206: يعودوا ('they return') who adds الى محبة مصر ('to the love of Egypt') and another ويصيروا فى الاحزاب ('and they will be among the nations', ed. Schroeter 39:15).

The addition of the prepositional phrase עליהם 'against them' after אגמעהם 'I will gather' (17a:7) clarifies the context: God gathers the nations against Israel; see also Yefet: אגמעהם עליהם (ed. Birnbaum 128:4; ed. Polliack and Schlossberg

202). Also Ibn Ezra interprets this 'gathering' in a negative sense: they will be gathered in Egypt to be punished, whereas, in Qimḥi's view, the nations are gathered to effect Israel's exile.

The beginning of the difficult text וַיָּחֵלּוּ מְעָט מִמַּשָּׂא מֶלֶךְ שָׂרִים has been rendered literally ואבתדו קליל מן חמל 'and they began a little from the load'. Instead of identifying מֶלֶךְ שָׂרִים as the title of the Assyrian king, the translator only suspends the asyndeton *king chiefs* by joining the words with the preposition מע 'with': מלך מע רווסא 'kings with chiefs' (17a:8); similarly most version which add 'and': LXX, Peshitta, Vulgate, Aquila, some MSS of the Targum and many Kennicot and de Rossi MSS insert here the connective conjunction 'and', i.e. 'kings and princes'. R. Tanchum: ويحلون ويخففون ما عليهم من ثقل كلف الملك وروساه الذى هم الان مطلبون بها ('and they will loosen and alleviate the heavy load which the king and his chiefs put on them, and which they now demand from them'). Yefet and Cod. Hunt. 206 take the two nouns as components of a construct chain and add the article before 'chiefs' when rendering: מלך אלרוסא (ed. Birnbaum 128:4–5; ed. Polliack and Schlossberg 202)/ملك الروساء 'the kings of the chiefs' (ed. Schroeter 39:16); see also Macintosh 1997:319. Some modern commentators change the vocalization into וְיֶהֱלוּ 'and they will show weakness' (v. Hoonacker; Macintosh 1997:319; Vielhauer 2007:64, 66).

Hosea 8:11

The reconstruction of מדאבח 'altars' (17a:9) is based on the author's usual rendering of מִזְבֵּחַ and on מדאבח in the second half of the verse.

ליכטי, literally 'so that he sins' (17a:9) as rendition of the infinitive לַחֲטֹא has been reconstructed according to the following identical ליכטי vs. Yefet: ללכטא (ed. Birnbaum 128:17; ed. Polliack and Schlossberg 202) and Cod. Hunt. 206: لِلْخَطَأ (ed. Schroeter 39:17). The author renders לַחֲטֹא twice by creating a subordinate clause ליכטי 'so that he sins' (17a:9).

By adding עליהא 'on them' twice (17a:9) vs. Yefet (cf. ed. Polliack and Schlossberg 202 עליה) and Cod. Hunt. 206, the translator emphasises that Ephraim committed the sin upon the altars. Probably he likes to indicate that Ephraim's sin had cultic connotations.

By the additional תום 'then' (17a:9), the author's signals his interest in a temporal sequence: first they increased altars to commit their sin upon them; then they had (other) altars for the same purpose.

TEXTUAL NOTES

Hosea 8:12

Since the lacuna at the beginning of the line cannot be filled with a simple אכתוב, I suggest the restoration כנת אכתוב 'I wrote' (17a:10) as rendition of אֶכְתָּוב-; see also Yefet: כנת אכתב (ed. Birnbaum 129:12; ed. Polliack and Schlossberg 202) and Cod. Hunt. 206: كنت اكتب (ed. Schroeter 39:17).

The restoration of מתל 'like' (17a:10) for כְּמוֹ is based on the author's rendition in Hosea 7:4; 13:7.

כְּמוֹ-זָר is rendered with מתל אלגריב 'like the stranger'; R. Tanchum chooses the same noun though a different preposition: كالغريب vs. Yefet מתל אלאגנבי (ed. Birnbaum 129:12; ed. Polliack and Schlossberg 202) and Cod. Hunt. 206: مثل الاجنبي (ed. Schroeter 39:18).

Hosea 8:13

The reconstruction of דבאיח 'offerings' (17a:11) as translation of the construct זִבְחֵי instead of possible קראבין (T-S Ar.24.7 fol. 2 recto 14) is based on the translator's usual rendering (see Hosea 3:4; 6:6; 9:4); see also Yefet: דבאיח (ed. Birnbaum 130:5; ed. Polliack and Schlossberg 203)/Cod. Hunt. 206: ذباع (ed. Schroeter 39:18); Qimḥi: מתנות ('gifts'), i.e. the gifts that they deem to be given to Me.

The translation of the *hapax legomenon* הַבְהָבַי may be restored as עטאיא 'my gifts' (17a:11), as in T-S Ar.22.128 fol. 1 verso 13: ולדלך קאל הבהבי עטאיאי, or as עטאיי (T-S Ar.24.7 fol. 2 recto 14); see also Yefet: אלעטיה (ed. Birnbaum 130:5; ed. Polliack and Schlossberg 203 [which reads אלעטייה]) and Cod. Hunt. 206: العطايا 'the gifts' (ed. Schroeter 39:18).

The reconstruction of ירצי ענהם 'he accepts them' (17a:11) as translation of רָצָה is tentative though the diacritic point over the צ and the final י seem to be recognisable. Though Cod. Hunt. 206 renders with لم يقبلهم and adds قربيا 'he does (not) accept a sacrifice from them', he explains in his notes: רצם رضيهم (ed. Schroeter 39:22); Yefet has קבלהא (ed. Birnbaum 130:6; ed. Polliack and Schlossberg 203).

The reconstruction of דנבהם 'their sins' (17a:12) as rendition of עֲוֹנָם is likely because of the author's usual translation (see Hosea 5:5; 7:1; 9:9; 12:9; 14:2, 3, especially 4:8 with identical דנבהם as rendition of עֲוֹנָם; text missing: Hosea 9:7; 13:12). See Yefet: דנובהם (ed. Birnbaum 130:6; ed. Polliack and Schlossberg 203 [which reads דֻנבהם]).

The reconstruction of ויפתקד (17a:12) for וַיִּפְקֹד is based on the usual rendition of the root פקד *qal* with the Arabic cognate فقد VIII (see Hosea 2:15; 4:9,

14; 12:3; translation missing: Hosea 1:4; 9:9); see also Yefet: ויפתקד (ed. Birnbaum 130:7; ed. Polliack and Schlossberg 203) and Cod. Hunt. 206: وَيفتقد (ed. Schroeter 39:19).

The restored rendering כטאיאהם 'their sins' (17a:12) as rendition of חַטֹּאותָם is based on the translation of חַטָּאת with כטייה in Hosea 10:8; 13:12 (translation missing in Hosea 9:9; see also כטא for חֲטָא in Hosea 12:9); see also Yefet: כטאיאהם (ed. Birnbaum 130:7; ed. Polliack and Schlossberg 203) and Cod. Hunt. 206: خطاياهم (ed. Schroeter 39:19).

By adding בל 'rather' (17a:11) before the phrase אלסאעה ידכר 'now he will remember', the author emphasises the antithesis: God does not accept their sacrifices, on the contrary, He will remember their sins.

In the exegesis, the reconstruction of the verb ויאכלוהא 'and they ate them' (18b:7) can be justified when comparing T-S Ar.22.128 fol. 1 verso 16: ויאכלוהא לאנפסהם.

Hosea 8:14

The translator renders וַיִּשְׁכַּח literally with פנסי 'he forgot' (17a:12) whereas Yefet: ואטרח (ed. Birnbaum 131:22; ed. Polliack and Schlossberg 204) and Cod. Hunt. 206: واطرح (ed. Schroeter 40:1) have chosen a semantically stronger equivalent 'he threw far away', 'he discarded'.

The translator adopts the Arabic cognate هيكل 'temple', 'large building' (17a:13) when rendering הֵיכָלוֹת with היאכל; see also Yefet: היאכל (Birnbaum 131:22; ed. Polliack and Schlossberg 204) and Cod. Hunt. 206: هياكل (ed. Schroeter 401). הֵיכָלוֹת can have two meanings (1) 'idolatric temples' (Targum) and (2) 'palaces'; see Ibn Ezra: היכלות לבצר בהם ('palaces to fortify in them'); Qimḥi mentions both options: ובן היכלות לעבוד בהם ע״ז ויתכן לפרש ויבן היכלות להשגב בהם מפני האויב ('He built temples, in order to do idiolatry in them; it is possible to explain "he built temples", in order to find shelter from the enemy in them').

הִרְבָּה has been rendered with כתר 'he has multiplied' (17a:13), from كثر II, whereas Yefet and Cod. Hunt. 206 have the IV form: אכתר (ed. Birnbaum 131:23; ed. Polliack and Schlossberg 204)/أكثر (ed. Schroeter 40:1).

The translation of בְּצֻרוֹת with the feminine plural חציןאת 'fortified' (17a:13) echoes Hebrew grammar where the adjective is congruent with the feminine plural antecedent עָרִים, whereas Yefet and Cod. Hunt. 206 apply CA rules according to which the antecedent القرى demands the feminine singular: אלמחצנה (ed. Birnbaum 131:23; ed. Polliack and Schlossberg 204)/الحصينة (ed. Schroeter 40:2).

TEXTUAL NOTES   193

The translator renders וְשִׁלַּחְתִּי with פסא אוסרח 'and I will send' (17a:13–14) to emphasise the future tense vs. Yefet: ואנא ארסל (ed. Birnbaum 131:23; ed. Polliack and Schlossberg 204) and Cod. Hunt. 206: فانا ارسل (ed. Schroeter 40:2).

The rendering of אַרְמְנֹתֶיהָ with קצורה '*his* palaces' (17a:14) harmonises the suffix pronoun with the preceding קוריה '*his* cities', whereas Yefet and Cod. Hunt. 206 render literally: קצורהא (ed. Birnbaum 132:1; ed. Polliack and Schlossberg 204)/قصورها '*her* palaces' (ed. Schroeter 40:2).

Hosea 9:1

The unusual אֶל־גִּיל has been rendered literally אלי טרב 'unto a joy' (18b:19); see also Yefet: אלי אלטרב (ed. Birnbaum 132:14; ed. Polliack and Schlossberg 205) and the author's translation of Hosea 10:5 in connection with the cult of the calves. Cod. Hunt. 206 employs the same root for his rendition with the verb وتطرب (ed. Schroeter 40:4) which he sets in parallel with 'do not rejoice!' LXX's rendering μηδὲ εὐφραίνου ('and do not exult!') suggests a negated imperative אַל־תָּגֵל; see also Targum: לא תבועון, Vulgate: *noli exultare*, Peshitta: ܘܠܐ ܬܚܕܐ.

The translator renders מֵעַל אֱלֹהֶיךָ with ען טאעה אלאהך 'from *obeying* your God' (18b:19) (see his addition in the translation of Hosea 7:14), probably for theological reasons: it is impossible that man strays from God: he is only able to refrain from obeying Him. A similar reason can be assumed for Yefet: מן עבאדה אלאהך (ed. Birnbaum 132:15; ed. Polliack and Schlossberg 205 [where one manuscript lacks the word מן]) and Cod. Hunt. 206: من عبادة ربك (ed. Schroeter 40:4–5): 'from worshipping your God'/'your Lord'.

The translator adopts the asyndetic Hebrew syntax by rendering אָהַבְתָּ with אחבת 'you loved' (18b:19), whereas Yefet and Cod. Hunt. 206 add the connective conjunction 'and': ואחבבת (ed. Birnbaum 132:15; ed. Polliack and Schlossberg 205)/واحببت (ed. Schroeter 40:5).

The noun אֶתְנָן is rendered with גועל 'payment' (18b:20), which is also used as rendition of אֶתְנָה (Hosea 2:14), whereas Yefet has אלעטיה 'the present' (ed. Birnbaum 132:15; ed. Polliack and Schlossberg 205) and Cod. Hunt. 206: الجدر 'the fee' (ed. Schroeter 40:5). The author refers to the noun אלגדור 'the fee' in his commentary (19a:16).

Instead of retaining the preposition עַל in the phrase עַל כָּל־גָּרְנוֹת דָּגָן, as does Cod. Hunt. 206: على كل انادر الدجن (ed. Schroeter 40:5), the author introduces the prepostion מע 'with': מע כל אנדאדר דגן 'with all threshing-floors of grain' (18b:20); see also Yefet: מע כל אנאדר אלדגן (ed. Birnbaum 132:15–16; ed. Polliack and Schlossberg 205). Peshitta translates with ܡܢ ܟܠ ('from every').

The reconstruction אלכרוג מן טאעתה 'the walking away from obeying Him' (19a:11) in the exegesis is based on similar phrases in 16b:17; 20b:27.

Hosea 9:2

The translator adds פלדלך 'and therefore' at the beginning of the verse (18b:20); see also his exegesis (19a:18). Presumably his intention is to characterise the following sentence as expressing the consequent punishment for their actions: since they expected the threshing-floor to pay for their harlotry, the same threshing-floor (and the wine-press) will not provide any food for them at all.

The translator derives יִרְעֵם from רעה I 'to pasture', 'to graze', 'to tend', 'to feed', as shows his translation ירעאהם (18b:20); see also Yefet: ירעאהם (ed. Birnbaum 133:12; ed. Polliack and Schlossberg 205), Cod. Hunt. 206: يرعاهم (ed. Schroeter 40:6), Vulgate: *non pascet eos* ('he will not feed them'); in a passive sense: Peshitta: ܠܐ ܢܣܒܥܘܢ ('they will not be satisfied [from the threshing-floor]'); Targum: לא יתזנון ('they will not be nourished [from the threshing-floor]'). Ibn Ezra, however, says that the threshing-floor and the wine-press will no pay attention to them (יכירם), i.e. he derives the verb from the root רעה III 'to take pleasure', 'to watch', 'to regard' (BDB). When discussing Hosea 12:2 (אֶפְרַיִם רֹעֶה רוּחַ), also Ibn Janāḥ suggests the meaning of 'thought', 'review', 'attention': אלפקר ואלתפקקד ואלראעת. LXX: οὐκ ἔγνω αὐτούς ('he did not know them') reflects a misreading ot יִרְעֵם as יֵדָעֵם. Some modern commentators derive the verb יִרְעֵם from רעה II 'to associate with' (Nyberg; Wolff). LXX ἔγνων read ידעם.

After the phrase 'he will not graze them', the tanslator adds the explanatory note כל ואחד מנהא 'every single one of them' (18b:21), obviously to emphasise that there is no exception: not a single threshing-floor and not a single wine press will provide food for them.

The verb יְכַחֶשׁ 'he will deceive', 'he acts deceptively' (BDB) is rendered with פינכתם 'and it will be concealed' (18b:21), whereas Yefet: יגחדהא (ed. Birnbaum 133:12; ed. Polliack and Schlossberg 205) and Cod. Hunt. 206: يجحدها (ed. Schroeter 40:6) think of 'to refuse', 'to reject'. See also LXX: ἐψεύσατο αὐτούς ('he deceived them'); Vulgate: *mentietur*; Peshitta: ܘܡܫܚܐ ܢܕܓܠ ('and oil shall deceive [them]'); Targum: לא יסופיק ('[wine] will not be sufficient [for them]').

The translator interprets the pronominal object בָּהּ of the biblical text (*it will fail in her*) as referring to the land: פינכתם מנהא 'it will be concealed from it', i.e. the land (18b:21); see also his exegesis in 19a:19–20. All versions render with the 3rd plural masculine.

Hosea 9:3

The translator interprets the Hebrew connective conjunction 'and' in וְשָׁב as
בל 'rather' (18b:22) to emphasise the antithesis between the dwelling *in YHWH
land* and the exile in Egypt and Assur; Yefet translates literally with: וירגע (ed.
Birnbaum 134:2; ed. Polliack and Schlossberg 205); Cod. Hunt. 206: لا يجلسوا (ed.
Schroeter 40:6).

The translator retains the word order of the Hebrew טָמֵא יֹאכֵלוּ by rendering נגס יאכלו 'unclean (things)—they will eat' (18b:22); see also Yefet: נגס יאכלון
(ed. Birnbaum 134:3; ed. Polliack and Schlossberg 205), whereas Cod. Hunt. 206
prefers the usual syntax of a verbal clause, i.e. finite verb, subject, object: يأكلوا
النجس (ed. Schroeter 40:7).

The attribute אלכאץ in the phrase פי אלבלד אלכאץ (19a:22) in the exegesis has
been inferred from the phrase in 19a:27.

Hosea 9:4

The additional introductory לאן 'for' (18b:22) links this verse more closely with
the preceding one (see Hosea 4:4) to assure that it is understood as the reason
for Israel's unclean status.

The translator adds הודא 'behold' (18b:23) twice probably to anticipate the
הִנֵּה of the following verse and to draw special attention to Israel's libation offering and their ethical behaviour.

יֶעֶרְבוּ is rendered with the Arabic cognate יערובו 'they will be pleasing'
(18b:23) vs. Yefet: ילדו (ed. Birnbaum 135:4; ed. Polliack and Schlossberg 206);
Cod. Hunt. 206: تلذ (ed. Schroeter 40:8).

The translator adds the subject אפעאלהם 'their deeds' (18b:23) to the phrase
'and they will not be pleasing to Him', because, as he regarded זִבְחֵיהֶם obviously as the subject of the following phrase, he missed a subject in the phrase
וְלֹא יֶעֶרְבוּ־לוֹ. By introducing the new subject 'their deeds', the author seems
to express his view that God's dissatisfaction is not a fundamental one, as
expressed in LXX: οὐχ ἥδυσαν αὐτῷ ('they have not pleased Him') and Vulgate:
non placebunt ei ('they will not please Him'), but refers to their (evil) deeds only.
Peshitta, on the other hand, regards 'their offerings' as subject of the verbal sentence: ܠܐ ܢܒܣܡܢ ܠܗ ܕܒܚܝܗܘܢ ('their offerings will not please Him'). Cod.
Hunt. 206 regards 'their sacrifices' as subject of the phrase: ولا تلذ له ذبايحهم 'their
sacrifices do not please him' (ed. Schroeter 40:8). Targum solves the difficulty by
presenting two translations of 'their offerings': לא יתקבלון לרעוא קורבנהון ודבחיהון
כלחים מרחק ('their offerings will not be received with favour, and their sacrifices
will be like unclean bread').

The translator introduces 'their sacrifices' with another לאן 'for' (18b:24), thus giving the reason for God's disfavour: He is not pleased with their deeds, 'because their sacrifices are like bread of unbelievers for them'. Yefet appears to retain the Hebrew syntax: דבאיחהם מתל דבאח אלכפאר || ולא ילדו לה (ed. Birnbaum 135:4–5; ed. Polliack and Schlossberg 206 [where one manuscript reads טעאם אלגצב in place of דבאיח אלכפאר]).

אוֹנִים is usually interpreted as a plural masculine participle ('mourners') or as an abstract plural ('mourning'); see LXX: ἄρτος πένθους ('bread of mourning'); Peshitta: ܕܐܒܠܐ ('[bread of] affliction'); Vulgate: *lugentium* ('of mourners'); Cod. Hunt. 206: الغضب ('wrath', 'fury', 'anger', ed. Schroeter 40:8); R. Tanchum: طعام الاحزان ('food of sadness'). However, the Targum renders with מרחק ('unclean', 'abominable'). The author's translation כופאר 'unbelievers' (18b:24) appears to draw from the same exegetical idea, since 'unbelievers' are involved in 'unclean', 'abominable' food, deeds etc.; see also Yefet: אלכפאר (ed. Birnbaum 135:5; ed. Polliack and Schlossberg 206 [cf. previous reference]).

The orthography אַי in אַיכְלִיה (18b:24) for long *ā* (= آكِلِه) is noteworthy; see on the other hand Yefet: אכליה (ed. Birnbaum 135:5; ed. Polliack and Schlossberg 206).

Hosea 9:5

The translator changes the preposition of the phrases לְיוֹם ... וּלְיוֹם into: פי יום ... ופי יום 'on (the) day of ... and on (the) day of' (18b:26), whereas Cod. Hunt. 206 retains the biblical phrase by rendering ليوم ... وليوم (ed. Schroeter 40:9–10); Yefet combines two different prepositions: ליום ... ופי יום (ed. Birnbaum 136:8; ed. Polliack and Schlossberg 206).

מוֹעֵד has been rendered with the Arabic cognate מועד 'appointed time' (18b:26); see also Cod. Hunt. 206: الموعد (ed. Schroeter 40:10) vs. Yefet: אלמוסם 'time of the year', 'festive season' (ed. Birnbaum 136:8; ed. Polliack and Schlossberg 206).

The translator interprets חַג-יהוה 'the festival of YHWH' as צחייה אלרב 'the sacrifice of the Lord' (18b:26), whereas Yefet: (חג̇ רב אלעא למין) (ed. Birnbaum 136:8; ed. Polliack and Schlossberg 206) and Cod. Hunt. 206: حج الله (ed. Schroeter 40:10) translate חג with the Arabic cognate.

The reconstruction יקתול 'he will kill' (19b:7) in the exegesis draws on Yefet's phrase: מן אג̇ל מא קתל אלעדו פיהם (ed. Birnbaum 136:21–22; ed. Polliack and Schlossberg 207).

The verb קאל 'he said' (19a:25) in the exegesis has been restored from the following formula פכאנה קאל (19a:26).

אלסוקע (19b:12) see Yefet: אלסקע (ed. Birnbaum 76:22), Hava 326: 'Lower part of a well, Country, House'.

Hosea 9:6

By adding the connective conjunction פ (twice) and the adverbs תום and ואיצא (18b:27–28), the translator obviously tries to establish a temporal structure of the asyndetic sentences of the Hebrew source text.

The translator replaces the preposition מן in מִשֹּׁד by מן ענד, literally 'from with' (18b:26) vs. Yefet: מן גהה (ed. Birnbaum 137:11; ed. Polliack and Schlossberg 207) and Cod. Hunt. 206: من جهة (ed. Schroeter 40:10).

תְּקַבְּרֵם has been rendered with the Arabic cognate תקברהם 'she will bury them' (18b:27); see also Yefet: תקרבהם (ed. Birnbaum 137:12; ed. Polliack and Schlossberg 207), instead of possible תדפנהם as in Cod. Hunt. 206: تدفنهم (ed. Schroeter 40:11).

The translator understands מַחְמַד 'the desirable' as *nomen loci*: פאלמואצע אלמתמנאה 'and the desirable places' (18b:27); see also Targum: בית חמדת כספהון ('the house of their desired silver'); see also Yefet: ומואצ׳ע תמני (ed. Birnbaum 137:12; ed. Polliack and Schlossberg 207 [where one manuscript reads ומואצׄע]) and Cod. Hunt. 206: وموضع تمني (ed. Schroeter 40:11).

Whereas Yefet and Cod. Hunt. 206 render לְכַסְפָּם literally with פצתהם (ed. Birnbaum 137:12; ed. Polliack and Schlossberg 207)/فضتهم 'their silver' (ed. Schroeter 40:11), the translator prefers a paraphrastic rendition: לאמואלהם 'for their wealth'.

קִימּוֹשׂ 'thistles' is rendered with חרשף (18b:28) 'scales (of fish)' (Wehr p. 168), 'swarm of locusts', 'young ones of animals', 'fish-scales' (Hava p. 119), 'troupe', 'bande troupeau', 'multitude'; 'petits de bestiaux ou d'oiseaux ou petites créatures'; 'viellards débiles ou hommes faibles', 'débiles'; 'piétons'; 'artichaut'; 'écaille de poisson'; 'cotte de mailles'; 'ornements', 'divers objets qu'on attache aux armes, en guise d'ornement' (Kazimirski p. 408). Yefet and Cod. Hunt. 206 have אלעוסֹג (ed. Birnbaum 137:12; ed. Polliack and Schlossberg 207 [where one manuscript reads אלעתיג])/العوسج (ed. Schroeter 40:12) 'boxthorn' respectively. R. Tanchum: قريص 'stinging nettle'.

The translator adds the verb ינבות 'it will grow' (18b:28) *ad sensum*.

For rendering בְּאָהֳלֵיהֶם, the translator chooses פי אכבייתהם 'in their tents' (18b:28; see also Hosea 12:10), whereas Yefet: פי מצׄאברהם (ed. Birnbaum 137:13; ed. Polliack and Schlossberg 207) and Cod. Hunt. 206: في مضاربهم (ed. Schroeter 40:12) think of a 'large tent'.

The visible final ן after the preposition מן may suggest that the last word of the *lacuna* in the text of the exegesis could be אלאנסאן or אנסאן 'man' (20a:18).

Hosea 9:7

The translator chooses ואפו 'they have come' (18b:29) twice as rendition of בָּאוּ, whereas Yefet and Cod. Hunt. 206 have the more familiar verb גאת (ed. Birnbaum 138:14 [2×]; ed. Polliack and Schlossberg 208 [which reads גֹאת]))/جاأت (ed. Schroeter 40:12, 13).

מְשֻׁגָּע has been rendered with מווסוס 'foolish' (19a:2); see Cod. Hunt. 206 who has the accusative موسوسا (ed. Schroeter 40:14), whereas Yefet has מגנון (ed. Birnbaum 138:18; ed. Polliack and Schlossberg 208 [which reads מוסוס]).

The restoration of the translation in 19a:1 is difficult because only the upper parts of some *lamed*s are visible in the middle and at the end of the line. The length of the *lacuna* between גאיל 'fool' (19a:1) and מווסוס 'foolish' (19a:2) suggests, however, that the translator has expanded the biblical text considerably by providing a more interpretative translation, possibly similar to Yefet and Cod. Hunt. 206 who dissolve the parallelism of the biblical source text by rendering: אן גֹאהל אלמדעי אלנבוה מגנון (ed. Birnbaum 138:18; ed. Polliack and Schlossberg 208 [which reads אן גֹאהל אלמדעי מוסוס אלמדעי אלנבוה])/ان الجاهل المدعى نبوة رجلا موسوسا 'the ignorant who pretends prophecy is a foolish man' (ed. Schroeter 40:13–14).

The restoration of עלי כתרה 'because of the multitude' (19a:2) as rendition of עַל רֹב is based on Hosea 10:13 where עלי כתרה is the rendition of בְּרֹב vs. Yefet: בסבב כתרה (ed. Birnbaum 138:19; ed. Polliack and Schlossberg 208)/Cod. Hunt. 206: بسبب كثرة (ed. Schroeter 40:14).

The conjecture דנבך 'your sin' (19a:2) as rendition of עֲוֺנְךָ is based on the usual translation of עָוֺן (see Hosea 4:8; 5:5; 7:1; 9:9; 12:9; 14:2, 3; translation missing: Hosea 8:13); see also Cod. Hunt. 206: ذنوبك (ed. Schroeter 40:14) vs. Yefet: וזרך (ed. Birnbaum 138:19; ed. Polliack and Schlossberg 208).

The reconstruction מחאקדה 'hatred' (19a:2) in the translation was possible because of the preserved rendition of מַשְׂטֵמָה in the following verse Hosea 9:8; Yefet and Cod. Hunt. 206 render this word which occurs only in Hosea (but see 1QS III:23; CD XVI:5), with the noun אלחקד (ed. Birnbaum 138:19; ed. Polliack and Schlossberg 208)/الحقد 'the hatred' (ed. Schroeter 40:15) respectively. All translations refer to the variant Hebrew root סטן/שטן, as do modern commentators, e.g. Macintosh 1997:352: 'The cognate verb appears to be a variant form of the root סטן'.

The restoration באלריח 'with the spirit' (19b:19) in the exegesis is based on the context.

The reconstruction of כתרה דנבך 'the multitude of your sin' (19b:24) in the exegesis is based on the translation (19a:2).

Hosea 9:8

Parts of the translation have been completed by using the phraseology of the exegesis: מע אלאהי 'with my God' (19a:3) from 19b:27; see also Yefet: מע אלאהי (ed. Birnbaum 140:10; ed. Polliack and Schlossberg 208) and Cod. Hunt. 206: مع الالهى (ed. Schroeter 40:15); פך 'snare' (19a:3) from 20a:2; see also Yefet: אלפך (ed. Birnbaum 140:10; ed. Polliack and Schlossberg 208) and Cod. Hunt. 206: الفخ (ed. Schroeter 40:15); יוהק 'he is thrown' (19a:3) from 20a:3; see also Yefet: יוהק (ed. Birnbaum 140:11; ed. Polliack and Schlossberg 208) and Cod. Hunt. 206: يوهق (ed. Schroeter 40:16).

The translator renders צוֹפֶה 'watching', 'watchman' with the *nomen agentis* דידבאן 'guard' (19a:3), a Persian loanwoard. Yefet: מדידב (ed. Birnbaum 140:10; ed. Polliack and Schlossberg 208)/Cod. Hunt. 206: مديدب (ed. Schroeter 40:15) reflect the Hebrew source text more closely by using the participle. In T-S Ar.28.174 recto 9, the noun אלדידבאן can be found as explanation of the top-onym Mizpah in Hosea 5:1.

The author changes the nominal clause of the Hebrew source text into a verbal clause by adding the finite verb אנצב 'he has been set up' (19a:3) between 'watchman' and 'Ephraim'.

For יוהק 'it is thrown' (19a:3) see Saadiah's rendition of the roots נקש/יקש with והק (Deuteronomy 7:25; 12:30; Isaiah 28:13; Proverbs 6:2) and with בהק (Isaiah 8:15).

Hosea 9:9

The restoration of the text of the translation גמקו 'they made deep' (19a:4) as rendition of הֶעְמִיקוּ is based on the translation of Hosea 5:2 (11b:1). From the author's exegesis which explains הֶעְמִיקוּ and שִׁחֵתוּ separately (20a:6–7), it may be assumed that the translator did not interpret גמקו as a relative verb, which had to be construed asyndetically with the following main verb אפסדו, thus functioning as adverb: 'they were deeply corrupted' (19a:4), but preferred a syn-detic syntax: גמקו ואפסדו 'they deepened and corrupted'; see also Yefet: גמקו ואפסדו (ed. Birnbaum 141:8; ed. Polliack and Schlossberg 209)/Cod. Hunt. 206: عمقوا وافسدوا (ed. Schroeter 40:16).

ואפסדו 'and they corrupted' (19a:4) has been restored because the verb also occurs in the exegesis (20a:7).

The reconstruction of כאיאם 'as days of' (19a:4) is based on the author's usual rendition of יום vs. Yefet and Cod. Hunt. 206: מתל זמאן (ed. Birnbaum 141:8; ed. Polliack and Schlossberg 209)/مثل زمان (ed. Schroeter 40:17).

By adding פלדלך 'and therefore' (19a:5) before *He will remember their iniquity*, the author indicates that he understands the preceding sentences as giving the reason for God's remembering.

By adding תום 'then' before the announcement of punishment (19a:5), the translator achieves a temporal sequence: first remembering, then punishing.

Hosea 9:10

מָצָאתִי is rendered with אצבת 'I obtained' (20a:14) (see also Hosea 12:9 [2×]; text missing: Hosea 5:6); only for נִמְצָא in Hosea 14:9, he chooses the root وجد, which is the preferable rendering of Yefet: וגדת (ed. Birnbaum 141:23; ed. Polliack and Schlossberg 209 [which reads וגّד]) and Cod. Hunt. 206: وجدت (ed. Schroeter 40:18) here and elsewhere.

The restoration of פי אלתין 'on the fig tree' (20a:14) as rendition of בִּתְאֵנָה is based on Yefet: פי אלתין (ed. Birnbaum 142:1; ed. Polliack and Schlossberg 209) and Cod. Hunt. 206 في التين (ed. Schroeter 40:18).

The same applies to פי אבתדאהא 'in its beginning' (20a:14); see Yefet and Cod. Hunt. 206: פי אבתדאהא (ed. Birnbaum 142:1; ed. Polliack and Schlossberg 209)/ في ابدائها (ed. Schroeter 40:18) and Vulgate: *in cacumine eius* ('in its top'), whereas LXX prefers the adverb πρόιμον ('early') and Targum creates a relative clause: דבאול מאבבה ('which ripens in early season').

The translator renders וַיִּנָּזְרוּ with פתנגבו 'they were devoted' (20a:15) + מן (Hava p. 750; Lane p. 2765), whereas Yefet and Cod. Hunt. 206 have ותנסכו (ed. Birnbaum 142:2; ed. Polliack and Schlossberg 209)/وتنسكوا 'and they were devoted', 'and they devoted themselves' (ed. Schroeter 40:19); LXX: ἀπηλλοτριώ-θησαν ('to ally with a foreign god').

The restoration אלכזי 'the shame' (20a:15) as translation of לַבֹּשֶׁת is based on the author's translation of Hosea 2:7; 10:6 (בָּשְׁנָה—כזייה); see Yefet: ללכזי (ed. Birnbaum 142:2; ed. Polliack and Schlossberg 209) and Cod. Hunt. 206: للخزى (ed. Schroeter 40:19).

The translator provides a direct object of the phrase כְּאָהֳבָם 'as they loved' when rendering ענד מחבתהם דלך 'when they loved that' (20a:16) wheras Yefet and Cod. Hunt. 206 provide a literal translation: כמחבתהם (ed. Birnbaum 142:3; ed. Polliack and Schlossberg 209)/بمحبتهم (ed. Schroeter 41:1).

TEXTUAL NOTES 201

Hosea 9:11

The reconstruction of כאלטאיר 'like the bird' (20a:16) as rendering of כָּעוֹף is based on the author's usual rendering of עוֹף (see Hosea 2:20; 4:3; 7:12); see Yefet: מתֿל אלטאיר (ed. Birnbaum 143:20; ed. Polliack and Schlossberg 210) and Cod. Hunt. 206: مثل الطير (ed. Schroeter 41:1).

The reconstructed verb יתטאיר 'he will fly' (20a:16) draws on Yefet: יתטאיר (ed. Birnbaum 143:20; ed. Polliack and Schlossberg 210)/Cod. Hunt. 206: يطير (ed. Schroeter 41:1).

The restored translation אחשא 'womb' (20a:17) is based on Hosea 9:16; 12:4; see also Yefet and Cod. Hunt. 206 who have the definite noun אלאחשא (ed. Birnbaum 143:21; ed. Polliack and Schlossberg 210 [where one manuscript reads אלבטן]/ الاحشاء (ed. Schroeter 41:2).

The restoration ומן חבל 'and from pregnancy' (20a:17) as translation of וּמֵהֵרָיוֹן is based on Hosea 14:1 (וחבאלאה for וְהָרִיּוֹתָיו; see also Hosea 2:7; text missing: Hosea 1:3, 6, 8); see also Yefet: ומן אלחבל (ed. Birnbaum 143:21; ed. Polliack and Schlossberg 210); Cod. Hunt. 206: ومن الحبل (ed. Schroeter 41:2).

Hosea 9:12

The restoration of ירבו 'they bring up' (20a:17) as rendition of יְגַדְּלוּ is based on Yefet: ירבון (ed. Birnbaum 144:19; ed. Polliack and Schlossberg 210)/Cod. Hunt. 206: يربون (ed. Schroeter 41:2).

פאני (20a:18), i.e. the Hebrew personal pronoun 1st person singular, combined with the Arabic connective conjunction ف, is probably an erroneous orthography for פאנא 'and I' (see also 20b:21).

The lacuna after אתכלהם מן 'I will bereave them from' (20a:18) indicates that the translator must have provided a longer paraphrase to a possible literal rendering מן אלנאס as Yefet: מן אלנאס (ed. Birnbaum 144:19; ed. Polliack and Schlossberg 210) and Cod. Hunt. 206: من الناس (ed. Schroeter 41:3). The final ן could be the last letter of אנסאן 'man' (20a:18), possibly: בני אלאנסאן. The versions render: LXX: ἐξ ἀνθρώπων ('from men'); Peshitta: ܡܢ ܒܕ ܐܢܫܐ; Targum: מלמהוי גברין ('from becoming men'); Vulgate: in hominibus ('among men').

By adding the finite verb קד חצל 'it was' (20a:18), the translator transfers the 'Woe' into the past.

The translator derives כְּשׂוּרִי from the root סור, as is evident from his rendering ענד זואלי, literally 'with my abandoning' (20a:18–19) and his grammatical note (21a:1–3); see also Yefet: ענד זואלי (ed. Birnbaum 144:20; ed. Polliack and Schlossberg 210) and Cod. Hunt. 206: عند زوالي (ed. Schroeter 41:3); Aquila and

Symmachus: ἐκκλίναντός μου ἀπ' αὐτῶν ('when I turn away from them'); Ibn Harūn on Hosea 9:12: הו בשין ומשהור לגה אלזואל בסמך ('which has *sin*, but the lexical class of "passing away" normally has *samekh*') (1.28.7). In the past context (קד חצל), the translator understood the withdrawal of God's care and protection as a matter of the past (see also his exegesis 20b:24 and 21a:1).

Hosea 9:13

The restored כמא 'as' (20a:19) as translation of כַּאֲשֶׁר follows Yefet: כמא (ed. Birnbaum 145:14; ed. Polliack and Schlossberg 211 [where one manuscript reads באלדי]); the other option כאלדי (see Cod. Hunt. 206: كالذى, ed. Schroeter 41:4) is less likely because of the limited space between כאן and ראית (20a:19).

By adding a verb in the past tense: קד כאן (20a:19), the translator emphasises that the comparison between Ephraim and Tyre refers to a situation in the past.

The author's identification of צוֹר as the name of the city 'Tyre' in South Lebanon is shared by Yefet: צור (ed. Birnbaum 145:14; ed. Polliack and Schlossberg 211), Cod. Hunt. 206: صور (ed. Schroeter 41:4), Vulgate: *Tyrus erat fundata in pulchritudine* ('[Ephraim] was as Tyre grounded in excellence'), Peshitta: ܠܚܨܝ ܐܝܟ ܨܘܪ ܕܢܨܝܒܐ ܒܒܢܝܢܗ ('[Ephraim] was like Tyre planted in its buildings') and Targum: דמיא לצור באצלחותה בשליותה ('like Tyre in her prosperity and ease'). The reading of צוֹר as צוּר 'rock' can be found in Theodotion: ἐφραιμ καθὼς εἶδον εἰς πέτραν πεφυτευόμενοι οἱ υἱοὶ αὐτῆς ('Ephraim, her sons are planted as a rock') and LXX: εἰς θήραν παρέστησαν τὰ τέκνα αὐτῶν ('[Ephraim] has presented its children as prey'); these versions would demand a text like לְצַיִד שָׁת לֹה בָּנָיו instead of MT: לְצוֹר שְׁתוּלָה בְנָוֶה.

The translator adds אלאן 'now' (20a:20) before the statement about Ephraim's slaughtering their children, probably to emphasise the contrast between the past and the present. Also Macintosh 1997:370 supplies the temporal adverb 'now' in his translation *ad sensum* 'to draw out the contrast of the time' (Macintosh 1997:371).

The translator renders the infinitive לְהוֹצִיא with the modifying verb אלתגא (20a:20), followed by a subordinate clause אן יכרג 'that he brings forth' (20a:20), whereas Yefet: לאכראג (ed. Birnbaum 145:15; ed. Polliack and Schlossberg 211) and Cod. Hunt. 206: لاخراج (ed. Schroeter 41:4) provide a literal translation of the Hebrew source text.

Hosea 9:14

The translator adds after the imperative אועטיהם יא רב 'give them, Lord' (20a:20–21) the indefinite relative clause מא יסתחקו, which could be the object of the following verb: 'what they deserve, you may give them' (20a:21). In the context, this sentence appears to function as parenthesis, since the following imperative extends the initial imperative by adding the direct objects.

מכמשה 'shrunk' (20a:21) as rendering of צֹמְקִים is derived from كمش 'she was, or became, small in her breast', v 'to shrink (skin)' (Lane 2637). Yefet/Cod. Hunt. 206 render with צָאמרה (ed. Birnbaum 146:13; ed. Polliack and Schlossberg 211)/ضامرة 'shrinking' (ed. Schroeter 41:6) respectively.

Hosea 9:15

The translator transforms the nominal clause *all their evil (is) in Gilgal* into a verbal clause by adding the finite verb דכרת 'I have remembered' (20a:22) *ad sensum* vs. the literal translation of Yefet/Cod. Hunt. 206: כל בליתהם פי אלגלגל (ed. Birnbaum 147:10; ed. Polliack and Schlossberg 211)/كل بليتهم فى الجلجل (ed. Schroeter 41:9).

The following verb שְׂנֵאתִים has been rendered with Arabic cognate שניתהם 'I hated them' (20a:22), whereas Yefet and Cod. Hunt. 206 translate with בגצתהם (ed. Birnbaum 147:10; ed. Polliack and Schlossberg 211) / بغضتهم (ed. Schroeter 41:9).

The restored רדא 'evil' (20a:23) as rendition of the *hapax legomenon* (in Hosea) רֹעַ is based on the translator's rendering of the phrase רָעַת רַעַתְכֶם (Hosea 10:15); see also the translation of Hosea 9:15 in T-S NS 227.32 recto 20. Yefet and Cod. Hunt. 206 have: קבה (ed. Birnbaum 147:11)/قبح (ed. Schroeter 41:9).

סֹרְרִים is rendered with זאיגין 'wandering astray' (20a:24); see also Yefet: זאיגין (ed. Birnbaum 147:12; ed. Polliack and Schlossberg 211), while Cod. Hunt 206 has زائلين 'going away' (ed. Schroeter 41:10).

Hosea 9:16

The addition of לאַן 'for' (20a:24) at the beginning of the verse introduces the reason why Ephraim is smitten: their root is withered (see Hosea 4:4).

By adding the copula קד חצל between *their root* and *dry* (20a:24), the translator ensures that the withering of their root has to be understood as an event of the past.

The translator renders שָׁרְשָׁם with אצלהם 'their root' (20a:24), whereas Yefet and Cod. Hunt. 206 prefer the same noun عرق 'root', 'stem', though they differ in the number: singular ערקהם (ed. Birnbaum 148:18; ed. Polliack and Schlossberg 212) vs. plural عروقهم (ed. Schroeter 41:11).

The additional personal pronoun אנא before the verb *I will slay* (20a:25) emphasises the subject, literally: 'It is I who will slay'.

The orthography of מתמנאאת 'delights' (20a:25) as rendition of מַחֲמַדֵּי is identical with Cod. Hunt. 206: متمنّاات (ed. Schroeter 41:12) vs. Yefet: מתמניאת (ed. Birnbaum 148:19; ed. Polliack and Schlossberg 212 [which reads מתמנאיאת]).

Hosea 9:17

The rendering מא סמיעו 'they did not hear' (20a:26) reflects the Hebrew source text לֹא שָׁמְעוּ literally, whereas Yefet and Cod. Hunt. 206 offer the paraphrase: לא יקבלו אמרה ונהיה 'they did not accept His commandment and His prohibition' (ed. Birnbaum 149:15; ed. Polliack and Schlossberg 213 [which reads לם instead of לא]/ما قبلوا امره ونهيه (ed. Schroeter 41:13).

By rendering מצטרבין 'fugitives' (20a:27), the translator emphasises the aspect of 'disturbance', 'confusion' and 'restlessless' of the Hebrew נֹדְדִים. Yefet: מתנודין (ed. Birnbaum 149:16; ed. Polliack and Schlossberg 213 [where one manuscript reads מתנו]) points to the 'swinging back and forth' and Cod. Hunt. 206: مثغورين (ed. Schroeter 41:13) to 'being dispersed'.

בַּגּוֹיִם has been rendered with פי אלאחזאב, literally 'among the groups' (20a:27); see also Yefet: פי אלאחזאב (ed. Birnbaum 149:16; ed. Polliack and Schlossberg 213), whereas Cod. Hunt. 206 translates with بين الأمم (ed. Schroeter 41:13).

Hosea 10:1

It is controversial if the attributive participle בּוֹקֵק is to be understood alternatively in a positive or negative sense.

(1) The positive option, i.e. בּוֹקֵק denoting 'healthy and luxuriant growth' (Macintosh 1997:383) has been adopted from early times; see LXX: εὐκλη-ματοῦσα, Jerome: *bonas habens propagines, et flagella fructifera, quae multos botros tulit, et uvarum foecunditas ramorum magnitudinem coaequavit*, Vulgate: *frondosa* ('abundant in leaves'), Peshitta: ܕܣܘܟܐ ('[vine of] shoots'). In this understanding, the metaphor refers to an exuberant and luxuriant vine with its fruit.

(2) The alternative view has been adopted by some versions and rabbinic commentators; according to them, בּוֹקֵק denotes the poor quality, deficiency, damage or decay of the vine; see Symmachus: ὑλομανοῦσα ('run to wood'), Aquila: ἔνυδρος ('watery'), Targum: בְּזִיזָא ('plundered', 'empty', 'despoiled', 'devastated'), Rashi: ישראל דומין לגפן המשיר כל פריו הטוב כך עזבו אותי שאני פרי הטוב והשוה לו ('Israel is similar to a vine that has thrown off all its good fruit; likewise they have left Me though I am a good fruit for him and it has become similar to it'), Qimḥi: גפן רק שאין בו שים לחלולית וכן בוקה ומבוקה ('an empty vine in which is no humours. In the same sense the word occurs in Nahum 2:11'). Ibn Barūn compares the root בקק with Arabic بوق 'to bring misfortune, disaster' (Lane 1, p. 276) rather than with the cognate بق 'to give off in abundance'; see also Syriac: ܚܡܡ 'to be worm-eaten, rotten, decayed'. R. Tanchum explains בּוֹקֵק as فاسد بائر لا خير فيه ('spoilt, uncultivated, in which is no good'). Also Macintosh translates 'a damaged vine' (1997:383).

The commentator prefers the second option: גפן באיר 'an uncultivated vine' (21b:3); see also his exegesis (21b:18–20). Similar Yefet: גפן מבור (ed. Birnbaum 150:4; ed. Polliack and Schlossberg 214 [which reads מבוור])/Cod. Hunt. 206: جفن بائر (ed. Schroeter 41:15); however, see Cod. Hunt. 206's grammatical note where he states that the meaning is بوره العذ 'Unkultur des Fruchtlandes' and not بائر (Schroeter II, 26:20–21, 32). T-S Ar.22.128 fol. 2 verso 2 explains בּוֹקֵק as באיר ואלבור.

יְשַׁוֶּה is reflected in a wide range of renderings:

(1) LXX: εὐθηνῶν ('flourishing'); Rashi: פרי אשר ישוה לו וייטב לו ('fruit which is beneficial for him and good for him').

(2) Aquila/Symmachus: ἐξισώθη ('became equal'); Vulgate: *fructus adaequatus est ei* ('the fruit became equal to it'), i.e. the verb is derived from שוה I 'to be like', 'to resemble'; see Yefet: יסוי לה (ed. Birnbaum 150:4; ed. Polliack and Schlossberg 214) and Cod. Hunt. 206: يساويه (ed. Schroeter 41:15), Jerome.

(3) According to Qimḥi יְשַׁוֶּה is equivalent to שוא ושקר; also Ibn Janāḥ derives it from שוא 'emptiness', 'nothingness', 'vanity'.

(4) Peshitta: ܕܐܥܒܕܬ ('which produced'), i.e. the verb is derived from שוה II pi. 'to set', 'to place', 'to make', 'to produce'; Ibn Ezra: ישוה לו יחשוב כי יפרה את פריו והיה שוה כגפן שהוא בוקק כי כאשר הרביתי פריו הרבו למזבחות ('i.e. it thinks that it will multiply its fruit; however, it is like a vine which is empty; for as I have multiplied its fruit, they have multiplied altars'). Probably also Targum: פירי עובדיהון גרמו להון דיגלון ('the fruits of their actions brought about their exile').

The translator appears to have adopted the interpretation that the fruit 'was similar to', 'resembled' (כאן יסווי) the uncultivated, degenerated vine (21b:3).

Taking into consideration the usual style of the translator and the rendering of the following verb יְשֻׁוֶּה with כאן יוסוי 'it was similar' (21b:3), a copula in the past tense, such as קד חצל, may also be suggested between גפן באיר and אל אסראיל (21b:3; see Hosea 4:4).

The restoration תמרה 'its fruit' (21b:4) as translation of לְפִרְיוֹ reflects the author's preference for masculine nouns; see also his translation of פְּרִי with תמר 'fruit' (21b:3) and Yefet: תֿמרה (ed. Birnbaum 150:5; ed. Polliack and Schlossberg 214), whereas Cod. Hunt. 206 has the feminine noun ثمره (ed. Schroeter 41:15).

Hosea 10:2

The reconstruction of לדלך at the beginnig of the verse (21b:5) is tentative.

The translator understands the verb חָלַק as being derived from the root חלק II 'to divide' rather than from חלק I 'to be smooth'; his rendering אנקסם 'it is divided' (21b:5) suggests an intransitive (passive) meaning. See also Aquila/Symmachus: ἐμερίσθη καρδία, Vulgate: *divisum est cor eorum*, Peshitta: ܐܬܦܠܓ ܠܒܗܘܢ ('their heart is divided'), Targum: אתפליג לבהון, Ibn Ezra: כי אין להם חלק אחד ('they have not only one part [but more, therefore their heart is not one, but divided])', Qimḥi: מיראת אל ומתורתו חלק לבם חלק פעל עומד כמו נחלק ('their heart is detached from the fear of God and His Torah. חָלַק is a transitive verb in the sense of נְחְלַק'). Cod. Hunt. 206 in his translation has تقسم 'he has been devided' (ed. Schroeter 41:16); however, in his grammatical notes, he states لذلك فسرته قسمهم قلبهم ولم افسره انقسم قلبهم 'therefore I have explained: their heart has divided them, and I have not explained: their heart is divided' (ed. Schroeter II, 27:2–3). LXX: ἐμέρισαν καρδίας αὐτῶν ('they have divided their hearts') adopts a transitive meaning with the plural subject remaining unclear; see also Yefet: קסם (ed. Birnbaum 151:5; ed. Polliack and Schlossberg 214).

The reconstruction יואכדו 'they will be punished' (21b:6) as the equivalent for יֶאְשָׁמוּ is likely because of the visible last letter. The author provides several equivalents for the root אשם: Hosea 5:15 (ינדמו), 13:1 (פלמא אתם), 14:1 (תואכד). The translator adopts the root اخذ, literally 'to take', here in the sense اخذ بذنبه 'to punish s.o. for his offense', whereas Yefet: יאתמו (ed. Birnbaum 151:5; ed. Polliack and Schlossberg 214)/Cod. Hunt. 206: ياثمو (ed. Schroeter 41:16) use Arabic cognate root اثم 'to sin', 'to err'.

The renderingof הוּא יַעֲרוֹף with הו יקפיהם 'he will break them' (21b:6) demonstrates that the translator regarded the verb as a denominative from עֶרֶף 'neck'; see also Yefet: הו יקפי (ed. Birnbaum 151:5; ed. Polliack and Schlossberg 214)/Cod.

Hunt. 206: هو يقفو (ed. Schroeter 41:15–16); R. Tanchum: يهدم ويخرب 'he will destroy and devastate' (Schroeter 33 n. 2).

Who is subject of הוּא יַעֲרוֹף 'he (it) will break etc.?'

(1) Rashi, Ibn Ezra, Qimḥi suppose that the personal pronoun הוא refers to the heart; i.e. the destruction of the altars has been caused by Israel itself.

(2) Or the pronoun refers to God. This is the preference of Jerome, though he suggests that God achieves this purpose through the agency of other nations. This is the view which is most likely shared by the commentator.

The translator adds a suffix pronoun יקפיהם 'he breaks them' (21b:6), since he probably regards the verb ערף as referring to people rather than to altars. Having provided a direct object of the verb, he has to connect the now isolated noun 'their altars'. This he achieves by inserting the preposition מע 'with' (see also T-S NS 285.9 verso 23). His rephrasing of this part of the verse may indicate that he intends to add to the punishment as announced in the biblical source text: God will not only break down their altars, but also the people themselves, thus corresponding to the announcement in the same verse that 'they will be punished'.

The rendition ינהב 'he will plunder' (21b:6) reflects the singular Hebrew verb יְשֻׁדָּד; see also Yefet: ינהב (ed. Birnbaum 151:5; ed. Polliack and Schlossberg 214), whereas Cod. Hunt. 206 translates with the plural verb يَنهبوا (ed. Schroeter 41:17).

The reconstruction of ומא שאכל דלך 'and similar' (22a:9) in the exegesis is based on the same phrase in 18b:7; 19a:10; see also 25a:23 (ומא שאכלהא) and 25a:25 (ומא שאכלה).

Hosea 10:3

מא כשינא 'we have not feared' (21b:7) is the literal translation of the Hebrew לֹא יָרֵאנוּ; see also Yefet: לם נכן כאשיין (ed. Birnbaum 151:22; ed. Polliack and Schlossberg 215), whereas Cod. Hunt. 206 has the imperfect لا نخشاه (ed. Schroeter 41:18).

It is noteworthy that the translator renders לָנוּ 'to us' with בנא 'among us' (21b:8), as do Yefet: בנא (ed. Birnbaum 151:23; ed. Polliack and Schlossberg 215) and Cod. Hunt. 206: بنا (ed. Schroeter 41:18).

Hosea 10:4

The first letter ד of דנב 'sin' (21b:8) is partly visible, so that the reconstructed noun seems to be justified. By adding דנב 'sin (is)' at the beginning of the verse, the author qualifies the following list *expressis verbis* as sin from the outset. The enumeration of sinful acts has been introduced by an additional פהי, literally: 'and they are' (21b:8).

אָלוֹת has been rendered with הוּרג (21b:8); see also Yefet: חרג (ed. Birnbaum 152:21; ed. Polliack and Schlossberg 215) and Cod. Hunt. 206: حرج (ed. Schroeter 42:1).

שָׁוְא has been rendered with גזאף 'parole ou action inconsidérée, irréfléchie, faite à la légère' (Kazimirski I, 289) (see also Hosea 12:12), whereas Cod. Hunt. 206 translates with وزور 'and lie' (ed. Schroeter 42:1) and Yefet has אלכדב (ed. Birnbaum 152:21; ed. Polliack and Schlossberg 215).

The translator renders וּפָרַח with פסא ינפרע 'and it will sprout' (21b:8–9) by using a similar root فرع 'to surpass', II 'to branch', V 'to branch off'; see also Yefet: ינפרע (ed. Birnbaum 152:21; ed. Polliack and Schlossberg 215 [where one manuscript reads יתפרע with no *waw*]) and Cod. Hunt. 206: ويتفرع (ed. Schroeter 42:1). Saadiah uses the same verb for rendering the root פרח (فرع I; Genesis 40:10; Isaiah 27:6; 35:1; 66:14; فرح V: Isaiah 35:2); see also the translation of Hosea 14:6, 8 again with פרע VII.

By adding פיהם 'among them' (21b:9), the translator apparently wants to indicate that the poisonous judgement is to be found among the people.

Hosea 10:5

The translator changes the singular שְׁכַן of MT into the plural סוכאן 'the inhabitants of' (21b:10), thus harmonising the subject with the plural verb: יָגוּרוּ/יגאורו; see also LXX: οἱ κατοικοῦντες ('dwellers'); Peshitta: ܥܡܘܪܝ; Yefet and Cod. Hunt. 206: סכאן (ed. Birnbaum 154:10; ed. Polliack and Schlossberg 216 [which reads סאכן])/سكان (ed. Schroeter 42:2).

The translator adds the phrase תורי = ترى [*turā*] to indicate the following as a question. 'Ces expressions s' emploient dans la langue vulgaire ... comme des adverbes exclamatifs. Elles indiquent une interrogation à laquelle est joint le plus souvent une désire' (Dozy I, 497). 'Die unvermittelte Direktheit einer Frage wird [durch ترى] ... abgeschwächt' (Fischer 1986 II, 87).

His rendering of יָגוּרוּ with יגאורו 'they will be in immediate vicinity' (21b:10), suggests that the translator derived the verb from גור I, as do LXX: παροικήσουσιν ('they dwell near'); Peshitta: ܢܥܡܪܘܢ; Yefet: יגאורון (ed. Birnbaum

154:10); ed. Polliack and Schlossberg 216 [which reads יגאורו]); Cod. Hunt. 206: يجاوروا (ed. Schroeter 42:2). However, most commentators derive it from the root גור III 'to be in dread', 'to fear', 'to worship'; see already Symmachus/Theodotion: ἐφοβήθησαν, Aquila: ἐσεβάσθησαν ('they feared'), Vulgate: *coluerunt* ('they worshipped'), Targum: פלחו with direct object 'the calves'.

The translator retains the Hebrew word וּכְמָרָיו, i.e. the officials of an idolatrous cult, when rendering with וכמארה 'and its priests' (21b:11) vs. Yefet and Cod. Hunt. 206: ושמאמסתה (ed. Birnbaum 154:11; ed. Polliack and Schlossberg 216)/وشمامسته (ed. Schroeter 42:3).

The translator introduces the second half of the verse by adding אי האת 'that is to say, Come' (21b:10), thus regarding the following as interpretation of the initial question.

The translator contrasts the former exultation of the priests because of the splendor of Samaria with their lamentation over its lost glory at the present time, by adding אלאן הודא יחזנו 'now, behold, they are mourning' (21b:11); see also Rashi: 'its priests who continually rejoice over it, now lament over its lost glory'; Ibn Ezra, Qimḥi.

כְּבוֹדוֹ has been rendered with כרמה 'his honour' (21b:12); a similar translation has Yefet: כרימה (ed. Birnbaum 154:12; ed. Polliack and Schlossberg 216 [which reads גלילה]), whereas Cod. Hunt. 206 has again وقاره (ed. Schroeter 42:4).

The reconstruction of the phrase אהל שמרון 'the people of Samaria' (22a:18) in the exegesis draws on Yefet: אהל שמרון (ed. Birnbaum 154:21; ed. Polliack and Schlossberg 216).

Hosea 10:6

The translator imitates the topicalized Hebrew pronominal object (object marker plus enclitic pronoun) אוֹתוֹ by rendering איאה 'him' (21b:12) despite the passive verb יוּבָל which he renders literally with יוגלב 'it will be brought' (21b:13); see also Yefet: איצא איאה לאשור יגלב (ed. Birnbaum 155:10; ed. Polliack and Schlossberg 216). A phrase similar to the translation in Cod. Hunt. 206: وهو يجلب (ed. Schroeter 42:6) can be found in the author's exegesis: הו יוגלב (22a:24).

The addition of a second ואיצא 'and also' before הדייה למלך ירב 'a gift to the king of Yareb' (21b:13) seems to emphasise that presents have been sent to Assur *and also* to Yareb at the same time, i.e. the translator does not identify *the king of Yareb* as the Great King of Assur (see Hosea 5:13), but regards him as a different king.

לְמֶלֶךְ has been rendered literally with למלך 'for the king' (21b:13), whereas Yefet and Cod. Hunt. 206 change the preposition: אלי מלך (ed. Birnbaum 155:10; ed. Polliack and Schlossberg 216)/الى ملك 'to (the) king' (ed. Schroeter 42:4).

The translator understands יָרֵב as a proper name, whereas Yefet: אלי מלך יכאצם (ed. Birnbaum 155:10; ed. Polliack and Schlossberg 216)/Cod. Hunt. 206: الى ملك يخاصم 'to a king who brings legal action' (ed. Schroeter 42:4–5) take the word as being derived from the root ריב; see also Aquila/ Theodotion: δικάζοντι; Symmachus: ὑπερμαχοῦντι; Targum: מלכא דייתי לאתפרעא ('the king who will come to take vengeance [for them])'; see Hosea 5:13. In his exegesis, the author refers also to מלך יכאצם ענהם (22a:25) thus combining the two options in his work.

By using the feminine noun כזייה 'shame' (21b:13) as rendition of בָּשְׁנָה, the author provides another example of imitating the Hebrew source text vs. the masculine noun אלכזי/الخزا in Yefet (ed. Birnbaum 155:11; ed. Polliack and Schlossberg 216) and Cod. Hunt 206 (ed. Schroeter 42:5). Whereas in his grammatical note after the exegesis of Hosea 10:6, the author only states that בָּשְׁנָה stands for בּוּשָׁה (22a:26–27), Ibn Ezra qualifies the nun as pleonastic: בשנה בָּשְׁנָה בתוספת הנון כמו שבענה בנים ('בָּשְׁנָה with pleonastic nun as in Job 42:12'); see also Qimḥi: בשנה כמו בושה והנון נוספת ('בָּשְׁנָה is like בּוּשָׁה and the nun is pleonastic') and Yefet: والنون فيه ואלנון פיה זאיד (ed. Birnbaum 230:14–15). Cod. Hunt. 206: زايد مثل שבענה בנים ('the nun in it is pleonastic as in Job 42:12', ed. Schroeter 11, 27:12–13). Saadiah in his commentary on Job 42:13 (ed. Qafah, Jerusalem 1973, pp. 207–208). At the end of a list of remarks on the prophets in the Firkovitch Collection, St. Petersburg (Firkovitch II, Evr.–Ar. I, 1756, page 97a, lines 19–22), we find an address ascribed to Ibn Nūḥ referring to Hosea 10:6: מן אלנאס מן קאל אן בשנה אלנון פיה זאיד ואצלה בשה והדא אלנון אלזאיד מתל אלדי פי וקבנו לי משם ופי הדשנה מחלב ופי יעברנהו ('Some say that the nun in בָּשְׁנָה is pleonastic and the root is בשׁה and this pleonastic nun is like that in Numbers 23:13; Isaiah 34:6 and Jeremiah 5:22'); see also the Karaites Daniel al-Qūmīsī and David b. Abraham al-Fāsī.

מֵעֲצָתוֹ has been rendered with מן משוורתה, literally 'from his counsel' (21b:14), whereas Yefet and Cod. Hunt. 206 have מן תדבירה (ed. Birnbaum 155:10–11; ed. Polliack and Schlossberg 216)/من تديره (ed. Schroeter 42:5).

Hosea 10:7

נִדְמֶה can be interpreted in different ways:
(1) The author's rendition קד שבה 'it is similar' (21b:14) indicates that he understands נִדְמֶה here as being derived from דמה 'to be like', 'to resemble';

Cod. Hunt. 206 refers to this option in his grammatical notes: ويجوز ان يفسر مشبه which may be explained as 'einer der ähnlich gemacht ist' (Schroeter II, 27:14–15); also: Abarbabel.

(2) Yefet: אנבכם (ed. Birnbaum 156:9; ed. Polliack and Schlossberg 217 [which reads אנכרם]) and Cod. Hunt. 206: انكمت (ed. Schroeter 42:5) derive the verb from the root דמם 'to be silent'; see also Cod. Hunt. 206 in his grammatical notes: يجوز ان يفسر منبكم which may be explained as 'einer der zum Schweigen gebracht worden ist' (ed. Schroeter II, 27:14); also Rashi: השתתק מלך שמרון ('the king of Samaria has been silenced').

(3) A third option 'to come to an end', 'to be ruined', 'to perish' is favoured by Qimḥi: שמרון נפעל עומד כי הוא בסגול והוא ענין כריתה ('the *nif'al* is intransitive, for it is vocalized with *segol* and has the sense of "destruction"') and Vulgate: *transire fecit Samaria regem suum* ('Samaria has made her king to vanish'). See also Macintosh: 'will fade away' (1997:406).

In his commentary, the author quotes two options: דמם 'to be silenced' (sc. by the rulers and king) and his favoured option 'to be similar' (22a:27–22b:1).

Instead of rendering שֹׁמְרוֹן literally, the translator prefers the phrase עב שמרון 'the people of Samaria' (21b:14). Moreover, he avoids the asyndesis שֹׁמְרוֹן מַלְכָּהּ 'Samaria, its king' in favour of the syndetic phrase שומרון מע מלכהא 'Samaria together with its king' (21b:14); see also Yefet: שמרון מע מלכהא (ed. Birnbaum 156:9; ed. Polliack and Schlossberg 217) and Cod. Hunt. 206: شومرون مع ملكها (ed. Schroeter 42:6).

The *hapax legomenon* כְּקֶצֶף is rendered with כזבד 'like foam' (21b:14); see also Yefet: מתֹל אלזבד (ed. Birnbaum 156:9; ed. Polliack and Schlossberg 217), Cod. Hunt. 206: مثل الزبد 'like the foam' (ed. Schroeter 42:6) and his grammatical notes (ed. Schroeter II, 27:17–18); Vulgate: *quasi spumam* ('like foam'), Targum, Rashi, R. Tanchum. An alternative interpretation is represented by LXX/Theodotion: ὡς φρύγανον ('like firewood') and Peshitta: ܐܝܟ ܚܘܛܪܐ ('like a stick'). In his explanatory note, Cod. Hunt. 206 considers the option that קֶצֶף (קצף׳) ويجوز ان يكون قصف سخط بان سخط انسان على سيما رما على وجه الماء may mean 'anger': 'can also have the meaning "anger", for if someone is angry at something, he throws it on the surface of the water', ed. Schroeter 42:7–8). This interpretaion can also be found in Aquila: ὡς ἀφρόν, Symmachus: ὡς ἐπίζεμα ('boiling') and Targum: כרתחא.

Hosea 10:8

The translator links verse 7 and 8 by adding לאן 'for' (21b:15) at the beginning; see Hosea 4:4.

בָּמוֹת 'heights', 'high places' is rendered with ביע 'temples' (21b:15) (plural of بيعة); see also Yefet: ביע (ed. Birnbaum 157:6; ed. Polliack and Schlossberg 217 [which reads בייע]), Cod. Hunt. 206: بِيَع (ed. Schroeter 42:9). Saadiah uses the same equivalent occasionally (e.g. Leviticus 26:30; Numbers 21:28; 22:41; Isaiah 15:2; 36:7). See also Peshitta: ܒܝܬ ܕܚܠܬܐ ('idol sanctuary'); LXX: βωμά ('platforms', 'altars'); Vulgate: *excelsa* ('heights'); Targum: במת ('altar').

The translator does not interpret אָוֶן as the abbreviated toponym 'Beth-Aven', referring to Beth-El, as does Cod. Hunt. 206: اون (ed. Schroeter 42:9), but as an abstract noun גל 'wickedness' (21b:15). Yefet translates with אלותן 'the idol' (ed. Birnbaum 157:6; ed. Polliack and Schlossberg 217 [where one manuscript reads אוּן]); Vulgate: *idoli* (plural).

The translator links the following phrase חַטַּאת יִשְׂרָאֵל *the sin of Israel* with בָּמוֹת אָוֶן by including it in a relative clause with an additional verb in the past tense: אלדי כאנו סבב 'which have been (the) reason' (21b:15–16). Whereas Yefet and Cod. Hunt. 206 identify the 'temples of Aven' with the actual ongoing 'sin of Israel': ביע אלותן אלדי הו כטיה ישראל (ed. Birnbaum 157:6; ed. Polliack and Schlossberg 217 [which reads כטייה]/بيع اون الذى هى خطية اسرائل) (ed. Schroeter 42:9), the translator emphasises that they *have been* the reason for Israel's sin in the past.

The Arabic cognate ודרדר 'and thorn' (21b:16) echoes the Hebrew וְדַרְדַּר; see Cod. Hunt. 206 who translates with the definite noun والدردر (ed. Schroeter 42:10), and Saadiah's translation of Genesis 3:18, whereas Yefet has ואלחסך 'and the thorns' (ed. Birnbaum 157:7; ed. Polliack and Schlossberg 217 [which reads ואלדרדר])

יַעֲלֶה has been rendered with יטלע 'he ascends' (21b:16), whereas Yefet and Cod. Hunt. 206 prefer יצעד (ed. Birnbaum 157:7; ed. Polliack and Schlossberg 217)/يصعد (ed. Schroeter 42:10).

Hosea 10:9

The translator understands the preposition מִן in מִימֵי הַגִּבְעָה in a temporal connotation: 'from (i.e. since) the days of Gibeah' (22b:8); also Vulgate: *ex diebus* ('from the days'); see LXX: ἀφ᾽ οὗ ('from when'); Vulgate: *ex diebus* ('from the days'); Peshitta: ܡܢ ܝܘܡܬܐ; Targum: מיומי. Ibn Ezra argues, however, that מִן has a comparative force: 'you have sinned more than at the time of Gibeah'; see also R. Tanchum; Yefet: אכתׄר מן איאם אלגבעה (ed. Birnbaum 158:3, 7; ed. Polliack and Schlossberg 218) and Cod. Hunt. 206: اكثر من ايام الجبعة 'more than in the days of Gibeah' (ed. Schroeter 42:11) also prefer the comparative interpretation, though Cod. Hunt. 206 concedes that the temporal understanding is possible: ويجوز ان يقال من زمان الجبعة 'it is possible to interpret: since the time of Gibeah' (ed. Schroeter 42:13).

The reconstruction of קד אכטאת 'you have sinned' (22b:9) as translation of חָטָאתָ is based on the author's usual rendering of the Hebrew verb חטא with the Arabic cognate خطئ (Hosea 4:7; 8:11; 13:2); see also Yefet: אכטאת (ed. Birnbaum 158:3; ed. Polliack and Schlossberg 218 [which reads אבטית])/Cod. Hunt. 206: أخطئت (ed. Schroeter 42:11) and T-S Ar.22.127 fol. 2 verso 16: קד אכטאת.

The negation before כאן תלחקהם can be restored as מא (22b:9), since the same phrase including the negation can be found in the exegesis (see 23a:25–26). On the other hand, modern commentators regard לֹא as an asseverative particle ('surely'), developed from its use in rhetorical questions; e.g. Wolff 1974:178 with reference to R. Gordis, Studies in the Relationship of Biblical and Rabbinic Hebrew, in: *Louis Ginzberg Jubilee Volume*, New York 1945, pp. 181–183; R. Gordis, The Text and Meaning of Hosea 14:3, in: *Vetus Testamentum 5* (1955), pp. 88–90; Macintosh 1997:411.

The translator connects the asyndetic Hebrew construction שָׁם עָמְדוּ with the antecedent 'Israel' by creating a syndetic relative clause אלדי תמה תבתו '(the people of Israel) who stood there' (22b:9), whereas Yefet and Cod. Hunt. 206 provide a literal translation: תם וקפו (ed. Birnbaum 158:4; ed. Polliack and Schlossberg 218)/ ثم وقفوا (ed. Schroeter 42:11–12). For שָׁם, which he usually renders with תם, the author chooses here תמה 'there' (ثمَّ) (22b:9) vs. Yefet: תׄם (ed. Birnbaum 158:4; ed. Polliack and Schlossberg 218) and Cod. Hunt. 206: ثم (ed. Schroeter 42:11).

תַּשִּׂיגֵם has been rendered with the compound verb form כאן תלחקהם (22b:9), whereas Yefet and Cod. Hunt. 206 have תדרכהם (ed. Birnbaum 158:4; ed. Polliack and Schlossberg 218)/ تدركهم (ed. Schroeter 42:12). It is noteworthy that the translator uses the 3rd masculine כאן in connection with a feminine singular verb instead of כאנת.

The translator retains the Hebrew מִלְחָמָה as a loanword מלחמה 'war' (22b:10; see also his translation of Hosea 2:20); see also Yefet: אלמלחמה (ed. Birnbaum 158:4; ed. Polliack and Schlossberg 218 [where one manuscript reads מלחמה without the definite article]), whereas Cod. Hunt. 206 translates with حرب (ed. Schroeter 42:12).

Unique is the rendering of בְּנֵי־עַלְוָה (see also 2 Samuel 3:34; 7:10) with ד̈יי גור, literally 'owners of unrighteousness' (22b:10), whereas Yefet and Cod. Hunt. 206

prefer אהל אלגור (ed. Birnbaum 158:5; ed. Polliack and Schlossberg 218)/اهل الجور (ed. Schroeter 42:12).

In his grammatical notes, the author explains עֲלָוָה as metathesis of עַוְלָה 'injustice', 'iniquity' (25a:15–16; see Hosea 10:13); see also Qimḥi: עלוה כמו הפוך ('עלוה) עולה וכן זועה וזעוה כבש וכשב שמלה ושלמה והדומים להם stands by metathesis for עולה and likewise we find זועה for זעוה (Deuteronomy 28:35), כֶּבֶשׂ for כֶּשֶׂב, שִׂמְלָה for שַׂלְמָה and many similar') and Vulgate: *iniquitatis*; LXX: ἀδικίας ('injustice'); Peshitta: ܒܥܘܠܐ. This is also the assumption of modern authors; see Wolff 1974:174 who refers to the root עול I 'to deal unjustly'. However, Rashi derives the noun from the root עלה and translates it as 'haughtiness'; see also Koehler-Baumgartner p. 707 (from עלה II).

Hosea 10:10

The addition of אלאן 'now' (22b:10) at the beginning of the verse characterises the following sentence as happening at this very moment of the present.

The translator understands בְּאַוָּתִי to be a noun, as indicated in his rendition בשהותי 'by my desire' (22b:10); see also Yefet: בשהותי (ed. Birnbaum 159:13; ed. Polliack and Schlossberg 218); Cod. Hunt. 206: بشهوتي (ed. Schroeter 42:14); Rashi, Jerome ('according with my good pleasure'), Vulgate: *iuxta desiderium meum* ('according to my wish'), Peshitta: ܒܟܐܬܝ ('in my censure'). Some versions interpret the word as a verb from the root בוא, e.g. LXX: ἦλθεν ('he came'); Targum: במימרי ('through my Memra').

The additional verb אסלמהם 'I will hand them over' (22b:10) seems to indicate that God is not directly the subject exercising the judgement. Rather He delivers Israel into the hands of their enemies who on their part will carry out the punishment.

The translation ארבטהם 'I will bind them' (22b:10) demonstrates that the translator understood the verb וְאֶסֳּרֵם to be an imperfect from of the root אסר 'to bind', i.e. אֶאְסְרֵם; see also Yefet: ארבטהם (ed. Birnbaum 159:13; ed. Polliack and Schlossberg 218), whereas the versions and rabbinic commentators derive it from the root יסר 'to discipline', e.g. LXX: ἦλθεν παιδεῦσαι αὐτούς ('he came to chastise them'), Vulgate: *corripiam eos* ('I shall censure them'); Peshitta: ܐܪܕܐ ܐܢܘܢ ('I will chastise them'); Targum: איתיתי עליהון יסורין ('I brought chastisement upon them'), Cod. Hunt. 206: اؤدبهم (ed. Schroeter 42:14), Qimḥi: שרשו יסר מן הקל וכן יוסר לך ודגש הסמך לתפארת הקריאה לחסרון היוד פ"א הפעל כמו אצק מים על צמא ובמקבות יצרהו ('אֱסֹר is the *qal* of the root יסר, and likewise Proverbs 9:7; and the *dagesh* in the *samekh* is put because of euphony in order to replace the *yud* of the first radical, like אֶצָק and יִצְּרֵהוּ [Isaiah 44:12]').

Whereas the Hebrew paratactic syntax וְאֶסְפּוּ has also been adopted by Yefet: וחשרת (ed. Birnbaum 159:13; ed. Polliack and Schlossberg 218) and Cod. Hunt. 206 واجتمعوا (ed. Schroeter 42:14), the translator creates a subordinate clause by introducing the preposition חתי: חתי יוחשרו 'until they will gather' (22b:11). He obviously intends to achieve a temporal sequence; see Yefet's paraphrase: יסלמו חתי ... (ed. Birnbaum 160:6–7; ed. Polliack and Schlossberg 219).

After deriving וְאֶסְרֵם from the root אסר 'to bind', the translator also renders בְּאָסְרָם with בסבב רבטהם literally with 'because of their binding' (22b:11). See also Targum: כמיסר ('as one binds'); Yefet and Cod. Hunt. 206 render with ענד רבטהם (ed. Birnbaum 159:13–14; ed. Polliack and Schlossberg 218)/عند ربطهم (ed. Schroeter 42:14). On the other hand, LXX: ἐν τῷ παιδεύεσθαι αὐτούς ('when they are disciplined'), Vulgate: *cum corripientur* and Peshitta: ܟܕ ܡܬܪܕܝܢ again prefer the derivation from the root יסר.

עִינֹתָם (*ketiv*) has been rendered with the Arabic cognate מעניתיהם 'their two furrows' (22b:11) < מעניה (see 25a:21), see Cod. Hunt. 206: معنياتهم (ed. Schroeter 42:15) and his grammatical notes: وهو اسم للمعنية 'it is a noun for "furrow"' (ed. Schroeter 11, 27:19) and Yefet: לכלתי מענאתהם (ed. Birnbaum 159:14; ed. Polliack and Schlossberg 218). In his grammatical notes, the author refers to 1 Samuel 14:14 and Psalms 129:3 (25a:21); see also Cod. Hunt. 206 who lists three nouns as equivalents of מעניה, namely מַעֲנָה (1 Samuel 14:14), מַעֲנִית (Psalms 129:3) and עוֹנָה (Hosea 10:10) (ed. Schroeter 27:19–21), Ibn Ezra: לשתי קשורים יאסרו כמו ואסרם כבחצימענה האריכו חמעהיתם כמו עונותם ('And I will bind them, like they bind a strap on the two furrows. עונות has the same meaning as 1 Samuel 14:14 "like a half furrow" and Psalms 129:3 "they made long their furrows"'). Also in Ibn Janaḥ's view, the word means 'furrow' and has to be linked with the two biblical verses quoted above. The *Qere* עֲוֹנֹתָם 'their wickednesses' is reflected in LXX: ἐν ταῖς δυσὶν ἀδικίαις ('on account of their two wickednesses'), Peshitta: ܥܠ ܬܪܬܝܢ ܥܘܠܘܬܗܘܢ and Vulgate: *propter duas iniquitates suas*; see also Ibn Janaḥ ('their wicked policies')

The restoration in the text of the commentary (23b:5) is based on the general historical situation and a similar phrase in Yefet: ואחד פי בית אל וואחד פי דן (ed. Birnbaum 74:1–2; ed. Polliack and Schlossberg 220).

Hosea 10:11

The reconstruction of the lacuna מועלמה 'trained' (22b:12) is based on the author's phrase in his exegesis (23b:8); see also Yefet and Cod. Hunt. 206: מעלמה (ed. Birnbaum 162:7; ed. Polliack and Schlossberg 220)/معلمة (ed. Schroeter 42:15) and the versions LXX: δεδιαγμένη, Vulgate: *docta*, Peshitta: ܡܠܦܬܐ ('taught'), Targum: דמלפין לה ('which men teach [to plough]').

The restored מחבה 'loving' (22b:12) as translation of the participle form אֹהַ֫בְתִּי (with *yod compaginis*) can also be found in Yefet: מחבה (ed. Birnbaum 162:7; ed. Polliack and Schlossberg 220), in Cod. Hunt. 206: كانت محبة (ed. Schroeter 42:15) and in his grammatical notes: وتفسيره محبة 'and its rendition is "loving"' (ed. Schroeter II, 28:1).

עָבַ֫רְתִּי has been rendered with the Arabic cognate פעברת 'I have passed over' (22b:12) which has also been adopted by Yefet and Cod. Hunt. 206: עברת (ed. Birnbaum 162:8; ed. Polliack and Schlossberg 220)/عبرت (ed. Schroeter 42:16), LXX: ἐπελεύσομαι ('I will come down upon'), Vulgate: *transivi*, Peshitta: ܐܥܕܝܬ; see however Targum: אעדיתי ('[I redeemed them from slavery in Egypt] I removed [the hard yoke from their necks]').

The translator renders טוב with the masculine noun גוד 'good' (22b:13), whereas Yefet and Cod. Hunt. 206 prefer the feminine equivalent: גֹּודה (ed. Birnbaum 162:8; ed. Polliack and Schlossberg 220 [which reads גִּידה])/جودة (ed. Schroeter 42:16).

The phrase 'I will make Ephraim to ride' is introduced by an additional פקלת 'and I said' (22b:13) in order to label the following sentence explicitly as God's speech.

After rendering אַרְכִּ֫יב with the cognate אורכב 'I will make ride' (22b:13), the translator adds the direct object אלניר 'the yoke' (22b:13). Yefet and Cod. Hunt. 206 and Yefet translate with ארכב עלי אפרים (ed. Birnbaum 162:8–9; ed. Polliack and Schlossberg 220)/اركب على افرئم 'I ride on Ephraim' (ed. Schroeter 42:16). Cod. Hunt 206 he provides a similar addition to the previous verb: عبرت بنيري 'I passed with my yoke [upon her beautiful neck]' (ed. Schroeter 42:16).

יְשַׂדֶּד is rendered with יכרוב 'he will harrow' (22b:14); the author probably thinks of a pun of the roots רכב/כרב. See also Yefet: יכרב (ed. Birnbaum 162:9; ed. Polliack and Schlossberg 220) and Cod. Hunt. 206: يكرب (ed. Schroeter 42:17). The same understanding is reflected in Vulgate: *confringet* ('he will harrow'). LXX read apparently ישדד since the translation is ἐνισχύσει ('he will strengthen', 'prevail'), whereas Peshitta: ܢܒܗܐ ('he will plunder') derived the verb from the root שוד. לה 'for him' (22b:14) as rendition of לֹו reflects the *dativus ethicus* (see also לָכֶ֫ם in Hosea 10:12); see also Yefet: לה (ed. Birnbaum 162:9; ed. Polliack and Schlossberg 220).

Hosea 10:12

Similarly to the introduction פקלת 'and I said' in Hosea 10:11 (22b:13), the translator adds here an additional phrase וכדי קלת להם 'and thus I said to them'

(22b:14) also at the beginning of this verse, in order to label the following as a direct speech in God's lips, addressed to Ephraim and Jacob.

By adding פאנכם 'and you' (22b:15) before 'you will harvest', the translator appears to emphasise the subject of the sentence.

The indefinite noun חֶסֶד has been rendered with the definite noun אלאחסאן 'the good deed' (23b:16) which has been reconstructed on the basis of 22b:15. The noun is followed by an additional attributive clause אלדי תעמלו '[the good deeds] you do' (22b:15). Thus the translator clarifies that, in his view, חֶסֶד does not refer to God's lovingkindness, but to Israel's 'good deeds' (see Leviticus 19:9–10; 23:22; Deuteronomy 24:19) which ensure a good harvest, metaphor for reward (see 23b:14–17). See also Targum: עבידו לכון עובדין טבין ('do good deeds!'). Yefet renders: מקדאר (ed. Birnbaum 164:3; ed. Polliack and Schlossberg 221); Cod. Hunt. 206 adds an inseparable preposition: بمقدار (ed. Schroeter 42:19).

The author contrasts the two activities 'sowing'/'harvesting' with the following 'ploughing'/'setting a time' by introducing the particle ליכן 'but', 'however' (23b:15). The orthography ליכן for לכן or لكن/لاكن [lākin] can also be found on 23a:11; 25a:19.

The translator adds another imperative ואגעל 'and make!', 'and attribute!' (22b:16), since the preceding imperative אחרתו 'plow!' with the direct object 'ploughing' deemed to be inappropriate in connection with a direct object 'time'. See R. Tanchum: واجعلوا لطلبه وقتا (see Schroeter p. 179 note 3).

The infinitive לִדְרוֹשׁ is rendered with the unusual לאילתמאס 'to seek' (22b:16); see the rendering of דִּרְשׁוּ יהוה (Psalms 105:4) with אלתמסו אללה in T-S AS 141.24 verso 13. Yefet and Cod. Hunt. 206 use the more common root طلب when rendering: לטלבה (ed. Birnbaum 164:4; ed. Polliack and Schlossberg 221)/مطالبة (ed. Schroeter 43:1).

עַד has been rendered with מהמא 'whenever' (22b:16), whereas Cod. Hunt. 206 has الى ان 'until' (ed. Schroeter 43:1) and Yefet's translates with מא דאם (ed. Birnbaum 164:4; ed. Polliack and Schlossberg 221).

The verb יגי 'He comes' (22b:17) in the translation has been reconstructed following 23b:20; see Yefet and Cod. Hunt. 206: יגי (ed. Birnbaum 164:5; ed. Polliack and Schlossberg 221)/يجيء (ed. Schroeter 43:1).

The translator does not interpret וְיוֹרֶה as a noun meaning 'former rain', but as a verb from the root ירה hi., as shows the translation ויעלמכם 'and he will teach you' (22b:17); see also Cod. Hunt. 206: ويرشدكم (ed. Schroeter 43:1), similarly Yefet: וירשד לכם (ed. Birnbaum 164:5; ed. Polliack and Schlossberg 221), Vulgate: *cum venerit qui docebit vos iustitiam* ('when He comes who will teach you righteousness'), Peshitta: ܥܕ ܢܐܬܐ ܘܢܚܘܐ ('until He comes and declares [righteousness to you]'); see also Wolff.

הודא 'behold' in the exegesis (23b:16) has been reconstructed on the basis of the translation in 22b:16; the discourse marker is an addition to the biblical text; see also Yefet: מהמא הודא (ed. Birnbaum 165:6; ed. Polliack and Schlossberg 221).

Hosea 10:13

By adding the phrase פמא קבלתום בל 'and you have not obeyed rather' at the beginning of the verse (22b:17), the translator achieves a contrast from the outset: instead of obeying the conduct to be expected of Israel—, they acted in exactly the opposite way, as the following metaphors are going to unfold.

The translator retains the word order of the Hebrew source text חֲרַשְׁתֶּם־רֶ֖שַׁע עַוְלָ֣תָה קְצַרְתֶּ֑ם by rendering חרתתם טולם [...] אלגור חצרתם (22b:17–18), whereas Yefet and Cod. Hunt. 206 prefer the usual word order predicate-subject-object: חרתתם אלטלם חצרתם אלגור (ed. Birnbaum 165:23; ed. Polliack and Schlossberg 222)/حرثتم الظلم حصرتم الجور (ed. Schroeter 43:2).

The reconstruction at the beginning of 22b:18 after טולם (22b:18) is uncertain, possibly: בעד הדה since the translator often opts for a temporal sequence of actions.

The rendition of פְּרִי with the masculine noun תמר 'fruit' (22b:18) fits the style of the translator; see also Yefet: ثمر (ed. Birnbaum 165:23; ed. Polliack and Schlossberg 222), whereas Cod. Hunt. 206 prefers the feminine equivalent ثمرة (ed. Schroeter 43:2).

בָטַחְתָּ has been rendered with אתכלת 'you trusted' (23b:18), whereas Yefet and Cod. Hunt. 206 have ותּקת (ed. Birnbaum 166:1; ed. Polliack and Schlossberg 222 [which reads ות'קתא])/وثقت (ed. Schroeter 43:2).

The reconstructed phrase עלי טריקך 'on your way' (22b:19) for Hebrew בְדַרְכְּךָ is due to the attachment of the preposition עלי to the verb وكل VIII; see also the following phrase which has the same preposition: עלי כתרה 'in the multitude' (22b:19) vs. Yefet: בטריקך (ed. Birnbaum 166:1; ed. Polliack and Schlossberg 222 [where one manuscript reads בטירקתך]).

The additional attribute אלסו after 'your way' emphasises that the way they trusted in, is not a 'neutral' way, but has to be qualified as 'evil' (22b:19); see the theological term ἐν τοῖς ἁμαρτήμασιν in LXX^B for בְדַרְכְּךָ, whereas LXX^AQ has τοῖς ἅρμασιν ('chariots').

The translator changes again the preposition of the phrase בְּרֹב into עלי כתרה 'on the multitude' (23b:19), due to the preposition joined with the verb وكل vs. Yefet and Cod. Hunt. 206: בכתרה (ed. Birnbaum 166:1; ed. Polliack and Schlossberg 222)/بكثرة (ed. Schroeter 43:3).

TEXTUAL NOTES

Hosea 10:14

The author may have chosen the verb יתסות 'the sound will arise' (22b:19) the orthography יתסות probably stands for יתצות with the change of *ṣade* into *samekh* because of the similar final consonants of the last word of the same verse פוקיסת 'and she was torn asunder' (22b:21) which stands for פוקצית. Thus he achieves a sort of inclusion. Yefet and Cod. Hunt. 206 prefer the more usual Arabic cognate: סיקום (ed. Birnbaum 166:20; ed. Polliack and Schlossberg 222) and وسيقوم (ed. Schroeter 43:3).

שָׁאוֹן has been rendered with רהג 'tumulte', 'emeute' (Kazimirski I, p. 936) (22b:19). Yefet and Cod. Hunt. 206 translate with צוֹצָא (ed. Birnbaum 166:20; ed. Polliack and Schlossberg 222)/ضوضا (ed. Schroeter 43:3) 'noise', 'uproar'.

By adding the explanatory note כל ואחד מנהא 'every single one of them' (22b:20), the author tries to harmonise the plural subject 'your fortresses' with the singular verb 'he will be plundered' and may also intend to include every single of the aforementioned fortresses, i.e. he emphasises the total destruction. See Yefet's phrase in his commentary: ויכון נהבהא נהם עטים (ed. Birnbaum 167:13; ed. Polliack and Schlossberg 222).

מִלְחָמָה has again been adopted as Hebrew loanword מלחמה 'battle' (22b:21) vs. חרב which occurs in Yefet and Cod. Hunt. 206 with the article: אלחרב (ed. Birnbaum 166:21 ed. Polliack and Schlossberg 222)/الحرب (ed. Schroeter 43:5).

עַל is rendered with מע 'together with' (22b:21); see also Yefet and Cod. Hunt. 206: מע (ed. Birnbaum 166:22; ed. Polliack and Schlossberg 222)/مع (ed. Schroeter 43:5).

רֻטָּשָׁה *dashed into pieces* (see Psalms 137:9; 2 Kings 8:12; Isaiah 13:16; Nahum 3:10) is rendered with פוקיסת 'and her neck has been broken' (22b:21); see also Hosea 14:1 (יופסקון—יְרֻטָּשׁוּ). Similar to the orthography of the root صوت in יתסות above (22b:19), the *samekh* seems to stand for *ṣade*. Yefet and Cod. Hunt. 206 render with בעגת (ed. Birnbaum 166:22; ed. Polliack and Schlossberg 222)/بعجت 'she has been slit open' (ed. Schroeter 43:5).

The translator changes the Hebrew asyndetic construction אֵם עַל־בָּנִים רֻטָּשָׁה 'a mother was dashed into pieces with (her) children' into a syndetic relative clause which links this event with the aforementioned military operation: אלדי אום מע בנין פוקיסת '(on the day of war) when a mother with (her) children was torn asunder' (22b:21).

Hosea 10:15

The author changes the prepositional phrase לָכֶם 'for you' into בכם 'among you' (22b:22); see also Yefet and Cod. Hunt. 206: בכם (ed. Birnbaum 167:18; ed. Polliack and Schlossberg 223)/ بكْ (ed. Schroeter 43:5).

The translator adds the noun אלעגל 'the calf' as the subject of the sentence and expands it by adding a relative clause including the subject of the Hebrew source text: אלעגל אלדי אנצבתום פי בית אל 'the calf which you have established in Beth-El' (22b:22). These changes indicate the author's view that is not Beth-El itself which has acted in that way, but the calf as the symbol of Beth-El's idolatrous cult.

מן קיבל 'because of' is a literal translation of מִפְּנֵי (22b:22); see also Yefet and Cod. Hunt. 206: מן קבל (ed. Birnbaum 167:18; ed. Polliack and Schlossberg 223)/ من قبل (ed. Schroeter 43:6).

רָעַת רָעַתְכֶם has been rendered literally with רדאה רדאתכם 'the evil of your evil' (22b:22–23), indicating a superlative, whereas Yefet and Cod. Hunt. 206 translate only the second component of the construct chain: רדאכם (ed. Birnbaum 167:19; ed. Polliack and Schlossberg 223)/ ردائكْ (ed. Schroeter 43:6).

The preposition in the phrase of the translation באלפגר 'at the dawn' (22b:23) has been corrected into פי which can also be found in Cod. Hunt. 206 وفي الفجر (ed. Schroeter 43:6), whereas Yefet translates with ענד אלפגר (ed. Birnbaum 167:19; ed. Polliack and Schlossberg 223).

The additional פלדלך 'and therefore' (22b:23) introduces the following punishment as a consequence of their great wickedness.

The translator renders the *figura etymologica* נִדְמֹה נִדְמָה almost slavishly by retaining the infinitive abolute: אינבכאם אנבכם 'he has utterly been silenced' (22b:23); see also Yefet and Cod. Hunt. 206: אנבכאם אנבכם (ed. Birnbaum 167:19; ed. Polliack and Schlossberg 223)/ انبكام انبكْ (ed. Schroeter 43:6).

Hosea 11:1

The translator interprets the conjunction כִּי in a causal sense: לאן 'for', 'because' (22b:24); see also LXX, Aquila, Symmachus: ὅτι ('because'); Vulgate: *quia*; Peshitta: ܡܛܠ ܕܗܘ; Targum: ארי, whereas modern commentators usually prefer a temporal sense 'when' (e.g. Macintosh 1997:436; Vielhauer 2007:15). However, see also Cod. Hunt. 206: لأنْ (ed. Schroeter 43:9).

By adding the copula כאן (22b:24), the translator obviously intends to clarify that the following sentence has to placed in the past: 'since the people of Israel *were* a young man'; see also Yefet and Cod. Hunt. 206: אן חדת ישראל

(ed. Birnbaum 168:17; ed. Polliack and Schlossberg 224)/لان حدث كان اسرائل (ed. Schroeter 43:9).

The translator renders קְרָאתִי with נאדית 'I called' (22b:24), whereas Yefet chooses סמית (ed. Birnbaum 168:17; ed. Polliack and Schlossberg 224); Cod. Hunt. 206 adds the suffix pronoun: سميته (ed. Schroeter 43:9) 'I called him', i.e. I named him 'my son'; see also Qimḥi, Peshitta, Targum.

לבני is rendered with באבני, literally 'in my son' (22b:24), by changing the preposition according to Arabic syntax which allows بـ III to be construed with ب or ه or على; see Cod. Hunt. 206: ابني (ed. Schroeter 43:9).

Hosea 11:2

As the addition of פלמא 'and when', 'and after' (22b:25) at the beginning of the verse indicates, the author is interested in establishing a temporal sequence; see also Hosea 7:15. LXX: καθὼς μετεκάλεσα ('as I called') and Peshitta: ܐܝܟ ܕ add the conjunction 'as' which corresponds to the following כֵּן.

By adding the preposition with enclitic pronoun אלי 'to Me', the author emphasises that the mediators did not only call Israel, but showed them the direction: to God (22b:25).

The translator chooses the Arabic cognate יוקתרו 'they burn incense' (22b:26) for rendering יְקַטֵּרוּן; see also Yefet: ויקתרו (ed. Birnbaum 169:13; ed. Polliack and Schlossberg 224 [where one manuscript reads ויברכו])/Cod. Hunt. 206: ويقتروا (ed. Schroeter 43:11).

Hosea 11:3

The *hapax legomenon* תִרְגַּלְתִּי (*tifʿel* for *hifʿil*) is understood to be a verb, as shows the translator's rendering פדדית 'and I pampered' (22b:26). LXX connects the verb with the noun רגל 'foot' when rendering: συνεπόδισα ('I bound their feet'); Qimḥi, Ibn Ezra: 'I taught to walk'; Symmachus: ἐπαιδαγώγουν ('I trained', 'I nurtured'); Vulgate: *ego quasi nutritius* ('I am like a tutor'). Also Peshitta: ܪܒܝܬ; Targum: דברית notice a connection with רגל causative 'to cause to walk'. In his exegesis, the author refers to (at least) two options for interpreting this verb, one of them being גססת 'I examined', 'I tested'. This option understands the verb as being derived from רגל *piʿel* 'to spy', as do Yefet: גססת (ed. Birnbaum 169:21; ed. Polliack and Schlossberg 224) and Cod. Hunt. 206: جسست (ed. Schroeter 43:11); see Saadiah's translation of the root רגל with جس (e.g. Genesis 42:9, 11, 14; Deuteronomy 1:24). According to Rashi, תִרְגַּלְתִּי is an equivalent of הרגלתי *hifʿil* (see H. Englander, Rashi's Grammatical Comments, in: *Hebrew Union College Annual* 17 (1942/43), p. 473); see also Ibn Ezra, Qimḥi, Parchon.

The subject of the biblical phrase קָחָם עַל זְרוֹעֹתָיו 'he took them on his arms' is not clear from the context: is the subject God or someone else? To avoid the possible understanding as anthropomorphism, the translator adds the subject אלנבי 'the prophet' (22b:27); see also his exegesis (24a:20).

The restoration of קד אשפיתהם 'I healed them' (23a:1) as translation of רְפָאתִים is based on a phrase in the exegesis (24a:23); see also Yefet: אשפיתהם IV (ed. Birnbaum 169:22; ed. Polliack and Schlossberg 224) vs. Cod. Hunt. 206: شفيتهم I (ed. Schroeter 43:12).

Hosea 11:4

The phrase בלחבאל אלנאס 'with the cords of man' (23a:1) as rendition of בְּחַבְלֵי אָדָם can be restored from 24a:25 (חבאל אלנאס); see also Yefet: בחבאל אלנאס (ed. Birnbaum 170:20; 171:1; ed. Polliack and Schlossberg 225) and Cod. Hunt. 206: بحبال الناس (ed. Schroeter 43:12).

The translator changes the present tense אֶמְשְׁכֵם into the compound verb form of the past כונת אגדבהם 'I drew them' or 'I permanently drew them' (23a:1); Yefet and Cod. Hunt. 206 retain the present tense in their translations אגדבהם (ed. Birnbaum 170:20; ed. Polliack and Schlossberg 225)/ آجذ بهم (ed. Schroeter 43:12).

The translator chooses the singular במוקט 'with a rope' (23a:1) (مُقْط pl. مقاط Hava 729; Dozy 613) as rendering of the plural בַּעֲבֹתוֹת 'with bonds'; see Saadiah's translation of Psalms 118:27 (בַּעֲבֹתִים). Yefet and Cod. Hunt. 206 render with a plural noun: בנסוע (ed. Birnbaum 170:20; ed. Polliack and Schlossberg 225)/ بنسوع (ed. Schroeter 43:12).

The visible remnants make it likely that the translator rendered וָאֶהְיֶה with וצרת 'and I was' (23a:2) vs. Yefet: פכנת (ed. Birnbaum 170:20; ed. Polliack and Schlossberg 225)/Cod. Hunt. 206: فكنت (ed. Schroeter 43:13).

כמרפעי 'like those who lift' (23a:2) as rendition of כִּמְרִימֵי has been reconstructed according to the author's usual rendering of the preposition כְּ with כ and of the root רום with the root רפע (see Hosea 13:6: וַיָּרֻם: ארתפע); see also Yefet: מתל מרפעי (ed. Birnbaum 170:21; ed. Polliack and Schlossberg 225)/Cod. Hunt. 206: مثل مرفعي (ed. Schroeter 43:13). Some versions translate the phrase as the singular: Aquila: ὡς αἴρων ('like one taking off'); Peshitta: ܐܝܟ ܗܘ ܕܡܪܝܡ '(like one who lifts') and Vulgate: *quasi exaltans*, opposed to Symmachus: ὡς ὁ ἐπιθείς ('like one who imposes').

לְחֵיהֶם has been rendered with כדיהם 'their two jaws' (23a:2); see also the exegesis: עלי אענאקהם 'on their necks' (24b:2). As is evident from their translation טראותהם (ed. Birnbaum 170:21; ed. Polliack and Schlossberg 225)/طراوتهم 'their freshness' (ed. Schroeter 43:13), Yefet and Cod. Hunt. 206 derive the word from לח, referring explicitly to Ezekiel 17:24 (עֵץ לָח). See also the grammatical notes in Cod. Hunt. 206 (ed. Schroeter II, 28:6); in the grammarian's view, the rendering خديهم 'their cheeks' would be the equivalent of Hebrew לְחֵיהֶם (ed. Schroeter II, 28:7).

The translation מילת 'I bowed down' (23a:2) proves that the translator understood וָאַט to be derived from the root נטה *hifʿil* 'to bend', 'to incline oneself towards', 'to stoop down to'. In his grammatical notes, Cod. Hunt. 206 refers to the imperative הַטֵּה (ed. Schroeter II, 28:8); see also Aquila: καὶ ἔκλινα, Symmachus/Theodotion: ἐξέκλινα ('I extended'), Ibn Ezra: ואט כמו אטה; Yefet: ואמיל (ed. Birnbaum 170:21; ed. Polliack and Schlossberg 225), Cod. Hunt. 206: واميل 'and I will bow down' (ed. Schroeter 43:13).

According to Ibn Ezra, אוֹכִיל is a noun: ומלת אוכיל שם דבר כמו אוכל בכסף והייתי מטה אליו אוכל ורבי מרינוס אמר כי אוכיל ראוי להיותו אאכיל כמו ויוסף עוד דוד את כל בחור בישראל ופרוש ואט כמשמעו שהייתי מאכילו אט ('The word אוכיל is a noun like Deuteronomy 2:28; the meaning is: I have offered him food. However, R. Marinus says that אוכיל is the same as אאכיל, see 2 Samuel 7:1. The explanation of ואט is according to the straight meaning: I have given food to them in a gentle way'). However, the translator appears to refer to the root יכל 'to be able', since the text is presumably אטיק 'I am able' (see Hosea 8:5). This assumption is supported by his exegesis אנא אקדר עליה 'I have power over him' (24b:7–8) and his grammatical notes which refer to the imperative הוֹכֵיל (25a:25); see also Cod. Hunt. 206's grammatical notes (ed. Schroeter II, 28:10). The same understanding can be found in LXX: δυνήσομαι αὐτῷ ('I will prevail over him'), Yefet: אוסע (ed. Birnbaum 170:21; ed. Polliack and Schlossberg 225), referring to 1 Kings 7:24 and Jeremiah 2:13, and Cod. Hunt. 206: اوسع 'I am able' (ed. Schroeter 43:14).

Hosea 11:5

The *lacuna* after מצר and before אשור (23a:3) suggests that the translator added one or two words; Yefet and Cod. Hunt. 206 render literally: לא ירגע אלי ארץ מצר ואשור הו מלכה (ed. Birnbaum 171:17; ed. Polliack and Schlossberg 225)/لا يرجع الى ارض مصر والموصل هو ملكه (ed. Schroeter 43:17).

Hosea 11:6

As can be concluded from his exegesis קד אבתדת סיף מלך אשור 'the sword of the king of Assur began' (24b:12), the translator appears to derive the verb וְחָלָה from the root חלל III 'to begin'; therefore the text of the translation has been reconstructed as ותבתדי סיף 'and the sword begins' (23a:4); see also Yefet: ותבתדי (ed. Birnbaum 172:5; ed. Polliack and Schlossberg 225 [where one manuscript reads תבתדי without *waw*])/Cod. Hunt. 206: وَبَتدِى (ed. Schroeter 43:18); Vulgate: *coepit* ('he began'). In his grammatical note (25a:26–27), the author derives the verb from the imperative חול, whom he attributes the same meaning 'to begin', i.e. חלל *hif'il*; see also Cod. Hunt. 206 in his grammatical notes: וחלה חרב אמר חול (ed. Schroeter 28:14) with the same meaning 'to begin'. Modern translators (e.g. Wolff 1964:259; Vielhauer 2007:15, 19) derive the verb from the root חול I 'to whirl', 'to dance'; Macintosh translates: 'The sword will fall upon' (1997:452); see also Aquila: ἔπεσεν and Targum: ולחול ('it whirls'. 'it is impending'). The phrase of the whirling sword indicates the devastation to come like the proverbial sword of Damocles. LXX: καὶ ἠσθένησεν and Peshitta: ܘܐܬܟܪܗ ('it became weak') derive the verb from the root חלה I 'to become sick', 'weak'. Symmachus: καὶ τραυματίσει ('it will wound') and Jerome: *vulnerabit* appear to derive the verb from חלל I BDB.

Since the translator's usual rendering of עיר is קורה (see Hosea 8:14; 13:10; text missing: Hosea 8:14; 11:6, 9), the restoration פי קוראה 'in his cities' for בְּעָרָיו appears to be likely, whereas Yefet and Cod. Hunt. 206 prefer פי בלדאנה (ed. Birnbaum 172:5; ed. Polliack and Schlossberg 225)/فى بلدانه (ed. Schroeter 43:18).

After the phrase וְחָלָה חֶרֶב בְּעָרָיו *a sword will begin in his cities*, the translator adds תום 'then' (23a:4) to create a temporal sequence, i.e. after destroying the cities, the sword will continue its devastation by devouring the people.

The rendering of בַּדָּיו with דהוקה 'his branches' (23a:5) indicates that the translator interpreted the Hebrew noun as 'bars', 'sticks' (from בד I), presumably influenced by Ezekiel 17:6. The same interpretation can be found in Ibn Ezra's explanation סעיפיו ('his branches') and Qimḥi: פירוש בדיו ענפיו ('the meaning of בַּדָּיו is "his branches"'); however, the latter remarks that the usage of the word is figurative and denotes 'villages', since 'villages are to cities what branches are to trees'. Some versions offer a figurative understanding: Targum: גיברוהי ('his warriors'), Vulgate: *electos eius* ('his chosen men'); Rashi; Cod. Hunt. 206: اجلاءه 'his great ones'.

The translator changes the connective conjunction in וְאָכְלָה into the conjunction לאנהא 'for it' (23a:5), thus suggesting a causal sequence.

מן משווראתהם 'because of their teachings' (23a:5) as rendition for מִמֹּעֲצוֹתֵיהֶם has been restored according to the translation of Hosea 10:6. Yefet and Cod.

Hunt. 206 have מן גהה תדביראהם (ed. Birnbaum 172:6; ed. Polliack and Schlossberg 225 [where one manuscript reads תדביראתה]/من جهة تدبيراتهم ('because of their counsels', ed. Schroeter 43:18–19), see also LXX: ἐκ τῶν διαβουλίων αὐτῶν; Symmachus: διὰ τὰς διαβουλίας αὐτῶν; Peshitta: ܡܢ ܬܪܥܝܬܗܘܢ ('because of their counsels'); Targum: ממלכי עצתהון ('because of the counsels of their advisers'), as opposed to Vulgate: *capita eorum* as direct object of וְאָכְלָה ('[and it will consume] their chief points').

Hosea 11:7

ושעבי 'and my people' (23a:5) has been restored according to the author's usual rendering of עַם; also Yefet and Cod. Hunt. 206 have here ושעבי (ed. Birnbaum 172:16; ed. Polliack and Schlossberg 226)/وشعبي (ed. Schroeter 43:19).

תְּלוּאִים is rendered with פמועלקין 'and hanging' (23a:6); see also Yefet: מעלקין (ed. Birnbaum 172:16; ed. Polliack and Schlossberg 226) and Cod. Hunt. 206: معلقين (ed. Schroeter 43:19; Schroeter II, 28:17).

The restoration of the translation לאיגל רגעתי 'about returning to Me' (23a:6) for לִמְשׁוּבָתִי is based on a phrase in the exegesis מועלקין באלרגעה 'undecided to return' (24b:15); see also the versions: Aquila: τῇ ἐπιστροφῇ μου; Theodotion: ἐπιστροφὴν αὐτοῦ; others introduce a preposition, e.g. Symmachus: εἰς τὸ ἐπιστρέφειν πρός με, Vulgate: *ad reditum meum* ('to My returning'), Peshitta: ܠܡܗܦܟ ܠܘܬܝ ('to return to Me'). Yefet translates: מן גהה אלעתו אלדי עתו מני (Birnbaum 172:16; ed. Polliack and Schlossberg 226 [where one manuscript reads אלתי instead of אלדי and another manuscript reads מנה instead of מני]).

The restoration ואלי אלעאלי 'and to the Most High' as rendering of וְאֶל עַל is based on 24b:18 (אלעאלי); see also Yefet: ואלי אלעאלי (ed. Birnbaum 172:16–17; ed. Polliack and Schlossberg 226)/Cod. Hunt. 206: والى العالى (ed. Schroeter 43:20). See Ibn Harūn on עַל: אסם הוא אלדי ('which is a noun', 1.5.4).

The translator adds והום 'and they' (23a:6) before גמיעא, probably for the purpose of emphasis: 'and they altogether there is no one among them ...'.

The translation of יְרוֹמֵם 'he will lift' is missing. The final י which is visible may indicate that the translator chose a finite verb with suffix pronoun 1. singular, as he may have felt a direct object missing in the biblical source text, possibly: ירפעני 'who praises Me'. See Cod. Hunt. 206 who has the same verb: يرفع (ed. Schroeter 43:20) vs. Yefet: ישרף (ed. Birnbaum 172:17; ed. Polliack and Schlossberg 226).

Hosea 11:8

The reconstruction of the beginning of the translation with כיף אגעלך יא אל אפרים (23a:7) is based on the following parallel phrase; see also T-S Ar.21.105 fol. 2 recto 18: כיף אתרכך יא אל אפרים; Yefet: כיף אגעלך יא אפרים (ed. Birnbaum 173:8; ed. Polliack and Schlossberg 226)/Cod. Hunt. 206: كيف اجعلك يا افرٓم (ed. Schroeter 44:2).

The translator renders both Hebrew verbs אֶתֶּנְךָ and אֲמַגֶּנְךָ with אגעלך 'I make you' (23a:7, 8). However, in his grammatical notes, he offers two options: (1) 'breaking' (כסר) and (2) 'handing over' (תסלים) (25a:27–25b:1); see Cod. Hunt. 206: اسلمك (ed. Schroeter 44:2). Ibn Nūḥ quotes Hosea 11:8 in connection with the first rendering: ודלך אן לא לגה אלכסר מן הדה אללגה מא וגדנא בלא מים אצלי כך אשר מִגֵּן צָרֶיךָ: אֲמַגֶּנְךָ ישראל ('This is because we do not find forms from the lexical class "breaking", to which this belongs, without a *mem* in the base, for example אֲשֶׁר־מִגֵּן צָרֶיךָ [Genesis 14:20], אֲמַגֶּנְךָ יִשְׂרָאֵל [Hosea 11:8]', *Diqduq* on Lamentations 3:65, ed. Khan 2000:482–483).

The translator adds another כיף 'how' before the second אגעלך (23a:7), in order to achieve a closer parallelism; see also the additional prepostion + connective conjunction in Yefet/Cod. Hunt. 206: וכיף (ed. Birnbaum 173:8; ed. Polliack and Schlossberg 226)/ وكيف (ed. Schroeter 44:3).

The restoration אגעלך 'I make you' (23a:8) as rendering of אֲשִׂימְךָ is based on the translation of Hosea 2:2, 5, 14. The fourfold occurrence of the same verb in the Arabic version, though quite monotonous, appears to be intended in order to focuss exclusively on the names Ephraim, Israel, Admah and Zeboim, rather to distract from them by a variation of the verbal forms. Yefet and Cod. Hunt. 206 translate with: אצירך (ed. Birnbaum 173:10; ed. Polliack and Schlossberg 226 [which reads אצײרך])/ اصورك (ed. Schroeter 44:3), as Saadiah does when rendering אָשִׂים in Genesis 46:3; Deuteronomy 1:13.

The phrase אנקלב עליי קלבי 'My heart has been turned around against Me' (23a:9) provides a pun in the translation that does not occur in the source text נֶהְפַּךְ עָלַי לִבִּי, since the verb قلب VII 'to be turned over' and the noun قلب 'heart' share identical root letters. The 'overturning' occurs as a complete 'overturning' in God's heart. His 'heart' is the 'turning point'.

יַחַד has been rendered with the adverbial accusative גמיעא 'together' (23a:9) as in Hosea 11:7 (23a:7), whereas the versions have: LXX: ἐν τῷ αὐτῷ; Vulgate: *pariter* ('at the same time'); Symmachus: ἐν τούτῳ; Targum: נחדא ('at once'). Yefet and Cod. Hunt. 206 have also: גמיעא (ed. Birnbaum 173:10; ed. Polliack and Schlossberg 226)/ جميعا (ed. Schroeter 44:3).

The translator renders נִכְמְרוּ with האגת 'she was stirred up' (23a:9). Yefet: האגת (ed. Birnbaum 173:11; ed. Polliack and Schlossberg 226) and Cod. Hunt.

206: هاجوا (ed. Schroeter 44:4); see also R. Tanchum: هاج. Ibn Janāḥ notes that the semantic range of the Hebrew כמר is identical with Arabic هيج; see Saadiah's translation of Genesis 43:30 (נִכְמְרוּ רַחֲמָיו—האגת רחמתה),

The reconstruction תעאזי 'My consolations' (23a:9) as rendition of נְחוּמָי has been suggested *ad sensum*. If this is correct, this rendering would point to Aquila/Symmachus: παράκλησίς μου; LXX: ἡ μεταμέλειά μου ('my regret', 'my repentance'); Vulgate: *paenitudo mea*; Peshitta: ܢܚܡܬܝ ('my tenderness'). Yefet: צפחאתי (ed. Birnbaum 173:11; ed. Polliack and Schlossberg 226)/Cod. Hunt. 206: صفحاتي (ed. Schroeter 44:4) refer to the root صفح 'to pardon', 'to forgive'.

Hosea 11:9

The phrase חֲרוֹן אַפּוֹ has been rendered literally with שדה גצבי 'the vehemence of My wrath' (23a:9–10); see also Yefet: שדה גצבי (ed. Birnbaum 175:21; ed. Polliack and Schlossberg 227), whereas Cod. Hunt. 206 adds the a preposition ب: بشدة عضبي 'in the vehemence of My wrath' (ed. Schroeter 44:4).

The restoration of לאפסאד 'to destroy' (23a:10) as rendition of לְשַׁחֵת seems to be most likely since the translator uses the same root in his translation of Hosea 13:9: אפסדך (for שִׁחֶתְךָ); see also Yefet: לאפסאד (ed. Birnbaum 175:21; ed. Polliack and Schlossberg 227)/Cod. Hunt. 206: لافساد (ed. Schroeter 44:5).

The restoration of טאיק 'Almighty' (23a:10) as rendition of אֵל is based on the translation of אֵל in Hosea 2:1 (text missing: Hosea 12:1); see also Yefet and Cod. Hunt. 206: טאיק (ed. Birnbaum 175:22; ed. Polliack and Schlossberg 227)/طائق (ed. Schroeter 44:5).

The translator rephrases the nominal sentence בְּקִרְבְּךָ קָדוֹשׁ by forming a verbal sentence with a verb form of the future פי וסטך אכון קדוס 'in your midst I will be holy' (23a:10–11), whereas Yefet and Cod. Hunt. 206 render literally פי וסטך קדוס (ed. Birnbaum 175:22; ed. Polliack and Schlossberg 227)/في وسطك قدوس (ed. Schroeter 44:5).

The gap after וליס אדכול פי קוריה 'I will not enter a city' (23a:11) in the translation can possibly be restored when taking into consideration Saadiah's paraphrase (according to Qimḥi): ולא אבא בעיר אחרת אלא בירושלם ('I do not enter a city other than Jerusalem') and Yefet's commentary: פליס אדכ̇ל בה אלי מדינה̇ אכרי לם אכ̇תאר במדינה̇ אסכן וקארי פיה גיר ירושלם (ed. Birnbaum 177:2–4; ed. Polliack and Schlossberg 228). The *alef* after the first *lacuna* could be part of אלא and the final *mem* which is visible before the *sof pasuq*, may be the last letter of ירושלם, i.e. the missing text may be read accordingly: וליס אדכל פי קריה אוכרי אלא פי ירושלם, meaning that God does not allow His presence to rest in any other city but Jerusalem. Yefet and Cod. Hunt. 206 provide a literal translation: ולא אדכ̇ל פי

ולא ادخل فى مدينة/(ed. Birnbaum 175:23; ed. Polliack and Schlossberg 227) מדינה (ed. Schroeter 44:5–6). The Targum reflects the same idea of God's predilection for Jerusalem: ולא אחליף בקריא אוחרי עוד ית ירושלם ('I will never exchange Jerusalem for any other city'), and also Jerome provides a similar interpretation: 'I am not one of those who inhabit cities, who live by human laws, who suppose that cruelty is justice ...'.

Hosea 11:10

The translator rephrases MT by creating a subordinate clause: ליכן פי אלוקת אלדי 'however, at the time when ...' (23a:11–12).

The rendering of יֵלְכוּ with יסלוכו 'they go' (23a:12) is, though not a cognate, closer to the consonants of the Hebrew verb than Yefet and Cod. Hunt. 206 who choose the equivalent יסירו (ed. Birnbaum 177:13; ed. Polliack and Schlossberg 228)/يسيروا (ed. Schroeter 44:6),

The translator changes the indefinite כְּאַרְיֵה into the definite noun כאלאסד 'like the lion', followed by a syndetic relative clause, introduced by the relative marker אלדי (23a:12); see also Cod. Hunt. 206: مثل الاسد الذى يزئر (ed. Schroeter 44:6).

Instead of providing a literal translation of the phrase כִּי־הוּא יִשְׁאַג for He will roar, the translator creates another relative clause with the personal pronoun הו 'he' as antecedent, thus emphasising that it is God Himself who roars, and he specifies God's roaring as being directed 'towards them' by adding אליהם 'to them': לאנה הו אלדי יזיר אליהם 'for He is the one who roars towards them' (23a:12–13). Yefet and Cod. Hunt. 206 translate in this instance literally: לאנה יזיר (ed. Birnbaum 177:14; ed. Polliack and Schlossberg 228)/لانه يزئر (ed. Schroeter 44:6–7).

וְיֶחֶרְדוּ 'they tremble' is rendered with פינזעגו 'and they will be stirred up' (23a:13). Also Ibn Janāḥ refers to the same Arabic root زع 'to be roused', 'to be stirred up' (אלאנזעאג), as opposed to אלקראר 'permanence', 'stability', 'rest', 'stillness', whereas Yefet: פיקלקו (ed. Birnbaum 177:14; ed. Polliack and Schlossberg 228) and Cod. Hunt. 206: فيقلقوا (ed. Schroeter 44:7) emphasise the aspect of 'unsteadiness'.

The translator renders מִיָּם with מן גהה אלגרב to denote the direction 'the west' (23a:13), whereas Yefet and Cod. Hunt. 206 expand: מן גזאיר אלבחר (ed. Birnbaum 177:14; ed. Polliack and Schlossberg 228)/من جزائر البحر 'from the islands of the sea' (ed. Schroeter 44:7), probably under the influence of Isaiah 11:11; see also Targum: גלותא ממערבא. The versions LXX: τέκνα ὑδάτων; Vulgate: filii maris; Peshitta: ܒܢܝ ܡܝܐ require Hebrew בני מים instead of MT: בנים מים.

Hosea 11:11

כְּצִפּוֹר has been rendered with the similar Arabic term כעצפור 'like a sparrow' (23a:13), whereas Yefet and Cod. Hunt. 206 provide the more general term: מתל אלטאיר (ed. Birnbaum 177:15; ed. Polliack and Schlossberg 228)/مثل الطائر 'like the bird' (ed. Schroeter 44:11–12).

From his rendering פאוגלסהם 'and I will settle them', it can be concluded that the translator derived וְהוֹשַׁבְתִּים from יש״ב; see also Yefet: ואגלסהם (ed. Birnbaum 177:16; ed. Polliack and Schlossberg 228) and Cod. Hunt. 206: واجلسهم (ed. Schroeter 44:9). The rendering of T-S Ar.21.105 fol. 2 recto 21: וארדהם ('and I will return them') indicates that he derived the verb from the root שו״ב.

The translator changes the unusual preposition of the phrase עַל־בָּתֵּיהֶם by rendering פי ביותהם 'in their houses' (23a:14); see also the same preposition, though combined with a different noun, in Yefet/Cod. Hunt. 206: פי מנאזלהם (ed. Birnbaum 177:16–17; ed. Polliack and Schlossberg 228)/في منازلهم (ed. Schroeter 44:9).

Hosea 12:1

The restoration of בגחוד 'with rejection' (25b:1) as translation of בְּכַחַשׁ is based on the author's translation in Hosea 4:2; 10:13; see also the definite noun in Yefet: באלגחד (ed. Birnbaum 180:2; ed. Polliack and Schlossberg 230) and the definite plural in Cod. Hunt. 206: بالجحود (ed. Schroeter 44:11).

The emendation ובמכר 'and with deception' (25b:1) as translation of וּבְמִרְמָה is based on the translation of מִרְמָה in Hosea 12:8 (25b:11), though in his exegesis of this verse, the author refers to the participle ממאכרה (26a:17). Also Yefet and Cod. Hunt. 206 render with the same noun; however, they add the definite article: באלמכר (ed. Birnbaum 180:3; ed. Polliack and Schlossberg 230)/بالمكر (ed. Schroeter 44:11).

The verb רָד only occurs here, Genesis 27:40; Psalms 55:3 these two biblical references are quoted in Yefet's commentary (ed. Birnbaum 182:1–2; ed. Polliack and Schlossberg 230–231) and Jeremiah 2:31. The translator renders it with אסתולא 'he made himself master', 'he is master', 'he overwhelmed' (25b:2), i.e. the author derives the Hebrew verb from the root רו״ד 'to rule', by-form of רד״ה 'to dominate', 'to rule'. The rendering possibly constitutes a reference to Jacob's prevailing when wrestling with the angel (Genesis 32:29). Ibn Janāḥ, Yefet and Cod. Hunt. 206 have the identical translation אלדי כאן טאיע (ed. Birnbaum 180:3–4; ed. Polliack and Schlossberg 230)/الذى كان طايع 'who was obedient' (ed. Schroeter 44:12). See also Rashi: אבל יהודה עודנו רד עם אל מושל עוד ביראת אלהים ('only

Judah rules with God, i.e. it rules still in the fear of God') and Aquila: ἐπικρα-
τῶν. Cod. Hunt. 206, however, notes a different option: وقال مفسر اخر ויהודה עד רד
:ויהודה עד רד 'another exegete explains ויהוּדָה עד רד وان یهوده ایضا صار والیا مع القادر: Judah has
also become a ruler with the Powerful One' (ed. Schroeter 44:15–16). See also
Yefet's exegesis: וקאל מפסר אבֿר ויהודה עד רד ואן יהודה איצׄא צאר ואלי מע אלקאדר
(ed. Birnbaum 182:11–13; ed. Polliack and Schlossberg 231) and Saadiah's translation of תָּרִיד with אסתולית (Genesis 27:40) and אָרִיד with אסתולי (Psalms 55:3).

The translator seems to have rendered the plural קְדוֹשִׁים literally with
אלקודוס (25b:2) without clarifying in his translation that he understood the
noun to be a majestic plural referring to God; see, however, his exegesis (26a:21).
Yefet/Cod. Hunt. 206 add another epithet to exclude any misunderstanding:
אלבארי אלקדוס 'the Creator, the Holy One' (ed. Birnbaum 180:4–5; ed. Polliack
and Schlossberg 230)/الرب القدوس 'the Lord, the Holy One' (ed. Schroeter 44:12–
13). Qimḥi who also refers to Joshua 24:19, notes: כי קדושים במקום אל אמר לשון
רבים כמו אלהים קדושים הוא ('for קְדוֹשִׁים stands instead of אֵל; however, he puts
the plural as in Joshua 24:19').

The reconstruction of אלטאיק 'the Powerful One' (25b:2) as rendition of אֵל is
based on the author's translation of אֵל in Hosea 2:1; 11:9, though, in his exegesis,
he uses a different root when phrasing אנא קאדר 'I am powerful' (26a:21); see
Yefet: אלקאדר (ed. Birnbaum 180:4; ed. Polliack and Schlossberg 2301) and Cod.
Hunt. 206 القادر (ed. Schroeter 44:12).

The reconstruction תאבת 'perservering' (25b:2) as rendering of נֶאֱמָן is based
on a phrase in the author's exegesis (26a:21) and the translation of נֶאֱמָנָה with
תאבתה in Hosea 5:9.

The translator imitates the inverted word order of the Hebrew source text
עִם-אֵל וְעִם-קְדוֹשִׁים נֶאֱמָן by rendering מע אלטאיק ומע אלקודוס תאבת, whereas Yefet
and Cod. Hunt. 206 change into the usual word order: ואלדי כאן תקה ענד אלבארי
אלקדוס (ed. Birnbaum 180:4–5; ed. Polliack and Schlossberg 230)/كان ثقة عند
الرب القدوس (ed. Schroeter 44:11–12).

Hosea 12:2

The Hebrew רֹעֶה has been translated literally with ראעי 'grazing' (25b:3); see
also Yefet: ראעי (ed. Birnbaum 182:19; ed. Polliack and Schlossberg 231); Cod.
Hunt. 206: راعي (ed. Schroeter 44:18); Vulgate: *pascit ventum* ('he grazes wind');
Peshitta: ܪܥܐ ܪܘܚܐ, as opposed to Targum: דמן לדרוח זרע ('[the House of
Israel] is like he who sows wind').

The reconstruction כל אליום 'all the day' (25b:3) for כָּל הַיּוֹם is based on the
author's usual rendering of יוֹם (see Hosea 2:5, 15, 17, 18, 23; 3:5; 4:5; 5:9; 9:5; 10:9,

TEXTUAL NOTES   231

14; 12:10; text missing: Hosea 1:1 [2×], 5; 3:4; 9:9); another option can be found in Yefet and Cod. Hunt. 206: כל אלזמאן (ed. Birnbaum 182:19–20)/كل الزمان (ed. Schroeter 44:18; ed. Polliack and Schlossberg 231).

The translator clarifies the ambivalent Hebrew קָדִים as רוח שרקי 'east *wind*' (25b:3); see also his exegesis in 26a:23 and Hosea 13:15, Yefet: אלשרקי (ed. Birnbaum 182:19; ed. Polliack and Schlossberg 231) and Cod. Hunt. 206: الشرق (ed. Schroeter 44:18).

The author retains the word-order כָּל־הַיּוֹם כֶּסֶף וְשַׁד יַרְבֶּה by rendering כל אליום כדב ונהב יוכתר (25b:3), whereas Yefet and Cod. Hunt. 206 adopt the usual word-order כל אלזמאן יכתֹר אלכדב ואלנהב (ed. Birnbaum 182:19–20; ed. Polliack and Schlossberg 231 [where one manuscript reads אלנהב ואלכדב].)/كل الزمان يكثر الكذب والنهب (ed. Schroeter 44:18–19).

For the phrase ועהד ... יקטעו 'they made a covenant' as rendition of Hebrew וּבְרִית ... יִכְרֹתוּ see Hosea 7:20. The translator retains the unusual Hebrew syntax וּבְרִית עִם־אַשּׁוּר יִכְרֹתוּ when rendering ועהד מע מלך אשור יקטעו (25b:3–4), whereas Yefet and Cod. Hunt. 206 change to the more usual word-order: ועהד יקטעו מע אשור (ed. Birnbaum 182:19–20; ed. Polliack and Schlossberg 231)/وعهد يقطعوا مع الموصليين (ed. Schroeter 44:19).

It is noteworthy that the translator adds מלך 'king' before 'Assur' to indicate the partner of the covenant (25b:4) whereas Yefet renders literally: מע אשור (ed. Birnbaum 182:20; ed. Polliack and Schlossberg 231).

The reconstruction of יוגלב 'he is carried' (25b:4) as translation of יוּבָל is based on the author's translation of Hosea 10:6; see also Yefet: יגלב (ed. Birnbaum 182:21; ed. Polliack and Schlossberg 231) and Cod. Hunt. 206: يجلب (ed. Schroeter 44:20).

Hosea 12:3

The reconstruction נטר ללרב 'the Lord has a lawsuit' (25b:4) for וְרִיב לַיהוה has been favourized because of the similar phrase in Hosea 4:1 (כִּי רִיב לַיהוה) which is rendered לאן נטר ללרב. Yefet and Cod. Hunt. 206 translate with ומנאטרה (ed. Birnbaum 183:20; ed. Polliack and Schlossberg 231)/ومناظرة (ed. Schroeter 44:20).

The translator adds איצא 'also' after 'Judah' (25b:5) *ad sensum*.

The rendering ולאפקתאד 'and to inspect' could be expected as equivalent of the infinitive וְלִפְקֹד see Yefet and Cod. Hunt. 206: ולאפתקאד (ed. Birnbaum 183:21; ed. Polliack and Schlossberg 231)/ولا فتقاد (ed. Schroeter 44:20)); however, the author prefers the finite verb form וסיפתקד 'and He visits' (25b:5). The reason for the unique orthography וסיף תקד, written in two words with a clearly legible final *pe*, is not clear.

The two nouns כשמאילה 'according to his deeds' and כטורקה 'according to his ways' can be reconstructed according to the almost identical formulation in Hosea 4:9. See also שמאיל as rendering of מעללים in Hosea 4:9 5:4; 7:2; 9:15 and טריק as rendering of דרך in Hosea 2:8; 4:9; 6:9; 12:3; 13:7; 14:10. Yefet and Cod. Hunt. 206 כִּדְרָכָיו with מדאהבה (ed. Birnbaum 183:21; ed. Polliack and Schlossberg 231)/مذاهبه (ed. Schroeter 44:21).

The reconstruction ירוד 'he will repay' as rendering of יָשִׁיב is based on the translation of יָשִׁיב with ירוד in Hosea 12:15 and on the similar phrase in Hosea 4:9; see also Yefet: ירד (ed. Birnbaum 183:22; ed. Polliack and Schlossberg 231) and Cod. Hunt. 206: يرد (ed. Schroeter 44:21).

Hosea 12:4

The author connects this verse closely with the previous one by introducing a relative clause (אלדי) with 'Jacob' of the preceding verse as antecedent (25b:6).

The translator understands the verb עָקַב as denominative from עָקֵב 'heel' in accordance with Genesis 25:26, as can be seen from his rendering אעתקב 'he grasped his heel' (25b:6); see also LXX: ἐπτέρνισεν. On the other hand, Yefet and Cod. Hunt. 206 translate with גרבז (ed. Birnbaum 184:9; ed. Polliack and Schlossberg 232)/جربز (ed. Schroeter 44:22) a denominative from Persian گرز 'fraud', 'deception'—thus interpreting the verb to denote 'to deceive', 'to trick' (see Genesis 27:36); see also Peshitta: ܢܟܠ ('he defrauded').

The reconstruction of the translation for וּבְאוֹנוֹ is problematic, since in Hosea 12:9, the only other occurrence of the noun, the author renders it with מנאל 'property' which does not fit in this context. The rendition with ובקותה 'and by his strength' (25b:6) seems preferable here, since, in his exegesis, the author interprets the phrase as אשתד וקוי, literally 'become strong and vigorous' by using the root قوى (26b:12); see also Yefet and Cod. Hunt. 206: ובקותה (ed. Birnbaum 184:10; ed. Polliack and Schlossberg 232)/وبقوته (ed. Schroeter 44:22); LXX: ἐν ἰσχύι, Vulgate: *in fortitudine*, and Saadiah's translation of אוֹנִי with וקותי in Genesis 49:3. Wolff, on the other hand, favours the option 'that here אוֹן denotes wealth' (1974:212) as in Hosea 12:9.

שָׂרָה is rendered with תראוס 'he gained mastery' (25b:7); see also Yefet: ראוס (ed. Polliack and Schlossberg 232); Cod. Hunt. 206: تراس (ed. Schroeter 44:22); LXX: ἐνίσχυσεν πρός ('he proved mighty towards'); Vulgate: *directus est cum*; Peshitta: ܐܬܪܘܪܒ ('he behaved arrogantly'); Targum: אתרב ('he claimed superiority'). Also Saadiah renders שָׂרִיתָ in Genesis 32:29 with תראסת; see Targum Onqelos: רברבת. The intention may have been that they tried to avoid the offensiveness which may have been felt in a *fight* of Jacob with God. The option שרה 'to strive' is represented in LXX and Aquila.

The rendition of אֶת־אֱלֹהִים with מע מלך (25b:7) stands in the tradition of Vulgate: *angelo*, Aquila: ἄγγελον and Targum: מלאכא, thus anticipating the following מַלְאָךְ (Hosea 12:5), whereas LXX (θεόν) and Peshitta (ܐܠܗܐ) translate with 'God'. Yefet: אלבארי (ed. Birnbaum 184:10; ed. Polliack and Schlossberg 232) and Cod. Hunt. 206: البارئ (ed. Schroeter 45:1) share the identical rendering 'the Creator'.

Hosea 12:5

By adding the conjunctions/adverbs פלמא 'and when', חתי 'until' and תום 'then' (2×), the translator achieves a temporal structure of the events.

The verb תראוס, lit. 'he became head', including the preposition מע 'with', (25b:7) has been restored according to the phrase תראוס מע מלך in Hosea 12:4. The translation indicates that the author derived the verb וַיָּשַׂר from the root שׂרר 'to reign', 'to rule' as in the previous verse; see also LXX: καὶ ἐνίσχυσεν (as in Hosea 12:4); Aquila and Theodotion: καὶ κατώρθωσε (as in Hosea 12:4); Peshitta: ܘܐܬܚܣܢ; Targum: ואתרב (as in Hosea 12:4); Symmachus: κατεδυνάστευσε ('he got control'); Vulgate: *invaluit*; Cod. Hunt. 206: وتراؤس (ed. Schroeter 45:1) vs. Yefet: ואתראס (ed. Birnbaum 184:11; ed. Polliack and Schlossberg 232 [where one manuscript reads אתראוס]): v with prosthetic *alif* (see Birnbaum xxxv).;

וַיֻּכַל is rendered with קדר עליה 'he overpowered him' (25b:7); see Yefet: וקדר (ed. Birnbaum 184:11; ed. Polliack and Schlossberg 232) without prepositional phrase, imitating slavishly MT, whereas Cod. Hunt. 206 translates with وطاق به (ed. Schroeter 45:1).

The translator creates a subordinate clause by rephrasing בָּכָה with חתי בכא 'until he wept' (25b:8); see also Cod. Hunt. 206: حتى بكى (ed. Schroeter 45:1), whereas Yefet adopts the paratactic syntax of the source text: בכא (ed. Birnbaum 184:11; ed. Polliack and Schlossberg 232).

The translator prefers the Arabic cognate תחנן אליה 'he implored him for a favour' (25b:8) as rendition of וַיִּתְחַנֶּן־לוֹ vs. Yefet: ואתצרע (ed. Birnbaum 184:11; ed. Polliack and Schlossberg 232) and Cod. Hunt. 206: وتضرع (ed. Schroeter 45:1) and with prothetic *alif* (see Birnbaum xxxv).

יִמְצָאֶנּוּ is rendered with יציבה 'he will find him' (25b:8), whereas Yefet and Cod. Hunt. 206 prefer the verb وجد: כאן יגדה (ed. Birnbaum 184:12; ed. Polliack and Schlossberg 232 [where one manuscript reads וגדה])/یجده (ed. Schroeter 45:2).

The translator transfers the present tense of יְדַבֵּר into the past by rendering with the frequentative כאן יכאטב 'he used to speak' (25b:9), whereas Yefet and

Cod. Hunt. 206: retain tie present tense: יכׄאטב (ed. Birnbaum 184:12; ed. Polliack and Schlossberg 232)/يخاطب (ed. Schroeter 45:2). It is noteworthy that only here the author uses the root خطب III as rendition of Hebrew דבר *pi'el*, whereas usually he chooses the root كلم V (see Hosea 2:16; 7:13; 10:4; 12:11; 13:1).

Hosea 12:6

The author translated הַצְּבָאוֹת literally with אלגיוש 'the legions' (25b:9); see also COd. Hunt. 206: الجيوش (ed. Schroeter 45:2), whereas Yefet has the characteristic phrase אלרב אלקיום 'the self-existing Master' (ed. Birnbaum 187:15; ed. Polliack and Schlossberg 233 [which reads אלאה אלקיום]); see also Yefet's commentary on Zechariah 8:14, 22, 23.

The translator renders Hebrew זִכְרוֹ *verbatim* with the Arabic cognate דכרה 'His remembrance', 'His name' (25b:9); see also Yefet: דכרה (ed. Birnbaum 187:15; ed. Polliack and Schlossberg 233) and Cod. Hunt. 206: ذكره (ed. Schroeter 45:3). For the parallelism of 'name' and 'remembrance' see Exodus 3:15; Psalms 102:13; 135:13.

Hosea 12:7

The translator mirrors the emphatic position of the personal pronoun וְאַתָּה by rendering ואנת פאלי אלאהך תרגע, lit. 'and you to your God you will return' (25b:10). Additionally, Yefet and Cod. Hunt. 206 focuss on the duty to do so: ואנת אלי מעבודך יגב אן תרגע (ed. Birnbaum 188:3; ed. Polliack and Schlossberg 233)/وانت يجب ان ترجع (ed. Schroeter 45:3).

The translator changes the preposition of the phrase בֵאלֹהֶיךָ 'in/with/by/through your God' into אלי אלאהך 'to your God' in order to indicate the direction of the Israel's returning (25b:10); see also Yefet: אלי אלאהך (ed. Birnbaum 188:4; ed. Polliack and Schlossberg 233) and Cod. Hunt. 206: الى الاهك (ed. Schroeter 45:3). Also Rashi, Ibn Ezra and Qimḥi understand the preposition in the same sense: returning to God; see also: Vulgate: *ad Deum tuum*; Peshitta: ܠܐܠܗܟ, whereas LXX and Targum adopt the exact equivalent of the Hebrew preposition: LXX: ἐν θεῷ; Targum: בפלחנא דאלהך ('in the service of your God').

חֶסֶד has been rendered with איחסאן 'kindness' (25b:10), whereas Cod. Hunt. 206 translates with الدين (ed. Schroeter 45:3) and Yefet adds the connective conjunction ו: ואלדין (ed. Birnbaum 188:3; ed. Polliack and Schlossberg 233 [which reads אלדין without *waw*]).

The reconstruction of וחוכם 'and justice' (25b:10) as rendition of וּמִשְׁפָּט is based on the author's usual translation (see Hosea 5:1; 6:5; 10:4; text missing: Hosea 5:11). Yefet and Cod. Hunt. 206 add the article: ואלחכם (ed. Birnbaum 188:3; ed. Polliack and Schlossberg 233)/والحكم (ed. Schroeter 45:3).

Hosea 12:8

For the connective particle לאן 'for' (25b:11) see on Hosea 4:4.

The translator understands כְּנַעַן as denoting אלתאגר 'trader', 'merchant' (25b:11; see Isaiah 23:8; Zechariah 14:21; Proverbs 31:24; Job 40:30) with the pejorative sense of 'trafficker', and not literally as the gentilic 'Canaan'; see also Yefet: אלתאגר (Birnbaum 188:15; ed. Polliack and Schlossberg 234) and Cod. Hunt. 206: التاجر (ed. Schroeter 45:4), the latter referring in his additional notes to Isaiah 23:8 (כְּנַעֲנִים); Aquila: μετάβολος ('trader'), Targum: לא תהון כתגרין ('do not be like merchants'), BT Pesaḥim 50a; Baba Batra 75a. R. Tanchum explains: يا من هو تاجر بيده موازين المكر اذ احب الغشم والجور ('O who is a trader in whose hand is the scale of deceit, for he loved oppression and injustice').

The lacuna after אלתאגר may be reconstructed as פבידה 'and in his hand' (25b:11); see Yefet: בידה (ed. Birnbaum 188:15; ed. Polliack and Schlossberg 234); Cod. Hunt. 206: بيده (ed. Schroeter 45:8).

In the phrase מואזן מכר 'scales of deceit' (25b:11) as opposite to 'scales of justice' (see Leviticus 19:36; Deuteronomy 25:13; Job 31:6), the term מכר (see Hosea 12:1) indicates 'cunning' and 'deception'. See Saadiah's translation of Proverbs 11:1 (מואזן אלמכר), 20:23 (מיזאן אלמכר) vs. Job 31:6 (מיזאן עדל).

Hosea 12:9

אַךְ has been rendered with כאן 'indeed' (also Hosea 4:4); see also Yefet: כאן (ed. Birnbaum 189:2; ed. Polliack and Schlossberg 234), whereas Cod. Hunt. 206 prefers the feminine equivalent خاصة (ed. Schroeter 45:9).

The author has crossed out his first translation כאן קד אדתגנית 'indeed I have become wealthy' (25b:12) as rendition of אַךְ עָשַׁרְתִּי to replace it with כאן קד אייסרת 'indeed I have become rich' (25b:13) which is similar to Yefet: כאן איסרת (ed. Birnbaum 189:2; ed. Polliack and Schlossberg 234) and Cod. Hunt. 206: خاصة ايسرت (ed. Schroeter 45:7).

The translator renders אוֹן in this context with מנאל, literally 'attainment', 'acquisition', i.e. 'wealth', whereas Yefet and Cod. Hunt. 206 prefer קוה (ed. Birnbaum 189:2; ed. Polliack and Schlossberg 234)/قوة ('power', 'strength', ed. Schro-

eter 45:7), as in Hosea 12:4; see also Rashi, Qimḥi, R. Tanchum: מצאתי في الوجود والا
און לי אן יכון אלפה מנדלה מן הא הון עשיר קרית עזי לקולה אך עשרתי אלא אן יקול אן קותה מן אגל
العشر ('The best assumption is that the *alef* in אוֹן stands for *he*, as in Proverbs
18:11, so that this is an equivalent to the preceding phrase אַךְ עָשַׁרְתִּי, except that
he says that his strenght has its cause in wealth').

אתעאבי, literally 'my hardships', 'my toils' (25b:13), as rendition of יְגִיעַי probably denotes not only 'toil', 'labour', but also the result of the labour, i.e. 'property', 'wealth' (see 27a:3), like Hebrew יְגִיעַ (see Isaiah 45:14; 55:2). Yefet and Cod. Hunt. 206 translate with כדי (ed. Birnbaum 189:3; ed. Polliack and Schlossberg 234)/كدى (ed. Schroeter 45:6). R. Tanchum interprets the noun as مكاسبي 'my profit': ما يتعب في تحصيله ('what someone gains in his aquisition').

Hosea 12:10

The vocalization אגלסך 'I will make you dwell' (25b:15), which is the rendition of אוֹשִׁיבְךָ, indicates that the author refers to جلس II instead of possible جلس IV; see Yefet and Cod. Hunt. 206: אגלסך (ed. Birnbaum 190:1; ed. Polliack and Schlossberg 234)/أَجْلِس (ed. Schroeter 45:10).

בָּאֳהָלִים has been rendered with פי אלאכביה 'in the tents' (25b:15), whereas Yefet and Cod. Hunt. 206 chose the noun אלמצארב (ed. Birnbaum 190:1–2; ed. Polliack and Schlossberg 234)/المضارب (ed. Schroeter 45:10); see also the translation of Hosea 9:6.

The translator provides a literal translation of כִּימֵי מוֹעֵד by rendering כאיאם מועד 'as (in) the days of an appointed time/season' (25b:15), i.e. 'assembly', 'festival'; see also LXX^AQ: καθὼς ἡμέρα ἑορτῆς ('according to the day of festival'); LXX^B: ἡμέραι ('days'); Vulgate: *in diebus festivitatis*. Yefet and Cod. Hunt. 206 translate *ad sensum*: מתל אלזמאן אלקדים (ed. Birnbaum 190:2; ed. Polliack and Schlossberg 234)/مثل الزمان القديم 'as in olden times' (ed. Schroeter 45:10–11); see also Targum: כיומי קדם and Peshitta: ܐܝܟ ܝܘܡܬܐ ܕܩܕܝܡ ('as in the days of old').

Hosea 12:11

The translator renders עַל־הַנְּבִיאִים with עלי אידי אלאנביא 'through (literally: the hands of) the prophets' (25b:16–17), thus achieving a closer parallelism to the following phrase וּבְיַד הַנְּבִיאִים which he translates with ועלי יד אלאנביא 'and through (literally: the hand of) the prophets'; see also Yefet: ... עלי יד אלאנביא

ועלי יד אלאנביא (ed. Birnbaum 191:3–4; ed. Polliack and Schlossberg 235); Cod. Hunt. 206: على يد الانبياء ... وعلى يد الانبياء (ed. Schroeter 45:11–12).

חָזוֹן has been rendered with the indefinite singular noun פוזחי 'and a vision' (25b:16), whereas Yefet has the definite noun אלוחי (ed Birnbaum 191:3; ed. Polliack and Schlossberg 235); see also Vulgate: *visionem*; LXX renders with the plural ὁράσεις; Peshitta: ܣܘܗܢܝ ('my visions'). Cod. Hunt. 206 emphasises a close connection of that vision with the prophecy by rendering النبوة (ed. Schroeter 45:11); a similar tendency can be noticed in Targum: נבואן ('prophecies').

The translator adds the verbal particle קד twice (קד תבלמת and קד כתרת) to emphasise the past tense (25b:16).

The translation אושבה 'I convey parables' (25b:17) indicates that the author derived the verb אֲדַמֶּה from the root דמה I *pi'el* 'to compare', 'to liken'. The absolute use possibly includes the technical meaning 'to use comparisons', i.e. 'to tell a parable'; see Yefet and Cod. Hunt. 206 denote the frequentative action in the past by rendering: כנת אשבה (ed. Birnbaum 191:4; ed. Polliack and Schlossberg 235)/ كنت أشبّه (ed. Schroeter 45:12).

Hosea 12:12

Instead of the elliptical biblical phrase 'If Gilead wickedness', the translator paraphrases אן כאן אהל גלעד אסתעמל גיל 'if the people of Gilead used wickedness' (25b:17); see also Yefet: אן אהל גלעד אסתעמלו אלגל (ed. Birnbaum 192:3; ed. Polliack and Schlossberg 235) and Cod. Hunt. 206: ان اهل جلعد استعملوا الغل (ed. Schroeter 45:12).

The translator chooses גזאף 'vanity' (25b:18) as rendition of שָׁוְא (see also Hosea 10:4). Yefet and Cod. Hunt. 206 have אלמחאל (ed. Birnbaum 192:3; ed. Polliack and Schlossberg 235)/ المحال (ed. Schroeter 45:13) 'absurd', 'crooked', 'impossible' (Hava p. 151).

The translator adds the copula קד צארת 'they became' (25b:19) after 'their altars' to ensure that the sentence refers to the past.

In his grammatical notes, the author links the plural שְׁוָרִים with the singular שׁוֹר which stands for שׁוֹר (28a:12); see also Yefet: פסרו שורים תיראן ואליחיד מנה שׁוֹר פצארת אצלין שור שורים שור שורים (ed. Birnbaum 192:16–18; ed. Polliack and Schlossberg 236) and Cod. Hunt. 206: وفسروا شورم ثيران. واليحيد منه شور: فصارت 'they explain שְׁוָרִים as "bulls"; its singular is שׁוֹר. There are two basic forms: שׁוֹר-שׁוֹרִים and שְׁוָר-שְׁוָרִים' (ed. Schroeter 45:15–16).

כְּגַלִּים has been rendered with כתלול 'like hills' (25b:19); see also Yefet and Cod. Hunt. 206 with the different plurals: מתל אתלאל (ed. Birnbaum 192:5; ed. Polliack and Schlossberg 235)/ مثل التلال (ed. Schroeter 45:14).

The phrase עַל תַּלְמֵי שָׂדָי which occurs *verbatim* also in Hosea 10:4 and had been rendered there with עלי אתלאם אלצחרא (21b:9), is translated here with עלי אתלאם צחרא 'on the furrows of a field' (25b:19), i.e. by an indefinite second component of the construct chain, whereas Yefet and Cod. Hunt. 206 have a definite second component also here: עלי אתלאם אלצחרא (ed. Birnbaum 192:4; ed. Polliack and Schlossberg 235 [where one manuscript reads על]/على اتلام الصحراء (ed. Schroeter 45:14).

Hosea 12:13

The noun שָׂדֶה has been rendered with ציעה 'domain' (25b:19) as distinct from שָׂדָי in Hosea 12:12, whereas Yefet and Cod. Hunt. 206 translate with צחראה (ed. Birnbaum 192:19; ed. Polliack and Schlossberg 236)/صحراة (ed. Schroeter 45:17).

By rendering וּבְאִשָּׁה with ובאימראה אוכרי 'and for *another* woman' (25b:20), the translator indicates that he does not regard the two *stichoi* as parallel statements within a *parallelismus membrorum*, but obviously links the first biblical statement *and Israel served for a woman* to Jacob's service for Leah and the second one *and for a woman he kept* to his service for Rachel (see Genesis 29). Yefet and Cod. Hunt. 206 render *verbatim*: בסבב מראה ובסבב מראה (ed. Birnbaum 192:20; ed. Polliack and Schlossberg 236 [where one manuscript reads מרה]/بسبب امرأة ... وبسبب امرأة (ed. Schroeter 45:17–18).

The translator understands שָׁמָר to be used elliptically with the meaning חפט אלגנם 'he kept the sheep' (25b:20) as in 1 Samuel 17:20; see Jerome and Targum: ובאיתתא נטר ענא 'and for a woman he kept sheep'. Yefet and Cod. Hunt. 206 render literally supplying an object: חפט (ed. Birnbaum 192:20; ed. Polliack and Schlossberg 236)/حفظ (ed. Schroeter 45:18). However, see Yefet's exegesis: יריד בה חפט אלמואקפה אלתי קאל לה לבן (ed. Birnbaum 193:21;).

Hosea 12:15

The translator adds a direct object to the verb הִכְעִיס 'he angered' by rendering אגאץ' אפרים רבה 'Ephraim angered his Lord' (25b:22), whereas Yefet and Cod. Hunt. 206 reflect the absolute use of the biblical verb by rendering literally: אגאץ' אפרים (ed. Birnbaum 195:17; ed. Polliack and Schlossberg 237 [where one manuscript reads אגאט']/اغاض افرٔم (ed. Schroeter 46:1).

The rendition פי מראראת, literally 'in bitterness', demonstrates that the translator understood the noun תַּמְרוּרִים as an abstract plural noun with adverbial function; however, he does not connect it with the preceding verb ('he angered his Lord *bitterly*'), but forms a new sentence, including the additional verb פחצל, which indicates the result of provoking God's anger: 'He became bitter' (25b:22). The meaning seems to be: they provoked God's anger with the result that He became bitter. God's anger is evident from the following retribution: his blood-guilt will spread over himself, and God will repay them the dishonour. Also Qimḥi derives תַּמְרוּרִים from the root מרר 'to be bitter'. Yefet and Cod. Hunt. 206 offer a different interpretation by rendering תַּמְרוּרִים with באלזעאראת (ed. Birnbaum 195:17; ed. Polliack and Schlossberg 237) and بالزعارات '[Ephraim has angered] through his maliciousness' (ed. Schroeter 46:1). This peculiar use of זער in the sense of 'feeling or causing bitterness' (see also Yefet Ruth 1:13, ed. Schorstein p. xv, Daniel 1:11) is one of the reasons for Birnbaum's thesis that Yefet is the author of Cod. Hunt. 206 (Birnbaum lii, note 124). Abu l-Walīd Lexicon explains תַּמְרוּרִים as عصيان وخلاف 'disobedience and contradiction'.

The verb יִטּוֹשׁ has been rendered literally with יוסייב 'it will be poured' (25b:23); see also Yefet: יסיב (ed. Birnbaum 195:18; ed. Polliack and Schlossberg 237)/Cod. Hunt. 206: يسيب (ed. Schroeter 46:1); LXX: ἐπ' αὐτὸν ἐκχυθήσεται ('it will be poured out on him'), Peshitta: ܢܬܠܚ ,ܢܣܝܟ, Vulgate: *super eum veniet* ('it will come upon him'). Qimḥi defines the meaning of the word as 'spreading out' (התפשטות).

The translator renders וְחֶרְפָּתוֹ with ומעיירתה 'and his disgrace' (25b:23); see also Yefet: ומעירתה (ed. Birnbaum 195:18; ed. Polliack and Schlossberg 237) and Cod. Hunt. 206 ومعيرته (ed. Schroeter 46:1).

Hosea 13:1

רְתֵת is *hapax legomenon*; however, it is attested in 1QH IV:33 parallel to רעד 'trembling' (רעד ורתת אחזוני 'shaking and trembling have seized me'); in Exodus 15:15, the Hebrew רעד is rendered in the Targum with רתיתא (Job 4:14). Symmachus and Theodotion translate רְתֵת with τρόμον 'trembling', Aquila: φρίκην, Peshitta: ܪܬܝ ܗܘܐ ('he was trembling'), Targum: רתיתא אחיד להון ('trembling seized them') and Vulgate: *horror invasit Israhel* ('trembling invaded Israel'). The translator rephrases the biblical text by creating a complete sentence: כאן יאכוד אלנאס רעדה 'trembling seized the people' (25b:24); see also Cod. Hunt. 206: الرعدة تقع على الناس (ed. Schroeter 46:4), whereas Yefet renders literally with אלרעדה (ed. Birnbaum 197:14; ed. Polliack and Schlossberg 238), only adding the definite article. In his grammatical notes, the commentator links רְתֵת with רֶטֶט (Jeremiah 49:24) (28a:13). Also Ibn Janāḥ apparently understands the noun as by-form of רֶטֶט with the same meaning. Ibn Ezra regards it as Aramaism with the meaning 'fear'. Qimḥi offers the paraphrase 'before Ephraim sinned, fear of him subdued all the surrounding peoples, for, when he spoke, trembling seized his hearers'.

The additional conjunction לאנה 'for' (25b:24) before כאן שריף 'he was honoured' indicates, that the author understands the following sentence נָשָׂא הוּא בְּיִשְׂרָאֵל as giving the reason for the trembling.

The verb נָשָׂא has been interpreted as כאן שריף 'he was honoured' (25b:24). Yefet and Cod. Hunt. 206 who both refer to the same root شرف, differ in their actual translation; whereas Yefet renders with the verb שרף II 'he honoured' (ed. Birnbaum 197:14; ed. Polliack and Schlossberg 238), Cod. Hunt. 206 has a noun: شرف كان له 'he had honour' (ed. Schroeter 46:4). Rashi and Ibn Ezra interpret the verb נָשָׂא in a passive or reflexive sense: 'he was exalted', 'he exalted himself'; see also Peshitta: ܘܗܘܐ ܪܒܐ ('and he was a great one') and Targum: מתרברבין הוו ('those who were great'), whereas Qimḥi retains the *qal* 'he lifted' and assumes an elliptical sense 'he lifted his head'.

וַיֶּאְשָׁם has been rendered with the Arabic cognate פלמא אתם 'when he sinned' (25b:25); see also Yefet and Cod. Hunt. 206: פאתם (ed. Birnbaum 197:15; ed. Polliack and Schlossberg 238)/فاثم (ed. Schroeter 46:5).

Instead of rendering בַּבַּעַל literally, the translator chooses the phrase בעבאדה אלותן 'in the worship of the idol' (25b:25), which can also be found in Yefet: בעבאדה אלותן (ed. Birnbaum 197:15; ed. Polliack and Schlossberg 238) and Cod. Hunt. 206: بعبادة الوثن (ed. Schroeter 46:5).

Whereas Yefet: ומאת (ed. Birnbaum 197:15; ed. Polliack and Schlossberg 238) and Cod. Hunt. 206: ومات (ed. Schroeter 46:5) provide a literal translation of וַיָּמֹת 'and he died', the translator moderates the verb by rendering עוקב 'he has been punished' (25b:25), leaving the type of punishment open for further interpretation; see also his exegesis (27b:4). Yefet adds this option in an explanatory note: יעני אנה עוקב (ed. Birnbaum 197:15–16; ed. Polliack and Schlossberg 238).

Hosea 13:2

The translator adds פהודא 'and behold' (25b:25) between the adverb 'and now' and the verb 'they increase'.

יוֹסִפוּ has been rendered with יזידו 'they increase' (25b:23), whereas Yefet and Cod. Hunt. 206 translate with יעאודן (ed. Birnbaum 198:9; ed. Polliack and Schlossberg 238)/يعاودوا (ed. Schroeter 46:12).

Instead of the infinitive with the preposition לַחֲטֹא, the translator chooses a noun: פי אלבטא (25b:26); similar Yefet and Cod. Hunt. 206: אלי אלבטא (ed. Birnbaum 198:9; ed. Polliack and Schlossberg 238)/الى الخطاء (ed. Schroeter 46:12).

The additional לאן 'for' (25b:26) before the second phrase of the verse *they made them molten images* indicates that the increase of their sin is due to their making molten images; Yefet and Cod. Hunt. 206 provide a literal translation: וצנעו (ed. Birnbaum 198:9; ed. Polliack and Schlossberg 238)/وصنعوا (ed. Schroeter 46:12).

The translator renders מַסֵּכָה literally with מסבוכה 'molten (image)' (25b:26); see also Saadiah's translation of מַסֵּכָה with מסבוכא in Exodus 32:4, 8.whereas Yefet: מעבוד מצבוב (sic; ed. Birnbaum 198:9–10; ed. Polliack and Schlossberg 238) and Cod. Hunt. 206: معبود مسبوك (ed. Schroeter 46:12) think of 'cast idols';

כִּתְבוּנָם has been rendered literally with כבנייתהם 'according to their pattern' (25b:27), whereas Yefet renders with כתמייזהם 'according to their preference' (ed. Birnbaum 198:10; ed. Polliack and Schlossberg 238) and Cod. Hunt. 206 paraphrases with: على قدر فهمهم ('according to the power of their understanding', ed. Schroeter 46:13). LXX: κατ' εἰκόνα εἰδώλων; Vulgate: *quasi similitudinem idolorum* ('according to the pattern of idols'); Peshitta: ܒܕܡܘܬܗܘܢ ('in their likeness'); Targum: כדמותהון ('according to their likeness').

The translator renders עֲצַבִּים with אצנאם 'idols' (25b:27), whereas Yefet and Cod. Hunt. 206 choose the equivalent אותאן (ed. Birnbaum 198:10; ed. Polliack and Schlossberg 238)/اوثان (ed. Schroeter 46:13).

חָרָשִׁים has been rendered with צונאע 'craftsmen' (25b:27); see Yefet: אלצנאע with article (ed. Birnbaum 198:10; ed. Polliack and Schlossberg 238), whereas Cod. Hunt. 206 thinks specifically of 'the carpenters' (النجارين, ed. Schroeter 46:13).

The difficult phrase זֹבְחֵי אָדָם is rendered *verbatim* with דאבחי [אלאנסאן] 'the sacrificers of the men' (25b:27–26a:1); Yefet: יא דאבחין אלנאס (ed. Birnbaum 198:11; ed. Polliack and Schlossberg 238 [which reads דָּאבחון])/Cod. Hunt. 206: يا ذابحين الناس (ed. Schroeter 46:14).

The author creates a temporal sequence by introducing תום 'then' before 'they shall kiss' (26a:1).

יִשָּׁקוּן has been rendered with יוקבלו 'they shall kiss' (26a:1); see Yefet and Cod. Hunt. 206: יקבלון (ed. Birnbaum 198:11; ed. Polliack and Schlossberg 238)/يقبّلون (ed. Schroeter 46:14); Peshitta: ܡܢܫܩܝܢ ('kissing [calves]'); Aquila: καταφιλοῦντες; Vulgate: *adorantes*.

The restoration of אסם אלבנייה 'a noun (meaning) "pattern"' in the grammatical notes (28a:13) is based on the author's translation (25b:27) and his stereotypical phrase when defining the meaning of a noun.

Hosea 13:3

The translation כגמאם צובח וכאלנדא אלדי הו מודלג סאלך (26a:1–2) is identical with the translation of Hosea 6:4 where the first two similes are used *verbatim*.

The translator reads the *po'el* יְסֹעֵר as *po'al* יְסֹעַר, as is evident from his rendering יועצף 'it is blown away' with 'chaff' as subject (26a:2); see also Yefet and Cod. Hunt. 206: יעצף (ed. Birnbaum 199:17; ed. Polliack and Schlossberg 239)/يعصف (ed. Schroeter 46:16). Also some versions prefer the passive rendering: LXX ἀποφυσώμενος ('blown away'); Vulgate: *turbine raptus* ('whisked away by the whirlwind') vs. the active interpretaion of Peshitta: ܕܦܗܙ ('which flies away') and Targum: דנסבא רוחא ('which the wind blows').

The translator renders מֵאֲרֻבָּה 'from a skylight' with מן רוזנה 'from a window' (26a:3), using the Persian loanword روزنه; see also Yefet: מן אלרוזנה (ed. Birnbaum 199:18; ed. Polliack and Schlossberg 239) and Cod. Hunt. 206: من الروزنة (ed. Schroeter 46:17). The rendition of the versions are: LXX^{AQ*}: ἐκ καπνοδόχης, Aquila: ἀπὸ καταράκτου ('from a smoke-hole'), Jerome and Vulgate: *de fumario*; Peshitta: ܡܢ ܟܘܬܐ; Targum: מכות נורא.

By adding the verb יכרוג 'it evades' (26a:3) to form an asyndetic relative clause, the translator achieves a closer parallelism to the preceding similes, which include a verbal form. Some modern authors also add a verb in their translation, e.g. Wolff: 'like smoke (that rises) from the window' (1974:219).

Hosea 13:4

וֵאלֹהִים has been rendered literally with ואלאה 'and gods' (26a:3), whereas Yefet and Cod. Hunt. 206 translate with ומעבוד (ed, Birnbaum 201:4; ed. Polliack and Schlossberg 240)/ومعبود (ed. Schroeter 46:18).

The translator renders וּמוֹשִׁיעַ אַיִן בִּלְתִּי by adding לך: 'there is no saviour *for you* but Me' (26a:4), apparently to emphasise the special relationship between God and Israel. A similar phraseology can be noticed in the exegesis where the author paraphrases ליס לכם מן גיתכם 'there is nobody *for you* who will deliver you' (27b:16). Yefet and Cod. Hunt. 206 translate literally: ומגית ליס גירי (ed. Birnbaum 201:5; ed. Polliack and Schlossberg 240)/ومغيث ليس غيرى (ed. Schroeter 46:18).

Hosea 13:5

By adding the relative marker אלדי after 'I', the translator creates a relative clause, thus emphasising the subject 'God', literally 'I am the one who knew you' (26a:4).

ערפתך 'I knew you' (16a:4) as translation of יְדַעְתִּיךָ is distinct from Yefet: נאגّיתך (ed. Birnbaum 201:12; ed. Polliack and Schlossberg 240) and Cod. Hunt. 206: ناجيتك 'I supported you' (ed. Schroeter 46:18), who refers to Deutoronomy 34:10.

The restoration of פי אלבר 'in the desert' (26a:5) as rendering of בַּמִּדְבָּר is based on the rendition of the noun in Hosea 2:16; 9:10; 13:15 (text missing in Hosea 2:5). Yefet and Cod. Hunt. 206 prefer the feminine noun: פי אלבריה (ed. Birnbaum 201:12; ed. Polliack and Schlossberg 240 [where one manuscript has the spelling אלברייה])/في البرية (ed. Schroeter 46:19).

The *hapax legomenon* תַּלְאֻבוֹת 'drought' is rendered with קפאר 'desolate', 'vacant', 'void', 'waterless regions' (26a:5); see also Yefet: אלקפאר (ed. Birnbaum 201:12; ed. Polliack and Schlossberg 240) and Cod. Hunt. 206: القفار (ed. Schroeter 46:19), Vulgate: *solitudinis* ('uninhabited'), Peshitta: ܐܬܪܐ ܕܠܐ ܥܡܘܪ ('dry and without inhabitant'), LXX: ἐν γῇ ἀνοικήτῳ.

Hosea 13:6

By adding למא 'when', 'after' before *they were satisfied* (26a:6), the translator creates a temporal, almost causal sequence of effects: being grazed → being sated → forgetting God; 4QpHos[a]III3 on Hosea 2:10 uses almost the same sequence when interpreting 'that they ate and were sated and forgot God'; see also Yefet and Cod. Hunt. 206: פענד מא שבעו (ed. Birnbaum 202:8; ed. Polliack and Schlossberg 240 [where one manuscript reads וענד])/فعند ما شبعوا 'and when they were sated' (ed. Schroeter 46:22).

וַיָּרֻם has been rendered literally with ארתפע 'it became elevated, exalted' (26a:6), whereas Yefet and Cod. Hunt. 206 translate: שמך (ed. Birnbaum 202:8; ed. Polliack and Schlossberg 240)/شمخ 'he was high', i.e. 'he became arrogant' (ed. Schroeter 46:22).

The translator renders שְׁכֵחוּנִי literally with נסיוני 'they forgot me' (26a:6), whereas Yefet and Cod. Hunt. 206 try to avoid the idea that Israel forgot God Himself by rephrasing אטרחו עבאדתי ונסיו אחסאני 'they have cast away My worship and have forgotten My benificience' (ed. Birnbaum 202:9; ed. Polliack and Schlossberg 240)/اطرحوا عبادتي ونسوا احساني (ed. Schroeter 47:1).

Hosea 13:7

The translator links this verse closely with the preceding one by adding פלדלך 'and therefore' at the beginning (26a:6), in order to indicate the following as the consequences of Israel forgetting God.

כְּמוֹ-שַׁחַל has been rendered with מתל אלאסד 'like the lion' (26a:7), whereas Cod. Hunt. 206 chooses the equivalent مثل الشبل ('like the lion [cub]', ed. Schroeter 47:1–2) and Yefet retains the Hebrew homonym: מתל אלשחל (ed. Birnbaum 203:1 ed. Polliack and Schlossberg 240). However, all translations prefer a definite noun.

The translator renders כְּנָמֵר with כאלבבר 'like the tiger' (26a:7), whereas Yefet and Cod. Hunt. 206 adopt an Arabic homonym: מתל נמר (ed. Birnbaum 203:1; ed. Polliack and Schlossberg 240 [where one manuscript readsl ומת'ל])/والنّر (ed. Schroeter 47:2).

The translator understands אָשׁוּר to be a verb from the root שור II 'to look', 'to gaze', 'to watch', as demonstrates his rendering אלמח 'I will lurk' (26a:7); see also Hosea 14:9 (וַאֲשׁוּרֶנּוּ—ואלמחה); Yefet: אלמח (ed. Birnbaum 203:1; ed. Polliack and Schlossberg 240) and Cod. Hunt. 206: الْمح (ed. Schroeter 47:2) despite Schroeter's translation 'auf betretenem (gebahntem) Wege' (Schroeter 188); Rashi: ...; Ibn Janāḥ: ... David al-Fāsī: אשור אלמח ואתרצד ואלאלף פיה אשארה אלי אלקאיל ('I will look and watch; the *alef* is a pronominal prefix' [Skoss p. 165:220]). Targum understands the root שור in the sense of 'to lie in ambush': כמין על שבילא ('lying in wait on the path'). The second option is to regard אָשׁוּר as an adjective (passive participle) from the root אשר 'to walk ahead', 'to advance', which functions as attribute to the antecedent 'road'; see Abu l-Walīd: على طريق مسلوك ('on the passable road'), Ibn Ezra: אשור תואר כמו עצום שילכו אשורי אדם בו ("אשור is an adjective like עצום and refers to a road on which the feet of people walk'). Among modern exegetes, e.g. Macintosh 1997:532: 'beside a well-trodden path'.

Hosea 13:8

The verb אֶפְגְּשֵׁם has been rendered with אפאגיהם 'I will suddenly come upon them', presumably in order to indicate the unexpected and surprising aspect of God's action; see also Yefet: אפאגיהם (ed. Birnbaum 203:2; ed. Polliack and Schlossberg 240) and Cod. Hunt. 206: افاجِئهم (ed. Schroeter 47:2). and Yefet See also Saadiah's translation of וּפְגָשׁוּ of Isaiah 34:14 with יפאגי (Derenbourg III, p. 51); Genesis 33:8 (פְּגָשְׁתִּי): פאגיתה [Derenbourg I, p. 52]); Exodus 4:24 (וַיִּפְגְּשֵׁהוּ: פאגא ולדה [Derenbourg I, p. 86]).

TEXTUAL NOTES   245

The author translateses וְאֶקְרַע 'I will tear open' (26a:8) and תְּבַקְעֵם 'she will split them open' (26a:9) with the same root שקק 'to split open': פאשוק and תושקקהם; see also Yefet: ואשק (ed. Birnbaum 203:2; ed. Polliack and Schlossberg 240) and תשקקהם (ed. Birnbaum 203:3) and Cod. Hunt. 206: واشقّ/تُشقّقهم (ed. Schroeter 47:2, 3).

Instead of choosing the possible rendition of גלק for סְגוֹר, the translator seems to have preferred the infinitive אגלאק the vowel sign *paṭaḥ* is visible (26a:8), since there is a small gap between פאשוק and גלק. See also Cod. Hunt. 206 grammatical notes: ويحتمل أنّه مصدر ويفسر اغلاق قلوبهم 'it can be an infinitive and means the enclosure of their heart' (ed. Schroeter 28:23); Yefet: גלק (ed. Birnbaum 203:2; ed. Polliack and Schlossberg 240).

The strong anthropomorphism וְאֹכְלֵם, suggesting God's direct involvement in devouring people, which is reflected in the literal translation תום אכולהם 'then I will eat them' (26a:8), can also be found in Yefet: ואכלהם (ed. Birnbaum 203:2; also Vulgate and Targum have the 1st person; ed. Polliack and Schlossberg 240), but has been avoided in Cod. Hunt. 206 who renders: وافنيهم هناك واللبؤ ووحوش الصحراء تُشقّقهم 'and I will annihilate them there, and the lioness and the animals of the field will tear them' (ed. Schroeter 47:3); see also LXX: καὶ καταφάγονται αὐτοὺς ἐκεῖ σκύμνοι δρυμοῦ ('and lion cubs of the forest will devour them there') and Peshitta: ܘܢܐܟܠܘܢ ܐܢܘܢ ('and it [= the lioness] will devour them').

Hosea 13:9

The translator seems to have understood the word שִׁחֶתְךָ to be a verb (*piʿel*), 3rd person singular perfect: אפסדך 'he/it has destroyed you' rather than a noun ('your destruction'); see also Yefet and Cod. Hunt. 206: אפסדך (ed. Birnbaum 205:3; ed. Polliack and Schlossberg 241)/افسدك (ed. Schroeter 47:4).

Who is the subject?

(1) Rashi understands Israel to be the implicit subject: חבלת עצמך ישראל ('You have destroyed yourself, Israel'); see Targum: כד מחבלין אתון עובדיכון ('when you corrupt your deeds').

(2) On the other hand, Qimḥi assumes that the calf is the subject who has destroyed Israel: שחתך העגל ('the calf has destroyed you').

(3) Peshitta's rendition: ܚܒܠܬܟ ('I have destroyed you') would correspond to Hebrew שִׁחַתִּיךָ, i.e. 1st person singular.

(4) The translator does not introduce the subject of the verb explicitly. From his exegesis, which links the vers 'it has destroyed you' with the preceding 'the beast of the field will tear them' (see 27b:24–25), it seems likely that it is not God but the wild animal that destroys Israel.

The translator replaces the obscure phrase כִּי-בִי בְעֶזְרֶךָ 'for in Me, your help' by two complete sentences: כִּי בִי has been transformed into לאן בי כאנת תסתעין 'for you turned to Me for help' (26a:9–10), and the phrase בְעֶזְרֶךָ became part of the other sentence פצירת פי עונך 'and I became your help' (26a:10). Cod. Hunt. 206 translates with الذي بي كانت نصرتك ('that your help was in Me', ed. Schroeter 47:4); similar Yefet: אלדי בי נצרצך (ed. Birnbaum 205:3; ed. Polliack and Schlossberg 241).

Hosea 13:10

The translator provides a twofold translation of אֱהִי: (1) As can be concluded from his translation with אין 'where?' (26a:10), he interprets אֱהִי by metathesis as the interrogative particle אַיֵּה; see also LXX: ποῦ ('where?'), Vulgate: *ubi*; Peshitta: ܐܝܟܐ; Targum: אָן. (2) His second translation with אכון 'I will be' (26a:11) indicates that he takes it also as denoting an apocopated form of the 1st person imperfect of the verb היה; see also Rashi, Ibn Ezra and Qimḥi though in a different sense; Yefet: אכון (ed. Birnbaum 205:17; ed. Polliack and Schlossberg 242), Cod. Hunt. 206: اكون (ed. Schroeter 47:4). Both renderings are the basic components of the author's elaborate sentence אין אלדי כאן יקול לך אנא אכון מליכך 'Where is the one who said to you: "*I will be* your king!"?' (26a:10–11). By interpreting 'I will be now your king' as direct speech, the translator achieves a close parallel to the following direct speech concerning the judges. It is noteworthy that after his translation, Cod. Hunt. 206 gives an additional explanation which is identical with the rendering of our translator: قوله אהי מלכך يريد به اين الذي كان يقول لك انا اكون ملكك (ed. Schroeter 47: 7–8).

The translator renders the enclitic particle אֵפוֹא with אלאן 'now' (26a:11), whereas Yefet translates it with אין הו האהנא 'where is he here' (ed. Birnbaum 205:17; ed. Polliack and Schlossberg 242) as if it were a compound of אֵי 'where' and פֹּה 'here' (see Birnbaum xxxiv) and Cod. Hunt 206 has هاهنا (ed. Schroeter 47:5).

The *waw* in וְיוֹשִׁיעֲךָ has been paraphrased with חתי 'so that' (26a:11); see also Yefet: חתי (ed. Birnbaum 205:17; ed. Polliack and Schlossberg 242) and Cod. Hunt. 206: حتّى (ed. Schroeter 47:5).

עָרֶיךָ has been rendered with קוראך 'your cities' (26a:11), whereas Yefet and Cod. Hunt. 206 translate again with בלאדנך (ed. Birnbaum 205:18; ed. Polliack and Schlossberg 242) and بلادنك 'your countries' (ed. Schroeter 47:5).

By adding another ואין 'and where?' before 'your judges', the translator creates a closer parallelism with the first half of the verse: 'Where is the one ...?

// And where are your judges ...?' (26a:11); see also Yefet: ואין חכאמך (ed. Birnbaum 205:18; ed. Polliack and Schlossberg 242 [where one manuscript reads ואן instead of ואין]) and Cod. Hunt. 206: واين حكامك (ed. Schroeter 47:5).

Instead of the simple imperative אגעל 'do!' as translation of תְּנָה so Yefet: אגעל (ed. Birnbaum 205:18; ed. Polliack and Schlossberg 242) and Cod. Hunt. 206: اجعل (ed. Schroeter 47:6)—, the translator adds an absolute infinitive איגעאל אגעל 'please, appoint' (26a:12), presumably for reasons of emphasis.

The same purpose may be assumed for the rendition of לִי with לנפסי, literally 'for my soul' (26a:12) vs. possible עלי; see Yefet: עלי (ed. Birnbaum 205:18; ed. Polliack and Schlossberg 242 [which reads עליי]) and Cod. Hunt. 206: علي (ed. Schroeter 47:6).

Hosea 13:11

The additional introductory personal pronoun אנא 'and I' before the finite verb 'I give' (26a:12) emphasises the subject: 'it was I'.

The present tense אֶתֵּן is rendered with the past tense פכונת אגעל 'I appointed' (26a:12–13), whereas Yefet and Cod. Hunt. 206 retain the biblical imperfect when rendering אולי (ed. Birnbaum 207:14; ed. Polliack and Schlossberg 243)/اولى (ed. Schroeter 47:9).

לְךָ has been rendered literally with לך 'for you' (26a:13), whereas Yefet and Cod. Hunt. 206, following the verb אולי/اولى, change the preposition into עליך (ed. Birnbaum 207:14; ed. Polliack and Schlossberg 243)/عليك (ed. Schroeter 47:9).

The translator renders וְאֶקַּח literally with ואוכד 'and I will take' (26a:13); see also Yefet: ואכֹד (ed. Birnbaum 207:14; ed. Polliack and Schlossberg 243), whereas Cod. Hunt. 206 interprets the verb as واسبى 'I will lead into captivity' (ed. Schroeter 47:9), referring to Genesis 14:11 (ed. Schroeter 47:10–11).

בחלטתי 'in my wrath' (26a:13) as rendering of בְּעֶבְרָתִי is identical with Yefet's translation בחלטתי (ed. Birnbaum 207:14; ed. Polliack and Schlossberg 243) vs. Cod. Hunt. 206: بزغمى (ed. Schroeter 47:9).

Hosea 13:12

The reconstruction דנב '(the) iniquity of' (28a:17) is based on the author's usual rendering of עָוֹן (see Hosea 8:13); see also Yefet: דנב (ed. Birnbaum 208:20; ed. Polliack and Schlossberg 243) and Cod. Hunt. 206: ذنب (ed. Schroeter 47:12).

The reconstruction אל אפרים 'people of Ephraim' (28:17) is tentative vs. Yefet and Cod. Hunt. 206 who translate the name 'Ephraim' only: אפרים (ed. Birnbaum 208:20; ed. Polliack and Schlossberg 243)/افرَّم (ed. Schroeter 47:12).

Hosea 13:13

By introducing the verse with an additional פלדלך 'and therefore' (28a:18), the translator characterises the following punishment as the result of Samaria's guilt (see also Hosea 13:15).

The phrase חֶבְלֵי יוֹלֵדָה has been rendered with אמכאץ ואלדה 'the labour pains of a woman giving birth' (28a:18); see also Yefet: אמכאץ אלנפסא (ed. Birnbaum 209:11; ed. Polliack and Schlossberg 243), whereas Cod. Hunt. 206 choses a different option: طلق النفساء (ed. Schroeter 47:12).

The reconstruction יגו לה 'they come for him' (28a:18) reflects the Hebrew יָבֹאוּ לוֹ, though the subject אמכאץ 'labour pains' would, according to CA, demand a verb form in the singular, as can be found in Cod. Hunt. 206: يجى ء عليه (ed. Schroeter 47:12–13) vs. Yefet: יגו עליה (ed. Birnbaum 209:11; ed. Polliack and Schlossberg 243). The reconstruction לה for לו despite Cod. Hunt 206 and Yetet's rendering, reflects the author's preference for a literal, sometimes slavish translation throughout his work.

The translator expands כִּי־עֵת into the phrase פאן יגיה וקת 'and if time comes to him (i.e. the unwise son)' (28a:18–10); see Cod. Hunt. 206 who specifies: فان يجيئه زمان الِلدة ('and even if the time of childbirth comes to him', ed. Schroeter 47:13), whereas Yefet renders literally: פאן יגיה זמאן (ed. Birnbaum 209:12; ed. Polliack and Schlossberg 243).

The rendition of מִשְׁבַּר בָּנִים may be reconstructed, by using the Arabic cognates, as מתבר בנין 'birthstool of children' (28a:19) vs. Yefet: מתבר אלאולאד (ed. Birnbaum 209:12; ed. Polliack and Schlossberg 243) and Cod. Hunt. 206: مثبر الاولاد (ed. Schroeter 47:14). Rashi defines this term as the place of delivery (*sella parturiensis*); see also Targum: כאיתא דיתבא על מתברא וחיל לית לה למילד ('like a woman who has positioned herself on the birthstool but has no strength to give birth'); Abu l-Walīd: مسقط الولد على الارض ('the place where the child falls down on the earth'); R. Tanchum: الكرسى التى تلد عليها المراة ('the chair on which the woman gives birth').

Hosea 13:14

By starting the verse with בעד אן כונת ... אפדיהם 'after I have ... redeemed them' (28a:19–20), the translator creates a temporal sequence of the events: after the redemption from Sheol and the liberation from death, death and Sheol themselves will die. It is noteworthy that the author changes the present tense of the biblical text אֶפְדֵּם into the past tense: כונת אפדיהם; see also Yefet: כנת אפדיהם (ed. Birnbaum 210:16; ed. Polliack and Schlossberg 244) vs. Cod. Hunt. 206: افديهم (ed. Schroeter 47:14). Modern commentators understand the sentences as questions, e.g. Wolff (after reconstructing his text) 'Shall I redeem them from the power of Sheol? Shall I ransom them from death? Where are your thorns, O Death? Where is your sting, O Sheol?' (1974:221); similarly Macintosh 1997:546.

אלתרא 'the netherworld' (28a:20) as rendition of שְׁאוֹל has been reconstructed on the basis of the following אלתרא (28a:21); see Saadiah's usual rendering of the term (e.g. Genesis 37:35; 42:38; Numbers 16:30, 33; Deuteronomy 32:22; Isaiah 5:14; 14:9, 11, 15; 38:10, 18); Yefet and Cod. Hunt. 206 have the orthography: אלתרי (ed. Birnbaum 210:16; ed. Polliack and Schlossberg 244)/الثرى (ed. Schroeter 47:14). The translator avoids the literal rendition of the metaphor מִיַּד שְׁאוֹל with possible מן יד אלתרא, as Yefet: מן יד אלתרי (ed. Birnbaum 210:16; ed. Polliack and Schlossberg 244) and Cod. Hunt. 206: من يد الثرى (ed. Schroeter 47:14), rather he rephrases מן מוצע אלתרא 'from the place of the netherworld' (28a:19–20).

After rendering the first verb of the verse אֶפְדֵּם with the past tense כונת ... אפדיהם, it is only consequent that the translator changes the second verb אֶגְאָלֵם into וכונת ... אפוכהם 'and I have ... liberated them' (28a:20) accordingly; see also Yefet: כנת אפכהם (ed. Birnbaum 210:16–17; ed. Polliack and Schlossberg 244), whereas Cod. Hunt. 206 retains the present tense: افكّهم 'I will redeem them' (ed. Schroeter 47:15).

The twofold Hebrew אֱהִי has been rendered twice with אכון 'I will be' (28a:20, 21) rather with an interrogative particle; see also Aquila/Symmachus: ἔσομαι and Vulgate: ero; Cod. Hunt. 206: اكون / واكون (ed. Schroeter 47:15). Moreover, the translator adds before the verbs the personal pronoun 1st person singular (אנא) and before the first verb also the temporal particle אלאן ... אלאן אנא אכון :אלאן אנא אכון; see also Yefet: ואלאן (ed. Birnbaum 210:17; ed. Polliack and Schlossberg 244).

The translator appears to have understood the Hebrew דְּבָרֶיךָ as derived from דֶּבֶר 'plague', 'pestilence', parallel to the following קָטָב 'destruction' (see also both nouns in parallelism in Psalms 91:6); a possible reconstruction of the missing term could be ובאך 'your disease' (28a:21) on the basis of Yefet: ובאך (ed.

Birnbaum 210:17; ed. Polliack and Schlossberg 244) and Cod. Hunt. 206: وباء
(ed. Schroeter 47:15). See also Symmachus: πληγή σου ('your calamity'), Vulgate:
mors tua ('your death') and Cod. Hunt. 206 in his grammatical notes (ed. Schroeter 29:1). The reconstruction of the syntax וכונת מן יד אלמות אפוכהם 'and I have
liberated them from the hand of the death' (28a:20) is based on the preceeding
phrase בעד אן כונת מן מוצע אלתרא אפדיהם 'after I have redeemed them from the
place of the netherworld' (28a:19–20).

The rendition of קָטָבְךָ seems to be חתפך 'your death' (28a:21), which would
be identical with Saadiah's usual rendering of קֶטֶב (e.g. Deuteronomy 32:24;
Isaiah 28:2; Psalms 91:6).

The reconstruction אלי אלמות (28a:21) is based on the phrase אלי אלתרא in
28a:21.

The reconstruction of the noun אלצפח 'the forgiveness' (28a:21) as rendition
of the *hapax legomenon* נֹחַם is based on the last visible consonant ח and on
Yefet: אלצפח (ed. Birnbaum 210:18; ed. Polliack and Schlossberg 244), whereas
Cod. Hunt. 206 translates with التعزية (ed. Schroeter 47:15).

The rendering מן חצרתי (28a:22) of MT מֵעֵינָי is opposed to Yefet: מן בין ידי (ed.
Birnbaum 210:18; ed. Polliack and Schlossberg 244) and Cod. Hunt. 206: من بين
يدى (ed. Schroeter 47:16).

Hosea 13:15

It is not absolutely clear if the commentator takes the phrase בֵּין אַחִים as
'among brothers', as do Yefet: בין אלאכוה (ed. Birnbaum 213:3; ed. Polliack and
Schlossberg 245) and Cod. Hunt. 206: بين الاخوه 'among the brothers' (ed. Schroeter 47:18), also: LXX: ἀνὰ μέσον ἀδελφῶν, Vulgate: *inter fratres*, Peshitta: ܒܝܬ
ܐܚܐ ('between brothers'). Since the preserved first vocalized letter א can
hardly be the first letter of the plural *'iḥwa* or *'iḥwān* 'brothers', which both
demand a *kasra*, the reading אַגַם (اجم|) collective 'thicket', 'jungle', 'reeds' has
been suggested (28a:22). The reconstruction אגם 'thicket' (28a:22) as rendering
of אַחִים is based on the *pataḥ* that is visible under the *alef*, i.e. the translator
read probably אֲחִים. The other option אַחִים seems to have been added in an
explanatory note: אכוה 'brothers'. Taking into consideration the visible letters א
and ה and the *lacuna*, this explanatory could have been יעני אכוה 'i.e. brothers'
(28a:22).

The translation יתמר 'he will bear fruit' (28a:22) indicates that the author
understood יַפְרִיא as to be derived from פרה 'to be fruitful'; see also Cod. Hunt.
206: يثمر (ed. Schroeter 47:18) and Yefet: יתמר (ed. Birnbaum 213:3; ed. Polliack
and Schlossberg 245).

TEXTUAL NOTES   251

The author adds פלדלך 'and therefore' before 'he will come' (28a:22) to indicate that the following phrase is to be understood as the consequent punishment for their evil deeds (see Hosea 13:13).

יָבוֹא has been rendered with יואפי 'he will come' (28a:23) vs. Yefet: וסיגי (ed. Birnbaum 213:3; ed. Polliack and Schlossberg 245) and Cod. Hunt. 206: وسيجيء (ed. Schroeter 47:18).

The translator adds the copula הו between 'the east wind' and 'the wind of the Lord' (28a:13) for syntactic reasons.

The reconstruction of the participle צאעד 'rising' (28a:23) as rendition of עֹלֶה is tentative, since the translation of the root עלה varies; three times the author renders with the root טלע (Hosea 2:2; 8:9; 10:8), twice with the root צעד (Hosea 2:17; 12:14; text missing: Hosea 4:15). The vicinity to Hosea 12:14 (אצעד) may suggest that צאעד is preferable; see also Yefet: צאעד (ed. Birnbaum 213:4; ed. Polliack and Schlossberg 245) and Cod. Hunt. 206 صاعد (ed. Schroeter 47:19).

As his rendering פייבס 'and it will become dry' (28a:23) confirms, the translator links the verb וַיֵּבוֹשׁ, which is usually derived from the root בוש 'to be ashamed', 'to be confounded', to the root יבש 'to be dry'; see also Yefet: חתי ייבס (ed. Birnbaum 213:5; ed. Polliack and Schlossberg 245), Cod. Hunt. 206: حتى ييبس (ed. Schroeter 47:19), LXX: καὶ ἀναξηρανεῖ ('and he will dry up' [causative]), Vulgate: *et siccabit*, Peshitta: ܘܢܬܝܒܫ, Targum: ויחריב. 4QXII reads ויבש (without waw) (see M. Testuz, Deux fragments inedits des manuscrits de la Mer Morte, in: *Semitica 5* (1955), pp. 38–39), also a number of Kennicott MSS.

מְקוֹרוֹ has been rendered with מעדה 'his fountain' (28a:24) vs. Yefet: נביעה (ed. Birnbaum 213:5; ed. Polliack and Schlossberg 245) and Cod. Hunt. 206: نبعه (ed. Schroeter 47:19).

The translator renders וְיֶחֱרַב with וינשף 'and it dries out' (28a:24), whereas Yefet and Cod. Hunt. 206 choose the root جف 'to dry out', 'to become dry': ויגף (ed. Birnbaum 213:5; ed. Polliack and Schlossberg 245)/ويجف (ed. Schroeter 47:19), so Peshitta: ܘܢܬܝܒܫ ('[the wind] will dry up'), as opposed to LXX: ἐξερημώσει ('he will lay waste'), Vulgate: *desolabit* (= ויחריב).

The reconstruction of the phrase הו יסתביח 'he will take as booty' (28a:24) as rendition of הוא יִשְׁסֶה is based on the visible remnants of the verb; see also Yefet: והו יסתביח (ed. Birnbaum 213:5; ed. Polliack and Schlossberg 245), Cod. Hunt. 206: وهو يستبيح (ed. Schroeter 47:20) and Vulgate: *diripiet* ('he will despoil').

חֶמְדָּה is rendered with מותמנאה (28a:24); see Yefet: אלתמני (ed. Birnbaum 213:6; ed. Polliack and Schlossberg 245); Cod. Hunt. 206: التمنى (ed. Schroeter 47:20).

The orthography ללשוך in the grammatical notes is obviously a writing error for אלשוך 'the thorns' (28b:18), since the author chooses usually a phrase including a noun with the definite article when defining the meaning of a noun.

Hosea 14:1

The rendering of תֶּאְשַׁם with תואכד [*tuʾāḫaḏu*] 'she will be punished' (28a:25) suggests that the author derived the verb from אשם 'to be guilty'. This is distinguished from his translation of Hosea 13:1, where he renders וַיֶּאְשַׁם with the Arabic cognate פלמא אתם 'when he sinned'; see also Yefet: סתואבֹד (ed. Birnbaum 213:21; ed. Polliack and Schlossberg 246) and Cod. Hunt. 206: ستؤاخذ (ed. Schroeter 47:22). derive the verb from שמם 'to be desolate', 'to be destroyed'; Peshitta: ܐܬܚܝܒܬ ('she incurred guilt'), Targum: תחוב. LXX, on the other hand, derives the verb from the root שמם, as can be concluded from their translation ἀφανισθήσεται 'it will be destroyed'; see also Vulgate: *pereat*.

מָרְתָה has been rendered with כאלפת 'she has disobeyed' (28a:23) vs. Yefet: עצת 'you disobeyed' (ed. Birnbaum 213:21; ed. Polliack and Schlossberg 246) and Cod. Hunt. 206: عصت (ed. Schroeter 47:22).

The translator renders בֵּאלֹהֶיהָ with אלאההא 'her God' (28a:25) whereas the plural in Yefet: במעבודהא (ed. Birnbaum 213:21; ed. Polliack and Schlossberg 246) and Cod. Hunt. 206: بمعبودات (ed. Schroeter 47:22) clarifies that they regard the noun as referring to idols, alien gods; see also Hosea 14:4.

יְרֻטָּשׁוּ has been rendered with יופקסו 'they will be dashed' (28a:26), whereas Yefet and Cod. Hunt. 206 translate with יבעגון (ed. Birnbaum 213:22; ed. Polliack and Schlossberg 246 [where one manuscript reads יובעגון])/يبعجون 'they are slit open' (ed. Schroeter 47:23).

Hosea 14:2

The translator renders יִשְׂרָאֵל with יא אל אסראיל 'O people of Israel' (28b:23), whereas Yefet and Cod. Hunt. 206 prefer the simple term יא ישראל 'O Israel' (ed. Birnbaum 214:10; ed. Polliack and Schlossberg 246)/يا اسرائل (ed. Schroeter 47:23).

The restoration קד תעתרת 'you have stumbled' (28b:24) for כָּשַׁלְתָּ is based on the author's usual rendering of the root כשל with עתר v (see Hosea 4:5 [2×]; 5:5; text missing: Hosea 5:5; 14:10), whereas Yefet: עתרת (ed. Birnbaum 214:11; ed. Polliack and Schlossberg 246) and Cod. Hunt. 206: عثرت (ed. Schroeter 48:1) prefer עתר I.

Hosea 14:3

The author has chosen כטוב 'words' as equivalent of דְּבָרִים; see also Yefet: כטב (ed. Birnbaum 215:2; ed. Polliack and Schlossberg 246), whereas Cod. Hunt. 206 translates with كلام (ed. Schroeter 48:1).

The translator adds the connective conjunction פ before the imperative פקולו 'and say!' instead of the asyndetic אִמְרוּ (28b:25); see also Cod. Hunt. 206 وقولوا (ed. Schroeter 48:2), whereas Yefet imitates the Hebrew asyndetic style by rendering קולו (ed. Birnbaum 215:2; ed. Polliack and Schlossberg 246 [which reads וקולו]).

The unusual word order of the biblical phrase כָּל-תִּשָּׂא עָוֺן 'all may you bear iniquity' has been rendered with כל דנב לנא תגפר, including an additional לנא: 'may you forgive *us* all iniquity' (28b:25). The author clarifies his view in his exegesis: כל תשא עון means כל-עון תשא (29a:23); see Ibn Nūḥ explicitly: נטיר כל תשא עון ומעניה כל עון תשא ('like כָּל-תִּשָּׂא עָוֺן וְקַח-טוֹב' [Hosea 14:3], the meaning of which is כָּל-עָוֺן תִּשָּׂא', Diqduq on Psalms 141:10, ed. Khan 2000:352–353). See also Cod. Hunt. 206: كلّ ذنب تغفر (not: تغفي; ed. Schroeter 48:2) and Yefet: כל דנב תגפר (ed. Birnbaum 215:3; ed. Polliack and Schlossberg 246).

וְקַח-טוֹב 'and accept good!' has been rendered with ואקבל מנא הדא אלכיר 'and accept this good from us!' (28b:25–26). In his exegesis, the commentator explains this by 'the good they have done'. Also Cod. Hunt. 206 interprets טוב as 'good deeds': فعال لاخير (ed. Schroeter 48:2), Yefet: פעל אלצואב 'the deed of rightness' (ed. Birnbaum 215:3; ed. Polliack and Schlossberg 246). For Ibn Ezra 'good' implies speech: דיבור טוב 'a good confession', whereas LXX: ἀγαθά ('good things') and Peshitta: ܛܒܬܐ prefer a neutral rendering (see also translation of Hosea 8:3). For the phrase 'a friendly speech' in the exegesis (29a:21) see Qimḥi: אינו שואל מכם בתשובה לא כסף וזהב ולא עולות אלא דברים טובים שתתודו בהם עונותיכם ('he does not demand from them when returning, neither silver nor gold nor offerings, but good words by which you confess your sins').

By adding the personal pronoun פנחן 'and we' (28b:26) before 'we will fulfil', the author appears to emphasise the active involvement and initiative of Israel in repentance; see already the additional לנא 'for us' and מנא 'from us' (28b:25).

The interpretation of פָרִים differs considerably in the exegetical tradition:

(1) Some derive the noun from פַּר 'young bull', e.g. Vulgate: *vitulos* ('calves'), Targum: כתורין ('like bullocks'), Cod. Hunt. 206: البقر ('the cattle', ed. Schroeter 48:3).

(2) Others appear to have read פֵּרִים, e.g. LXX: καρπόν ('fruit') and Peshitta: ܦܐܪܐ ('fruit'); the final *mem* has been explained as an archaic Canaanite case ending as attested in Ugaritic (see O'Callaghan, R.T., Echoes of Canaanite Literature in Psalms, in: *Vetus Testamentum 4* (1954), pp. 170–

171). In combination with the following, פָּרִים would form the familiar phrase פָּרִים שְׂפָתֵינוּ 'the fruit of our lips' (see Isaiah 57:19; Proverbs 12:14; 13:2).

The translator adopts the first option, as indicated by his rendering with אלרתות 'the bulls'; see also Yefet: אלרתות (ed. Birnbaum 215:4; ed. Polliack and Schlossberg 246). רת, originally 'swine', 'boar' is generally used by Judaeo-Arabic authors as equivalent of Hebrew פר; see e.g. T-S AS 160.22 recto 5: רותות for Hebrew פרים (Psalms 51:21).

Whereas the biblical text includes the metaphor *the bulls of our lips*, the translator forms an antithesis: 'instead of (בדל) the bulls the words of our lips' (28b:26), i.e. the words of the lips replace the offerings; see also Yefet: בדל תקריב אלרתות באקראר שפתינא (ed. Birnbaum 215:3–4; ed. Polliack and Schlossberg 246) and Cod. Hunt. 206: بدل تقريب البقر باقرار شفتينا (ed. Schroeter 48:3).

The reconstruction in the exegesis תובה 'his return' (29b:7) draws on Yefet (ed. Birnbaum 217:22; ed. Polliack and Schlossberg 246–247).

Hosea 14:4

Most of the text is completely missing or fragmentary. From the *lacunae*, it may be assumed that the author expanded his translation at several occasions.

The restoration אשור as rendition of the nomen proprium אַשּׁוּר is based on the author's usual rendering (Hosea 7:11; 8:9; 9:3; 10:6; 11:11; 12:2; text missing: Hosea 5:13; 11:5); see also Yefet: אשור (ed. Birnbaum 217:19; ed. Polliack and Schlossberg 248), whereas Cod. Hunt. 206 translates with الموصل (ed. Schroeter 48:3).

יגיתנא 'he will save us' (29a:1) has been suggested as rendition of יוֹשִׁיעֵנוּ, since the author usually renders the root ישע with גות (see Hosea 13:4, 10; text missing: Hosea 1:7 [2×]); see also Yefet: יגיתנא (ed. Birnbaum 217:19; ed. Polliack and Schlossberg 248), whereas Cod. Hunt. 206 obviously regarded the homonym as femine: تغيثنا (ed. Schroeter 48:3).

The rendering of סוס is not clear to me; only a final ס is visible; Yefet: אלכיל (ed. Birnbaum 217:19; ed. Polliack and Schlossberg 248 [where one manuscript just reads כיל]); Cod. Hunt. 206: الخيل (ed. Schroeter 48:4).

The rendition ליס נקול 'we will not say' (29a:1) as translation of וְלֹא-נֹאמַר has been suggested, because the author prefers the negation ליס vs. Yefet: ולא נקול (ed. Birnbaum 217:19–20; ed. Polliack and Schlossberg 248) and Cod. Hunt. 206: ولا نقول (ed. Schroeter 48:4).

The restoration זאדה 'yet' (29a:1) is based on the author's characteristic rendering of עוֹד (Hosea 2:18, 19; 3:1; 12:1, 10; 14:9; text missing: Hosea 1:4, 6) vs. Yefet:

אבדא (ed. Birnbaum 217:20; ed. Polliack and Schlossberg 248) and Cod. Hunt. 206: ابدا (ed. Schroeter 48:4).

Since the author usually translates אלהים with the Arabic cognate, the literal rendition אלאנא 'our God' (29a:2) for אֱלֹהֵינוּ has been suggested, like Targum: אלהא 'our God', whereas Yefet and Cod. Hunt. 206 translate with מעבודנא (ed. Birnbaum 217:20; ed. Polliack and Schlossberg 248)/معبودنا (ed. Schroeter 48:4) to ensure that foreign Gods are intended. The plural is adopted by LXX: θεοὶ ἡμῶν ('our gods'): Vulgate: *dei nostri*; Peshitta: ܐܠܗܢ (with *seyamē*).

לעמל 'to (the) work' (29a:2) has been restored as rendition of לְמַעֲשֵׂה because of the author's translation of מַעֲשֵׂה with עמל in Hosea 13:2; see also Cod. Hunt. 206 without preposition عمل (ed. Schroeter 48:4) and Yefet: לעמל (ed. Birnbaum 217:20; ed. Polliack and Schlossberg 248).

The partly reconstructed יורחם 'he finds mercy' (29a:2) reflects the author's usual rendering of the Hebrew root with the Arabic cognate رحم (Hosea 2:3, 25 [2×]; text missing: Hosea 1:6, 7; 2:6; and his translation of רחמים in Hosea 2:21); see also the translations of Yefet: ירחם (ed. Birnbaum 217:20; ed. Polliack and Schlossberg 248) and Cod. Hund. 206: يرحم (ed. Schroeter 48:5).

The lacuna after יורחם suggests that the author has expanded his translation before the final word יתים 'orphan', which is the equivalent of Hebrew יָתוֹם vs. Yefet and Cod. Hunt. 206: אליתים (ed. Birnbaum 217:21; ed. Polliack and Schlossberg 248)/اليتيم (ed. Schroeter 48:5).

Hosea 14:5

מְשׁוּבָתָם is rendered with עותוהם 'their impertinence' (29a:3); see also Yefet: עתוהם (ed. Birnbaum 219:16; ed. Polliack and Schlossberg 248) and Cod. Hunt. 206: عتوهم (ed. Schroeter 48:5). Also Saadiah uses the same root as translation of שוב (e.g. Isaiah 47:10; 57:17).

The translator adds תום 'then' (29a:3) after 'I will heal their impertinence' in order to achieve a temporal sequence (see also Hosea 14:7): firstly, God will heal their impertinence and then he will love them.

The rendering of נְדָבָה 'gratuiously', 'generously' is not clear, since only the first letter ה of the noun is visible after the additional preposition לאיגל 'because of' (29a:3). Therefore a possible rendition with סכא 'generosity' is unlikely; see Yefet: סכאוה (ed. Birnbaum 219:16; ed. Polliack and Schlossberg 248 סכאה) and Cod. Hunt. 206: سخاوة (ed. Schroeter 48:5). Likewise the rendering with תברע 'gift', 'donation' is doubtul; see R. Tanchum: احبّهم تبرعا ('I love them spontaneously'); see Saadiah's translation of נְדָבָה with תברעא [Exodus 35:29; Derenbourg I, p. 134:20] and with מתברעא [Deuteronomy 23:24; Derenbourg I,

p. 288:10]; see also Deuteronomy 12:6, 17. The author has possibly chosen as translation הדיה 'gift', 'present'; the context would be: 'I love them because of a gift'. If this assumption is correct, the question arises: Does the 'gift' refer to God's generous love *sola gratia* (see Vulgate: *spontane* 'spontaneously'; LXX: ὁμολόγως), or to Israel's 'generosity'? From the exegesis in which the author characterizes Israel's repentance as a sign of their generosity (29b:25), the latter option appears to be more likely.

The reconstruction of גצבי 'my anger' (29a:4) is based on Hosea 11:9; see also Yefet: גֹצְבִי (ed. Birnbaum 219:16; ed. Polliack and Schlossberg 248) and Cod. Hunt. 206: غضي (ed. Schroeter 48:5).

The reconstruction of מנה 'from him' (29a:4) as rendering of מִמֶּנּוּ takes into account the author's usual literal translation; see also LXX^B: ἀπ' αὐτοῦ ('from him'). While Yefet also has מנה (ed. Birnbaum 219:16; ed. Polliack and Schlossberg 248), Cod. Hunt. 206 harmonises the sentence with the plural context (see the suffixes מְשׁוּבָתָם, אֹהֲבֵם) by rendering عنهم 'from them' (ed. Schroeter 48:6); the same tendency of harmonisation can be observed in LXX: ἀπ' αὐτῶν ('from them'); Peshittaܡܢܗܘܢ; Targum: מנהון.

Hosea 14:6

כַּטַּל has been rendered with כאלטל (29a:4); see also Cod. Hunt. 206: كالطلّ (ed. Schroeter 48:6) vs. Yefet: מתל אלנדי (ed. Birnbaum 220:22; ed. Polliack and Schlossberg 249).

יִפְרַח has been rendered with the Arabic cognate פינפרח 'he will blossom' (29a:4), whereas Yefet and Cod. Hunt. 206 use a different root: ינפרע (ed. Birnbaum 220:22; ed. Polliack and Schlossberg 249 [where one manuscript reads ליתפרע/فيتفرّع]) 'and he branches out' (ed. Schroeter 48:6; see also Hosea 10:4).

כאלסוסנה 'like the lily (of the valley)' (29a:5) as rendition of כַּשּׁוֹשַׁנָּה has been restored according to the legible remnants of the word; see also Yefet: מתל אלסוסנה (ed. Birnbaum 220:22–23; ed. Polliack and Schlossberg 249) and Cod. Hunt. 206: مثل السوسنة (ed. Schroeter 48:4).

The restoration ויצרב 'and he will strike' (29a:5) as translation of וְיַךְ is based on the author's translation of Hosea 6:1 (יצרבהא for יַךְ); see also Yefet: ויצרב (ed. Birnbaum 220:23; ed. Polliack and Schlossberg 249) and Cod. Hunt. 206: ويضرب (ed. Schroeter 48:6).

The restoration of אצולה 'his roots' (29a:5) as rendition of שָׁרָשָׁיו has been chosen because of the author's rendering of שֹׁרֶשׁ with אצלהם in Hosea 9:16 vs. Yefet: סנוכה (ed. Birnbaum 220:23; ed. Polliack and Schlossberg 249) and Cod. Hunt. 206: سنوخه (ed. Schroeter 48:7).

Hosea 14:7

The translation רוֹאֲצָעה, literally 'his sucklings' (29a:5) imitates the Hebrew יוֹנְקוֹתָיו; see also Yefet: רואצעה (ed. Birnbaum 220:24; ed. Polliack and Schlossberg 249) and Cod. Hunt. 206: رواضعه (ed. Schroeter 48:7). The noun is used metaphorically to denote the fresh shoots, tender branches. R. Tanchum explains: והי الاغصان تشبيها لها بعوללים ויונקים ('they are branches; he compares them with "children" and "sucklings"'). The Targum understood the noun literally: יסגון בנין ובנן 'sons and daughters multiplied'.

The translator adds תום 'then' at the beginning of the verse (29a:5) to create a temporal sequence of events.

The translation of הוֹדוֹ has been restored as בהאיה 'his splendor' (29a:6); see also Cod. Hunt. 206: بهائه (ed. Schroeter 48:8); Yefet: בהאה (ed. Birnbaum 220:24; ed. Polliack and Schlossberg 249) and Saadiah's translation of הוד with בהא (Numbers 27:20 [Derenbourg I, 237:16]; Isaiah 30:30 [Derenbourg III, 46:6]; Job 37:22 [Derenbourg V, 109:10]; 39:20 [Derenbourg V, 115:19]; 40:10 [Derenbourg V, 117:15]).

Hosea 14:8

The translator renders בְּצִלּוֹ with פי פייוה 'in his shadows' instead of possible טלה; see Yefet: פי טלה (ed. Birnbaum 222:19; ed. Polliack and Schlossberg 250) and Cod. Hunt. 206: فى ظلّه (ed. Schroeter 48:9).

יְחַיּוּ has been rendered with יבקו 'they will preserve' (29a:7), whereas Yefet: ירבו (ed. Birnbaum 222:19; ed. Polliack and Schlossberg 250) and Cod. Hunt. 206: يربوا (ed. Schroeter 48:9) refer to the root ربا II 'to let grow'.

The author adds the conjunction לאן 'for' (29a:7) and the copula יכון 'he will be' (29a:7) to provide a reason: 'for his memory will be like the wine of Lebanon'.

Hosea 14:9

The translator provides an introduction to the following speech with 'Ephraim' as subject: 'when (אדא) Ephraim will say' (29a:8). The verse is understood to be part of a dialogue between Ephraim (verse 9a) and God (verse 9b); see also Yefet: קאל אפרים (ed. Birnbaum 224:10; ed. Polliack and Schlossberg 251), Cod. Hunt. 206: قال افرم (ed. Schroeter 48:10), Peshitta: ܢܐܡܪ ('[Ephraim] will say') and Targum: יימרון.

יכון 'he will be' (first word in line 29a:9) seems to be a slip of the pen for אכון 'I will be'.

The author translates אֲנִי עָנִיתִי with the future tense and adds the suffix pronoun 3. singular masculine אכון קד אגבתה 'I will answer him' (29a:9) in accordance with the following ואמלחה 'and I will look on him' (29a:9); see also Rashi, whereas Yefet renders with the past: אנא אגבת (ed. Birnbaum 224:11; ed. Polliack and Schlossberg 251); Cod. Hunt. 206: انا اجبت (ed. Schroeter 48:11).

כִּבְרוֹשׁ 'like he cedar' is rendered with כברות 'like a cypress' (29a:9) which seems to be the Aramaic בְּרוֹתָא 'cypress', 'pine tree' (Jastrow p. 198) and has been adopted as Arabic cognate. Yefet and Cod. Hunt. 206 translate with אלשרבין (ed. Birnbaum 224:12; ed. Polliack and Schlossberg 251)/الشربين (ed. Schroeter 48:12).

The translator adds the vocative יא באיס 'oh miserable one' (29a:9), presumably to smoothen the transition from God's speech referring to a 3rd person singular masculine (וַאֲשׁוּרֶנּוּ) to the direct address of a 2nd person singular masculine (פֶּרְיְךָ).

רַעֲנָן has been rendered with גץ 'fresh', 'tender' (29a:9); see also Yefet: אלגץ (ed/ Birnbaum 224:12; ed. Polliack and Schlossberg 251) and Cod. Hunt. 206: الغض (ed. Schroeter 48:12), who adds the explanation ويقال اكروثاء 'leafy', ed. Polliack and Schlossberg ויקאל אלברותא – see Kazimirski II, 882: 'être touffu (se dit des cheveux, de l'herbe, etc.').

The translator renders נִמְצָא with the perfect קד וגד (29a:10) instead with a participle, as do Yefet and Cod. Hunt. 206: מוגוד (ed. Birnbaum 224:12; ed. Polliack and Schlossberg 251)/موجود (ed. Schroeter 48:12).

Hosea 14:10

וְיָבֵן has been rendered with פיפהם 'and he understands'; Cod. Hunt. 206 translates with ويَعِزّ (ed. Schroeter 48:13); see Yefet: ויערפהם (ed. Birnbaum 226:1; ed. Polliack and Schlossberg 252).

The final letter י after the verb פיפהם can be restored as האולי 'these' (plural communis for persons). Though the feminine singular demonstrative pronoun הדה in combination with the following noun אלכטוב 'the things' should be expected according to CA see Yefet: הדה (ed. Birnbaum 226:1; ed. Polliack and Schlossberg 252) and Cod. Hunt. 206: هذه (ed. Schroeter 48:13)—, the author appears to interpret the vage object אֵלֶּה 'these' of the biblical text as referring to 'the words (of the prophet)', as his addition אלכטוב 'the words' (29a:10) indicates.

The author translates the plural masculine יְשָׁרִים verbatim with מוסתקימין 'upright ones', 'righteous ones' (29a:11) see also Yefet: מסתקימין (ed. Birnbaum

226:2; ed. Polliack and Schlossberg 252) and Cod. Hunt. 206: مستقيمى (ed. Schroeter 48:14) though the adjective as an attribute characterizing 'the ways of the Lord' should be, according to CA, feminine singular.

The same problem occurs when the translator renders בָּם twice literally with בהם 'on them', i.e. persons (29a:12), where פיהא or בהא should be expected, according to CA. Yefet and Cod. Hunt 206 have twice פיה twice (ed. Birnbaum 226:3; ed. Polliack and Schlossberg 252)/فيها (ed. Schroeter 48:15). The difference with CA grammar demonstrates the author's tendency to provide a literal translation of the Hebrew source text.

References

Baker, Colin F. and Polliack, Meira. 2001. *Arabic and Judaeo-Arabic Manuscripts in The Cambridge Genizah Collections: Arabic Old Series (T-S Ar.1a–54)*. Cambridge University Library Genizah Series 12. Cambridge: Cambridge University Press.

Beit-Arié, Malachi. 1976. *Hebrew Codicology: Tenative Typology of Technical Practices Employed in Hebrew Dated Medieval Manuscripts*. Études de Paléographie Hébraïque. Paris: Centre national de la recherche scientifique.

Birnbaum, Philip. 1942. *The Arabic Commentary of Yefet Ben 'Ali the Karaite on the Book of Hosea*. Philadelphia: Dropsie College.

Birnbaum, Solomon A. 1954. *The Hebrew Scripts*. London: Palaeographia.

Birnbaum, Solomon A. 1971. *The Hebrew Scripts*. Leiden: Brill.

Blau, Joshua, and Simon Hopkins. 1985. 'A Vocalized Judaeo-Arabic Letter from The Cairo Geniza'. *Jerusalem Studies in Arabic and Islam* 6: 417–476.

Blau, Joshua. 1978. 'Medieval Judeo-Arabic'. In *Jewish Languages, Theme and Variation*, edited by Herbert H. Paper, 85–96. Cambridge, MA: Association for Jewish Studies.

Blau, Joshua. 1980. *A Grammar of Mediaeval Judaeo-Arabic*. 2nd ed. Jerusalem: Magnes Press (in Hebrew).

Blau, Joshua. 1988. *Studies in Middle Arabic and Its Judaeo-Arabic Variety*. Jerusalem: Magnes Press.

Buber, Salomon. 1868. *Pesikta, Die älteste Hagada Redigirt in Palastina von Rab Kahana*. Lyck: Verein Mekize Nirdamim.

Derenbourg, Joseph. 1893. *Version Arabe Du Pentateuque de R Saadia Ben Iosef Al-Fayyoumi*. [Oeuvres Completes de R Saadia Ben Iosef Al-Fayyoumi 1. Paris.

Engel, Edna. 1999. 'Styles of Hebrew Script on The Tenth and Eleventh Centuries in The Light of Dated and Datable Geniza Documents,' *Te'uda* 15: 365–410 (in Hebrew), xxx–xxxi (English summary).

Frank, Daniel. 2000. 'Karaite Exegesis'. In *Hebrew Bible/Old Testament. The History of Its Interpretation, Volume 1: From the Beginnings to the Middle Ages (Until 1300)*, edited by Magne Sæbø, Christianus Brekelmans, and Menahem Haran, 110–128. Göttingen: Vandenhoeck & Ruprecht.

Gil, Moshe. 1983. *Palestine During The First Muslim Period (634–1099), Part II, Cairo Geniza Documents*. Publications of The Diaspora Research Institute 57. Tel-Aviv: University of Tel-Aviv (in Hebrew).

Haarbrücker, Theodor. 1843. *R. Tanchumi Hierosolymitani in Prophetas Commentarii arabici specimen primum*. Halle: Academia Fridericiana.

Harper, William Rainey. 1905. *A Critical and Exegetical Commentary on Amos and Hosea*. International Critical Commentary on the Holy Scriptures of the Old and New Testaments. Edinburgh: T. & T. Clark.

Hary, Benjamin. 1990. 'The Importance of The Orthography in Judeo-Arabic'. In *Proceedings of The Tenth World Congress of Jewish Studies Jerusalem, August 16–24, 1989, Division D. Vol. 1, The Hebrew Language, Jewish Languages*, 77–84. Jerusalem: World Union of Jewish Studies.

Kazimirski, Albert de Biberstein. 1860. *Dictionnaire Arabe-Français Contenant Toutes Les Racines de La Langue Arabe, Leurs Dérivés, Tant Dans l'Idiome Vulgaire Que Dans L'idiome Littéral, Ainsi Que Les Dialectes d'Alger et de Maroc*. Paris: Maison-neuve et cie.

Khan, Geoffrey. 1992a. 'The Function of the Shewa Sign in Vocalized Judaeo-Arabic Texts from the Genizah'. In *Genizah Research after Ninety Years: The Case of Judaeo-Arabic*, edited by Joshua Blau and Stefan Reif, 105–111. University of Cambridge Oriental Publications 47. Cambridge: Cambridge University Press.

Khan, Geoffrey. 1992b. 'Notes on The Grammar of A Late Judaeo-Arabic Text'. *Jerusalem Studies in Arabic and Islam* 15 (Festschrift for Joshua Blau): 220–239.

Khan, Geoffrey. 2000. *The Early Karaite Tradition of Hebrew Grammatical Thought: Including a Critical Edition, Translation and Analysis of the Diqduq of ʾAbū Yaʿqūb Yūsuf Ibn Nūḥ on the Hagiographa*. Studies in Semitic Languages and Linguistics. Leiden: Brill.

Khan, Geoffrey. 2011. 'The Grammatical Commentary on Hosea by the Karaite Yūsuf Ibn Nūḥ'. In *Studies on the Text and Versions of the Hebrew Bible in Honour of Robert Gordon*, edited by Geoffrey Khan and Diana Lipton, 387–418. Leiden; Boston: Brill.

Macintosh, Andrew Alexander. 1997. *A Critical and Exegetical Commentary on Hosea*. The International Critical Commentary. Edinburgh: T&T Clark.

Mays, James Luther. 1969. *Hosea: A Commentary*. Old Testament Library. London: SCM.

Neubauer, Adolf. 1875. *The Book of Hebrew Roots by Abū Al-Walīd Marwān ibn Janāḥ*. Oxford: Clarendon Press.

Polliack, Meira, and Eliezer Schlossberg. 2009. *Yefet Ben ʿEli's Commentary on Hosea. Annotated Edition, Hebrew Translation and Introduction*. Ramat Gan: Bar-Ilan University Press.

Polliack, Meira. 1996a. 'Medieval Karaite Views on Translating the Hebrew Bible into Arabic'. *Journal of Jewish Studies* 47: 64–84.

Polliack, Meira. 1996b. 'The Medieval Karaite Tradition of Translating the Hebrew Bible into Arabic: Its Sources, Characteristics and Historical Background'. *Journal of the Royal Asiatic Society* (Third series) 6: 189–196.

Polliack, Meira. 1997. *The Karaite Tradition of Arabic Bible Translation: A Linguistic and Exegetical Study of Karaite Translations of the Pentateuch from the Tenth and Eleventh Centries C.E.* Vol. 17. Études Sur Le Judaïsme Médiéval. Leiden: Brill.

Polliack, Meira. 1999. 'The Emergence of Karaite Bible Exegesis'. *Sefunot* NS 7 (22): 299–311 (in Hebrew).

Polliack, Meira, and Eliezer Schlossberg. 2009. *Yefet Ben ʿEli's Commentary on Hosea.*

Annotated Edition, Hebrew Translation and Introduction. Ramat Gan: Bar-Ilan University Press.

Qil, Yehuda. 1973. *Peruš Daʿat Ha-Miqra La-Tre ʿAsar*. Jerusalem: Mosad ha-rav Quq (in Hebrew).

Schroeter, R. 1867. 'Die in Cod. Hunt. 206 Aufbewahrte Arabische Uebersetzung Der Kleinen Propheten. I. Hosea'. In *Archiv Für Wissenschaftliche Erforschung Des Alten Testamentes*, edited by Adalbert Merx, 1:28–54, 153–194. Halle: Verlag der Buchhandlung des Waisenhauses.

Sharvit, Shimon. 1992. 'Studies in the Vocalization of Liturgical Fragments from the Cairo Genizah'. In *Language Studies 5–6 (Israel Yeivin Festschrift)*, edited by Moshe Bar-Asher, 501–518. Jerusalem: Magnes Press (in Hebrew).

Stuart, Douglas. 1987. *Hosea—Jonah*. Vol. 31. Word Biblical Commentary. Waco, Texas: Word Books.

Versteegh, Cornelis H.M. 1993. *Arabic Grammar and Qurʾānic Exegesis in Early Islam*. Studies in Semitic Languages and Linguistics 19. Leiden: Brill.

Vielhauer, Roman. 2007. *Das Werden Des Buches Hosea Elektronische Ressource Eine Redaktionsgeschichtliche Untersuchung*. Vol. 349. Beihefte Zur Zeitschrift Für Die Alttestamentliche Wissenschaft. Berlin-New York: de Gruyter.

Wechter, Pinchas. 1967. *Ibn Barun's Arabic Works on Hebrew Grammar and Lexicography*. Philadelphia: Dropsie College.

Wolff, Hans Walter. 1974. *Hosea: A Commentary on the Book of the Prophet Hosea*. Hermeneia—a Critical and Historical Commentary on the Bible. Philadelphia: Fortress Press.

Yardeni, Ada. 1997. *The Book of Hebrew Script: History, Palaeography, Script Styles, Calligraphy & Design*. Jerusalem: Carta.

Index of Cambridge University Library, Taylor-Schechter manuscripts

T-S NS		
29.172	2	
29.199	6	
29 minute	6	
59.1	10	
261.4	7, 10	
261.5	5	
261.6	6	
261.7	5	
261.8	2	
261.9	1	
261.10	6	
261.11	3	
261.12	5	
261.13	1	
261.14	5	
261.15	4	
261.16	3	
261.17	2, 3, 10	
261.18	7	
261.19	7	
261.20	7	
261.21	3	
261.22	8, 10	
261.23	4	
261.24	5, 10	
261.25	5	
261.26	5, 10	
261.27	7, 10, 12	
261.28	7, 10	
261.29	5, 10	
261.30	5	
261.31	5, 8	
261.32	2, 5, 12	
261.33	5	
261.34	5	
261.35	6	
261.36	4	
261.37	7, 10	
261.38	3	
261.39	4	
261.40	7, 10, 12	
261.41	7, 6	
261.42	6, 8, 10	
261.43	2, 9, 10	
261.44	3	
261.45	3, 10, 12	
261.47	4, 10	
261.48	2, 3	
261.49	5, 10	
261.50	3, 10	
261.51	6, 10	
261.52	6, 10	
261.53	4, 10	
261.55	4, 10	
261.56	5, 10, 12	
261.57	4, 10	
261.58	7, 10	
261.59	2, 3	
261.60	3	
261.61	1	
261.62	2, 3	
261.63	2, 3	
261.64	7	
261.65	5	
261.66	4	
261.67	2, 9	
261 minute	2, 3, 4, 5, 6, 7, 8	
277.32	203	
285.9	207	
341.13	4	
341.18	3, 10	
339 minute	8	
341 minute	2, 5, 6	

T-S AS		
90.189	7	
140.87	7	
140.113	4, 7	
140.114	7	
141.47	155	
154.79	7	
155.450	6	
156.162	6	
156.443	6, 7	
159.51	4	
159.303	4	
160.22	254	

INDEX OF CAMBRIDGE UNIVERSITY LIBRARY

164.138	6	Ar.9.5	1
164.307	3	Ar.21.105	226, 229
164.308	6	Ar.21.137	1
167.34	6	Ar.21.179	1
167.209	2	Ar.21.182	127, 129, 130
167.217	2	Ar.22.119	1
164.325	3	Ar.22.127	132, 136, 213
167.325	2	Ar.22.128	191, 192, 205
169.93	5	Ar.23.18	1
172.378	6	Ar.24.7	149, 180
173.444	3	Ar.24.165	118, 119
175.152	6	Ar.28.174	149, 150, 151, 152, 153, 192
201.310	5	Ar.31.221	1
202.95	4	Ar.31.228	1
202.490	4	Ar.54.1	1
217.172	6		
218.301	4	**T-S 13J & 18J**	
221.313	4	13J11.5	8
221.315	7	18J3.9	8
222.41	7		
224.208	4	**T-S 24**	
225.265	6	24.7	185, 191
225.272	6		

T-S Ar.
Ar.1b.23	147
Ar.1c.24	1

Index of Biblical Verses

Genesis

3:18	212		
6	140		
7	140		
8	140		
13:7	120		
14:11	247		
14:14	124		
14:20	97, 119, 226		
14:22	119		
16:13	119		
17:1	119		
18:27	156		
18:31	156		
22:17	19		
22:18	182		
25:8	140		
25:17	140		
25:26	232		
27:23	135		
27:36	232		
27:40	229, 230		
28:17	103		
29	238		
31:23	124		
31:34	137		
32:27	103		
32:29	103, 229, 232		
33:8	244		
33:20	119		
35:9	103		
35:29	140		
37:35	249		
40:10	208		
42:8	135		
42:9	221		
42:11	221		
42:14	221		
42:38	249		
43:30	227		
46:3	226		
49:1	138		
49:3	232		

Exodus

1:10	21
2:15	105
2:21	156
3:15	234
4:24	244
14:8	124
15:15	239
19:5	93
19:6	93
19:7	91
19:16	154
19:19	154
20:5	67
20:18	154
21:10	21
22:15	130
24:7	29
24:12	67
32:4	241
32:14	111
32:20	65, 186
33:19	138
34:15	122
35:29	255

Leviticus

19:9	217
19:10	217
19:36	235
20:6	122
23:22	217
25:9	154
26:30	83, 212
26:31	43
27:16	136

Numbers

10:2	154
10:8	154
10:9	154
10:10	154
11:12	93
12:11	156
14:24	182
16:30	249

INDEX OF BIBLICAL VERSES

16:33	249	32:22	249
17:13	105	32:24	29, 250
21:28	212	33:9	135
22:41	212	34:10	243
23:13	210		
24:14	138	**Joshua**	
27:20	257	22:17	77
31:6	154	24:19	109, 230
32:40	51		
		Judges	
Deuteronomy		2:10	140
1:5	156	6:32	158
1:10	19	15:5	137
1:13	226	18:31	89
1:24	221	20:22	89
2:28	223		
4:13	67	**1 Samuel**	
4:30	103, 138	14:14	95, 215
5:2	29	15:23	137
5:3	29	17:20	238
5:18	67	19:16	35
7:12	182		
7:13	125	**2 Samuel**	
7:25	199	3:34	213
8:14	107	7:1	223
9:24	77	7:10	213
10:22	83	23:1	93
11:13	59		
11:14	125	**1 Kings**	
12:6	256	7:24	223
12:17	125, 256	15:20	53
12:30	199	17:20	63
14:23	125		
16:3	33	**2 Kings**	
18:4	125	2:9	81
23:19	128	8:12	219
23:24	255	9:11	73
24:19	217	19:19	15
25:13	235	19:35	15
27:17	155	13:6	65
28:33	47	22:20	140
28:35	214		
28:47	59	**Isaiah**	
28:48	59	1:21	122
28:49	63	2:2	138
28:51	125	2:11	25
29:11	29	2:17	25
30:10	103	5	135
31:9	67	5:14	249

Isaiah *(cont.)*

8:15	166, 199
9:5	119
10:21	119
11:11	228
13:16	219
14:9	249
14:11	249
14:15	249
15:1	141
15:2	212
16:7	135
18:3	154
19:8	166
19:13	156
21:8	95
23:8	235
26:9	161
27:6	208
27:13	154
28:2	250
28:10	117
28:13	199
29:4	179
30:14	65
30:16	115
30:30	257
34:6	210
34:14	244
35:1	208
35:2	208
37:7	212
38:9	163
38:10	249
38:18	249
42:2	156
42:4	49
44:12	214
45:14	236
47:10	255
54:15	179
55:2	236
57:3	122
57:17	255
57:19	254
58:1	154
63:10	111
66:14	208

Jeremiah

2:13	223
2:31	107, 229
5:22	210
11:13	83
12:6	73
15:1	23
17:9	166
23:15	95
23:32	181
29:17	168
29:26	73
38:2–13	1
38:3–7	1
40:1–6	1
40:7–8	1
40:7–12	1
40:8	1
49:24	109, 239
51:51	1
51:52–53	1
51:54–55	1

Ezekiel

16:7	83
17:6	224
17:24	223
20:8	91
20:9	91
20:35	27, 130
21:31	172
45:14	35

Hosea

1:1	2, 231
1:2	2, 33, 122, 146
1:3	2, 146, 201
1:4	2, 15, 118, 128, 131, 175, 192, 254
1:5	15, 19
1:6	15, 122, 131, 175, 201, 254, 255
1:7	15, 122, 254, 255
1:8	15, 21, 118, 201
1:9	15, 19, 21, 31, 119, 175
2:1	15, 19, 118, 120, 135, 153, 160, 227
2:2	15, 19, 118, 119, 121, 153, 226, 251

… INDEX OF BIBLICAL VERSES

2:3	11, 17, 21, 25, 119, 120, 122, 255	4:5	2, 37, 124, 141, 152, 230, 252
2:4	17, 21, 25, 120, 122, 125, 134, 140, 152	4:6	2, 37, 119, 120, 142, 152, 153, 182
2:5	17, 23, 118, 119, 121, 226, 230, 243	4:7	2, 37, 118, 143, 213
2:6	17, 23, 118, 120, 122, 147, 153, 255	4:8	2, 37, 119, 144, 175, 191, 198
		4:9	2, 37, 118, 128, 131, 144, 170, 191, 232
2:7	17, 21, 23, 25, 120, 122, 135, 200, 201	4:10	2, 37, 120, 122, 145, 146, 175
2:8	17, 23, 25, 122, 123, 232	4:11	2, 37, 125, 139, 146
2:9	11, 17, 23, 25, 27, 120, 124, 152, 153, 163	4:12	2, 37, 119, 120, 121, 122, 147, 151
2:10	17, 23, 120, 122, 125, 150, 151, 243	4:13	2, 120, 122
		4:14	2, 120, 122, 128, 192
2:11	17, 21, 23, 124, 125, 126, 127, 146, 160, 230	4:15	2, 37, 51, 122, 147, 251
		4:16	39, 119, 120, 125
2:12	17, 23, 25, 125, 127	4:17	39, 123, 129, 147
2:13	17, 21, 23, 25, 127, 130	4:18	39, 121, 122, 147
2:14	17, 23, 25, 27, 69, 121, 124, 128, 135, 175, 193, 226	4:19	39
		5:1	39, 41, 120, 135, 148, 178, 199, 235
2:15	17, 21, 25, 123, 124, 126, 128, 133, 191, 230	5:2	39, 41, 43, 57, 149, 199
		5:3	39, 41, 120, 122, 125, 150, 151
2:16	25, 121, 123, 124, 130, 234, 243	5:4	41, 120, 121, 122, 145, 147, 150, 151, 170, 177, 232
2:17	25, 27, 118, 130, 230, 251	5:5	41, 43, 47, 118, 124, 135, 151, 177, 191, 198, 252
2:18	27, 120, 129, 131, 133, 175, 230, 254	5:6	41, 43, 152, 200
2:19	27, 121, 126, 131, 254	5:7	41, 43, 120, 125, 153, 175
2:20	27, 29, 132, 133, 201, 213	5:8	43, 47, 124, 139, 154, 155
2:21	27, 29, 124, 133, 255	5:9	43, 47, 118, 135, 151, 154, 230
2:22	27, 29, 133, 151	5:10	43, 47, 118, 119, 124, 155, 171
2:23	29, 31, 129, 131, 133, 230	5:11	43, 47, 123, 156, 157, 235
2:24	29, 31, 125	5:12	43, 47, 118, 157
2:25	31, 119, 120, 122, 124, 134, 255	5:13	45, 47, 49, 115, 158, 209, 210, 254
3:1	31, 33, 118, 119, 131, 134, 153, 254	5:14	45, 49, 119, 159, 160, 175
		5:15	45, 49, 160, 164, 177, 206
3:2	31, 33, 135	6:1	45, 49, 159, 161, 163, 169, 256
3:3	31, 35, 122, 136, 152		
3:4	31, 35, 118, 120, 137, 153, 160, 171, 175, 191	6:2	45, 49, 161, 162
		6:3	45, 51, 118, 151, 161, 163
3:5	33, 35, 118, 135, 137, 152, 153, 230	6:4	45, 51, 118, 161, 164, 165, 174, 242
4:1	2, 37, 118, 120, 135, 138, 153, 160, 175, 231	6:5	45, 51, 164, 166, 235
		6:6	45, 51, 165, 191
4:2	2, 37, 134, 138, 229	6:7	45, 51, 118, 165, 182
4:3	2, 37, 139, 152, 201	6:8	45, 51, 105, 166
4:4	2, 37, 118, 119, 140, 195, 203, 206, 212, 235	6:9	45, 51, 118, 166, 170, 232
		6:10	45, 51, 135, 141, 150, 168

Hosea (*cont.*)

6:11	45, 53, 55, 119, 152, 169
7:1	53, 55, 119, 135, 159, 163, 169, 191, 198
7:2	53, 55, 145, 152, 169, 170, 232
7:3	53, 55, 125, 170, 171
7:4	53, 55, 119, 134, 171, 175, 191
7:5	53, 57, 171, 173
7:6	53, 57, 59, 118, 119, 174, 175
7:7	55, 57, 59, 119, 160, 175
7:8	55, 57, 59, 119, 175
7:9	55, 59, 150, 151, 152, 175, 176, 187
7:10	55, 59, 135, 151, 152, 177
7:11	55, 59, 118, 130, 160, 175, 177, 254
7:12	55, 59, 63, 118, 119, 152, 178, 201
7:13	59, 63, 77, 79, 141, 179, 183, 234
7:14	59, 63, 121, 125, 170, 179, 193
7:15	59, 63, 139, 180, 221
7:16	61, 63, 118, 143, 180
7:20	231
8:1	61, 63, 119, 154, 179, 182
8:2	61, 65, 135, 139, 151, 183
8:3	61, 65, 124, 143, 151, 163, 184, 253
8:4	61, 65, 109, 184
8:5	61, 65, 83, 139, 159, 184, 185, 223
8:6	61, 65, 69, 186
8:7	61, 65, 69, 139, 153, 160, 175, 176, 187
8:8	61, 65, 118, 125, 160, 175, 187
8:9	61, 65, 69, 71, 141, 188, 189, 251, 254
8:10	61, 67, 125, 152, 171, 189
8:11	61, 67, 124, 190, 213
8:12	61, 67, 69, 119, 153, 182, 191
8:13	61, 67, 125, 139, 144, 150, 175, 191, 198, 247
8:14	61, 69, 71, 118, 175, 192, 224
9:1	69, 71, 118, 119, 122, 125, 128, 135, 193
9:2	69, 71, 125, 143, 184, 194
9:3	69, 71, 139, 175, 195, 254
9:4	69, 73, 118, 123, 139, 163, 175, 191, 195
9:5	69, 73, 196, 230
9:6	71, 73, 123, 124, 197, 236
9:7	71, 73, 75, 118, 128, 135, 151, 163, 191, 198
9:8	71, 75, 81, 198, 199
9:9	71, 75, 119, 128, 144, 191, 192, 198, 199
9:10	75, 77, 118, 119, 121, 135, 158, 163, 200, 243
9:11	75, 77, 119, 201
9:12	75, 77, 119, 141, 152, 153, 179, 201, 202
9:13	75, 79, 153, 158, 202
9:14	75, 79, 81, 203
9:15	75, 79, 139, 145, 169, 170, 203, 232
9:16	75, 79, 139, 141, 152, 201, 203, 256
9:17	77, 81, 118, 150, 204
10:1	81, 83, 85, 119, 204
10:2	81, 83, 125, 206
10:3	81, 83, 125, 160, 175, 207
10:4	81, 83, 118, 132, 208, 234, 235, 237, 238, 256
10:5	81, 83, 119, 123, 193, 208
10:6	81, 85, 115, 135, 146, 152, 200, 209, 210, 224, 231, 254
10:7	81, 85, 91, 118, 152, 210
10:8	81, 85, 118, 135, 139, 144, 192, 212, 251
10:9	85, 89, 95, 118, 124, 132, 135, 153, 212, 230
10:10	85, 89, 95, 119, 214, 215
10:11	85, 89, 124, 182, 215, 216
10:12	85, 89, 123, 163, 216
10:13	85, 91, 124, 139, 198, 214, 218, 229
10:14	87, 91, 118, 153, 119, 219, 231
10:15	87, 91, 135, 142, 143, 203, 220
11:1	87, 91, 135, 153, 175, 220
11:2	87, 91, 126, 129, 143, 180, 221
11:3	87, 91, 146, 151, 159, 221
11:4	87, 93, 97, 119, 222
11:5	87, 93, 223, 254
11:6	87, 93, 97, 124, 139, 175, 224
11:7	87, 93, 119, 175, 225, 226

INDEX OF BIBLICAL VERSES

11:8	87, 93, 97, 95, 119, 121, 135, 226	14:1	109, 111, 122, 201, 206, 219, 252
11:9	87, 95, 163, 224, 227, 256	14:2	111, 113, 135, 191, 198, 252
11:10	87, 95, 118, 123, 152, 153, 228	14:3	111, 113, 146, 184, 191, 198, 213, 253
11:11	87, 95, 118, 129, 229, 254	14:4	111, 115, 117, 122, 131, 252, 254
12:1	97, 101, 107, 109, 131, 227, 229, 235, 254	14:5	113, 115, 124, 159, 255
12:2	97, 101, 115, 124, 132, 163, 194, 230, 254	14:6	113, 115, 118, 208, 256
		14:7	113, 118, 124, 152, 255, 257
12:3	97, 101, 119, 145, 170, 192, 231, 232	14:8	113, 117, 118, 125, 139, 208, 257
12:4	97, 101, 105, 109, 201, 232, 233, 236	14:9	113, 117, 118, 131, 200, 244, 254, 257
12:5	97, 101, 124, 180, 233	14:10	113, 152, 179, 232, 252, 258
12:6	97, 103, 234	**Joel**	
12:7	97, 103, 234	1:1	117
12:8	97, 103, 109, 139, 229, 235	1:2	1, 117
12:9	97, 103, 105, 191, 192, 198, 200, 232, 235	1:3	1, 117
12:10	97, 103, 118, 131, 197, 231, 236, 254	1:4	1, 117
		1:5	1, 117
12:11	97, 105, 234, 236	1:6	1, 117
12:12	99, 105, 109, 118, 139, 152, 208, 237, 238	**Amos**	
12:13	99, 105, 124, 135, 238	8:14	89
12:14	99, 105, 251	**Jonah**	
12:15	99, 105, 141, 232, 238	4:2	91
13:1	99, 105, 109, 119, 126, 139, 180, 206, 234, 239, 252	**Micah**	
13:2	99, 105, 109, 118, 123, 139, 213, 240, 255	1:7	128
		2:1	57
13:3	99, 107, 109, 118, 161, 174, 188, 242	**Nahum**	
13:4	99, 107, 151, 160, 242, 254	2:11	205
13:5	99, 107, 109, 121, 151, 243	3:6	127
13:6	99, 107, 109, 119, 221, 243	3:10	219
13:7	99, 107, 118, 119, 143, 191, 232, 244	**Habakkuk**	
		1:15	166
13:8	99, 107, 109, 118, 124, 175, 244	**Zephaniah**	
13:9	99, 107, 135, 227, 245	1:11	141
13:10	99, 107, 224, 246, 254	3:9	167
13:11	99, 107, 247		
13:12	109, 144, 156, 191, 192, 247	**Zechariah**	
13:13	109, 111, 143, 153, 248, 251	8:14	234
13:14	109, 111, 117, 249	8:22	234
13:15	109, 111, 121, 143, 163, 231, 243, 248, 250	8:23	234
14	1		

Zechariah (cont.)

11:15	134
14:21	235

Malachi

1:1–2:13	1
3:18–21	1

Psalms

10:14	115
19:7	163
51:21	254
55:3	229, 230
63:2	161
73:1–3	1
73:19–28	1
77:1–5	1
77:14–21	1
78:34	161
78:41	189
80:2–3	1
80:9	83
80:11–17	1
80:15–20	1
82:1–8	1
82:4–8	1
83:1–5	1
83:4–12	1
84:1–13, 1–2	1
86:1–2, 1–11	1
86:7–17	1
87:6	19
89:1	1
91:6	249, 250
102:10	25
102:13	234
105:4	217
118:27	222
129:3	97, 215
135:13	234
137:9	219
141:10	253

Proverbs

4:25	178
6:2	199
9:7	214
11:1	235
12:4	158
12:14	254
13:2	254
14:30	158
17:22	49, 159
18:11	236
20:23	235
25:12	25, 129
25:20	25
30:15	39, 69
31:24	235

Job

4:14	239
5:8	119
8:5	119
18:5	49, 186
31:6	235
37:22	257
39:20	257
40:10	257
40:30	235
42:8	127
42:12	210
42:13	210

Song of Songs

2:11	51
3:7	33
3:10	33

Ruth

1:13	239

Lamentations

3:65	226
5:3	115

Daniel

3:22	69, 186
5:17	69
7:9	186

1 Chronicles

27:23	19

2 Chronicles

7:3	49
15:3	35

Printed in the United States
by Baker & Taylor Publisher Services